HISTORY OF RUSSIAN PHILOSOPHY

HISTORY OF RUSSIAN PHILOSOPHY

by

N. O. LOSSKY

*Professor of Philosophy
Russian Orthodox Seminary of New York*

*Formerly Professor of Philosophy
University of St. Petersburg*

INTERNATIONAL UNIVERSITIES PRESS, INC.

New York (1951) New York

Copyright 1951, by International Universities Press, Inc.

*Sponsored by St. Vladimir Orthodox
Theological Seminary and Academy,
New York*

Manufactured in the United States of America

CONTENTS

CHAPTER		PAGE
I.	Russian Philosophy in the Eighteenth Century and in the First Part of the Nineteenth Century	9
II.	Slavophils	15
	1. I. Kireyevsky	15
	2. A. Khomiakov	29
	3. K. Aksakov—Y. Samarin	41
III.	Westernizers	47
	1. P. Chaadaev	47
	2. N. Stankevich	51
	3. V. Belinsky	53
	4. A. Hertsen	56
IV.	Russian Materialists in the Sixties—Nihilism	59
	1. M. Bakunin	59
	2. N. Chernyshevsky	60
	3. D. Pisarev	62
	4. I. Sechenov	63
V.	Russian Positivists	65
	1. P. Lavrov—G. Virubov—E. de Roberty	65
	2. N. Mihailovsky	66
	3. K. Kavelin—M. Troitsky—N. Kareyev—N. Korkunov	68
VI.	Degeneration of Slavophilism	70
	1. N. Danilevsky	70
	2. N. Strakhov—K. Leontiev	72
VII.	Precursors of Vladimir Soloviev	73
	1. P. Yurkevich—V. Kudriavtsev	73
	2. N. Fedorov	75
VIII.	Vladimir S. Soloviev	81
IX.	Epistemology, Logic and Metaphysics in the Last Quarter of the Nineteenth Century	134
	1. B. Chicherin	134
	2. N. Debolsky	143
	3. P. Bakunin	144
	4. M. Karinsky	145
	5. N. Grot	149
X.	Princes S. and E. Trubetskoy	150

XI.	The Russian Personalists	158
	1. A. Kozlov	158
	2. L. Lopatin	160
	3. N. Bugayev—P. Astafiev—E. Bobrov	161
XII.	The Russian Neo-Kantians	163
	1. A. Vvedensky	163
	2. I. Lapshin	166
XIII.	The Changing Mentality of Russian Intellectuals in the Beginning of the Twentieth Century	171
XIV.	Father Pavel Florensky	176
XV.	Father Sergius Bulgakov	192
XVI.	N. Berdyaev	233
XVII.	The Intuitivists	251
	1. N. Lossky	251
	2. S. Frank	266
	3. A. Losev	292
	4. D. Boldyrev—S. Levitsky	296
	5. V. Kozhevnikov	297
XVIII.	L. Karsavin	299
XIX.	Studies in Logic	315
XX.	Transcendental-Logical Idealism in Russia and Its Critic, V. Ern	318
	1. Representatives of Transcendental-Logical Idealism	318
	2. Shestov's Irrationalism	325
	3. V. Ern	326
XXI.	Scientist-Philosophers	329
XXII.	Jurist-Philosophers	333
XXIII.	Philosophical Ideas of Poet-Symbolists	335
	1. Andrei Belyi	335
	2. V. Ivanov—N. Minsky	336
	3. D. Merezhovsky	337
	4. V. Rozanov	342
XXIV.	Dialectical Materialism in the U.S.S.R.	345
	1. Hegel's Dialectical Method	345
	2. Dialectical Materialism	347
XXV.	The Influence of E. Mach and R. Avenarius on Marxists	378
XXVI.	Recent Developments in Russian Philosophy	381
	1. S. Alexeyev (Askoldov)	381
	2. V. Szylkarski	383
	3. L. Kobilinsky	384
	4. B. Vysheslavtsev	385
	5. I. Ilyin	387
	6. Father Vassili Zenkovsky	389
	7. Father George Florovsky	391
	8. V. Lossky	395
XXVII.	Characteristic Features of Russian Philosophy	402
	Index	411

ACKNOWLEDGMENTS

In these uncertain times it is no easy task to publish a long book on philosophy. I wish, therefore, to express my profound gratitude to all those who have helped in various ways with the production of this book: the St. Vladimir's Orthodox Theological Seminary in New York and its Dean, Father George Florovsky; Professor B. Bakhmeteff of Columbia University; Dr. P. Zouboff; Mrs. N. Duddington; Miss H. Iswolsky; and Professor A. S. Kagan of the International Universities Press, New York.

N. O. Lossky

Chapter 1

RUSSIAN PHILOSOPHY IN THE EIGHTEENTH CENTURY AND IN THE FIRST PART OF THE NINETEENTH CENTURY

The Russian culture of the nineteenth and the beginning of the twentieth century has a world-wide significance. Such significance may be said to attach to a nation's culture when the values developed in it hold for humanity as a whole. Such was the culture of ancient Greece and Rome, and, in modern times, of England, France, Germany, America; Russian culture in the form it had before the Bolshevik revolution undoubtedly also has a universal significance. To see the truth of this it is sufficient to recall the names of Pushkin, Gogol, Turgenev, Tolstoy, Dostoevsky, or of Glinka, Tchaikovsky, Mussorgsky, Rimsky Korsakov, or the achievements of Russian theatrical art in the drama, the opera, the ballet. In the realm of science it is enough to mention the names of Lobachevsky, Mendeleyev and Mechnikov. The beauty, wealth, and subtlety of the Russian language give it an incontestable right to be considered one of the world languages. In the domain of political culture, e.g., in rural and municipal self-government, law and executive justice, imperial Russia created values which will prove to have a universal significance when they are sufficiently studied and understood, and above all, when they are reborn in the postrevolutionary development of the Russian state. For persons capable of religious experience it is unquestionable that Orthodoxy in the Russian form of it contains values of exceptionally high order of excellence; they can be most easily detected in the aesthetic aspect of the Russian-Orthodox worship.

It would be strange if so high a culture had produced nothing original in the domain of philosophy. True, according to Hegel's apt remark, Minerva's owl does not begin to fly till evening dusk, and the development of Russian thought conforms to this rule: Russian philosophy began to develop only in the nineteenth century, when the Russian state was a thousand years old.

The Russian people accepted Christianity in 988 and as soon as the works of the Fathers of the Church began to be translated into church slavonic language, they got their first introduction to philosophy. As early as the twelfth century a translation was available of St. John Damascene's system of theology, the third part of his book πηγὴ γνώσεως, under the title *The Word About the True Faith*. The philosophical introduction to this book was translated in the fifteenth century, but fragments from it appeared in Sviatoslav's Izbornik in 1073. In the fourteenth century the works of Dionysius the Areopagite with commentaries by St. Maxim the Confessor were translated. These books and also the works of other Eastern Fathers were available in many Russian monasteries.[1]

With the help of these writings some of the Russian clergy attempted to continue the theological and philosophical work of Byzantium, e.g., the Metropolitan Pyotr Mogila in the seventeenth century and Bishop Feofan Prokopovich at the beginning of the eighteenth. Among laymen mention should be made of Grigory Skovoroda (1722-1794), a moralist who based his doctrine primarily upon the Bible, but also made use of certain neo-Platonic theories (e.g., in his interpretation of matter), of Philo, the Fathers of the Church and the German mystics (in his teaching about the outer and the inner man, the abyss of the human spirit and of the Divine being, of the "spark" in the heart of man—a favorite simile of the German mystics.[2]

The centuries of the Tartar domination and then the isolationism of the Moscow state prevented the Russian people from becoming acquainted with Western-European philosophy. Not until Peter the Great had "cut a window into Europe" was Russian society introduced to the western culture on a wide scale. The western influence at once affected the attitude toward the Church. Voltairian freethinking became widespread among the Russian nobility, but on the other hand there appeared a striving to find greater depths in the religious life, to find the meaning of "the true Christianity" and realize it in practice. In the first half of the eighteenth century freemasonry appeared in Russia and by the second half it had become widespread. The chief philosophical tendencies by which it was influenced were connected with the names of the French mystic Saint-Martin (1743-1803) and the German mystic Jacob Boehme (1575-1624). Saint-Martin's book *On Errors and Truth* was published in a Russian translation as early as 1785. There was also a translation of Thomas à Kempis's *Imitation of Christ* and of a book

---

1. The list of them is given in the first volume of Golubinsky's *History of the Russian Church*.
2. G. S. Skovoroda, *Collected Works*, Petersburg 1912; Ern, *G. S. Skovoroda*, Moscow 1912; D. Chizhevsky, *The Philosophy of G. S. Skovoroda*, Warsaw 1934.

by a Lutheran theologian Johann Arndt (1555–1621) *True Christianity*. Many translations of Jacob Boehme's works were circulated in manuscript and some were published.

Freemasons understood true Christianity as the development of spiritual life, moral self-improvement and active love for one's neighbors. N. T. Novikov (1744–1818) worked particularly hard in spreading the ideas of true Christianity; he published many books, edited masonic periodicals and organized libraries. I. G. Schwarz (1751–1784), a German who was professor of philosophy at the Moscow University from 1779–1782, should be mentioned alongside of Novikov. Schwarz was a believer in the Rosicrucian doctrines, and in the lectures which he delivered at his house he explained obscure passages in the works of St. Martin by references to Jacob Boehme's *Mysterium Magnum*. He maintained that God created the world not out of nothing, but out of His own inner essence. He preached the need for man's moral and spiritual improvement and denounced political and ecclesiastical abuses and defects of the clergy. His early death saved him from government persecution. Novikov also denounced the wrongs of the Russian political and ecclesiastical life, and in 1792 was incarcerated by Catherine II in the Schlüsselburg fortress. Four and a half years later he was liberated by Paul I, after Catherine's death, but the imprisonment had shattered him both physically and mentally. In 1790 Catherine the Great exiled to Siberia another famous critic of the wrongs of Russian life—A. N. Radishchev; after her death he too was liberated by Paul I.[3]

Radishchev (1749–1802) was a highly cultured man. With eleven other young men he was sent by the Empress Catherine to the University of Leipzig to study jurisprudence and other allied subjects. He spent six years at that university (1766–1772). He was familiar with the social and philosophical theories of Rousseau, Locke, Montesquieu, Helvetius, Leibniz, Herder. He was opposed to autocracy, and the institution of serfdom roused his indignation. He expressed his ideas on the subject most forcibly in his book *The Journey from Petersburg to Moscow* and was punished for it by exile to Siberia.

Radishchev's book *On Man and His Mortality and Immortality*, has a philosophical significance. It consists of four parts. In the first two the author expounds materialistic arguments against immortality, intended to prove that material properties belong to mental processes as well, that mental life depends upon the body and that, therefore, destruction

---

3. V. Tukalevsky, "Philosophical Tendencies in the Russian Society of the Eighteenth Century," *Journal of the Ministry of Public Education*, May 1911; S. G. Vernadsky, "Russian Freemasons During the Reign of Catherine II," *Annals of the Petersburg University Faculty of Arts*, 1917; V. Bogolubov, *N. Novikov and His Times*, Moscow 1916.

of the body must involve destruction of the mental life also. In the third and fourth parts he disproves these contentions and shows that the human soul is "an independent entity, distinct from the body;" it is "simple, nonextended, and indivisible among all feelings and thoughts." If it had no such unity "the man at this moment would not know whether he was the same as he had been the moment before. He would not be the same to-day as he was the day before;" he could not "either remember, or compare, or reason."[4]

Radishchev says that Helvetius was wrong in reducing all knowledge to sensuous experience. When I look at an object now with one, and now with the other eye, I see it every time. If I look at it with both eyes, I have two impressions, but "although the sensations in my eyes are two, the sensation in the soul is one, hence, the sensation of the eyes is not the same as that of the soul, for what is two in the eyes is one in the soul." Similarly, when I see a bell, hear it ringing and touch its hardness, I have three different sensations and nevertheless I "form one single conception of the bell" (253 f.).* Thus, Radishchev clearly saw the difference between sensuous experience and nonsensuous thought about the object.

Having arrived at the conclusion that the soul was simple and indivisible, Radishchev deduces from it that it was immortal. His reasoning is as follows: The purpose of life is the striving after perfection and bliss. The all-merciful Father did not create us in order that we should find this purpose to be a vain dream. It is therefore reasonable to suppose that after the destruction of his present body man shall possess another, a more perfect one, corresponding to the stage of development attained by him and that he will go on growing in perfection (293). In expounding the doctrine of reincarnation Radishchev refers to Leibniz who compared the transition from one incarnation to another to the transformation of a hideous caterpillar into a chrysalis and the appearance of a lovely butterfly out of the chrysalis (288).[5]

Radishchev was opposed to mysticism and therefore did not join the freemasons. The famous statesman, M. M. Speransky (1772–1839) was a freemason from 1810 till 1822 when the masonic movement was forbidden in Russia. He knew the works of the Western-European

---

4. Radichev, *Collected Works*, II, 245, Moscow 1907; I. Lapskin, *Radichev's Philosophy*, 1922.

* *Editorial Note:* Throughout this book, Arabic numerals refer to page references, while Roman numerals indicate the number of the volume; the words "page" and "volume" were omitted throughout.

5. See N. Lossky's article "Leibniz's Doctrine of Reincarnation as Metamorphosis," *Collected Works of the Russian Scientific Institute in Prague*, II, 1931; in German: "Leibniz' Lehre von der Reinkarnation als Metamorphose," *Archiv für Geschichte der Philosophie*, XI, 1931.

mystics—Tauler, Ruysbruck, Jacob Boehme, Pordage, St. John of the Cross, Molinos, Mme Guyon, Fénélon. He translated into Russian Thomas à Kempis's *Imitation of Christ* and selections from Tauler. The ultimate reality was for him spirit free from space and possessing unlimited freedom of will. The triune God is in His inmost being an abyss, "eternal silence." The feminine principle, Sophia or Wisdom, is the contemplation of the Divine knowledge, the mother of all that exists outside of God. The Fall of angels and of man gave rise to impenetrable matter and to its spatial form. Speransky was in sympathy with the theory of reincarnation; he says that although it has been condemned by the Church, it is found in many of the Fathers, e.g., in Origen, St. Methodius, Pamphilius, Synesius and others. In the domain of the spiritual life he condemned the practice of replacing inner fasting by the outer, spiritual prayer by vain repetition of words. He regarded the worship of the letter of the Bible rather than of the living word of God as pseudo-Christianity.[6]

The continuous development of Russian philosophical thought began in the nineteenth century when the Russian society had passed through a period of enthusiasm for the German idealism of Kant, Fichte, Schelling and Hegel. Schelling's philosophy of nature and aesthetics was expounded by Professors M. G. Pavlov, D. M. Vellansky, A. I. Galich, N. I. Nadezhdin. Pavlov (1773–1840) was professor of physics, mineralogy and agriculture at the Moscow University. He maintained that the main principles of the structure of nature are discovered through intellectual intuition, and experience merely confirms it. He interpreted intellectual intuition as the self-contemplation of the Absolute. Nadeshdin (1804–1856) was professor of aesthetics at the Moscow University. He introduced to his students Schelling's doctrine of the unconscious organic creativeness of genius. Vellansky (1774–1847) was professor of anatomy and physiology in the Petersburg Medico-Surgical Academy, and Galich (1783–1848) was, from 1805, professor at the Petersburg Pedagogical Institute reconstituted in 1819 as a University. In 1821 he was made to resign because "he preferred the godless Kant to Christ, and Schelling to the Holy Spirit."[7]

The beginnings of independent philosophical thought in Russia date back to the Slavophils Ivan Kireyevsky and Khomyakov. Their philosophy is an attempt to overcome the German type of philosophizing on the strength of the Russian interpretation of Christianity based upon the works of the Eastern Fathers and nourished by the national

6. See A. Yelchaninov, "The Mysticism of M. M. Speransky," *Theological Review* 1906.
7. On the influence of Schelling see V. Setschkareff, *Schellings Einfluss in der russischen Literatur der 20er und 30er Jahre des XIX. Jahrhunderts.* Leipzig 1939.

peculiarities of Russian spiritual life. Neither Kireyevsky nor Khomyakov worked out a system of philosophy, but they set out the program and established the spirit of the philosophical movement which is the most original and valuable achievement of Russian thought—I mean the attempt of the Russian thinkers to develop a systematic Christian world conception. Vladimir Soloviev was the first to create a system of Christian philosophy in the spirit of Kireyevsky's and Khomyakov's ideas. He was followed by a whole galaxy of philosophers in the same line. Religious philosophers include Prince S. N. Trubetskoy, his brother Prince Eugene Trubetskoy, N. Fyodorov, Father Pavel Florensky, Father Sergius Bulgakov, Ern, N. Berdyaev, N. Lossky, L. P. Karsavin, S. L. Frank, J. A. Ilyin, Father Vassili Zenkovsky, Father George Florovsky, V. Vysheslavtsev, N. Arseniev, P. Novgorodtsev, E. Spektorsky. This movement goes on developing and increasing up to the present day. Since it began with I. Kireyevsky and Khomyakov, I propose to give a detailed account of the life and teachings of these two men.

Chapter 2

SLAVOPHILS

1. I. V. KIREYEVSKY

Speaking of Russian philosophers, I will make short references to their social origin and the conditions of their life in order to give an idea of Russian culture in general. Ivan Kireyevsky was born in Moscow on 20th March, 1806, the son of a nobleman landowner, and died of cholera in St. Petersburg on 11th June, 1856. Almost the whole of his childhood, part of his youth and much of his later life he spent in his native village Dolbino, near Belev in the Tula province. In the countryside he received a good home education, firstly under the romantic poet V. A. Zhukovsky and afterwards from his stepfather, A. A. Elagin. The extent of his talents may be seen in an ability to play chess excellently at the age of seven. In 1813 the captive French general, Bonami, "declined to play with him, fearing to lose to a seven-year-old boy; for several hours he followed with curiosity the play of the boy who easily beat the other French officers."[1] At ten years of age he was well acquainted with the best writings in Russian literature and with classic French literature in the original; by twelve he knew German thoroughly. He began to learn Latin and Greek at sixteen in Moscow, but mastered these languages only in his forties, in order to read the Fathers of the Church in the original so that he might advise and criticize the Russian translation of St. Maxim the Confessor.

His interest in philosophy began already when he was a lad and was due to A. A. Elagin, who became acquainted with Schelling's works in 1819. Attracted by them Elagin began translating his *Philosophical Letters on Dogmatism and Criticism* (1796).

In 1822 all his mother's family moved to Moscow. Here Kireyevsky heard, among others, the public lectures of Schelling's disciple, Pavlov, on the philosophy of Schelling.

---

1. Kireyevsky, *Complete Works*, 2 vols., edited by Gershenson, I, 4, Moskow 1911. The reference is to the captive Frenchman of Napoleon's army after the campaign of 1812.

In Moscow he was one of a group of young scholars (Shevyrev, Pogodin), poets and writers (D. Venevitinov, Prince V. Odoevsky, etc.). He benefited by the influence of this cultured atmosphere, but himself produced hardly any literary work. This was chiefly due to the fact that like many gifted Russians, he was satisfied with the inner life and did not trouble to express himself either in writing or even in lecturing. For instance, in correspondence with friends on an offer to become editor of the paper *Muscovite* in 1845 he writes that it would be useful to him; "I need some external and even urgent compulsion to arouse my activity."[2]

Kireyevsky did not have any of the negative traits of character that impel many people to strenuous external activities—traits such as ambition, rivalry, love of dispute, a thirst to expose an opponent's weak points and triumph over him. His sensitive nature above all sought peace, calm and love. A monk of Optina Pustyn remarked to C. Leontiev: "He was all soul and love."[3] The blows of fate, obstacles to a literary career did not produce a strong reaction in him but drove him into himself, into submission to Providence, to that "Master who knows better than we how the human reason must develop." The central place in the life of the personality according to his view was the "heart," feeling. Of all feelings and dispositions he preferred sadness; the feeling of sadness, he thought, gave a particular insight into the meaning and the richness of life (I, 7).

In 1829 Kireyevsky fell in love with Natalya Petrovna Arbeneva, and asked for her hand, but, because of a distant relationship between the two families, he was refused. He was badly shaken by this; "he spends his life on a couch with coffee and a pipe," says Pogodin.[4] His relatives and doctors began to fear a decline. He was sent as a diversion on a journey abroad, where he spent the year 1830, visiting Berlin, Dresden and Munich. In Berlin he met Hegel and his followers, Hans and Michelet, and attended their lectures. In Munich he met Schelling and Oeken, likewise attending their lectures. Returning to Russia he began to publish in 1831 the magazine *The European* but the magazine was banned after the second number on account of Kireyevsky's article "The Nineteenth Century." The reason given for the ban—based on the words of the Emperor Nicholas I, who had read the article[5]—was that the author alleged that he was not speaking of politics but of literature, but his intention was something quite different: by "education" he

---

2. Letters to Zhukovsky (II, 236), to Khomiakov (II, 231). He wrote the same to Shevyrev on October 26, 1831 with reference to the publication of *The European*.
3. Gershenzon, *Historical Notes*, 10.
4. Barsukov, *The Life and Works of Pogodin*, II, 310.
5. Gershenzon, *Historical Notes*, 6.

meant "freedom" and by "the activity of the reason" he meant "revolution," while his artificial middle line was nothing less than constitutional government. This astonishing reason sounds like the ravings of a madman suffering from persecution mania. Kireyevsky might even have been exiled from the capital, had not Zhukovsky defended him. For eleven years after this blow Kireyevsky wrote practically nothing.

In 1845 he was co-editor of *The Muscovite* but soon gave it up as he had not received official permission to hold the post. In 1852 the Slavophils began to publish *Moscow Miscellanies* but after the first book this publication was forbidden for "disseminating absurd and harmful notions." The chief reason was Kireyevsky's article "The Character of European Civilization." Kireyevsky himself was placed under open police surveillance. It is not surprising that this man, who was conscious of his vocation to serve his country in literature, showed "signs of secret grief upon his brow." Hertzen, the famous Russian publicist and émigré who published the revolutionary magazine *The Bell*, wrote of Kireyevsky's appearance that it brought to mind "the melancholy calm of the sea swell over a sunken ship."

When you know the substance of Kireyevsky's teaching and ideals, you will be surprised that it was possible in this ridiculous manner to cramp the thought of a noble thinker, whose writings were in no sense a danger to the social order. You think perhaps that a denial of free speech such as existed in Russia in the reign of Nicholas I is possible only under primitive barbaric conditions. But you would be very much mistaken. Even in western Europe today after an age-long struggle for freedom, when an apparently high level of culture has been reached, there are once more harsh persecutions of free speech and thought, for example, in the Fascist countries. Do not, then, when you hear about the severities during the reign of Nicholas I, jump to general conclusions about Russian culture, the Russian state and the Russian mind.

While living in the country Kireyevsky prepared in the last years of his life *A Course of Philosophy*. He often went from his estate to Optina Pustyn; he was bound to the monastery by his close relations with the Elders, particularly with Father Makary, and also by his literary work, advising on translating and publishing the Fathers of the Church. (Optina Pustyn was a monastery in the Kaluga province, famous for its "Elders." Those who are unacquainted with Russian culture can obtain a picture of an Elder from Father Zossima in Dostoevsky's *Brothers Karamazov*.)

After the death of Nicholas I and the accession of Alexander II the air breathed freedom. In 1856 in Moscow was founded the magazine *Russian Conversation*, edited by Kireyevsky's friend, the Slavophil

Koshelev. There Kireyevsky published an article on "The Possibility and Necessity of New Principles in Philosophy." The article was intended as an introduction to a large work but actually it was Kireyevsky's last. He went to visit his son at St. Petersburg in June, was taken ill with cholera and died. He was buried at Optina Pustyn.

Already at the age of twenty-eight Kireyevsky had laid plans (in a letter to A. I. Koshelev in 1827) to join his friends in literary work for the good of his native land. "What can we not do, if we work together!" "We shall restore the right of true religion, we shall reconcile external refinement with morality, we shall arouse love of truth, we shall replace a stupid liberalism with respect for law and we shall raise the purity of life above the purity of style" (I, 10).

The religion, of which Kireyevsky speaks at this moment of his life, was not Orthodoxy. That is clear because seven years later, in 1834, when he married Natalya Petrovna Arbeneva, he was not pleased with her observing church rites and practices. "She, on the other hand," said Koshelev, "was grievously surprised by his lack of faith and his utter neglect of all the practices of the Orthodox Church." As he respected her religious feelings, he promised not to scoff in her presence.[6] Not before 1840 is it possible to speak of his return to the Orthodox Church. He obviously had retained from his youth some religion, but it is difficult to say what it consisted in. Koshelev says that in the Philosophical Society, of which Kireyevsky was a member, "German philosophy completely replaced religion in the young men."[7]

It is obvious, however, that even at that time the Gospel was the book which Kireyevsky read most. In 1830, when in Berlin, he asked his sister to copy out in each letter some text from the Gospels; he wanted in the first place to give her further occasion to study the Gospels and in the second place to make her letters "as much as possible flow from the heart" (II, 218).

At the same time he showed an ability to observe those subtle nuances in the mental life, which are close to mystical experience and compel us to recognize the presence of deep and intimate bonds between people and between all beings generally. He wrote to his sister about his dreams in Berlin: "They are no trifle to me, the best part of my life has been spent in dreams. . . . In order that you may know how to confer a dream, I must teach you to know the qualities of dreams in general." Dreams "depend on those to whom they refer" (1830, II, 221).

He expresses an even more striking thought with regard to the death in war of Count Michael Vyelgorsky: "If there is the feeling in

---

6. Koshelev, *The Story of Kireyevsky's Conversion,* I, 285.
7. Barsukov, *The Life and Works of Pogodin,* I, 302.

our heart which was part of his inner life as well, obviously our heart becomes the place where he abides, being not only in ideal but in *actual* contact with it" (1855; II, 290). Such thoughts are not the result of logical inference; they are first suggested to us by the experience we have after the death of those we love.

Religion on a philosophical basis, connected with personal mystical experience went side by side in the young Kireyevsky with a strong love of Russia and faith in her great destiny. He says that in modern history there always has been some one State which was, so to speak, the metropolis of the others; it was the heart from which comes and to which returns all the blood, all the living forces in the civilization of the peoples. "Now England and Germany stand at the pinnacle of European civilization; at present they are characterized by the one-sidedness of maturity." After them, he thinks, will come the turn of Russia, who will possess herself of all sides of European enlightenment and become the spiritual leader of Europe.[8]

Returning from abroad he founded his magazine *The European,* the very name of which shows how highly Kireyevsky rated Russia's task of assimilating the principles of European enlightenment. In a letter to Zhukovsky he says that, by getting all the best magazines and books, "I should like to make my study into the class room of a European university, and my magazine, like the notes of an assiduous student, would be useful to those who have neither the time nor the means to take lessons at first hand" (1831, II, 224).

We must not assume, however, that his journey to Western Europe, where he met the best minds of that time, enslaved Kireyevsky to Europe. The culture of Western Europe impressed him adversely by its one-sidedness, its narrow rationalism. He valued German scholarship highly, yet in general Germany struck him as stupid (II, 223; I, 28), wooden (II, 221) and dense.

Kireyevsky's repugnance to petty rationalism can be seen from a letter in which he criticizes the lecture of Schleiermacher on the resurrection of Jesus Christ. This subject, says Kireyevsky, leads a Christian philosopher to the summit of his world conception, there, where faith and philosophy must be shown "in their antithesis and consequently in all their fullness and completeness. The necessity of such a confession of faith is contained in the subject itself. He could not act otherwise, even if he wanted to; the proof is that he did want to but could not." "It was as though he wanted to avoid the central idea of his teaching;" "instead of embracing his subject at once in a single question, he revolved around it in a series of incomplete, irrelevant questions. He asked, e.g.:

---

8. *A Review of Russian Literature for the Year of 1829,* II, 38.

Did corruption begin in the body of Jesus Christ or not? Was there left in Him an unnoticeable spark of life? Or was there complete death? and so on" (I. 31). Kireyevsky did not doubt that Schleiermacher was a sincere believer and as his translations from Plato showed, a man of high intelligence. The superficiality of his lecture is explained by the fact that "the convictions of his heart are formed separately from his intellectual convictions" (I. 32). "He believes with his heart and wants to believe with his head. His system is like a pagan temple, converted into a Christian church, where all the externals, every stone, every adornment, speaks of idolatry, while within are sung hymns to Jesus and the Mother of God" (I. 32). In these critical considerations we can already observe the basic principle of Kireyevsky's subsequent thought—the principle, which he afterwards recognized as the essential virtue of the Russian cast of mind and character.

That principle is wholeness. Wholeness in the working of the mind consists in man's effort to bring together "all his different powers;" the condition of this collectedness is "that he should not regard his abstract logical capacity as the one and only instrument for the apprehension of truth; that the voice of ecstatic feeling unco-ordinated with the other powers of the spirit, should not be looked upon as an unerring indication of truth; that the promptings of aesthetic thought taken in isolation should not be considered independently of other concepts as a sure guide to the comprehension of the ultimate nature of the world; [that even the inner judgment of a more or less purified conscience should not be accepted in defiance of the other intellectual faculties as the final judgment of the highest justice];[9] not even must the ruling love of the heart be thought of separately from the other claims of the spirit as an infallible instructor in the achievement of the highest good; man must constantly seek in the depth of his soul that inner root of understanding, where all the separate faculties unite in one living whole of spiritual vision."[10]

At a high stage of moral development, reason is raised to the level of "spiritual vision," without which Divine truth cannot be seen (I, 251); thought is lifted up "to a sympathetic agreement with faith" (I, 249); faith (and Revelation) is for thought in this condition "an authority external and internal, the highest reasonableness, enlivening the mind" I, 250). "Faith is not credulity in other people's assurances," it is "a real communion with the Divine, with the world above, with

---

9. The sentence in brackets was struck out by the censor; I conjecture that it should be inserted here. See I, 287.

10. I, 249. "The Possibility and Necessity of New Principles in Philosophy," *Russian Conversation*, 1856.

heaven, with God" (Extracts I, 279). In other words Kireyevsky believes that, having united into a harmonious whole all his spiritual powers, "thought, feeling, aesthetic sense, love of the heart, conscience, and a disinterested will for truth," man acquires a capacity of mystical intuition and contemplation which makes accessible to him superrational truths about God and His relation to the world. The faith of such a man is not a trust in external authority, in the letter of written revelation but "a living and whole vision of the mind."

Kireyevsky finds the germ of such a philosophy in the Fathers of the Church; the ultimate development of their teaching "responsive to the present state of science and corresponding to the claims and questions of the modern mind" would get rid, he says, of "the morbid contradiction between reason and belief, between inner convictions and external life" (Extracts I, 270). Such knowledge must "reconcile faith and reason," "confirm spiritual truth by its visible supremacy over natural truth and elevate natural truth by its correct relation to spiritual truth, and at last bind both truths in one living thought" (Ext. I, 272). This knowledge based on the full unity of all the spiritual powers, differs fundamentally from the knowledge elaborated by the abstract "logical reason divided from the will." True, "the thinking man must conduct his knowledge through the domain of logic," but he must "know that this is not the summit of knowledge but only a stepping stone; knowledge is hyperlogical, where light is not a candle but life. Here the will grows side by side with thought" (1840, Letter to Khomyakov, I, 67). In such knowledge we arrive at those principles which are "inexpressible," to that in the soul which is related to the region of "the unsolved" (I, 67). Obviously, Kireyevsky has in view here the apprehension of the "metalogical" principles of being, lying deeper than qualitative and quantitative determinations. Such determinations, taken by themselves would be disunited in space and time and connected only by *external* relations expressible in rational concepts. Only the presence of metalogical principles such as the Absolute or God, in so far as He creates the world as an integral whole, and such principles as the individual substantial ego, creating real existence as its manifestations in space and time, makes possible intimate *internal* relations in the world, the bonds of love, of sympathy, of intuitive insight, mystical experience and so on.

The mind which does not see this side of the world, which abstracts from its content only the rational elements, qualitative and quantitative determinations, relations in time and space, etc., is poor and one-sided and inevitably gets into a blind-alley. Western-European civilization recognizes as the source of knowledge only personal experience and reason;[11] the result is in some thinkers a formal abstractness, i.e., *rationalism*, in others an abstract sensuousness; i.e., *positivism*.[12] In social life these qualities are expressed in the logical system of Roman Law but in social and family life it distorts the natural and moral relations of people (186 "European Civilisation"). In the Roman Church the rational quality leads to the result that her theologians see the unity of the Church in "the external unity of the episcopate;" they ascribe "an essential worth" to "the external actions of man;" among the means of salvation they admit "a definite term of purgatory;" they work out a doctrine of "a superabundance of good in external actions" and the possibility of utilizing this superabundance for the shortcomings of others" (I, 189). In philosophy the medieval philosophers try to express the whole system of knowledge in the form of a chain of syllogisms (I, 194); even the originator of modern philosophy, Descartes, "was so strangely blind to living truth that he did not consider his inner direct consciousness of his own existence as convincing until he had deduced it by abstract syllogistic inference."[13] France might have developed an independent positive philosophy thanks to Pascal and Fénélon, and the Port-Royal philosophers. Pascal pointed to ways of thought more lofty than Roman scholastics and rationalist philosophy (the "logic of the heart," religious experience, etc.). Fénélon defended Madame Guyon and collected the teachings of the Fathers of the Church about the inner life. But the Jesuits destroyed this movement. The "cold logic of Bossuet" compelled Fénélon "by the authority of the Pope to recant his sacred beliefs out of respect to Papal infallibility." What was the result? France surrendered to "Voltaire's laughter" and to doctrines destroying religion.[14]

Spinoza, formulating his philosophical system in a chain of syllogisms, could not find the "living Founder" of the world or detect in man his "inner freedom" (I, 196). Leibniz, pursuing the connection of abstract concepts, did not observe the living causal connection between bodily and mental processes, and had recourse to the theory of the pre-established harmony. Fichte saw in the external world the phantom of imagination (I, 197). Hegel developed the whole of his philosophy by the dialectical method as a system of the logical self-development of reason; but, carrying that method to its extreme limit, he perceived the limits of philosophical thought; he observed that the whole dialectical process "is only a potential, not an actual truth," "demanding for its realization another kind of thinking capable of positive and not only

11. "The Character of European Civilization," *Moscow Miscellanies*, I, 177, 1852.
12. *An Answer to Khomiakov*, I, 111, written in 1839.
13. I, 196. Kireyevsky is wrong in thinking *cogito ergo sum* to be a syllogism.
14. *New Principles*, I, 231, 1856.

of hypothetical comprehension and standing as far above the logical self-development as actual fact stands above mere possibility" (*New Principles*, I, 259). One must observe that Kireyevsky knows how Hegel defended his philosophy from the accusation of rationalism; he says that according to Hegel reason "deduces its knowledge through the laws of intellectual necessity, not from an abstract concept but from the very source of self-consciousness, where being and thought unite in one unconditional identity" (I, 258). Nevertheless he is right in accusing Hegel of overemphasizing the logical activity, since Hegel wants to understand everything in accordance with the laws of intellectual necessity; on that ground I add for myself that in his system God is not the Creator of the world and his system is not theism but pantheism. Schelling at the height of his development understood "the limited nature of rational thought" (I, 198) and founded a new system of philosophy, which "unites in itself two opposite aspects," one true and negative, showing the "insolvency of rational thought," the other positive and, in Schelling, a failure; it consists in recognizing the necessity of "Divine Revelation" and "living faith, as the highest form of reason." But Schelling did not turn directly to Christianity (*New Principles*, I, 261). He understood the limitations of Protestantism which rejected tradition, but he could not turn to the Roman Church which confused the true tradition with the false. He had with his own powers "to acquire from the confused Christian tradition that which corresponded to his inner understanding of Christian truth; it is a sorry task to compose one's own faith." He sought in ancient mythology "the traces of corrupted Revelation" and his philosophy, therefore, differs from Christianity in the understanding of the most important dogmas, while in the very method of understanding he did not rise to a "full consciousness of the believing reason" (I, 260–264), to that condition in which "the highest truths of the mind, its living visions" are revealed (I, 178). Accordingly the philosophy of Schelling together with German philosophy can serve the Russians only as a "convenient stepping stone" for the transition to an "independent philosophizing" (I, 264), wherein the Fathers of the Church must serve as a positive support.

Such in fact was the history of Kireyevsky's own development of thought. His friend, the Slavophil Koshelev, tells us that, having married in 1834, Kireyevsky gave his wife in the second year of their marriage some Cousin to read; she obeyed his wishes but said that while there was much good in the book, in the Fathers of the Church "all this is put more profoundly and more satisfyingly." Later they began to read Schelling together and here too more than once she found passages in the Fathers more significant in her opinion. Kireyevsky began to borrow her books from her in secret and was interested in them. Afterwards he entered into relations with the monk Philaret, an elder and *skhimnik* (hermit) of the Novospassky Monastery. By 1842 Kireyevsky had already set his foot firmly within the circle of the ideas of Orthodoxy.[15]

Kireyevsky did not regard the philosophy of the Fathers as final, requiring no further development. Granovsky ascribes to him the thought that in the Fathers of the Church "there is nothing to add, everything is said."[16] This is an example of the customary unfairness to the Slavophils. In his article on the possibility and necessity of new principles in philosophy Kireyevsky says that it would be a great mistake to think that we have in the Fathers of the Church a ready-made philosophy; our philosophy has yet to be created—and not by one man.

The attitude of mind found by Kireyevsky in the Eastern Fathers is "a serene inner wholeness of spirit" as the basis of all conduct and thought (I, 201). Together with Christianity this type of spiritual culture was received by the Russian people, whose culture was particularly high in the twelfth and thirteenth centuries (I, 202). Wholeness and reason are its fundamental traits, while in the West we find dualism and rationalism (I, 218). This distinction is sharply drawn in a multitude of instances: First, in the West an abstract rationalist theology, the demonstration of truth by a logical concatenation of concepts, in old Russia a striving after truth "by means of the inner elevation of self-consciousness to a warm-hearted wholeness and concentration of the intellect;" secondly, in the West a State system founded on violence and conquest, in old Russia a State system founded on the natural development of the national life; thirdly, in the West a hostile separation of the classes, in old Russia their single-minded combination; fourthly, in the West landed property as the basis of civic relations, in old Russia property only as the accidental expression of personal relations; fifthly, in the West a formal logical legality, in old Russia a legality derived from life. Generally speaking, in the West a dualism of spirit, science, state, classes, family rights and obligations; in Russia a striving for wholeness of the internal and external mode of life, "a perpetual consciousness of the relation of the temporal to the eternal, of the human to the Divine." Such was the life of old Russia, the traces of which are conserved even now in the people (*Extracts*, I, 265).

Having abandoned the search for the infinite and set himself petty tasks, "Western man is almost always satisfied with his condition;" he is "ready to say to himself and to others proudly clapping him-

---

15. *The Story of Kireyevsky's Conversion*, I, 285.
16. T. Granovsky, *A. Stankevich*, 112.

self on the chest, that his conscience is completely at rest, that he is quite clean before God and man, that he only asks of God that all other men might be like him." If he collides with generally accepted principles of conduct, he thinks out for himself an original system of morality and is once more at peace." "The Russian on the contrary always feels keenly his shortcomings and the higher he is on the moral scale, the more he demands of himself and the less pleased he is with himself" (I, 216).

It must not be supposed that Kireyevsky is an obscurant, recommending Russians to turn their backs on Western-European civilization. "The love of European culture," he says, "and the love of our own coincide in the last point of their development into a single love, a single tendency to a living, full, pan-human and Christian civilization."[17] When they reject one another both cultures become one-sided.[18] The task of the creative civilization of the future consists in this, that the "highest principles" of the Orthodox Church, transcending European civilization without supplanting it but on the contrary embracing it in their fullness, should give it the highest meaning and the final development (I, 222). In his maturity Kireyevsky said "now too I still love the West," "I belong to it by training, manners and tastes" (I, 112, letter to Khomiakov). More than that, he valued so highly the exact scientific methods of Western-European thinkers that in 1839 he wrote (in answer to Khomiakov): it would be a good thing if "some Frenchman were to understand the originality of Christian teaching as it is contained in our Church and were to write an article about it for a big magazine, the German would believe him and would study our Church more profoundly, as something which is necessary now for Europe, and then doubtless we should believe the Frenchman and German and should ourselves come to know what we have" (I, 120). It is remarkable that in our time the wish of Kireyevsky is being fulfilled; in Germany there is a widespread study of Russian culture and Russian religion, as a result of which there is growing up among Russians themselves an interest in the riches of their culture which they had not sufficiently valued in the past.

As is apparent from this survey, Kireyevsky has much to say about the right method of approaching truth, but he did not work out a system of philosophy. He has left only fragments of valuable ideas, which in part are elaborated in later Russian philosophy, in part await their elaboration.

At the end of his life, while he prepared a work on the history of philosophy, he said: "The direction of philosophy depends in the first

---

17. *A Review of Contemporary Literature*, I, 162, 1845.
18. *The Character of European Civilization*, I, 162, 1845; I, 222, 1852.

place on that concept which we have of the Holy Trinity" (I, 79). This thought, at first sight paradoxical, acquires profound meaning if we read such works as Vladimir Soloviev's *Lectures on Godmanhood* and *The Spiritual Foundations of Life*, Father Paul Florensky's *Pillar and Foundation of Truth*, Father Sergius Bulgakov's *Tragedy of Philosophy*, N. Lossky's *Value and Existence*. With these works we shall become acquainted in the later chapters.

Kireyevsky undoubtedly connected the idea of consubstantiality, expressed in the dogma of the Trinity, with the idea that the structure of the created spiritual world also has the character of immediate inner unity. "Each moral victory in the inmost depths of one Christian soul," he says, "is a spiritual triumph for the whole Christian world" (*Extracts*, I, 277); "in the physical world each being lives and is maintained only by the destruction of others, while in the spiritual world the construction of each personality constructs all, and each lives by the life of all" (I, 278). He asserts "the spiritual communion of each Christian with the plenitude of the whole Church" (I, 278). We find in these ideas the conception of *sobornost,* the commonalty principle, the doctrine of which was elaborated by Khomiakov. Undoubtedly the communal ideal presented itself to Kireyevsky as the guiding principle also of the social order. He says that "the distinctive type of the Russian outlook on every type of order" is "the combination of personal independence with the general order as a whole," but the mind of the Western European "does not comprise order without uniformity" (I, 76—To C. S. Aksakov, June 1, 1855).

The wholeness of society, combined with the personal independence and the individual diversity of the citizens, is possible only on the condition of a free subordination of separate persons to absolute values and in their free creativeness founded on love of the whole, love of the Church, love of their nation and State, and so on.

From this same understanding of wholeness as *sobornost* or commonalty springs Kireyevsky's negative attitude to exaggerating the importance of the hierarchy in the Church; of the Theology of Bishop Makarius he remarks that the Introduction contains a doctrine incompatible with our Church "concerning the infallibility of the hierarchy, as if the Holy Ghost appeared in the hierarchy independently of the Totality of all Christianity" (1851, To Koshelev, II, 258).

From the same understanding of wholeness as free commonalty springs Kireyevsky's teaching about the relation of Church and State which he developed in a letter to Koshelev (Oct.–Nov. 1853, II, 271, 280). "The State is the organization of society, having as its aim life on earth, in time; the Church is the organization of the same society, having as its aim life in heaven, in eternity." The temporal must serve the eternal; consequently the ordering of society by the State must serve the Church (II, 251). "The hegemony of the Church I do not understand in the form of an inquisition or of persecution for faith;" it consists in the State's setting itself the task (1) to become imbued with the spirit of the Church; and (2) to see in its existence only a means for the fullest and best establishment of the Church of God on earth" (II, 271). In fact in so far as the state realizes justice, morality, sanctity of the law, the dignity of man and so on, it serves not temporal but eternal ends. Only in such a State can freedom of the personality be guaranteed. On the contrary, a State existing for a petty earthly purpose cannot respect freedom. Political freedom is a relative and negative concept; if it is given a substantive and positive meaning, it is based on respect for moral freedom and human dignity, on a recognition of "the sanctity of the moral person" combined with the sanctity of eternal moral truths. Such ideas can only have a religious basis. The free and lawful development of personality therefore, can be guaranteed only in a State subject to religious faith (II, 280). The subordination of the State to the Church may be turned under the excuse of public security into the supremacy of the State; the priesthood may be converted into a body of officials, the citizens may be compelled to go to the sacraments, and there may be similar limitations of freedom; but these are abuses (II, 274).

In order to ascertain whether Kireyevsky's thought was significant or represented a negligible episode in the history of Russian culture, let us subject his basic idea to a critical examination.

He does not rate highly "abstract logical thought;" for the possession of truth, he says, it is essential to gather together all one's capacities into a single whole, logical thought, feeling ("the heart"), aesthetic sense, the conscience, love. Truth is unfolded only to the whole man; "the inner root of understanding" is there "where all the separate faculties unite in one living whole vision."

At first sight these expressions may appear empty, even meaningless. What bearing have feeling and aesthetic sense upon knowledge as a system of judgments with subjects, predicates, adequate grounds and so on? Must we not go further and say that the whole man must seize truth also with his hands, his feet and his mouth?

In answer to that I recall that precisely in contemporary philosophy many of the most varied thinkers insist on the necessity of developing Pascal's thought that besides the "logic of the mind" there is a "logic of the heart." It may be said that there is only one logic, and it is nonsense to think that there are many logics; I agree, but I still maintain that Pascal with his insistence on using the "heart" for knowledge, and

Kireyevsky with his claim to add also the will and indeed all the faculties of man, present a perfectly fair methodological demand and one very difficult to fulfill. Philosophy sets itself the task to embrace the world as a whole together with the supercosmical principle. Skill in dealing with logical forms and relations is not enough to achieve this end; if we are really to succeed, these forms must be filled with an all-round meaning, which can be given only by the fullness of experience, by the use of experience in all its diversity. There is a sensory experience, of the eyes, the ears, the touch; there is a nonsensory experience of the soul, self-observation and observation of the psychic life of others; there is a spiritual experience, the contemplation of ideas, e.g., mathematical ideas; there is an experience of feeling, bringing into the consciousness the value aspect of the world. M. Scheler has developed a whole theory on the subject that feelings are irreducible to subjective experiences but in their "intentional" aspect put us in communion with objective values; he calls his teaching "emotional intuitivism." One variety of such an experience of feeling is aesthetic receptivity, leading to the realm of beauty; then there is moral experience, and, finally, religious and mystical experience, establishing communion with the Kingdom of the Holy and the Divine.

Contemporary philosophy begins to develop the theory of these varieties of experience. If experience in all its completeness includes religious experience, a philosophy working on the right lines must be religious and Christian, since indisputably Christianity is the highest stage of religion achieved by man in the historical process of his development.

It was precisely this task of developing a Christian world conception that Kireyevsky set himself in the middle of the nineteenth century; now it is recognized by Russian and many European philosophers as the urgent problem of the day.

Kireyevsky, one may say, almost confined himself to setting problems, pointing the way; he did not develop them. Nevertheless the correct setting of a problem is already a great service. That Kireyevsky rendered this service, is to be seen in the fact that in a marvelous way almost a century ago he cast a programme, with the development of which Russian philosophy began to occupy itself thirty years later and continues to occupy itself with success to this day.

In fact the task of developing a Christian world conception has become almost the general theme of Russian philosophy. The most many-sided attempt to solve it belongs to Vladimir Soloviev; the works of his youth, *The Philosophical Principles of Integral Knowledge* and *The Critique of Abstract Principles,* show that he went the way pointed out by Kireyevsky, the way of overcoming abstract rationalism and acquiring knowledge through the integral unity of all man's faculties. The further development of Christian philosophy has been carried on by the Princes Sergius and Eugene Trubetskoy, Father Paul Florensky, Father Sergius Bulgakov, N. Berdiayev, Ern, Lossky, Frank, V. Ivanov, Merezhkovsky, Alexeyev (Askoldov), Karsavin, Zenkovsky, Florovsky, Novgorodtsev, I. A. Ilyin, Vysheslavtsev, Spektorsky.

In particular the idea of *sobornost* or commonalty, so clearly indicated by Kireyevsky, is further elaborated by Khomiakov, Soloviev, the Trubetskoys and other Russian philosophers.

The doctrine of the Trinity and of consubstantiality is set at the base of metaphysics by Florensky and Bulgakov; I make use of it for the purposes not only of metaphysics but also of axiology.

The doctrine of metalogical knowledge as the essential complement to logical knowledge particularly occupies Florensky, Bulgakov and Berdiayev; it is developed in the greatest detail and conviction by Frank in his book *The Object of Knowledge*. Interest in the metalogical principles of existence is closely combined in Russian religious philosophy with an insistence upon the *concreteness* and *wholeness* of existence.

As you see, Kireyevsky's ideas did not die with him. They actually, as it were, note the programme of Russian philosophy and the fact that different parts of his programme have been realized by many Russian philosophers who often were not even acquainted with the works of Kireyevsky shows that there exists an astonishing superempirical unity of a nation and that Kireyevsky was a true representative of the inmost depths of the Russian spirit. That is why I have devoted so much space to the exposition of his teaching.[19]

2. A. S. KHOMIAKOV

The immediate successor of Kireyevsky in philosophy was Alexey Stepanovitch Khomiakov, the most prominent of the Slavophils. Born on May 1, 1804 he died of cholera on September 23, 1860. Like Kireyevsky he came of the class of landed gentry.[1] His mother, Marie Alexeyevna, was a Kireyevsky by birth. Khomiakov says that he owed to her his unswerving devotion to the Orthodox Church and to the Russian national spirit. His mother was a woman of great character: her husband lost

---

19. On I. Kireyevsky see: V. Liaskovsky, *Kireyevskie*, 1899; A. Koyre, *La philosophie et le problème national en Russie au début du xix siècle,* Paris 1929; I. Smolitsch, *I. V. Kirevskej, Leben und Weltanschauung,* Breslau 1934; A. Caats, *I. Kireyevsky,* Paris 1937; N. Dorn, *I. Kireyevsky,* Paris 1938.

---

1. Until the great reforms of Alexander II in the sixties Russian culture was chiefly represented by the class of the landed gentry.

more than a million roubles at cards at the English Club in Moscow; she took the management of the estates into her hands and restored the family fortunes. As an expression of her patriotic feelings she built a church out of her personal savings to commemorate the deliverance of Russia from Napoleon in 1812.

Khomiakov was deeply religious as a boy; when, at the age of eleven he was taken to Petersburg he pictured this town as a pagan city and intended to suffer martyrdom there for the Orthodox faith. At about the same time he was taking Latin lessons from a French abbé, Boivin; discovering a misprint in a papal bull, he asked his teacher "how can you believe in the infallibility of the Pope?" Khomiakov was very keen about the liberation of the Slavs and used to dream of a rebellion against the Turks. At the age of seventeen he ran away from home in order to join the Greeks in their struggle for independence but was caught in the neighborhood of Moscow.

He was educated at the Moscow University and graduated in mathematics in 1822. From 1823 to 1825 he served as an officer in a cavalry regiment. His commander wrote of him after his death: "He had a remarkably good education. What beautiful and lofty poetry he wrote! He never succumbed to the fashion for sensuous poetry. His work is moral, spiritual and exalted throughout. He was a splendid horseman. He used to leap over barriers the height of a man. He was excellent at fencing. When quite young he had the strong will of a man tempered by experience. He strictly observed all the fasts prescribed by the Orthodox Church and went to all the church services on Sundays and holidays. There were a good many freethinkers among his comrades and many of them jeered at church observances saying that they were meant for the lower orders. But Khomiakov inspired such affection and respect that no one presumed to mock his faith. When not on duty he never wore fine cloth and never took advantage of the permission to wear a tin cuirass instead of the iron one weighing 18 pounds, although he was short in stature and of slight build. He was a true Spartan in bearing physical pain and hardships."[2]

In 1825 Khomiakov retired and went abroad to Paris where he studied painting and wrote a tragedy, *Yermak* (Yermak was the leader of the Kosaks who conquered Siberia in 1582). He went to Italy, Switzerland and to the land of the Western Slavs in Austria. In 1828 he joined a hussar regiment and took part in Russia's war against Turkey. During the war he got to know the life of the Bulgarian people. Khomiakov's fellow officers said that he was noted for "cold, brilliant courage." It

2. Count Osten-Saken in the almanach *Utro* 1866; V. Zavitnevich, *A. S. Khomiakov*, I, 101.

was remarkable that when going into attack he merely raised his sword but never struck the enemy as they ran.

When the war was over Khomiakov retired again and took to farming on his estates; the winters he spent in Moscow. In 1847 he went with his family to Germany and Bohemia. In Berlin he met Schelling and Neander with a view to find out their interpretation of Christianity but, as he says, "got nothing out of them." In Prague he met Czech scholars, Hanka and Safarik and was charmed by them.

Khomiakov's literary heritage consists chiefly of poems, tragedies, political and religious-philosophical articles. For the last twenty years of his life he was working at a great book on the philosophy of history *Thoughts on Universal History*. His friends jokingly referred to it as "Semiramis" because Gogol happened to see the name of Semiramis in Khomiakov's manuscript and spread the rumor that it was all about her.[3]

His chief philosophical and theological articles are "The Church Is One" (written in the forties, published after the author's death in 1864) and three pamphlets *An Orthodox Christian on Western Denominations,* published in French in Paris in 1853 and in Leipzig in 1855 and 1858 under the name of *Ignotus:* "The Pamphlet of Mr. Lorancey:" "The Message of the Archbishop of Paris:" "Certain Romanist and Protestant Writings." In Russia they were only allowed to be printed in 1879, though the Emperor Nicholas I had himself read the first pamphlet and approved of it.[4]

Khomiakov was a man of great versatility. M. Pogodin, a Russian historian, says of him that like Pico Mirandola he could hold disputes *de omni re scibili*. He studied theology, philosophy, history, theory of language (he compiled a dictionary of Russian words akin to the Sanskrit). He was a successful farmer and had a number of other practical abilities; he invented some sort of steam engine and sent it to be exhibited in London, taking out a patent for it (he had called it a "silent mover" but when the model was completed, it appeared that it "screeched dreadfully"); he invented a long range rifle, was extremely fond of horses and dogs and a good judge of them.

As opposed to Kireyevsky, Khomiakov had a passion for arguing. He completely crushed his opponents by his brilliant dialectic and enormous knowledge. He had an excellent memory. In a theological dispute with Kireyevsky, Khomiakov referred to a passage in the writings of St. Cyril of Jerusalem which he had read fifteen years before in the library of the monastery Troitskaya Lavra and which were not to

---

3. Khomiakov, *Completed works,* 8 vols.
4. Khomiakov, *Works,* 3rd ed., II, 90.

be found anywhere else. Kireyevsky doubted the accuracy of the quotation and said jokingly, "You like to make quotations that cannot be verified." Khomiakov replied that it was on page 12 or 13, in the middle of the page. The reference was verified later on and proved to be correct.[5]

Khomiakov liked to emphasize his love of everything Russian by wearing a beard and dressing in the old Russian style.

Like Kireyevsky's, Khomiakov's leading idea is the *concreteness* and *wholeness* of reality. In his two articles about Kireyevsky, Khomiakov entirely agrees with the latter's condemnation of the formal, dry and rationalistic character of European culture and with his contention that ancient Russian culture was inspired by the ideals of reason and wholeness (I, 199).

He regarded the philosophy of Hegel as the culminating point of rationalism, and said that his logic "ascribed spirit to abstractions." Hegel, he said, takes "the formula of a fact to be the cause of it" and thought that "the earth turned round the sun not because of the struggle of opposing forces but owing to the mathematical formula of the ellipse."[6] Hegel wants to deduce everything from the development of the thought—i.e., from the laws of thinking—forgetting that "a concept is that which is conceived by the conceiving mind," that the *object* conceived precedes the concept and the conceiving subject transcends it; the laws of thought cannot therefore be taken to be the laws of "spirit as a whole"[7] (I, 295).

In order to know objects in their living reality, the subject must go beyond himself and transfer himself into the object "through the moral power of sincere love" (I, 272). Thus enlarging his life by another life he acquires "living knowledge," not cut off from reality but interpenetrated by it. Being "inward" and "immediate," living knowledge differs from mediate cognition as much as the actual vision of light by a man who can see differs from the knowledge of the laws of light by one born blind (I, 279).

No "living truth" and especially no Divine truth can be fitted into the framework of logical understanding (II, 247). It is an object of faith, not in the sense of subjective certainty but in the sense of immediate givenness (I, 279, 282). In spite of its being metalogical, faith does not

5. Quoted by V. Zavitnevich, 6.   6. I, 37, 144, 267.
7. Like many other philosophers Khomiakov wrongly interprets Hegel's system as abstract panlogism (see N. Lossky's article *Hegel als Intuitivist, Blätter für Deutsche Philosophie, IX, 1, 1935*. In truth Hegel's philosophy is concrete ideal-realism (see I. A. Ilyin's book *The Philosophy of Hegel as a Concrete Theory of God and Man*, 1917). Hegel's terminology, however, shows that he was not sufficiently conscious of concrete entities and consequently underestimated such aspects of reality as force, individual supertemporal personal existence, etc.

contradict understanding (II, 247); indeed, it is necessary that the infinite wealth "of data acquired through its insight" should be analyzed by understanding (I, 282). Only where a harmony of faith and understanding is achieved is there "a wholeness of reason" (I, 279, 327). By the word "faith" Khomiakov obviously means intuition; i.e., the faculty of immediately cognizing actual living reality, things in themselves. The word "faith" has been used in this sense in the German philosophy by Jacobi before Khomiakov, and in the Russian by Vladimir Soloviev after him.

Living knowledge gives us knowledge of that which lies at the basis of existence—*force*. At the lower levels of reality it manifests itself in the form of material processes and at the higher, in the spiritual world, force is free will conjoined with reason. Force cannot be apprehended through the understanding because it is not an object; it belongs to the pre-objective realm. In other words, it is a *metalogical* principle (I, 276, 325, 347).

Man is a finite being endowed with rational will and moral freedom. Freedom means the freedom of choice between the love of God and selfishness, in other words, between righteousness and sin. This choice determines the ultimate relation of finite reason to its eternal source; i.e., God. But the whole world of finite minds, the whole creation is in the state of sin, either actually or potentially, having been saved from it solely by the absence of temptation and by the grace of God (II, 216). In so far as the creature is sinful, it is subject to *law*, but God has come down to the creature and showed it the way of liberty and salvation from sin: He entered the historical process as the God-man, He became "in Christ a limited being" who nevertheless "by the sole power of His human will realized all the fullness of Divine righteousness." This is why the God-man Jesus Christ is the supreme judge of the sinful creature, the bearer of "the righteousness of the eternal Father," awakening in man the full consciousness of his guilt, but at the same time He is "the infinite love of the Father." "He unites Himself to every creature that does not reject Him" (II, 216) and every being that has recourse to Him and loves His truth is included by Him within His Body the Church.

These general positions contain the germ of the metaphysical system that has subsequently been worked out in detail in Russian philosophy. Khomiakov barely indicated its main principles, yet, starting with them, it is easy to grasp the essence of his doctrines about the Church which form the most valuable part of his theological and philosophic reflections. He works out the conception of the Church as a truly *organic whole,* as a Body the head of which is Jesus Christ. Those who love

Christ and God's truth belong to the Church and become members of the Body of Christ. In the Church they find a new, fuller and more perfect life than they would have had apart from it. In order to understand this, we must remember that the Church is an organic whole spiritualized by Our Lord Himself. "A grain of sand, it is true, does not receive any new life from the heap upon which it had, by chance, been blown." "But every particle of matter assimilated by a living body becomes a part of the organism and receives new life and new meaning from it: this is the case of man in the Church, in the Body of Christ, the organic basis of Which is Love." Christ saves mankind not only because of His atoning sacrifice but because by accepting a sinner who loves Him into His Body, He unites Himself to him inwardly and allows him to share in His perfection (II, 112, 217).

Since all the faithful have in common their love for Christ as the bearer of perfect truth and righteousness, the Church is the *unity* of many persons, but a unity in which the *freedom* of each individual is preserved. This is possible only because this unity is based upon disinterested, self-renouncing love. Those who love Christ and His Church renounce all self-conceit, all proud claims of solitary understanding and acquire that rational vision of faith which makes manifest to us the meaning of the great truths of the Revelation.

A loving union with the Church is a necessary condition of understanding the truths of faith, because the complete truth belongs only to the *Church as a whole.* "Ignorance and sin are the inevitable portion of every person taken in isolation; fullness of understanding as well as spotless holiness belong only to the unity of all the members of the Church" (II, 58).

Such is the paradoxical but nevertheless true conclusion arrived at by Khomiakov. We must begin by loving "with one's heart" the completeness of truth and righteousness of Christ and the Church, and then our eyes will be opened and we shall possess "reason in its entirety" which comprehends superrational principles and their connection with the rational aspects of existence. Freedom of the faithful is preserved because in the Church man finds "himself, but not himself in the impotence of his spiritual isolation but in the power of his spiritual wholehearted union with his brethren and His Saviour. In the Church he finds himself in his perfection, or, rather, he finds in it that which is perfect in himself—namely, the Divine inspiration which is always evaporating in the coarse impurity of every isolated personal life. This purification takes place through the invincible power of the Christians' mutual love in Jesus Christ, for that love is the Holy Spirit" (II, 111).

Not obedience to external authority but *commonalty (sobornost)* is the basic principle of the Church. *Sobornost* is the free unity of the members of the Church in their common understanding of truth and finding salvation together—a unity based upon their unanimous love for Christ and Divine righteousness (II, 59, 192; I, 83). "Christianity is nothing else than freedom in Christ" (II, 192). Those who love God's truth and find it in Christ and His Church, *freely* and joyfully accept it, and this creates unity. "God is *freedom* for all pure beings. He is *law* for the unregenerated man; He is *necessity* for demons only" (II, 212). Hence it is clear that our true connection with the Church is bound to be free: "In matters of faith a unity by compulsion is a lie, and enforced obedience is death" (II, 192).

The principle of commonalty implies that the absolute bearer of truth in the Church is not the patriarch who has supreme authority, not the clergy, and not even the ecumenical council, but only the Church as a whole. "There have been heretical councils," says Khomiakov; "for instance, those in which a half-Arian creed was drawn up; externally, they differed in no way from the ecumenical councils—but why were they rejected? Solely because their decisions were not recognized by the whole body of the faithful as the voice of the Church." Khomiakov is referring here to the epistle of the Eastern Patriarchs to Pope Pius IX (1848), which says: "The invincible truth and immutable certainty of the Christian dogma does not depend upon the hierarchs of the Church; it is preserved by the whole of the people composing the Church which is the body of Christ" (A letter to Palmer, October 11, 1850. II, 363).

In using the word "Church" Khomiakov always means the Orthodox Church: being the Body of Christ, the Church is bound to be *one*. Catholicism and Protestantism have departed from the fundamental principles of the Church not through distortions of the truth by private individuals but as a matter of principle, and he therefore does not apply the term "church" to them but speaks of Romanism, Papism, Latinism, Protestantism, etc. But this by no means implies that he believes the Orthodox Church has realized all the fullness of truth *on earth*. Thus he speaks, for instance, about our clergy having a tendency towards "spiritual despotism." He rejoices that the Orthodox Church preserves in its depths the true *ideal,* but "in reality," he says, "there has never been a single nation, a single state or country in the world" which has realized to the full the principles of Christianity (I, 212).

He carefully disproves any false accusations against the Orthodox Church. Thus he shows, for instance, that the Russian Orthodox Church is not headed by the Emperor. "It is true," he says, "the expression *the head of the local church* has been used in the Laws of the Empire but in a totally different sense than it is interpreted in other countries" (II, 351). The Russian Emperor has no rights of priesthood, he has no claims to infallibility or "to any authority in matters of faith or even of church discipline." He signs the decisions of the Holy Synod, but this right of proclaiming laws and putting them into execution is not the same as the right to formulate ecclesiastical laws. The Tsar has influence with regard to the appointment of bishops and members of the Synod, but it should be observed that such dependence upon secular power is frequently met with in many Catholic countries as well. In some of the Protestant states it is even greater (II, 36–38, 208).

Although Khomiakov regarded Orthodoxy as the one true Church he was in no sense a fanatic. He did not believe that *extra ecclesiam nulla salus (there is no salvation outside the church)* in the sense that every Roman Catholic, Protestant, Jew, Buddhist, etc., is doomed to perdition. "The mysterious bonds that unite the earthly Church with the rest of mankind are not revealed to us; therefore we have neither the right nor the inclination to suppose that all who remain outside the visible Church will be severely condemned, especially as such a supposition would contradict the Divine mercy" (II, 220). "In confessing one baptism, as the beginning of all the sacraments we do not reject the other six;" but in addition to the seven, "there are many other sacraments; for every work done in faith, hope and love is inspired by the spirit of God and evokes God's invisible grace" (II, 14). "He who loved truth and righteousness and defended the weak against the strong, who fought against corruption, tortures and slavery, is a Christian, if only to some extent; he who did his best to improve the life of the workers and to brighten the wretched lot of the classes oppressed by poverty whom we cannot as yet make quite happy, is a Christian, if only in part." "Apart from Christ and without love for Christ man cannot be saved, but what is meant here is not the historical appearance of Christ, as Our Lord Himself tells us (II, 160, 220): Whosoever speaketh a word against the Son of man, it shall be forgiven him; but whosoever speaketh against the Holy Ghost, it shall not be forgiven him, neither in this world, neither in the world to come" (Matt. XII. 32). "Christ is not only a fact, He is a law, He is the realized idea; and therefore a man who, by the dispensation of Providence has never heard about the Righteous One who was crucified in Judea, may yet be worshipping the essence of Our Saviour though he cannot name Him or bless His Divine name. He who loves righteousness loves Christ; he whose heart is open to love and compassion is His disciple though he does not himself know it. All Christian sects contain men who in spite of their mistaken beliefs (for the most part inherited) honor with their whole life, with their thoughts, words and deeds Him who died for the sake of His criminal brethren. All of them, from the idolater to the sectarian, are more or less in darkness; but all see in the gloom some glimmering rays of the eternal light which reaches them in various ways" (II, 221).

In his criticism of Roman Catholicism and Protestantism Khomiakov takes for his starting point the principle of *sobornost* or commonalty; namely, the combination of unity and freedom based upon the love of God and His truth and the mutual love of all who love God. In Catholicism he finds unity without freedom and in Protestantism freedom without unity. In these denominations only an external unity and an external freedom are realized.

The legal formalism and logical rationalism of the Roman Catholic Church have their roots in the Roman State. These features developed in it more strongly than ever when the Western Church without consent of the Eastern introduced into the Nicean Creed the *filioque* clause. Such arbitrary change of the creed is an expression of pride and lack of love for one's brethren in the faith. "In order not to be regarded as a schism by the Church, Romanism was forced to ascribe to the bishop of Rome absolute infallibility." In this way Catholicism broke away from the Church as a whole and became an organization based upon external authority. Its unity is similar to the unity of the state: it is not super-rational but rationalistic and legally formal. Rationalism has led to the doctrine of the works of superarogation, established a balance of duties and merits between God and man, weighing in the scales sins and prayers, trespasses and deeds of expiation; it adopted the idea of transferring one person's debts or credits to another and legalized the exchange of assumed merits; in short, it introduced into the sanctuary of faith the mechanism of a banking house. Roman Catholicism rationalizes even the sacrament of the Eucharist: it interprets spiritual action as purely material and debases the sacrament to such an extent that it becomes in its view a kind of atomistic miracle. The Orthodox Church has no metaphysical theory of Transsubstantiation, and there is no need of such a theory. Christ is the Lord of the elements and it is in His power to do so that "every thing, without in the least changing its physical substance" could become His Body. "Christ's Body in the Eucharist is not physical flesh."

The rationalism of Catholicism which established unity without freedom gave rise, as a reaction against it, to another form of rationalism —Protestantism which realizes freedom without unity. The Bible, in itself a lifeless book, subjectively interpreted by every individual believer, is the basis of the Protestants' religious life. This is the reason why "Protestants have not that serenity, that perfect certainty of possessing the word of God which is given by faith alone." It attaches too much importance to the historical study of the Scriptures. It is a matter of vital importance to them whether the Epistle to the Romans was written by Paul or not. This means that Protestantism regards the Scriptures as an infallible authority, and at the same time as an authority external to man.

The attitude of the Orthodox Church to the Scriptures is different: "It regards the Scriptures as its own testimony and looks upon them as an inward fact in its own life." "Suppose it were proved today that the Epistle to the Romans was not written by Paul; the Church would say 'it is from me' and the very next day the epistle would be read aloud in all the churches as before, and the Christians would listen to it with the joyful attention of faith; for we know whose testimony alone is incontrovertible."

Khomiakov regards the Protestants' rejection of prayers for the dead, of the worship of the Saints and of the value of good works as the expression of utilitarian rationalism which fails to see the organic wholeness of the visible and the invisible Church.

The defects of Roman Catholicism and of Protestantism spring, he thinks, from the same psychological source: fear, the fear of one to lose the unity of the Church and the fear of the others to lose their freedom. Both think of heavenly things in earthly terms: " 'There is bound to be schism if there is no central power to decide on questions of dogma,' says the Roman Catholic; 'there is bound to be intellectual slavery if everyone considers himself bound to remain in agreement with others,' says the protestant."

Khomiakov describes the difference between the three Christian denominations as follows:

Three voices are heard more distinctly than others in Europe:

"Obey and believe my decrees," says Rome.

"Be free and try to create some sort of faith for yourself," says Protestantism.

And the Church calls to the faithful:

"Let us love one another that we may with one accord confess the Father, the Son and the Holy Ghost."

What is particularly valuable in Khomiakov's religious and philosophical writings is his emphasis upon the indissoluble union between love and freedom: Christianity is the religion of love and therefore it presupposes freedom. The dogmas of the Church are inviolable, as is clear to everyone who understands the conditions of the Church's life, but in matters of "opinion" Khomiakov freely seeks for new ways. "I often permit myself," he says in a letter to Aksakov, "to disagree with so-called opinions of the Church." It is not surprising that soon after Khomiakov's death the reactionary paper *Moscow News* called him a teacher of heresy.

Khomiakov's views on the historical development of mankind and on social life are closely connected with his religious philosophy. In his *Notes on Universal History* ("Semiramis") he reduces the whole historical process to the struggle of two principles—the Aryan and the Cushite. The Aryan principle is spiritual worship of the "freely creating spirit," the Cushite principle (the home of which is Ethiopia) is subjection to *matter*, "to the organic necessity determining its products through inevitable logical laws." The Aryan principle in religion is lofty monotheism, the highest expression of which is Christianity. The Cushite principle in religion is pantheism without a morally determined deity. The struggle of these two principles in history is the struggle between freedom and necessity.

The realization of Christian ideals in the historical development of Western Europe is hindered by their rationalistic distortion and by the proud conceit of her peoples. Russia received Christianity from Byzantium in its "purity and wholeness," free from one-sided rationalism. The Russian people's humility, their piety and love of the ideal of holiness, their liking for communal organization in the form of the village commune and the *artel*, based upon the duty of mutual help, give grounds to hope that Russia will go further than Europe in realizing social justice and, in particular, will find ways of reconciling the interests of capital and labor.

Khomiakov attached the greatest value to the Russian village commune, the *mir* with its meetings that passed unanimous decisions and its traditional justice in accordance with custom, conscience, and inner truth.

In Russian industrial life the *artel* was the parallel of the commune. In the Law Code an *artel* was defined as a company formed for carrying on certain work or trade by the personal labor of its members, at common expense and on joint responsibility (X, 1). Khomiakov's follower, Samarin, thought that the ancient Russian social and communal life was an embodiment of the principle of *sobornost*.

The aristocratic regime of warlike nations was foreign to the Slavs, an agricultural people, says Khomiakov. "We shall always remain democrats, standing for purely human ideals and blessing every tribe to live and develop in peace in its own way." Most of all Khomiakov hated slavery: "Demoralization is one of the chief punishments of slavery. Speaking relatively, the slaveowner is always more demoralized than the slave: a Christian may be a slave but must not be a slaveowner." In this passage Khomiakov is referring, among other things, to serfdom in Russia, insisting on the necessity of abolishing it (this was done six years later, in 1861).

In contradistinction to Kireyevsky and K. Aksakov, Khomiakov does not slur over the evils of the Russian life but severely condemns them. At the beginning of the Crimean War (against Turkey, France and England, 1854–1855) he denounced with the fire and inspiration of a prophet, the Russia of his day (before the great reforms of Alexander II) and called her to repentance.

Western Europe has failed to embody the Christian ideal of the wholeness of life through overemphasizing logical knowledge and rationality; Russia has so far failed to embody it because complete, all-embracing truth from its very nature develops slowly, and also because the Russian people have given too little attention to working out *logical* knowledge, which must be combined with the superlogical understanding of reality. Nevertheless Khomiakov believes in the great mission of the Russian people when it comes fully to recognize and express "all the spiritual forces and principles that lie at the basis of the Holy Orthodox Russia." "Russia is called to stand at the forefront of universal culture; history gives her the right to do so because of the completeness and manysidedness of her guiding principles; such a right given to a nation imposes a duty upon every one of its members." Russia's ideal vocation is not to be the richest or most powerful country but to become "the most Christian of all human societies."

In spite of Khomiakov's, and Kireyevsky's, critical attitude toward Western Europe it remained for them the treasure house of spiritual values; Khomiakov speaks of it in one of his poems as "the land of holy miracles." He was particularly fond of England. The best things in her social and political life were due, he thought, to the right balance being maintained between liberalism and conservatism. The conservatives stood for the organic force of the national life developing from its original sources while the liberals stood for the personal, individual force, for analytical, critical reason. The balance between these two forces in England has never yet been destroyed because "every liberal is a bit of a conservative at bottom because he is English." In England, as in Russia, the people have kept their religion and distrust analytical reason. But Protestant skepticism is undermining the balance between the organic and the analytic forces, and this is a menace to England in the future. In Russia the balance between these forces was disturbed by the hasty reforms of Peter the Great.

Khomiakov had genuine affection for other Slav races. He considered them inclined by nature to a communal and democratic organization. He hoped that all the Slavs, liberated with the help of Russia, will form a steadfast union.

The most valuable and fruitful of Khomiakov's ideas is his conception of *sobornost*. *Sobornost* means *the combination of freedom and unity of many persons on the basis of their common love for the same absolute values*. This idea may be applied to the solution of many difficult problems of social life. Khomiakov indicated its application to the Church and the commune. In analyzing the essence of Christianity he put in the foreground the indissoluble connection we find in it between love and freedom: Christianity is a religion of love, consequently it is the religion of freedom.

A complete understanding of the connection between love and freedom, requires a fully worked out system of metaphysics—a theory about the ontological structure of personality and of the world, about the final ideal, the connection between God and the world, etc. Khomiakov did not develop these theories. This work was done much later by Vladimir Solovyov who may be regarded as the first Russian thinker to have created an original system of philosophy.[8]

3. K. AKSAKOV—Y. SAMARIN

After an exposition of Ivan Kireyevsky's and Khomiakov's philosophical theories, a few words should be said about K. S. Aksakov and Yuri Samarin to give an idea of the older Slavophils' political views.

Konstantin Aksakov was the son of Sergei Timofeyevich Aksakov, the author of the famous *Family Chronicles*.[1] He was born on March 29, 1817 and died December 7, 1860. He spent the first nine years of his life at the Aksakov's country place, described in the *Chronicles* under the name of Bagrovo. After 1826 he lived almost all the time in Moscow with his parents to whom he was devoted, especially to his father. Between 1832 to 1835 he was a student at the Moscow University in the Faculty of Arts. From 1833 to 1840 he belonged to Stankevich's circle from which the so-called "Westernizing" movement originated. He was greatly influenced by Stankevich and Belinsky, and enthusiastically

---

[8]. On Khomiakov see: V. Zavitnevich, *A. S. Khomiakov*, 2 vols., 1903, 1913; E. Skobtsova, *A. Khomiakov*, Paris, Y.M.C.A. Press, 1929; N. Zernov, *Three Russian Prophets: Khomiakov, Dostoevsky, Soloviev*, 1937; A. Gratiaux, *A. S. Khomiakov, et le mouvement slavophile*, Paris, 1939 (in French); P. Baron, *Un Théologien laie orthodox russe au XIX s.: Alexis S. Khomiakov*, Rome, Pontif. Institutum Orient. Studiorum, 1940; S. Bolshakoff, *The Doctrine of the Unity of the Church in the Works of Khomiakov and Moehler*, London, 1946; N. Berdyaev, *A. Khomiakov* (in English).

[1]. Translated into English by Duff as *The Russian Gentleman* and *The Russian School-boy*, Clarendon Press.

studied German philosophy, especially Hegel's. After Stankevich's death (1840) the members of his circle became increasingly critical of conditions in Russia. Aksakov became intimate with Khomiakov, Kireyevsky and Samarin, who were close to him in spirit, and parted company with Belinsky. Aksakov was of passionate temperament, straightforward and fanatically devoted to his ideas; one day he said to Belinsky that owing to the difference in their opinions he could no longer visit him. The breach was painful to both; they kissed each other with tears in their eyes and parted forever. It should be noted that Belinsky too was fanatically intolerant; he used to say about himself "I am a Jew by nature, I can't be friends with the Philistines." In his love for the Russian people and their ways, K. Aksakov was the first to begin wearing top boots and the Russian shirt and to grow a long beard; in 1848 the police ordered him to shave it off.

The historian of Russia, S. Soloviev, who was very good at sharply summing up people's character, said of K. Aksakov "a powerful creature, loud-voiced, frank, kind-hearted, gifted, but dull-witted." Aksakov was of athletic build; Pogodin nick-named him a *pecheneg* (a nomad of the steppes), but at the same time there was in him to the end of his life something childish, infantile; he was a virgin, always lived with his parents, adored his father. Sergei Timofeyevitch Aksakov died on April 30, 1859; his son Konstantin grieved for him so much that he went into consumption and died on December 7, 1860 at the isle of Zante in the Greek Archipelago.

K. Aksakov's literary and scholarly activities were many: He translated Schiller and Goethe, whose humanism filled him with admiration. He wrote poems on patriotic and political subjects (e.g., in praise of free speech), a drama *The Liberation of Moscow in 1612*, a play *Oleg at Constantinople*, a comedy *Prince Lupovitsky* in 1856. He also wrote critical essays. He studied Russian history and philology. In 1840 he published his master thesis *Lomonosov in the History of Russian Literature and Russian Language*. His chief historical works are *The Manners and Customs of Ancient Slavs in General and of Russian Slavs in Particular* (1852); *The Hero Warriors of Prince Vladimir*, written in 1853, but owing to censorship restrictions published later; articles about "the basic principles of Russian history."

In his historical works K. Aksakov argues against the views of Evers and S. Soloviev that at the beginning of Russian history the social unit was a kinship group; he says that the clan should not be confused with the family. The development of the clan life interfered with the family and the state. The social structure characteristic of the Slavs, and of the Russian Slavs in particular, combines strongly developed family life not with a clannish or patriarchal system, but with a communal political order based upon the will of the people. In the case of Russian Slavs this can be seen in the way the state was founded by calling in the *Varangians,* in the institution of the *Veche* (City Assembly in the Middle Ages) and later of the *Zemski Sobors* (Estates General).

The Russian people, according to K. Aksakov, sharply distinguish between *land* and *state.* "Land" means the commune; it lives in accordance with the inner moral law and prefers the way of peace, in keeping with Christ's teachings. But the presence of warlike neighbors forced the people at last to build up a state. For this purpose the Russians called in the Varangians and separating the "land" from the state entrusted political power to the elected sovereign. The state lives in accordance with external law: it creates external rules of behavior and makes use of compulsion. The predominance of external righteousness over the inward is characteristic of Western Europe, where the state arose through conquest. In Russia, on the contrary, the state arose owing to the people voluntarily calling in the Varangians. Hence there is in Russia a union between "the land" and the state. "The land" has a consultative voice, the power of "public opinion," but the power of taking final decisions belongs to the sovereign (e.g., the relation between the Zemski Sobors and the Tsars in the Moscow period). The reforms of Peter the Great disturbed this ideal order. Aksakov began by extolling Peter the Great as the liberator of the Russians "from national exclusiveness" but afterwards he came to hate his reforms (see, e.g., his poem "To Peter" in *Rus* 1881), though he was still opposed to national exclusiveness. He thought the Russian nation superior to all others precisely because the universally human principles were more developed in it, and it was characterized by a "Christianly human spirit." The Western nations suffered from national exclusiveness, or, as a reaction against it, from cosmopolitanism; i.e., a denial of the national principle, which also is an error.

K. Aksakov idealized Russian history beyond all bounds and said that it is "a universal confession" and "can be read as one reads the lives of the saints." The humility of the Russian people finds expression in the fact that they ascribe their every victory and achievement not to themselves, but to God, glorifying Him by special church services, processions, building of churches, instead of erecting monuments to the nation and its great men. K. Aksakov's hatred of Western Europe was as passionate as his love of Russia. Kireyevsky and Khomiakov, though they pointed out the defects of the Western civilization, were aware of its achievements; they loved it and insisted upon the necessity of synthesizing the valuable elements of the Western and the Russian spirit. K. Aksakov saw only the dark side of the Western civilization: violence, hostility, erroneous faith (Catholicism and Protestantism), tendency toward theatrical effects, "debility."

Aksakov thought that the basis of the high morality of the Russian life was to be found in the peasantry unspoiled by civilization. He expressed this idea most vividly in his comedy *Prince Lupovitsky*. The prince who always lives in Paris and is an admirer of the Western-European culture decides that he ought to go to his estate in Russia in order to enlighten the peasants and bestow upon them "the pleasures of civilization." Thus, for instance, he says to his friends: "A Russian peasant if he wants to help a beggar gives him a copeck in the street; that's crude; in Western Europe they organize charity balls and concerts, and distribute the proceeds to the needy." The prince goes to his country place in Russia and begins by calling his bailiff Anton and talking to him. He advises him, among other things, to organize in the village a charity country dance with small money contributions for the poor. Anton answers that money for the poor is collected in the church, and that if a dance is organized, the money will be given not for God's sake but for the sake of amusement. When the prince suggests providing the peasants with books of various kinds, the bailiff replies that they do occasionally read very good religious books, but there are few of them in the village, and that if the prince buys them those kinds of books, that will certainly be very useful. The prince is particularly interested to know how the village meeting will deal with the question of providing a recruit for the army. It is proposed at the meeting to send for a soldier a young man called Andrey, an orphan, but a much respected peasant intercedes for him, saying that as an orphan he ought to be protected by the whole commune against injustice. The bailiff Anton has many sons, but all the villagers are fond of Anton and do not want to grieve him. So the village meeting finds a solution which pleased everyone though it means a financial burden for the community: It is decided to buy a "recruit's license" for 800 silver roubles. Aksakov strives to show that the peasants have a religiously moral outlook, thanks to the Orthodox faith, and in social matters they aim at justice, trying to satisfy both the interests of the commune as a whole and of each individual member of it.

S. Vengerov, in his critical study of Aksakov, comes to the conclusion that the qualities which Aksakov praised so highly and ascribed to the Russian people might be described as "democratic altruism" and that he was a preacher of "mystical democratism."

K. Aksakov was against the idea of limiting the autocratic power of the Tsar, but at the same time he championed the *spiritual* freedom of the individual. On the accession of Alexander II to the throne in 1855

Aksakov submitted to him, through Count Bludov, a report "On the Inner Condition of Russia." In it he reproached the Government for suppressing the people's moral freedom and following the path of despotism which has led to the nation's moral degradation. He pointed out that this might popularize the idea of political freedom and create a striving to attain it by revolutionary means. To avoid these dangers he advised the Tsars to allow freedom of thought and of speech and to re-establish the practice of calling Zemski Sobors.

A study of the philosophical and political theories of the older Slavophils—I. Kireyevsky, Khomiakov, K. Aksakov and Y. Samarin—shows that it is profoundly unjust to accuse them, as is often done, of being political reactionaries. They were all convinced democrats and considered Slavs, and especially Russians, as particularly adapted for embodying democratic principles in life. True, they defended autocracy and did not set much value on political freedom. In this respect they sharply differed from the Westernizers who wanted the political development of Russia to follow the same path as that of Western Europe. The Slavophil doctrine certainly did contain the three principles proclaimed by Count Uvarov, a reactionary minister of Public Education (1833–1849) under Nicolas I, to be the foundations of Russia's life: Orthodoxy, autocracy, nationality. But the older Slavophils interpreted those ideas in a peculiar and by no means reactionary sense. A Russian historian, Miliukov, a Westernizer and an impartial scholar, definitely maintains that the older Slavophils were not at all reactionary. He says that Orthodoxy meant for them a free community of spiritual Christians. They defended autocracy because they regarded the state as a dead and purely external form, merely serving to secure for the people the possibility of devoting themselves to the search of "the inner truth." For this purpose they demanded civic liberties—freedom of conscience, freedom of speech, freedom of the press. The nation was in their view not "a passive material for governmental measures, but an active force developing in accordance with its own inner laws; its freedom of self-determination might be violated but cannot be destroyed."

It is not surprising that the censorship was suspicious of the Slavophils and prevented them from freely expressing their ideas in the press. This was the reason, Miliukov thinks, why the Slavophils could not clearly define in print the difference between their doctrines and the reactionary views of the professors Shevyryov and Pogodin. Gershenson in his book *Historical Notes* makes it abundantly clear how unjust was the westernizers' interpretation of the older Slavophils' ideals.

Yuri Fyodorovitch Samarin (1819–1876), the son of a Kammerher, was a student in the faculty of Arts of the Moscow University from 1834 to 1838. After writing his dissertation on "Stefan Yavorsky and Feofan Prokopovich," Samarin began the study of Hegel's philosophy and was so taken up with it that he wanted to give up his former work, saying that "the Orthodox Church cannot exist outside of Hegel's philosophy." As early as 1844, however, Khomiakov cured him of his enthusiasm for Hegel and drew him to the Slavophil ideas.

Samarin's life was devoted to political and social activities. He took part in working out the conditions for the liberation of the serfs and waged a hard struggle against the claims of the Germans in the Baltic provinces. At the end of his life, in 1876, while staying in Berlin he became acquainted with Max Müller's theories of the origin of religion and wrote two articles against them, published in German. A Russian version of them is to be found in volume VI of his works, edited by his son, D. Samarin. In those articles and in a letter to his brother Samarin says: "At the core of the conception of God lies the *immediate perception* of His action upon every human being—the primary form and the precondition of His further revelation;" hence, the basis of religion is *"personal experience"* (485, 505). This gives rise to the idea of Providence, of the moral vocation and personal duty of each individual. Providence so orders the events of every man's life that they have a bearing upon his calling. "Only if there is such a relation between that which a man *ought* to be and that which *happens* to him does each human life form a *reasonable* whole" (507).

The protest raised by Samarin, a dilettante, against a famous scholar is particularly interesting because Samarin's conception of the origin of religion is a truly scientific solution of the problem, while the theories of Spencer, Max Müller, Taylor and others, prevalent in the nineteenth century, are typically pseudoscientific. According to those theories religion in its early stages is polytheistic, and the transition to monotheism is slow and gradual. In 1898 Andrew Lang in his book *The Making of Religion,* and after him Wilhelm Schmidt in the book *Der Ursprung der Gottesidee,* have shown, on the strength of ethnographical research, that the religion of the most primitive tribes is monotheism. They have thus laid a firm foundation for a scientific solution of the problem. Indeed, if God, the Creator of the world and of man, exists, it is natural to think that the source of religion is religious experience which in its deep and pure form leads to the conception of the One Supreme Being, and that only as the life of mankind becomes more complex is this idea supplemented by various presentations that distort it.

Chapter 3

WESTERNIZERS

1. P. CHAADAEV

In the history of Russian philosophy and especially of Russian political thought it is usual sharply to contrast two mutually opposed tendencies represented by the Slavophils and the Westernizers. The Slavophils strove to work out a Christian world conception, basing it on the teaching of the Eastern Fathers of the Church and on Orthodoxy in the particular form given to it by the Russian people. They immoderately idealized Russia's political past and Russian national character. They highly valued the specific peculiarities of Russian culture and insisted that Russian political and social life had developed and must go on developing along its own paths, different from those of the Western nations. In their opinion Russia's task in relation to Western Europe consisted in imparting health to it through the spirit of Orthodoxy and Russian social ideals, and in helping Europe to solve its political problems, both internal and international, in accordance with Christian principles.

The Westernizers, on the contrary, believed that Russia had to learn from the West and go through the same process of development. They wanted Russia to assimilate European science and secular enlightenment. They took little interest in religion or, if they were religious, they did not see the value of Orthodoxy and were inclined to exaggerate the shortcomings of the Russian Church. With regard to social problems some of them greatly valued political freedom and others supported socialism in one form or another.

Some historians of Russian culture believe that these two opposed tendencies have been preserved to this day under different names and in different forms. It should be noted that some Westernizers passed through several stages in their development and, either at the beginning or at the end of their life, considerably departed from the typical Westernizers' standpoint. The first thinker to be discussed in the present chapter, Chaadaev, affords a clear instance of this.

Pyotr Yakovlevich Chaadaev (1794–1856), the son of a wealthy landowner, studied at the Moscow University, but left it before graduating and went into the army. He took part in the war of 1812 and in the foreign campaigns that followed it. In 1820 when he was an officer in a Hussar regiment of the Guards he was sent to the Congress at Troppau to report to Alexander I on the mutiny in the Semyonovsky regiment. A few months after this, in 1821, he resigned his commission. Conflicting rumors as to what had passed between Alexander I and Chaadaev at Troppau and why he left the army are discussed in detail in Quénet's book *Tchaadaev* (54–72). From 1823 to 1826 he lived abroad and therefore did not take part in the Decembrist revolt. At Karlsbad he met Schelling with whom he kept up a correspondence. In France he met Lamennais.

At the end of 1829 Chaadaev began writing in French a treatise entitled *Philosophical Letters*. This work, consisting of eight letters, was finished in 1831. The letters are ostensibly addressed to a lady who is supposed to have asked Chaadaev's advice on the ordering of her spiritual life. In the first letter Chaadaev advises the lady to observe the ordinances of the Church as a spiritual exercise in obedience. Strict observance of church customs and regulations may only be dispensed with, he says, when "beliefs of a higher order have been attained, raising our spirit to the source of all certainty;" such beliefs must not be in contradiction to the "beliefs of the people." Chaadaev recommends a well-regulated life as favorable to spiritual development and praises Western Europe where "the ideas of duty, justice, law, order" are part of the people's flesh and blood and are, as he puts it, not the psychology, but the physiology of the West. He evidently has in mind the disciplinary influence of the Roman Catholic Church. As to Russia, Chaadaev is extremely critical of it. Russia, in his opinion, is neither the West nor the East. "Lonely in the world, we have given nothing to the world, have taught it nothing; we have not contributed one idea to the mass of human ideas." "If we had not spread ourselves from Behring Straits to Oder, we would never have been noticed." We do not, as it were, form part of the human organism and exist "solely in order to give humanity some important lesson."

This first "Philosophic Letter," dated December 1, 1829, was published in 1836 in the magazine *Telescope*. The censor who allowed it to be printed was dismissed from his post, the magazine was suppressed, and the editor, Professor Nadeshdin was exiled to Ust-Sysolsk and then to Vologda, whence he returned in 1838. Chaadaev was declared by the Emperor Nicolas I to be mad; for a year he was a prisoner in his own house under medical and police supervision. The censors were ordered not to pass any critical comments on Chaadaev's *Letter*. It was reprinted only in 1906 in the magazine *Voprosi Filosofii i Psihologii* and in Chaadaev's collected works, edited by Gershenson. Chaadaev's other *Letters* have been recently discovered by Prince D. Shahovskoy and the second, third, fourth, fifth and eighth were published in 1935 in the *Literaturnoe Nasledstvo,* XXII–XXIV. The sixth and the seventh letters were not printed, probably because in them Chaadaev speaks of the beneficial influence of the Church; fanatical atheists who rule U.S.S.R. would regard those letters as "opium for the people."

Chaadaev's philosophical outlook had a strongly marked religious character. He says that in order to combine "the ideas of truth and of goodness" one must thoroughly assimilate "the truths of the Revelation." It is best to rely on those not infrequent moments when, under the influence of religious feeling, "we fancy that we have lost our personal power and are involuntarily drawn toward the good by some higher power which draws us away from the earth and raises us to heaven;" then "the highest truths of all will flow into our heart of themselves" (Letter II, 27).

Two forces are active in our life: one force is "imperfect" and within us, another, "perfect," outside us, and from it we receive "the ideas of goodness, duty, virtue, law" (III, 31). They are handed down from generation to generation, thanks to the unbroken succession of minds which form one universal consciousness. "There is no doubt," Chaadaev writes, "the totality of all beings forms an absolute unity;" "it is a fact of enormous importance," "but it has nothing in common with the kind of pantheism proposed by most modern philosophers" (V, 46). "As nature is one, so—in Pascal's imaginative phrase—the whole succession of human generations is one man who abides eternally" (49).

Egoism separates man to some extent from the cosmic unity. Time and space are forms in which, in consequence of this separation, the external world appears to us (III, 34 f.). Similarly, there are no quantities in reality: "Absolute units exist in the mind only" (IV, 38). In reading Kant's *Critique of Pure Reason* Chaadaev scratched out the title and wrote instead *"Apologete adamitischer Vernunft."* He evidently meant that Kant expounded the doctrine not of pure reason but of reason distorted by sin.

The Christian teaching demands that we should attain "the regeneration of our being;" "it consists in the abolition of our old nature, and the birth in us of a new man, created by Christ" (III, 30). "The wonderful interpretation of life brought to the earth by the Founder of Christianity; the spirit of self-renunciation; abhorrence of division; passionate longing for unity; this is what keeps Christians pure under any circumstances. This is how the idea, revealed from above, is preserved, and through it there is accomplished the great work of merging the souls and the different moral forces in the world into one soul, one force. Such mergence is all that Christianity is intended for." The attainment of it is "the Kingdom of God," "the realized moral law" (VIII, 62). "Christianity was established without the help of any book." "The basis of Christianity is not a book, but Christ Himself" (60). The dogma of the real presence of Christ's body in the Eucharist "is particularly important." It may serve perhaps "as a means of uniting different Christian denominations" (62).

Serfdom aroused Chaadaev's indignation more than anything. His attitude to monarchy was expressed in a proclamation which he wrote in 1848 at the time of revolutions in Europe and hid inside a book in his library. In this proclamation, written in would-be peasant language, he expresses joy at the fact that the peoples have risen against their sovereigns. It ends with the words "We don't want any King except the King of heaven" (*Liter. Nasl.* XXII–XIV, 680).

Chaadaev's negative attitude to Russia, expressed so sharply in his first "Philosophical Letter" became less pronounced under the influence of Prince Odoevsky and other friends. In 1837 he wrote "A Madman's Apology" which was published in Paris after his death by a Russian Jesuit, Prince Gagarin in the book *Oeuvres choisies de P. Chaadaief*, 1862. Chaadaev came to the conclusion that the sterility of the Russian historical past is, in a sense, a virtue: the Russian people, unfettered by petrified forms of life, have freedom of spirit for carrying out a great task in the future. The Orthodox Church has preserved the essence of Christianity in its original purity; Orthodoxy can therefore vivify the body of the Catholic Church which is too much mechanized. The vocation of Russia is to bring about the final religious synthesis. When Russia, having assimilated all that is of value in Western Europe, begins to realize her God-given mission, she will be the center of intellectual Europe.

It must not be supposed that these ideas occurred to Chaadaev for the first time in 1836, after the catastrophe that befell him. The French Revolution of 1830 made him less inclined to idealize the West than he was when he wrote his "First Letter." In September 1831 he wrote to Pushkin: Mankind has before it the task of realizing "something like the political program preached by St. Simon in Paris or like the new kind of Catholicism which a few daring priests try to put in the place of the old one, sanctified by time." In a letter to A. I. Turgenev in November 1835—i.e., a year before the publication of the first "Letter"—Chaadaev answers the question as to who is to accomplish that task:

"We need not trouble about the ups and downs of the West, for we are not of the West." "If only Russia understood her mission, she ought to take the initiative in putting all generous ideas into practice, for she is free from Europe's ties, passions, ideas and interests." "Russia is too great to pursue a national policy; her task in the world is the politics of mankind; the Emperor Alexander understood this beautifully and that is his greatest glory. Providence has made us too strong to be selfish, it has put us beyond national interests and entrusted to us the interests of humanity; all our thoughts in life, science and art must start from this and culminate in this; in this lies our progress and our future." "This will be the logical result of our long solitude: all great things came from the desert" (*Lit. Nasl.* XXII–XIV, 16 f.). These ideas of Chaadaev's which bring him close to the Slavophils were expressed by him before the Slavophils had worked out their theory.[1]

2. N. STANKEVICH

The rise of the "Westernizing" movement in the strict sense is connected with the activity of Stankevich's "circle." It was formed in 1831 when N. V. Stankevich became a student at the Moscow University, and consisted chiefly of his fellow students. Hertsen and Ogaryov, who were also Westernizers, had at that period a circle of their own. Stankevich's circle included Belinsky, K. Aksakov, the poet Koltsov, the poet Lermontov, M. Bakunin (from 1835), V. Botkin, Katkov, Granovsky, Kavelin. Their main interests were philosophy, poetry and music. At first they enthusiastically studied the philosophy of Schelling, and after 1835 took up Hegel. In poetry their attention was centered upon Goethe, Schiller, Hoffmann and especially Shakespeare, and in music upon Beethoven and Schubert. The moving spirit of the circle was Stankevich who attracted everyone by his remarkable intelligence, kindness, and his courteous and unaffected manner. Not all the members of the circle became Westernizers, and probably Stankevich himself would not have remained one wholeheartedly had not early death from consumption cut short his spiritual development.

Nikolay Vladimirovich Stankevich (1813–1840) was the son of a rich landowner in the province of Voronesh. In his student years in Moscow (1831–1834) he lived in the family of Professor Pavlov. Pavlov introduced him to Schelling's philosophy of nature, and Professor Nadezhdin to Schelling's aesthetics. Having begun to study the philoso-

---

1. *Chaadaev's Works and Letters*, 2 vols., edited by Gershenson, 1913–14; M. Gershenson, *P. T. Chaadaev: Life and Thoughts*, 1908; Charles Quenet, *Tchaadaev et les Lettres Philosophiques*, Paris 1931; E. Moskoff, *Chaadaev* (in English).

phy of Hegel, Stankevich went abroad and in 1838–1839 attended private lectures in Hegel's Logic by Professor Werder in Berlin. Stankevich published very little. Some idea of his philosophic views may be gathered from his letters and from the reminiscences of his contemporaries. P. V. Annenkov published his correspondence and wrote his biography.[1] In a letter to M. Bakunin, Stankevich says that the whole of nature is one single organism evolving toward reason (596). Love is the feeling that lies at the basis of nature. He regarded woman as a sacred being. It is not for nothing, he says, that the Virgin and Mother is the fundamental symbol of our religion (592). In a letter to Miss L. A. Bakunin a propos of self-education he advises her "not to try crushing out one's defects one by one; it is better to notice their common source, the lack of love, and to think not of one's imperfection, but of what is beautiful in the world" (512).

When philosophy recombines that which it has broken up into elements, it becomes poetry (610). In other words, Stankevich thinks that philosophy discovers the truth about the real concrete being, and this being is the living personal spirit; otherwise, as he puts it, we should have to regard as concrete such things as railways, while actually they are only means to real being (367). He writes to Granovsky: "Remember that *contemplation* is necessary for the development of *thought* . . . a thing can be fully grasped only through general living feeling" (187). The study of Hegel convinced Stankevich that his conception of the cosmic process as the development of the Absolute idea is not abstract panlogism; i.e., not a theory of the dialectical self-movement of *impersonal* abstract notions. He detected that in Hegel the bearer of abstract notions always is in the last resort the spirit as a concrete living person.

Both in Germany and in other countries Hegel's philosophy has often been interpreted as abstract panlogism. The fact that Stankevich interpreted it as concrete ideal-realism is an expression of the general tendency of Russian philosophy toward concreteness. It is significant that one of the best works on Hegel is that by a Russian philosopher I. A. Ilyin, *The Philosophy of Hegel As a Concrete Doctrine of God and Man* (1918). N. Lossky's article "Hegel As an Intuitivist" is devoted to the same subject.[2]

Stankevich was not a convert to Hegel's philosophy. Observing that Hegel denied personal immortality, he wrote to Bakunin: His philoso-

---

1. N. V. Stankevich, *Correspondence and Biography*, written by P. V. Annenkov, Moscow 1858. This book is the source of my information about Stankevich's philosophical ideas.
2. *Proceedings of the Russian Scientific Institute in Belgrade*, IX, 1933; "Hegel als Intuitivist," *Blätter für Deutsche Philosophie*, IX, 1.

phy now "blows cold on me" (624). There is no doubt that in his further intellectual evolution Stankevich would have worked out an original system of Christian philosophy and not have been a typical Westernizer like Belinsky and Hertsen.

3. V. BELINSKY

Vissarion Grigoryevitch Belinsky (1811–1848) was a gifted literary critic. While a student at the Moscow University he joined Stankevich's circle. In it he became acquainted with Schelling's philosophy of nature; in 1836, under M. Bakunin's influence, he was for a short time interested in the philosophy of Fichte, and then through Stankevich and Bakunin became an enthusiastic Hegelian and remained so from 1837 to 1840. The way he used Hegel's philosophy in his critical articles may be seen for instance from his argument about poetry in his article "On *Woe From Wit*," 1839: "Poetry is truth in the form of contemplation;" hence, "poetry is the same as philosophy;" it is concerned with absolute truth, though not in the form of "the dialectical development of the idea out of itself, but in the form of the immediate manifestation of the idea in an image."

In 1839 Belinsky moved from Moscow to Petersburg and began working for Kzaevich's magazine *Otechestvenniya Zapiski*. In that year he published in the magazine three articles on the lines of "reconciliation with reality," "The Anniversary of Borodino," about the German critic Menzel and about Griboyedov's *Woe From Wit*. He makes use in them of Hegel's idea that "everything real is rational" and "everything rational is real." Extolling autocracy, Belinsky writes "with us the Government was always in advance of the people." Monarchic power "always acted in mysterious accord with the will of Providence—with rational reality" ("The Anniversary of Borodino"). "A man serves his Tsar and country from a lofty conception of his duty toward them, from the desire to be a means for truth and goodness, from the consciousness of being a part of society, of his physical and spiritual kinship with it—this is the world of reality" ("On *Woe from Wit*").

Belinsky was bitterly attacked for these articles by the opponents of autocracy. Living in Petersburg he came to know better the reactionary nature of Nicolas I's regime. In June 1841 in a letter to Botkin he speaks sharply not only against autocracy but against monarchy in general.

"Reconciliation with reality" expressed in his articles in 1839 should not be interpreted as a misunderstanding of Hegel's theory. People with a superficial knowledge of Hegel imagine that Hegel equates "reality" with every empirical fact. It would then have to be supposed that, e.g., the army punishment of beating a soldier to death, practiced under Nicolas I, was "real" and therefore rational. But in Hegel's complex philosophical system not everything that is present in the world is called real. Hegel distinguishes three levels of being: reality, appearance, and semblance; i.e., something like the Hindu Maya (*Wirklichkeit, Erscheinung und Schein*).

Belinsky did not know German, but he acquired his knowledge of Hegel from such experts as Stankevich and M. Bakunin and so he knew what Hegel meant by "reality." This can be seen from the following statement of his: "Reason in consciousness and reason in appearance, in short, the spirit manifesting itself to itself, is reality; whereas everything particular, accidental, irrational is a phantom as opposed to reality, and is its negation, a semblance and not being. A man eats, drinks, dresses himself—all this is the realm of phantoms, since his spirit has no part in it" ("On *Woe Wrom Wit*"). In the same article Belinsky writes: "Society is always more right than the individual and superior to him." So little did he value personality at that period of his activity.

Belinsky finally rejected Hegel's philosophy only when he came to recognize the supreme value of the individual. In a letter to Botkin in 1841 he says: "In Hegel the subject is not an end in himself, but a means for a momentary expression of the universal, and that universal is a kind of Moloch in relation to the subject, for after parading about in him (in the subject) for a time, it flings him away like a pair of old trousers." "Thank you very much, Yegor Fyodorovich[3]—I salute your philosopher's night-cap, but with all proper respect for your philistine philosophy, I have the honor to report to you that even if I did succeed in climbing to the topmost rung of the ladder of evolution, I would ask you from there to account to me for all victims of accidents, superstition, Philip II's Inquisition, etc., etc.; otherwise I will dash myself head downwards from the topmost rung. I do not want happiness even if it is given me unless I feel reassured about each of my brothers by blood —bone of my bone and flesh of my flesh," "the destiny of the subject, of the individual, the person, is more important than the destinies of the whole world and the health of the Chinese emperor (i.e., of Hegel's Universality)."[4]

In 1841 Belinsky was introduced to the French socialism of St. Simon and Leroux, and by 1848 socialism was for him "the idea of ideas." The "frantic Vissarion," as he was nicknamed for his passionate

---

3. A Russianized form of Hegel's Christian name.
4. I. Billig, *Der Zusammenbruch des deutschen Idealismus bei den russischen Romantikern* (Bjelenski, M. Bakumin), Berlin 1930.

temperament, forgetting his recent concern for the victims of history, wrote to Botkin: "I am beginning to love humanity in Marat's style: to render the smallest fraction of it happy, I believe I could exterminate the rest of it by fire and sword."[5]

In 1843–44 one of Belinsky's friends translated for him Feuerbach's *Essence of Christianity* which greatly appealed to him. Soviet writers maintain that at the end of his life Belinsky adopted under Feuerbach's influence, the standpoint of "anthropological materialism."[6] But since they are directed by the Soviet Government to find as many materialists as possible among the representatives of the Western-European and Russian culture, one cannot take their word for it; they consider even such a philosopher as Spinoza a materialist. Belinsky's writings do not show that he became a materialist, though it is true that during the last years of his life he completely ceased to refer to the supersensuous bases of the world's being. In February 1847 he wrote to Botkin: "To the devil with metaphysics, that word means the supernatural and therefore an absurdity;" it is necessary "to free science from the phantoms of transcendentalism and theology." In the article "A Survey of Russian Literature," written in 1846 he says: "Psychology not based upon physiology is as invalid as a physiology that knows nothing about the existence of anatomy." These words about the connection of mental life with physiological processes may be interpreted in several different ways, having nothing to do with materialism. Indeed, in the same article Belinsky writes: "The highest in man is his spirituality—i.e., feeling, reason, will—which express his eternal, abiding and necessary essence." "When someone you love dies, there does not die with him that which was best and noblest in him, what you called in him moral and spiritual —only the accidental, the crudely-material has died." "What is personality? The more clearly I contemplate within myself the essence of personality, the less I know how to define it in words."

It may also be questioned whether Belinsky really became an atheist at the end of his life. In a letter to Gogol à propos of his book *Correspondence With Friends,* Belinsky speaks most unfavorably about the Russian Orthodox Church and maintains that the Russian people "by nature are profoundly atheistic." In France, he says, many who have renounced Christianity still obstinately cling to some "sort of God" (15. VII. 1847). But six months after that letter, in the article "Survey of Russian Literature in 1847," written shortly before his death, he speaks as follows: "The Redeemer of mankind came into the world for the sake of all men." "He—the Son of God, humanly loved men and had

---

5. Belinsky, *Letters*, II, 244–247,
6. See M. Iovchuk, *Belinski, His Philosophical and Social Views*, Gosuld. izd. 1939.

compassion for them in their destitution, filth, shame, depravity, vices and crimes." "It was not in vain that the Divine word of love and brotherhood was spoken in the world."

In the course of his short but active life Belinsky often changed his philosophical views, and each of them profoundly affected his writings as a critic and publicist. He has, however, done nothing to further the development of philosophy as such, and I have spoken of him at such length only because he exercised great influence upon Russian culture as a remarkable literary critic endowed with fine aesthetic taste.

Another Westernizer to exercise great influence upon Russian political thought and the revolutionary movement was A. I. Hertsen.

4. A. HERTSEN

Alexander Ivanovich Hertsen (1812–1870) was an illegitimate son of a rich Russian landowner Yakovlev and a German girl Luise Haag brought by him to Russia from Stuttgart. As a boy of thirteen, during the coronation of Nicolas I in Moscow after the execution of the Decembrists, standing in the crowd "before the altar defiled by bloodstained prayers," as he puts it in his Memoirs, he vowed "to avenge the victims and to devote himself to the struggle against this throne, this altar and these cannons." Hertsen was a graduate of the Physico-Mathematical Faculty of the Moscow University. As a student he was much attracted by the socialism of St. Simon, and in 1834 was imprisoned and afterwards exiled to the northeast of Russia where he had to work in a Government office. In 1842 Hertsen retired, settled in Moscow and devoted himself to serious reading and literary work. In 1847 he emigrated to France. In 1855 he began publishing a magazine *Polarnaya Zvezda* (the Polar Star) and then *Kolokol* (the Bell). Hertsen's influence on Russian public life was considerable, but he made no original contributions to philosophy. The only philosophical things he wrote are essays on *Dilettantism in Science,* 1843, *Letters on the Study of Nature,* 1845, and *Letter To My Son* (about freedom of will), 1867.[1]

Hertsen's ideology was influenced by St. Simon's socialism, Schiller's philosophical views, Goethe's works on natural science and afterwards by the philosophy of Hegel, Feuerbach and finally of Proudhon. Hertsen was interested not in working out philosophical theories but in applying them in practice, in the struggle for the freedom and dignity of personality and for the realization of social justice.

---

1. Hertsen, *Collected Works,* 22 vols., ed. by Lemke, 1920. Hertzen, *Selected Philosophical Works,* 2 vols., Ogiz 1946. In making quotations I shall refer to the pages in this edition.

Lenin characterized Hertsen's ideology as follows: "He went beyond Hegel, towards materialism, after Feuerbach" . . . "Hertsen came right up to dialectical materialism and stopped short of historical materialism. This 'stoppage' was the cause of Hertsen's spiritual collapse after the revolution of 1848."[2] Lenin's words express the typical bolshevik tendency to regard as a materialist any writer who recognizes the close connection between mental and bodily processes. In truth, however, one can only find in Hertsen a negative attitude to religion, to the idea of a personal God and of personal immortality, but not the classical materialism according to which mental processes are passive and wholly dependent upon material processes. Having had a scientific education Hertsen highly valued the connection between philosophy and natural science, but he maintained that nature should be interpreted not by the method of "sensuous certainty" only (94), but of "speculative experience" used by Goethe in his works on natural science (112). Materialist metaphysicians, says Hertsen, "spoke only about the external processes; they thought that was all, and they were mistaken: the theory of sensuous thinking was a kind of mechanical psychology, just as Newton's view was a mechanical cosmology." "Materialists in general could never understand the objectivity of reason, . . . with them, thought and existence either fall apart or affect each other externally." Limited rationalistic thinking leads to "materialism which understands nothing except substance and body, and therefore does not understand either substance or body in their true meaning."[3] "Descartes could never rise to the idea of life;" the body is for him a machine (239).

Hertsen recognized the presence of objective reason at the basis of nature and called Hegel's theory that everything real is rational and everything rational real "a great idea" (78). But he was opposed to the false interpretation of this thesis and attacked those who preached "acceptance of all the dark side of contemporary life, calling everything trivial, accidental, outlived, in short everything one comes across, *real* and therefore having a right to recognition" (78).

Hertsen was not a materialist either in his youth or at the end of his life. When his son, a physiologist, gave a lecture in which he argued that all human and animal activities were reflexes and that consequently there was no free will, Hertsen wrote *A Letter To My Son*. All organic expressions, he says, "have a physiological basis, but go beyond it." "The historical process consists precisely in the constant emancipation of human personality from one form of slavery after another, one

---

2. These words serve as the epigraph to L. Piper's book *Hertsen's World Conception*, Moscow 1935.
3. *Lectures on the Study of Nature*, I, 270, 283 f.

authority after another, until the greatest correspondence is attained between reason and activity—a correspondence in which man *feels free.*" "Moral freedom is thus a psychological reality" (II, 281 f.). The conception of freedom developed in this letter is only relative and apparently fitted into a framework of determinism. But a determinist conception of psychological *moral* freedom cannot be worked out within a materialistic system; it presupposes the presence of *objective reason* at the basis of nature.

Hertsen sharply criticized the doctrines of the Slavophils, in so far as they idealized Orthodoxy and supported autocracy; but when, after the suppression of the revolutionary movement in 1848 he was disappointed with Western Europe and its "petty bourgeois" spirit, he came to the conclusion that the Russian village commune and the *artel* hold a promise of socialism being realized in Russia rather than in any other country. The village commune meant for him peasant communism.[4] In view of this he came to feel that reconciliation with the Slavophils was possible. In his article "The Moscow Panslavism and Russian Europeanism" (1851) he wrote: Is not socialism "accepted by the Slavophils as it is by us? It is a bridge on which we can meet and join hands" (I, 338).

Hertsen believed in the future of socialism, but he did not by any means regard it as a perfect form of social life. In 1849 he wrote: "Socialism will develop in all its phases to extremes, to the point of absurdity. Then once more a shout of protest will break forth from the titanic heart of the revolutionary minority—and once more there shall begin a deadly struggle in which socialism will take the place of the present-day conservatism, and will be overcome by a future, still unknown, revolution."[5]

In 1869 Hertsen wrote an article "To an Old Comrade," that is to M. Bakunin. He says in it that he does not believe "in the old revolutionary ways" (II, 294) and recommends "a gradual" social development. This article might well be read at the present day with advantage both by champions of violent revolutionary measures and by conservatives, who fail to see the necessity for social reforms ensuring to everyone material conditions of decent life.[6]

4. *The Russian People and Socialism*, II, 148, 1852.
5. "From the Other Shore," II, 99.
6. G. Spet, *Hertsen's Philosophical World Conceptions*, Moscow 1920; R. Gabry, *A. Hertsen, essai sur le formation et le developpement de ses idées*, Paris 1928.

Chapter 4

RUSSIAN MATERIALISTS IN THE SIXTIES—NIHILISM

I. MICHEL BAKUNIN

There have always been many materialists among Russian revolutionaries. In the twenties of the nineteenth century there were materialists among the Decembrists.[1] They had no significance whatever for the development of philosophy. In the sixties materialism was preached by M. Bakunin, Chernyshevsky, Dobrolubov and Pisarev and also by the famous physiologist Sechenov who took no part in the revolutionary movement. From the end of the nineteenth century down to the present day dialectical and historical materialism founded by Marx and Engels became widespread among Russian prerevolutionary emigrants as well as in Russia. This variety of materialism will be discussed in a different chapter.

Mihail Alexandrovich Bakunin (1814–1876), the son of a landowner, studied at the School of Artillery from 1828–1833, afterwards served as an officer in the army and retired in 1835. Joining Stankevich's circle he studied the philosophy of Kant, Fichte and Hegel. A convinced Hegelian, Bakunin interpreted reality as the eternal Divine Life, as the will and activity of the Spirit. The universal, taken in the abstract, remains lifeless and formal; it must be realized in the life of personality, in divinely human life penetrated by love. Bakunin interpreted at that time Hegel's thesis that "everything real is rational and everything rational is real" in the spirit of conservatism, and it was under his influence that Belinsky went through the phase of "reconciliation with reality."

In 1840 Bakunin went to Berlin for purposes of study. There he made friends with Arnold Ruge and other "Hegelians of the left." In 1842 he published in Ruge's magazine an article "Die Reaktion in Deutschland." He speaks in it of the absolute freedom of the spirit and,

---

1. Pavlov-Silvansky, Professor of Russian history, wrote an article about them in *Byloe*, VII, 1907, entitled "The Materialists of the Twenties."

maintaining that the negative is the condition of the positive, passes from conservatism to the other extreme and preaches the destruction of everything old. "Allow us to trust the eternal spirit," he writes, "which breaks up and destroys only because it is at the same time the inexhaustible and eternally creative source of all life. The passion for destruction is a creative passion."

This was the beginning of a stormy period in Bakunin's life. He took part in many political uprisings, was more than once sentenced to death, spent many years in prison after being handed over to the Russian government, was exiled to Siberia and escaped from there in 1861 to England; afterwards he lived in Italy and Switzerland. At that period of his life he became a materialist and began working out a peculiar form of anarchism. In 1868 he wrote in the magazine *Narodnoe Delo* which he published in Zürich: "The intellectual liberation of the individual is only possible on the basis of atheism and materialism; social and economic liberation is reached through abolishing hereditary property, giving the land to communes of laborers, and factories and capital to associations of workers, through abolishing marriage and family and organizing public upbringing of children." In his books *Fédéralisme, Socialisme et Antithéologisme* and *Dieu et l'Etat* he says that truly free men do not need the power of the state, for it is in their interest to support one another: they see in this the development of their own self; this is humane egoism. The social whole must be a free alliance of free communes.[2]

2. N. G. CHERNYSHEVSKY

Nicolay Gavrilovich Chernyshevsky (1828–1889) was the son of a priest and was educated at the clerical seminary at Saratov; from 1846 to 1850 he was a student at the Petersburg University in the Faculty of Arts. Chernyshevsky's world conception was formed under the influence of the French eighteenth century materialism, of the philosophy of Hegel, of the teachings of Proudhon, St. Simon, Fourier, Leroux and especially of Feuerbach, whose *Essence of Christianity* he read in 1849. Up to 1848 Chernyshevsky was deeply religious. He also believed at that period of his life that hereditary unlimited monarchy was specially intended for the protection of the oppressed, and transcended all class distinctions.[1]

2. M. Bakunin, *Collected Works and Letters*, 4 vols., 1934–35; *Oeuvres*, 6 vols., Paris 1907–1913; M. Nettlau, *The Life of M. Bakunin*, 3 vols., London 1894–1900; A. Kornilov, *M. Bakunin's Youth*, 1915; A. Kornilov, *M. Bakunin's Wanderings*, 1925; Y. M. Steklov, *M. A. Bakunin*, 4 vols., 1926; E. Carr, *M. Bakunin*, London, 1937.

1. "Diary," *Literaturnoe Nasledstvo*, Giz. I, 276 f., 1928.

At the age of twenty he became a materialist, an atheist, a democratic republican and a socialist. Nonexistence of God was proved for him by the fact of undeserved sufferings of men in general and of good men in particular. Abolition of monarchy by means of a pitiless peasant revolution was one of the main objects of his life. His revolutionary activity led to his arrest in 1862, to penal servitude in Siberia and afterwards to life there as a settler. In 1883 Chernyshevsky was allowed to return to European Russia and to live first in Astrakan, and afterwards in Saratov.

Hegel's influence upon Chernyshevsky was mainly confined to the fact that he greatly valued the dialectical method which compels the admission that "everything in the world changes" owing to the presence in life of opposed forces and qualities.[2] The most difficult problem for materialism is to explain how material processes can give rise to the mental. Chernyshevsky solves it by reference to Hegel's doctrine that quantitative changes result, at a certain stage, in the appearance of a new quality. His argument about the vibrations of ether and sensations of color is particularly interesting. In a letter to his sons from Siberia he says: "Naturalists wrongly imagine that ether waves are transformed into impressions of color. Color impressions are the same waves that go on moving along the optical nerve, reach the brain and continue their movement in it. There is no transformation here whatever."[3] If this statement does not imply an absurd identification between ether waves and colors, it must mean that even outside the human organism material processes contain sensory qualities of color, sound, etc.—i.e., those qualities are material and not mental realities. This theory is fairly widespread in modern philosophy.

In biology Chernyshevsky supported the doctrine of Transformism, but he was greatly scornful of Darwin's theory of struggle for existence as a factor in evolution. He maintained that the struggle for existence, owing to excessive reproduction and shortage of food, is bad for the organism and leads to degeneration and not to improvement. If this were the only factor in evolution, organic life would, he thinks, have disappeared altogether and been replaced by inorganic combinations, more stable than organisms.[4]

In ethics Chernyshevsky defended the theory of "rational egoism." A rational egoist understands that personal happiness coincides with the common good. Chernyshevsky propounded his ethical theories most

2. "Essays on the Gogol Period of Russian Literature," *Collected Works*, II, 122 f.
3. Steklov, *N. G. Chernyshevsky*, I, 243.
4. N. G. Chernyshevsky, "Origin of the Theory of a Beneficent Struggle for Life," *Collected Works*, X, part 2.

forcibly in his novel *What Is To Be Done?* One of the characters in that novel, Lopuhov, in sacrificing himself for the sake of others, says, "I am not a man to make sacrifices. And indeed there are no such things. One acts in the way that one finds most pleasant." A number of people regard this argument as an incontrovertible proof of the truth of eudeimonic and even of hedonistic theories of ethics. In truth, however, it contains the following fallacy of malobservation. The purpose of our every action is some real or fictitious value, loved by us, and the feeling of pleasure which we experience is merely a symptom of attaining the purpose, and certainly not the purpose itself. Materialists cannot explain the disinterested love for impersonal values such as truth or beauty or for the value of another's being, and therefore try to interpret every action as the consequence of striving for pleasure. The fact that men like Chernyshevsky, who devote their whole life to disinterested service of impersonal values, tend to explain their conduct by egoism is often due to a kind of chaste reserve which makes them avoid high-sounding words like conscience, honor, ideal, etc.

Chernyshevsky's chief object of study was political economy, but the thesis he submitted for the degree of Master of Philosophy at the Petersburg University in 1854 dealt with aesthetics: "The Aesthetic Relation of Art to Reality." He attacked in it the idealistic German theories of aesthetics. According to him "beauty is the fulness of life" (X, 115). The purpose of art is to reproduce reality and to explain it. The beauty of the living reality is higher than works of art.[5]

The rejection of the traditional bases of social life expressed in the works of Chernyshevsky and his co-believer Dobrolubov (1836–1861) has been aptly called *nihilism*. J. S. Turgenev, who coined the name, said once to Chernyshevsky in speaking about his movement, "You are a snake, and Dobrolubov is a cobra." The most striking representative of the movement was Pisarev.

3. D. PISAREV

Dmitri Ivanovich Pisarev (1840–1868) was the son of a landowner. He died early—he was drowned while bathing in the sea near Riga—but he had written many works that met with great success. He was a gifted essayist, literary critic, publicist and popularizer of theories on natural science. Like Chernyshevsky and Dobrolubov, Pisarev was deeply religious in his early youth. At the university he joined a circle of religious mystics who made a vow of lifelong celibacy. Perhaps this very excess of religious fervor was one of the reasons of his losing faith

5. N. G. Chernyshevsky, *Collected Works*, 10 vols., 1906. Y. M. Steklov, *N. G. Chernyshevsky, His Life and Works*, 2 vols., 1928.

two years later.[1] Having gone through this crisis he became a convert to the crude materialism of Vogt, Moleschott and Büchner. "One may make the bold surmise," he wrote, "that diversity of food, resulting in diversity of blood components, is the ground of intellectual many-sidedness and harmonious equilibrium between the divergent forces and strivings in a man's character." He explained the lively intellectual activity of the eighteenth century by the introduction of tea and coffee which act as stimulants.[2]

Pisarev explained human conduct by egoism and preached the liberation of the individual from all compulsion. To do good meant, according to him, to be useful to people and to enjoy such activity; i.e., to carry it out freely and not from submission to authority, from a sense of duty, etc.

Pisarev was contemptuous of art and philosophy, and declared that "a pair of boots is higher than Shakespeare." Like M. Bakunin he preached destruction: "What can be broken, should be broken; what will stand the blow, is fit to live; what breaks into smithereens, is rubbish; in any case, strike right and left, it will not and cannot do any harm." He hoped that social improvement will be brought about by a great increase in the number of "thinking realists" who, in building life, will be guided by the discoveries of natural science.[3]

4. I. SECHENOV

The physiologist Sechenov (1829–1905), in his book *Reflexes of the Cortex* tried to show that all human and animal actions are of the nature of reflexes. In his view, acts of thought have nothing at their basis "except a frequent excitation of the sense apparatus and the reproduction, connected therewith, of former similar impressions and their motor consequences."[1]

He said the same thing about the self as the modern English philosopher Bertrand Russell—namely, that the self is merely a grammatical form mistaken by people for a special psychic reality.[2]

---

1. See I. Lapshine, *La phénoménologie de la conscience religieuse dans la littérature russe*. Publ. by the Free Russian University, No. 35, 25–28, Prague.
2. L. A. Plotkin, *Pisarev and the Literary and Social Movement in the Sixties*, U.S.S.R. Academy of Sciences, 221, 1945.
3. D. I. Pisarev, *Collected Works*, 6 vols., 1894: *Selected Works*, 2 vols., Moskow-Leningrad 1934–35; L. A. Plotkin, *Pisarev*, 1940; F. Barghoorn, "D. I. Pisarev: A Representative of Russian Nihilism," *The Review of Politics*, II, April 1948.

---

1. Sechenov, "Who Is to Investigate Psychology, and How?" *Vestnik Europy*, April 1873, p. 597.
2. Sechenov, *Reflexes of the Cortex*, 1866; *Psychological Studies* 1873; Sechenov, *Selected Works*.

The doctrine that all human and animal actions are reflexes has flourished in Russia owing to the work of the physiologist J. P. Pavlov (1849–1936) and his school, and also of the psychiatrist V. M. Behterev (1857–1927). In his book *Collective Reflexology* Behterev tries to interpret the whole of social life as a system of reflexes. Pavlov's pupil Savich published in the *Review of the Biological Laboratory of P. F. Lesgaft* an article intended to prove that the highest creative manifestations of the human intellect are merely conditioned reflexes. As an instance he gives an analysis of Darwin's life and activity, attempting to show that all the great scientist's creative work may be interpreted as a series of conditioned reflexes.

Chapter 5

RUSSIAN POSITIVISTS

1. P. LAVROV—I. VIRUBOV—E. DE ROBERTY

The French positivism of Comte and the English positivism of John Stuart Mill and Herbert Spencer had many adherents in Russia. P. L. Lavzov was an influential representative of this trend of thought.

Pyotr Lavrovich Lavrov (1823–1900) was professor of mathematics at the School of Artillery. Owing to his connection with revolutionary circles he had to retire in 1866 and was exiled to the province of Vologda; he escaped from there in 1870 and settled in Paris. His philosophical views were formed under the influence of Comte, John Stuart Mill, Spencer and Feuerbach. According to Lavrov, only facts given in experience can be objects of scientific study. Science presupposes the real existence of objects apprehended through the normal activity of our sense organs, and a causal connection between them. Philosophy is a creative pursuit critically uniting all branches of knowledge into one whole. Lavrov called his philosophy anthropologism, because man was at the center of it. He believed that a striving for pleasure was innate in us; a cultured man, however, learns to enjoy moral activity and forms a conception of the dignity of personality. Lavrov was a determinist, but he maintained that the birth of consciousness leads to the appearance of a special kind of reality, namely, of personality which regards itself as free and responsible. The conception of free will is the *idealization* of human nature, necessary for human development. Progress means the development of consciousness and of critical thought in every individual and the increase of social solidarity. Social justice will be achieved by a socialistic revolution. The Russian village commune and the possibility of realizing in it common cultivation of land and joint use of the products of labor, made Lavrov hope that the Russian people will be the first to make a social revolution.[1]

---

1. Lavrov's chief works are "Historical Letters" (under the penname Mirtov) and "Essay on the History of Modern Thought" (unfinished). *Collected Works,* Petrograd 1918–1920.

G. N. Virubov (1843–1913) and E. V. de Roberty (1843–1915) who also were positivists, wrote chiefly in French, having spent most of their life in France. Virubov together with Littré edited in 1867 the magazine *Philosophie positive*.

2. N. MIHAILOVSKY

Nicolay Konstantinovich Mihailovsky (1843–1904), publicist, critic, and popularizer of scientific theories, had as much influence on Russian social thought as Lavrov. For a number of years he was editor of *Russkoe Bogatstvo,* the magazine of the "Populists" who eventually formed the socialist revolutionary party. Mihailovsky described the aim of his literary activity as follows: "Every time that the word *pravda* (truth) comes into my mind, I cannot help admiring its striking inner beauty. I don't think there is such a word in any European language. I believe it is only in Russian that truth and justice are called by the same word and as it were merge into one great whole." "Fearlessly to face reality and its reflection—the theoretical, objective truth—and at the same time to defend truth as justice, the subjective truth—this is my life's purpose."[1]

By objective truth Mihailovsky means the doctrine of mechanical causality in nature. But he considers that the objective method of investigation is insufficient in sociology. Man as a being capable of rational activity "brings a new force with him." He "is seldom satisfied with the combination of sensations and impressions received by him from the processes and results of the natural course of events."[2] He tries to change reality in conformity with his purposes and ideals, and this activity of his is subject to moral valuation. Moral categories, however, are subjective, and therefore in sociology not only the objective but the subjective method must be used, the last word belonging to the subjective method.[3] Mihailovsky does not uphold free will and does not deny that the historical process is subject to laws, but he nevertheless gives this advice to the individual: "Make history, move it in the direction of your ideal, for it is in this that obedience to the laws of history consists."[4]

Mihailovsky's ideal is a fully developed, many-sided personality and a society consisting of such personalities, capable of mutual understanding and mutual respect and of combining their powers in social activity for the attainment of happiness. In defining the conditions of social

1. N. K. Mihailovsky, *Collected Works*, I, 5. Preface to the third edition.
2. "Darwin's Theory and Social Science," *Collected Works*, I, 347, 4th ed.
3. "What Is Progress," *ibid.,* I, 164.
4. "Idealism, Realism and Idolatry," *ibid.,* IV, 69.

development in its approach to the ideal Mihailovsky distinguishes between the *type* of development and the *degree* of development. By the type of development he means the totality of the individual's different faculties, and points out that an individual who makes an almost exclusive use of one faculty, develops it to a high degree of perfection, but his other faculties become atrophied, so that his general type of development is lowered.[5] Starting with this conception, Mihailovsky attacks Spencer's theory of evolution and his view of society as an organism. Mihailovsky points out, on the authority of the zoologist Baer, that organisms develop and grow in perfection by means of the physiological division of labor which results in the greater complexity of the organism through the differentiation of its organs and tissues: every organ carries out perfectly some special function in serving the whole which, owing to this process of development, becomes a more and more complex individual entity. According to Spencer society also evolves through division of labor and specialization of its members' activity. Mihailovsky disputes this. He says that specialization leads to the regression of personality: the degree of development reached by a person who cultivates some one faculty in himself at the expense of other faculties may be very high, but the type of his development is lowered. In such a process of development society "tries to subordinate and to break up personality"; it transforms a man from an individual person into its own organ. One-sided specialists cease to understand the inner life of the representatives of other specialities; this leads to mutual indifference or even hostility, and a decrease in happiness. To avoid such undesirable consequences, "a man fights, or anyway ought to fight for his individuality, for the independence and many-sidedness of his self" (478). Thus a process that means progress in the life of organisms, means regression in the life of societies. Progress, according to Mihailovsky, is "a gradual approach to the wholeness of integers," to the greatest possible and many-sided division of labor between the organs of the body, and at the same time to the least possible division of labor between human beings.[6]

Criticizing the Darwinians who apply the law of the struggle for existence to the life of human society, Mihailovsky says that the human ideal is not adaptation to environment and elimination of the unfit; on the contrary, "you must adapt your environment to yourself, you must not eliminate the unfit, since struggle, natural selection and useful adaptation lead to the destruction both of yourself and of your society."[7]

The aim which Mihailovsky set himself was to work out a theory

---

5. "Struggle for Individuality," *ibid.*, I, 492 ff.
6. "What Is Progress?" *ibid.*, I, 166.
7. "Darwin's Theory of Social Science," *ibid.*, I, 308.

in which "truth-verity and truth-justice should appear hand in hand, completing each other." This goal is highly attractive. However, the fact that he was a positivist and therefore denied the possibility of metaphysics prevented Mihailovsky from giving a clear and consistent solution of the problem: had he worked out a theory of knowledge he would, like Kireyevsky, have come to the conclusion that the whole truth, in which truth-verity and truth-justice support each other, is revealed only to the whole man, capable of using all the varieties of experience—not only the sensory but also the experience of conscience, of aesthetic feeling and religious mystical intuition.

3. K. D. KAVELIN—M. TROITSKY—N. KAREYEV— N. KORKUNOV

Konstantin Dmitievich Kavelin (1818–1885) was inspired by a lofty ideal, but like Mihailovsky he could not justify it theoretically. Kavelin was a scholar and an expert on Russian history, a lawyer, a publicist and a philosopher. While doing government work he refused titles and orders of merit. In his youth he was interested in Hegel's philosophy, but after taking up historical research he learned to set great value upon the scientific method and came very near positivism; in his philosophical theories he avoided metaphysics. He wrote two philosophical works: *The Problems of Psychology*, 1872, and *The Problems of Ethics*, 1885.

Kavelin was opposed both to materialism and to metaphysical idealism, and tried to prove the relative independence of mental life. Consciousness and thought, he said, create an ideal world, lead man out of "the narrow circle of personal existence, raise him up to the universal, draw him to perfection, to an ideal ... the freedom of thoughts and actions is an organic property of human nature."[1] He believed, however, that the attempts to explain freedom of will had so far been unsatisfactory, and he did not work out any theory of the connection between material nature and mental events. Sechenov, a materialist and physiologist, wrote a long article "Who Is to Investigate Psychology and How?" as a crushing criticism of Kavelin's *The Problems of Psychology*. He concludes that all scientific investigation is based on the analysis of facts and that mental states are not accessible to scientific analysis, which can only be applied to physiological processes underlying those states; hence psychology should be the province of physiologists and not of psychologists. Kavelin made a detailed answer to Sechenov's article. Their dispute was published in *Vestnik Europy* in 1872–74.[2]

1. *The Problem of Ethics*, chap. II.   2. Kavelin, *Collected Works*, 1899.

The Slavophil Y. F. Samarin gave a detailed criticism of Kavelin's *The Problems of Psychology* from a point of view directly opposed to that of Sechenov. He pointed out that Kavelin had failed to establish the relative independence of mental life and had made many concessions to the materialists by exaggerating the importance of bodily processes for the life of the mind.[3]

M. M. Troitsky (1835–1899), professor at the University of Moscow, worked out a comprehensive system of psychology in the spirit of associationism. He sharply criticizes the philosophy of Kant and the post-Kantian German metaphysical idealism.[4]

N. I. Kareyev (1850–1931), professor of European history at the Petersburg University, in dealing with the problems of the philosophy of history, defended the theory of the significance of the individual in the historical process.[5]

Professor of jurisprudence, N. M. Korkunov (1853–1904), was the author of *The General Theory of Jurisprudence;* he expresses in it the following original and valuable idea. Mental processes have no spatial form. Therefore, although men's bodies are separated by space, their mental processes are interconnected, and this conditions the possibility of social life.

3. *Vestnik Europy*, 1875.
4. M. Troitsky, *Science of the Spirit; German Psychology in the Present Century*, 2 vols.
5. N. Kareyev, *The Fundamental Problems of the Philosophy of History*, 3 vols., 1883, 1890; *Essays on Sociology and the Philosophy of History*, 1895.

Chapter 6

DEGENERATION OF SLAVOPHILISM

1. N. DANILEVSKY

N. Y. Danilevsky (1822–1885), son of an army general, studied at the Tsarskoye Selo Lyceum from which he graduated in 1842. Being specially interested in natural sciences, he attended lectures at the faculty of natural sciences of the St. Petersburg University in 1843–47, and obtained his master's degree in botany. The ideas of Fourier having awakened his interest, he joined the revolutionary group of Petrashevsky, and was interned for one hundred days at the fortress of Saint Peter and Paul. It was proved at the inquest that Danilevsky envisaged Fourier's teaching as a purely economic, and not a revolutionary doctrine. He was released, but exiled from Petersburg and forced to work as a clerk in the offices of the governors of Vologda and Samara successively. From 1853, the Russian government assigned him a series of missions in order to survey the Volga and Caspian fisheries as well as those of the Black Sea and of the Russian North. In 1869, he began to publish in the review *Zarya* his work "Russia and Europe," which was later to appear in book-form. N. N. Strakhov, an admirer of Danilevsky, published in 1895 the fifth edition of this book, with a preface devoted to Danilevsky's life and works.

Danilevsky is considered as an epigon of Slavophilism, which at that time had entered the period of its decline. He is one of the most typical representatives of panslavism. In his book, *Russia and Europe* Danilevsky evolved in detail the theory concerning "the cultural-historical types" of mankind. This theory had previously been outlined by the German historian Rückert, and after Danilevsky, it was to become the topic of Spengler's writings. According to Danilevsky, there cannot be and there is no such thing as an all-human civilization. There are but various cultural-historical types of civilization, such as the Egyptian, Chinese, Assyria-Babylonian, Hebrew, Greek or Roman types. In contemporary history, Danilevsky was most interested in the Romano-Germanic and the Slavonic types, the last of which was beginning to take shape. The foundations of the civilization belonging to one type are not transmitted to another; there might only occur at times a survival of civilizations in a limited form and only in so far as minor traits are concerned. The period of growth of a cultural-historical type is undetermined in length, but the period of its flowering and fruition is brief; it exhausts once and for all the vital forces of a civilization (chap. V). Mankind, according to Danilevsky, is an abstract idea, not a living single whole. The relation of mankind to a people is that of species to kind. Species is an abstract and poor conception; the people is a concrete and living substance. The significance of cultural-historical types consists in the fact that each of them expresses in its own way the idea of man and these ideas taken as a whole are something all-human. The domination of one cultural-historical type extended to the entire world would mean the gradual exhaustion of life (chap. XV).

In our time, Danilevsky believes, the time has come for the development of the Slavonic race, as of a peculiar cultural-historical type. The original trait of this type will consist in the following: many cultural-historical types have one single basis; thus Hebrew culture is religious, Greek culture artistic, while Rome evolved a political culture. Romano-Germanic culture has a double basis: it is a political culture possessing a scientific and industrial character. The Slavonic type will be the first one possessing fully a quadruple basis: it will be 1) religious, 2) scientific, artistic, technological, industrial, 3) political, 4) economic and communal (chap. XVII).

In the future development of European history, Danilevsky states, Austro-Hungary will fall apart; there will arise an all-Slavonic federation, which will also include other racial bodies: Greece, Roumania and Hungary (chap. XIII). The Eastern problem will be solved following the struggle between the Romano-Germanic and the Slavonic world; Constantinople will become the capital of the Slavonic Union (chaps. XII and XIV).

In the first pages of his book Danilevsky devotes a great deal of attention to Western Europe's hostility toward Russia; he refutes the opinion that Russia is a rapacious conqueror. He demonstrates in detail that Russia never murdered nor mutilated nations (chap. I and II).

Dostoevsky started reading Danilevsky's book with vivid interest while this work was still appearing in the *Zarya* installments. But he was deeply disappointed when he discovered that Danilevsky rejected the oneness of mankind and the existence of all-human ideals. As we shall further see, Soloviev bitterly criticized Danilevsky's rejection of Christian universalism.

At the end of his life, Danilevsky devoted himself to the refutation of Darwinism. This work remained unfinished; in 1885, the first volume in two parts was published, and after the author's death one chapter of volume II appeared (1889). Danilevsky had presented his book to the Academy of Sciences in view of obtaining an award, but the latter was not granted. The Academy declared that this book was a round-up of the refutations of Darwinism having already been stated in Europe, though Danilevsky had developed them, adding new examples. Danilevsky conceived evolution as the consequence of an "organic goal-pursuing tendency," directed by a "reasonable cause." The idea and expression: goal-pursuing tendency (*Zielstrebigkeit*) were introduced into philosophy and biology by the famous zoologist Karl von Baer, with whom Danilevsky was on friendly terms.

Danilevsky stated the following aphorism concerning beauty: "God wanted to create beauty, and so He created matter."

2. N. STRAKHOV—K. LEONTIEV

N. N. Strakhov (1828–1896), having studied natural sciences, presented a dissertation for a master's degree in zoology in 1857. He did not choose a teaching career, but devoted himself to writing. His main works comprise philosophical essays, literary criticism and the study of the philosophical foundations of natural sciences in relation to Hegel's philosophy. In his book, entitled *The World as a Whole,* he demonstrates that the world is a "harmonious organic whole;" parts and phenomena of the world are not simply linked together, but submitted to each other, they form "a hierarchy of beings and phenomena;" the world is an organism in which the parts "serve each other, forming one whole," and man stands at the center. Strakhov struggled with peculiar insistence against the decline of spiritual culture, a decline manifested both in the West and in Russia, under the influence of materialism, positivism, nihilism. He demonstrated the fundamental error of these movements, which consists in the fact that they deny the higher spheres of being and tend to bring them down to the lowest levels of nature.[1]

K. N. Leontiev (1831–1891), a publicist and a writer, was not a Slavophil, but his ideas may be considered a degenerate form of Slavophilism. Vladimir Soloviev gave a good account and criticism of Leontiev's views in the *Russian Encyclopaedia* of Brockhaus and Efron. Berdyaev's book, *K. Leontiev* (G. Bles, London 1940) is also reliable.[2]

---

1. Strakhov's main works are: *A Method of Natural Sciences,* 1865; *The World as a Whole,* 1872; *The Struggle Against the West in Our Literature,* 3 vols., 1882, 1883, 1896; *Fundamental Ideas of Physiology and Psychology,* 1886; *Eternal Truths,* 1887; *From the History of Literary Nihilism,* 1892. Concerning Strakhov, see Chizhevsky, *Hegel in Russia,* pp. 266–283.

2. K. Leontiev, *Completed Works,* 8 vols.

Chapter 7

PRECURSORS OF VLADIMIR SOLOVIEV

1. P. D. YURKEVICH—V. D. KUDRIAVTSEV

Pamfil Danilovich Yurkevich (1827–1874) was professor of philosophy at the Moscow University from 1863 to 1874. Yurkevich sought in the spirit of platonism to discover behind the ever-changing phenomena perceived by the senses, the eternal idea of the object. In the idea, according to his teaching, thought and being are identical. Truth is revealed, not by thought alone, but also by the "heart;" that is in relation to man's religious and moral tendencies. In this process of ascension toward truth, knowledge is combined with faith which represents a factor more powerful than the merely empiric contents of thought. Without love, he declared, God cannot be known. The highest degree of the ascension toward the absolute, that is toward God, is mystical contemplation. That which can exist becomes actual through the media of that which *must* be, precisely through the aid of the Platonic idea of the Good.

Concerning Cernyshevsky's article "The Anthropological Principle in Philosophy," Yurkevich undertook a fundamental criticism of materialism. This criticism excited the hostility of the "progressive press" of his time, which started a slander-campaign against him. Chizhevsky, in his book *Hegel in Russia*, writes about Yurkevich. "His calm and efficient criticism of materialism (in the same way, he criticized "idealism" as well) did not encounter other methods of opposition than threats and imprecations. The most potent arm was slander: the enemies of Yurkevich discovered in his writings some lines stating that intellectual moments cannot be sufficiently active as methods of education . . . Life heeds more energetic foundations and methods than abstract conceptions of science—such as for instance man's dignity, a humane education." Yurkevich had doubtlessly in mind first of all religious faith and secondly, feeling. The champions of enlightenment saw in these lines the defense of corporal punishment. "The satirical press missed no occasion of attacking the hated philosopher, and the type of satire employed against him can be gathered from one of the slurs, comparing Yurkevich to the excrements of Diogenes. From 1859, to 1862, Yurkevich had published eight philosophical works; from 1862 to 1874, the year of his death, he wrote only one book" (253).

Yurkevich was a teacher of Soloviev who in his writings sympathetically appraised him, both as man and as philosopher.[1] Victor Dmitrievich Kudriavtsev (1828–1892) was professor of philosophy at the Moscow Theological School. Already as a student of this establishment, Kudriavtsev manifested exceptional abilities and obtained the Metropolitan Platon's scholarship; this gave him the right to add Platonov to his family name. In his work entitled *Religion, Its Essence and Origin,* Kudriavtsev-Platonov explains belief in God and the rise of religion by God's direct action on the spirit of man and by the religious experience resulting from this action. In the structure of the world, he declares, spiritual and material being differ profoundly from each other, but are nevertheless closely linked together. The attempts to understand the structure of the world through dualistic philosophy prove unsatisfactory; they lead to an issue where one of these two types of being is placed before the other, and the result is either materialism or idealism. We must discover a third principle which unifies spirit and matter. This principle is the absolutely perfect being, God, who created the world in such a way that matter serves as a substrata for the manifestation of the spirit. The goal of this world process is to draw nearer and nearer to absolute perfection. Kudriavtsev-Platonov gave his theory the name of transcendental monism.

Kudriavtsev-Platonov's idea was that it is possible to explain how psychical and material processes are tied together in spite of their profound difference only by discovering a third type of being standing above these two processes and uniting them; this idea is extremely valuable. However, the solution of the problem by reference to God yields no satisfying answer, as we know from the history of previous attempts: let us for instance recall Spinoza's pantheism, which, like all pantheistic doctrines is logically unsound; let us also recall the various forms of occasionalism, as well as the teaching of Leibniz concerning preestablished harmony. The link between the psychical and the bodily process in the life of man for instance, is so intimate that we have to discover in man's very structure the third principle, standing above these two types of process, and creating them in such a way that they are tied together.[2]

---

1. Soloviev, *Three Characteristics,* VIII. Works by Yurkevich: "The Heart and Its Significance in Man's Spiritual Life According to the Teaching of God's Word," *Trudy, Kiev, Theological School,* I, 1860. "The Idea," *Journal of the Ministry of Public Education,* 1860. "Reason, According to the Teaching of Plato and Experience According to the Teaching of Kant," *Moscow University Izvestia,* 1885.

2. *Collected Works of Kudriavtsev-Platonov,* published by the Theological School in three volumes, 1892–1894.

2. N. F. FEDOROV

In the evolution of Christian philosophy a place apart is held by Nikolay Fedorovich Fedorov (1828–1903) whose original ideas are still very little known, although at the time they made a great impression on V. Soloviev, Dostoevsky and Tolstoy.

The life of this man deserves a detailed study. There can be no doubt that he was a really righteous man, an uncanonized saint.

Fedorov, an illegitimate son of Prince P. I. Gagarin, was born in 1828. He studied in Odessa, at the Richelieu Lyceum, was a teacher of history and geography in provincial towns, then for many years the librarian of the Rumiantsev Museum in Moscow. A passionate bibliographer and lover of books he knew the whole contents of the Library and the places of books in it by heart. His erudition in all fields of knowledge was enormous. To people of most varied specialties working in the library he used to give, besides the books they ordered, several others bearing on the subject of their study, giving them also valuable advice and information. The accuracy and variety of his knowledge struck everybody who came into contact with him. In the early nineties several engineers, who were about to proceed to Siberia to make investigations for the tracing of the Trans-Siberian railway, paid a visit to the Rumyantsev Library. Fedorov at once referred them to a description of Siberia of which they had never heard, and throwing a glance at the projected railway line, found two mistakes in the map: in one case the altitude of a mountain was incorrectly given, in the other a rather important rivulet was completely omitted. On their return from Siberia, two years later, the engineers told Fedorov that he had been quite right. One can hear many similar stories about Fedorov told by historians, lawyers, philologists, physicians, technicians, etc.[1]

Living an intensive spiritual life and devoting himself entirely to public service, he reduced his own physical wants to the minimum. He occupied a tiny room and slept not more than four or five hours a day on a bare hump-backed trunk, resting his head on some hard object. His food consisted of tea with hard rolls, and of cheese or salted fish and often he would do for whole months on end without any hot food. Money was a nuisance to him. Receiving an insignificant salary (less than 400 roubles a year) and refusing any increase he used to give away the greater part of it, every month, to some "stipendiates" of his. He wanted to possess no property, and never had even a warm overcoat.

Fame and popularity he regarded as manifestations of immodesty.

1. *N. F. Fedorov: The Philosophy of Common Cause,* a biographical study compiled by Ostromirov, I, 13 ff., Kharbin 1928.

His articles appeared anonymously, and the majority of them were never published by him. His friends, V. Kozhevnikov and N. Peterson, published some of his writings after his death under the title *The Philosophy of the Common Cause* in 480 copies; they sent the book to the libraries and scientific societies and the remaining copies were distributed free of charge to all who wished to have it. A new edition of this book was published by Fedorov's admirers in Kharbin in 1928.

His modesty showed itself also in his refusal to be either photographed or painted. In order to have his portrait done his friends had to resort to a cunning device: the well-known painter Pasternak used to go to the Rumyantsev Library and, surrounding himself with books, pretend to read while now and then he would throw a glance at Fedorov and sketch his portrait (*ibid.*, XVIII).

In spite of his austere life he enjoyed excellent health and only fell ill when his friends compelled him to give up his habits. He never wore a fur coat and always walked; but in 1903, during severe December frosts, his friends made him put on a fur coat and take a cab. He contracted pneumonia and died.

All those who knew Fedorov felt a great respect for him and took a keen interest in his ideas. V. Soloviev wrote him: "Your plan is the first step forward made by the human mind on the path of Christ." Tolstoy used to say that by his way of life Fedorov was a pure Christian: "He is very poor, he gives away everything, and is always cheerful and meek."

Tolstoy's son, Ilya Lvovich, describing his father's relations with Fedorov, says: "He had extremely lively, keen and intelligent eyes, he seemed to radiate goodness which bordered on childish naivety. If there be saints they must be just like this." "It is remarkable that father, who always grew excited and easily lost his temper in argument, would listen to Nikolay Fedorovich with particular attention and never lost his temper with him."

Fedorov severely criticized Tolstoy's negative attitude toward higher cultural values, toward science and art. One day when Tolstoy came to the Library Fedorov started showing him its book treasures. "Don't people write a lot of silly things, all this ought to be burned," was Tolstoy's remark. Fedorov flew up at it: "I saw many silly men in my life," he said, "but no one as silly as you."

Fedorov connects his doctrine with the Christian religion, in particular with Orthodoxy as the religion which attaches especial value to the idea of resurrection (Easter) and everlasting life. Man's duty is to enter the path of *supramoralism*, to realize a synthesis of theoretical and practical reason and to become the reason of the Universe. Through knowledge and action man must transform all the forces of nature, at present blind and often hostile to him, into the instruments and organs of mankind. Having learned to control nature mankind will be able to overcome death; which is more, it can and must set itself the task of achieving *resurrection of all its ancestors*. After becoming multi-une, like the Tri-Unity of God the Father, the Son and the Holy Ghost, mankind will attain such "indivisibility" as to make impossible any disruption, any isolation—i.e., death.

The unbrotherly, hostile attitude of men and nations to one another is due, according to Fedorov, to the fact that under the pressure of the menacing, death-bearing forces of nature, every man becomes engrossed in the task of self-preservation; owing to this egotism the forces of men are divided and therefore insufficient for the solution of the great problem of ruling nature. Furthermore, they are to some extent actually directed to the struggle of man against man and of nation against nation. The social order arising out of egoism Fedorov designates as *zoomorphic*; it is based on the separation of the conscious and directing organs from the executive ones. Hence the distinctions of class and social standing. Owing to the discrepancy between thought and action the caste of scholars, engrossed in sheer contemplation, arrives at a false doctrine of the world and at a false orientation of all their scholarly activities; a contemplative scholar proclaims the world to be his presentation; he is engaged on the study of only that which *is,* taken in isolation from that which *ought to be* (p. 12); he is not interested in the final purpose of life; he does not investigate the causes of men's hostile attitude to each other, and so on. The false doctrine that the world is our presentation leads to false practices, such as e.g. morphinomania as a means of solving for oneself the cosmic problem by transforming unpleasant presentations into pleasant ones with the aid of drugs; or hypnotism as a means of "casting a spell," instead of educating a man's will and mind (p. 14 ff.). Great scientific discoveries and inventions, e.g. the explosives, are chiefly used in such a community not for common good but for mutual struggle.

The ideal social order must be based, according to Fedorov, on the unity of consciousness and action. There must be in it no class distinctions, no military or police coercion, no "demiurgical," i.e., industrial, activity giving shape to outward materials and relations. Under this ideal regime, which Fedorov calls "psychocracy," every one will do his duty fully aware of the necessity of the tasks with which he is faced.

The scientific activity under this regime will have as its special mission the study of the blind and deadly forces of nature with the object of turning them into lifegiving ones; all social work will be accompanied by the study of the corresponding region of the world.

Having learned to rule the forces of nature and so done away with hunger and all other wants, mankind, according to Fedorov, will at the same time do away with the causes of discord between men. It will concentrate all its forces on the common task of regulating the nature of the earth and even cosmos as a whole. The experiments with provoking rain by gun-firing, carried out in the United States in 1891, just at the time of the terrible famine in Russia due to drought, made a great impression on Fedorov. He speaks of the necessity of preserving armies under the future ideal regime, not for mutual destruction, but for the common task of regulating the forces of nature.

Fedorov's plans were very ambitious. He spoke of regulating meteorological processes and thus ensuring good harvests. He spoke further of utilizing solar energy and thus doing away with one of the hardest forms of industry—the coal-mining industry. But this is not all. He proposed to get hold of the electromagnetic energy of the earth so as to regulate its motion in space and turn it into a sort of vessel for cosmic cruises. The danger of the overpopulation of the earth did not terrify him, for he foresaw the possibility of colonizing other planets and heavenly bodies.

The supreme object to which the forces of nature must be made subservient is the resurrection of all our ancestors. Fedorov regarded as immoral the positivist theory of progress with its heartless attitude to the past generations and its building of the welfare of the posterity upon the corpses and sufferings of the ancestors (18–25). *"One must live not for oneself (egoism) and not for the others (altruism), but with everyone and for everyone; this is the union of the living (sons) for the resurrection of the dead (fathers)"* (II, 48). Even people who have no faith—e.g., the materialists—cannot prove that it is impossible to bring our ancestors to life, and have therefore, Fedorov thinks, no right to shirk the task. "Put together the engine, and consciousness will return to it," he says. The disintegration of the body and the complete dispersion of its particles cannot be an absolute obstacle to its reconstitution, for the particles of the body cannot go beyond the limits of space.

Fedorov designates the resurrection planned by him as *immanent;* he condemns the aspiration toward the transcendental existence of beyond. The ideal he proposes is the realization of God's Kingdom in this world.

N. A. Setnitsky, economist and philosopher, who was a professor at the University of Kharbin, in his book, *On the Ultimate Ideal* (1932), says that the bringing together of knowledge and action is being realized in Soviet Russia where scientific activity is understood as "a peculiar mission of expert men for carrying out the task of studying the blind and deadly forces of nature, in addition to which the demand is put forward that all people exercising this or that social function (employees and officials) should at the same time carry out the work of study in the sphere of activity ascribed to them." Similarly, in many technical plans of the Soviet Government he sees "a doubtless influence and fulfillment of Fedorov's ideas, though for the most part his name, having a strong religious coloring, is never mentioned and even the meaning of those works and their connection with Fedorov's plans are not realized. The most striking example of this is the attitude of the Soviets toward Fedorov's suggestions concerning the struggle against droughts." "The same is true of the most recent plans of utilizing the waterways of the U.S.S.R." (the problem of "Greater Volga," irrigation of Turkestan, etc.—82 ff.).

One could point to some still more daring plans discussed in the Soviet press; e.g., the plan of warming Siberia by altering the direction of the Gulfstream and diverting polar icebergs toward England in order to freeze that country which is the embodiment of hated capitalism.

In reality, as is well known, even the feasible technical projects do not lead to any increase of material welfare in Soviet Russia. Dostoevsky has long ago foretold that the attempt to build the "tower of Babylon" on sheer scientific foundations, "without God and religion," without a moral justification of social relations, as this is being done by the Communists in Soviet Russia, would merely lead to utter destitution and death.

Fedorov's philosophy strikes one by the singular blending in it of a deeply religious metaphysic—e.g., in the doctrine of the Holy Trinity as the ideal of loving unity of several persons—with a naturalist realism —e.g., in the doctrine of the methods of achieving the resurrection of our ancestors. What is meant is apparently the resurrection of man in a nontransfigured body, which would still need food; a question arises of colonizing other celestial bodies, and all this is attained by means of highly developed science and technique. From this point of view Fedorov's doctrine is akin to the modern teachings of the naturalists who think of prolonging life indefinitely through perfecting the art of medicine, improving the hygiene conditions of life, etc.

Fedorov's naturalism, in its combination with the Christian doctrine of the resurrection in the flesh, is inconsistent. Indeed, the body composed of impenetrable particles (atoms)—i.e., of particles performing the processes of repulsion in relation to the environment—is of necessity bound up with the struggle for existence and, therefore, with evil. The preservation of such a body for a long time requires a great deal of labor and a high degree of prevision. But the worst thing about it is that the eternal preservation of it, even had it been realizable, would amount to the perpetuation of evil and of lower forms of existence. Christianity sets up an infinitely higher ideal: it has in view the *transfigured* body, free from the processes of repulsion which create impenetrability; by its very conception this body is such that no force in the world can be found, or even conceived, capable of destroying it.

The transfigured body is not created by scientific techniques; it is created by the spirit of man loving God more than himself, and all other beings as much as himself, and therefore free from any selfish exclusiveness. At the basis of the Christian doctrine lies the conviction that the moral evil of pride and selfishness in general is primordial, and all the remaining forms of evil—imperfections of the body, the blindness of nature's forces and man's discord with it—are but a *consequence* of that primordial evil. Therefore the redemption from evil cannot be attained except through the elimination of its principal cause—the severance from God. Fedorov begs the question when he says that the struggle of every man for the preservation of his existence creates discord with other men; in fact, on the contrary, the discord between men and between man and nature brings about the struggle for existence.

Fedorov's philosophical works leave the impression of being the ideas of a gifted but untutored mind, not sufficiently systematic and consistent because of lack of learning and an extreme concentration on one pet idea. Yet they contain a wealth of original and profound reflections on various questions; e.g., on the imperfection of scientific knowledge when, severed from practice, of the positivist theory of progress; or, e.g., when he compares the old Gothic writing of the Germans and the old Russian writing with modern shorthand. It is possible that in our days, when mankind thanks to the extraordinary development of science and technique begins to set itself ever more daring tasks, Fedorov's philosophy will have a growing influence.

Chapter 8

VLADIMIR S. SOLOVIEV

Vladimir Soloviev was born in Moscow on January 16, 1853. His father Sergey Soloviev was a professor of the University of Moscow and a well-known Russian historian who wrote *The History of Russia*, in 29 volumes. Vladimir's grandfather, a priest, was a kind man and an ardent believer, a genuine Christian. Once, when his grandson was eight years old he took him to the altar and in a warm prayer blessed him for Lord's service.

At the age of seven Vladimir began reading, on the advice of his father, the lives of the saints. His religious feeling was so strong that he began exercising ascetic feats; sometimes, for instance, his mother would find him, in winter, lying in bed without a blanket. It was one of the exercises for vanquishing the flesh.[1]

In his early childhood Soloviev showed a liking for poetry, knew many songs and poems of Russian poets, was fond of Russian folklore, liked the peasants, the coachman, the beggars. A mythical attitude toward nature was very strongly developed in him. Even to inanimate objects he used to give proper names: his satchel he called Gregory, his pencil, Andrew. He sometimes had visions and prophetic dreams. In his tenth year he had a vision which was subsequently twice repeated and stands in close connection with his whole philosophical system. It was connected with his first love. The girl he was in love with turned out to be indifferent to him. Seized with jealousy he was standing at Mass in church. Suddenly all the immediate surroundings vanished from the field of his consciousness, and in the poem "Three Meetings," written not long before his death, he thus describes the unearthly vision he saw: he perceived suddenly the blue of the sky all around him, and in his own soul; and through this blue he saw the "Eternal Womanhood," woven as it were of blue ether, and holding in her hand a blossom from unearthly countries. She nodded in his direction, smiling at him with a radiant smile, and then disappeared in the mist. His soul became blind

---

1. See S. Lukyanov, *On V. S. Soloviev in his Young Years.*

to all worldly things, and the childish love which caused his jealousy became repugnant to him.[2]

That which he saw he subsequently interpreted as the vision of God's wisdom, Sophia—the Eternal and Perfect Feminine.

At the age of thirteen began the religious crisis in the life of Soloviev from which he emerged early in 1871 when he was eighteen. He succumbed to atheism, threw his ikons into the garden, became keen on Büchner's materialism and Pisarev's nihilism. Socialism and even communism became his social ideals. He gave up this simplified philosophy thanks to reading Spinoza, Feuerbach and J. S. Mill, who convinced him of the groundlessness of materialism. From Spinoza he turned to Schopenhauer and Hartmann, then to Schelling and Hegel, and ended by working out his own philosophical system. During this time (from 1869 to 1873) he was studying science and history and philology at the University of Moscow; after graduating he studied for a year at the Moscow Theological Academy.

His first important philosophical work was his master's thesis, "The Crisis of Western Philosophy: Against the Positivists," which he submitted in 1874. In his preliminary speech before the dissertation he said that absence of religion devastated the soul and led to suicide. He referred, no doubt, to his own mental crisis. On emerging from it he said in one of his letters (to Miss E. V. Romanov, of December 31, 1872), that rational philosophy was darkness, "death in life," but that this darkness could become a beginning of life: having come to the conclusion that he is "nothing," man can perceive that "God is everything," and then he will receive answers to all his questions in the Christian teaching which is based on Living God and not on abstract conceptions of reason.

Desirous of studying "Indian, gnostic and medieval philosophy," and being keen on the problem of Sophia, Soloviev on being sent abroad to complete his studies went to London in order to work at the British Museum. In his notebook of that time is to be found a prayer for the descent of Holy Divine Sophia. Here indeed he had, for the second time, a vision of Sophia. Its incompleteness did not, however, satisfy him. While he was thinking of this and eagerly desiring to see her more fully, he heard an inner voice which told him: "Be in Egypt!" Giving up all his work in London, Soloviev went to Egypt and took a room in a hotel in Cairo. After staying there for a time he went, one evening, on foot to Thebaide, without provisions, wearing a town dress,—top hat and overcoat. In the desert, twelve miles from the town, he met some Beduins who at first were frightened, taking him for the devil, but then

---

2. V. Soloviev, *God-manhood*, translated by P. Zouboff, Introduction by P. Zouboff, 13.

apparently robbed him and went away. It was night, jackals could be heard howling, Soloviev lay down on the ground. In his poem "Three Meetings" he thus relates what happened at the dawn:

> "All that was, and is, and ever shall be
> My steadfast gaze embraced it all in one.
> The seas and rivers sparkle blue beneath me,
> And distant woods, and mountains clad in snow.
> I saw it all, and all was one fair image
> Of woman's beauty, holding all as one.
> The boundless was within its form enclosed—
> Before me and in me is you alone."

The philosophical system to the working out of which Soloviev devoted his whole life may be, in the opinion of many students of his philosophy, called the philosophy of the Eternal Feminine.

In 1880 Soloviev received a degree of Doctor of Philosophy at the St. Petersburg University for his dissertation "A Critique of Abstract Principles."

Soloviev's professorial activity was a very shortlived one. He was Lecturer at the University of Moscow and then at the University of St. Petersburg and Professor at the Women's University until autumn 1881. After the murder of Alexander II on March 1, 1881 Soloviev gave in St. Petersburg a public lecture which he ended by courageously exhorting the Czar to pardon his father's assassins in the name of Supreme truth and not to inflict capital punishment on them.

After this he believed it necessary to resign from the Science Committee of the Ministry of Public Education, though the minister, accepting his resignation, declared: "I did not demand this."[3]

In his *curriculum vitae* for volume III of the Russian translation of Ueberveg's *History of Philosophy,* Soloviev wrote: "In March 1881 I gave a public lecture on capital punishment and was temporarily obliged to leave Petersburg . . . In 1882 I resumed my lectures on philosophy at the Petersburg University and at the Higher Women's School, but after a month I left Petersburg and gave up my teaching for good."[4]

He wrote to Professor Bestujev-Ryumin: "I decided to give up my professor's career, not only because of my wish to have the leisure of devoting myself to philosophical writings, there were other more pressing reasons which made my decision final."[5] About two years later he

---

3. See E. Radlov, "V. Soloviev: A Biographical Essay," *Soloviev's Collected Works,* IX, 9.
4. *Soloviev's Letters,* edited by E. L. Radlov, II, 338.
5. *Ibid.,* III, 36.

wrote to General Kireiev: "My idleness is becoming irksome to me, will you think of some practical activity for me (except teaching, for I do not want to resume it)?"[6] He could have been a professor as early as 1880, when Nekrassov, dean of the Historical Philological School of Odessa, offered him a post of assistant professor, and again in 1889 when the Warsaw District Commissioner of Education offered him a chair at the Warsaw University. Soloviev probably rejected a professor's career mainly because his fighting spirit urged him to discuss the burning topics of Russia's national politics, church problems, etc. He could not rest satisfied with a professor's life, demanding concentration on purely scholarly research.

In the eighties Soloviev took a particular interest in the problem of the reunion of Churches. At the invitation of Bishop Strossmayer, an eminent Roman-Catholic prelate, he went one summer to Zagreb in Croatia and there published his book *History and the Future of Theocracy*. In 1889 he once more visited Bishop Strossmayer in Zagreb and published in Paris a book called *La Russie et l'Eglise Universelle*. In this book Soloviev pronounced himself in favor of the Roman Catholic Church because it has created a universal super-state organization.

The Catholics regard Soloviev as having renounced Orthodoxy and joined the Roman Catholic Church. In fact Soloviev had never left the Orthodox Church; he merely came to the conviction that the Eastern and the Western Churches, despite the outward breach, had not severed their mystical bond. Prince Eugene Trubetskoy who was Soloviev's personal friend says, on the authority of Soloviev's own words, that the immediate impulse for Soloviev's change of attitude toward the Roman Catholic Church which he used to regard as the Church of the Antichrist's tradition, "was a prophetic dream which he saw a year before the coronation of the Emperor Alexander III." He had a clear vision of himself driving through the streets of Moscow, and he remembered well both the streets and the house in front of which his carriage had stopped. While entering the house he met a Roman Catholic ecclesiastical dignitary whom he at once asked for a blessing. The other seemed to hesitate, doubting whether it was possible to give a blessing to a Schismatic; but Soloviev overpowered his doubts by pointing out the mystical unity of the universal Church which in its essence had not been shattered by the apparent disunion of its two halves. The blessing was given.

"A year later the coronation of the Emperor Alexander III was, indeed, attended by the Papal Nuncio, and Soloviev relived his dream in reality. The blessing was asked for and given in exactly the same cir-

6. *Ibid.*, II, 110.

cumstances, the reality coinciding with the dream down to minor details. Soloviev recognized the streets through which he had driven, and the house which he had entered, and the Roman Catholic prelate who indeed after some hesitation, yielded to the same arguments as in his dream.[7]

In reality, Soloviev's new attitude toward the Catholic Church was formed before this dream and its fulfillment. In a letter to Martynov, dated July 18/30 1887, he wrote that eight years earlier he had read for the first time Y. F. Samarin's "Letters on the Jesuits." This work, he said, "considerably contributed to develop my sympathies toward the Catholic Church. The gross logical errors and obvious lack of good faith manifested by the author—otherwise so loyal and intelligent a man as Yury Samarin—made me seriously reflect upon our attitude toward Catholicism."[8]

Being convinced of the mystical unity of the Roman Catholic and Orthodox Church, Soloviev did entertain to the former such relations as might have left the Catholics under the impression that he had renounced Orthodoxy and become a Roman Catholic. It can, however, be proved beyond doubt that Soloviev remained faithful to the Orthodox Church.

In 1886, on his return from Zagreb, he wrote to Archimandrite Antony (the future Metropolitan of St. Petersburg): "To achieve the reunion of Churches, any outward union and any individual conversion are not only unnecessary, but would be even harmful. To the attempts at conversion, aimed at myself, I answered in the first place by confessing and communing (at an unusual time) at the Orthodox Serbian Church in Zagreb with its curate Rev. Father Amvrosy.—Generally speaking, I have returned to Russia—if one may say so *more of an Orthodox than when I left her.*"[9]

After the publication of his book *La Russie et l'Eglise Universelle,* it was rumored that he had joined the Catholic Church. Soloviev's spiritual director, Father Varnava, said to him: "Go to confession to your Catholic priests." The fact that Soloviev was for a long time deprived of the sacraments, which he deeply cherished, was so painful to him, that after several years had elapsed, he decided to undertake a very dangerous step. On February 18, 1896, he went to confession to Father Nicholas Tolstoy and received communion from this priest who had become a Catholic, but who shared Soloviev's teaching: the preservation of mystical unity of the Eastern and Western Churches, in spite of out-

---

7. Prince E. Trubetskoy, *The Philosophy of V. Soloviev.* I, 488 ff.
8. *Soloviev's Letters,* III, 25.
9. *Ibid.,* III, 189.

ward separation. This is why, before receiving communion, Soloviev, having read the decision of the Council of Trent, could add his declaration that the Eastern Church is the true Orthodox and Catholic Church.[10]

This means that he performed an act which can be approved neither by the Orthodox nor by the Catholic Church. Soloviev's further statements and acts clearly prove that he had not left the Orthodox Church.

In July 1900 Soloviev came to Moscow where he was taken ill. He left for the country home of Prince Peter Trubetskoy, located not far from Moscow, and where his friend, Professor S. N. Trubetskoy, was staying at that time. Stricken with serious kidney trouble, and aware that his end was near, Soloviev requested on July 30th (the eve of his death) that an Orthodox priest should be called from a nearby village to hear his confession and give him communion. Here is what Father Beliayev, the priest who administered the last rites to Soloviev, was to relate concerning this event: "One evening, a servant of the Trubetskoys' household was sent to me inviting me in the name of Serguei Nikolaievich (Trubetskoy) to celebrate Mass on the next day and administer a sick gentleman who had arrived from Moscow; I was to bring him the Holy Eucharist which I would consecrate at the Mass (according to Soloviev's personal wish)." The next day, "after having recited matins, I went to the Trubetskoys. Vladimir Sergueyevitch (Soloviev) made his confession with the true Christian contrition and said among other things that he had not received communion during three years; for when he last went to confession, he had an argument with the priest on a point of dogma and was forbidden the sacraments." "The priest was right," Soloviev added, "I argued with him only because of hot temper and pride; after this we corresponded for some time concerning this question, but I would not give in, though well aware that I was in the wrong; now I clearly realize my error and sincerely regret it."[11]

According to the rules of the Catholic Church, a Catholic *in extremis* may make his confession to an Orthodox priest and receive communion from him if there is no time or possibility of summoning a Catholic priest. Therefore, Catholics say that Soloviev's last communion does not prove that he had remained a member of the Orthodox Church. Of course, they are mistaken. Soloviev himself put off his confession and communion until the next day; he would have therefore had the time to summon a Catholic priest from Moscow. His mention of a dogmatic argument with an Orthodox priest and the fact of his having been for-

---

10. See D. Stremooukhov, *V. Soloviev, sa mission et son oeuvre*, 216, 230.
11. See "About Soloviev's Confession," *Letters*, III, 215.

bidden the Sacraments "during three years" prove that after his communion at the hands of Nicholas Tolstoy, he had wished to receive the holy species from an Orthodox priest; in any case, this shows that he had only once received communion from a Catholic priest. This is easy to understand if we take into consideration his condemnation of individual conversions from one Church to another.[12]

Professor Stroyev heard from a distant relative that several months before his death, Soloviev, speaking in a circle of his admirers, resolutely denied his conversion to catholicism.[13]

After the publication of his book *La Russie et l'Eglise Universelle* in 1889, Soloviev, it seems, grew temporarily indifferent to Church problems. In a letter to L. P. Nikiforov, probably written during the last year of his life, Soloviev declared: "I can tell you nothing about my works in French. Their fate interests me but little. Though there is nothing in them that contradicts objective truth, the subjective mood, the feelings and hopes which filled them when I was writing them, have been outlived by me."[14]

Meanwhile, Soloviev had become a friend of M. M. Stassiulevitch, director of the liberal review *Vestnik Evropy* (Courier of Europe) and devoted himself to philosophical publishing. His major philosophical writing during that last period of his life, *The Justification of the Good* (1897) contains a system of ethics. Two years before his death Soloviev planned a series of important works. In a letter to Tavernier (in French) he wrote: "I have published in a review the first chapter of my metaphysics and I hope to finish writing my book in fifteen months. Moreover, I am absorbed in Plato, whom I plan to translate. Having finished the Metaphysics, Plato and Esthetics, I shall entirely concentrate on the Bible . . . I do not know as yet, whether my final work will take the form of a new translation with lengthy commentaries, or whether this will become a system of historical philosophy founded on facts, in the spirit of the Bible."[15]

Of all these plans, Soloviev had only time to make the translation of a few of Plato's dialogues, with introductions leading into them and several chapters devoted to problems of epistemology (entitled *Theoretical Philosophy*). He moreover wrote his great work entitled *Three Conversations;* it is a study of the problems of evil, and in the chapter: "The Story of the Antichrist" he vividly depicts the union of the three Churches, Orthodox, Catholic and Protestant, which is to take place at

12. See *Letters*, III, 193.
13. Article in *Russkaya Mysl*, XXIX, 136, 1926.
14. *Letters*, edited by Radlov, additional volume, 6, 1823.
15. *Ibid.*, letter No. 15 to Tavernier, January 1898.

the end of times, and in which they appear as three organs of the whole, enjoying equal rights.

A detailed biography of Soloviev is still a work of the future. It is necessary because Soloviev was a great philosopher; it will be valuable because Soloviev was an extraordinary personality who was unquestionably in touch with the higher world. His friend Prince Evgeny Trubetskoy writes: "Whoever had the opportunity of seeing Vladimir Sergueevich Soloviev even once in his life forever retained the impression of having seen a man quite unlike ordinary mortals. Even his outward appearance, especially the expression of his large and beautiful eyes struck one by a unique combination of infirmity and power, of physical helplessness and spiritual depth."

"He was so shortsighted that *he could not see that which everybody saw*. Screwing his eyes from under his bushy eyebrows he could hardly discern the nearest objects. But when his eyes looked into the distance he seemed to penetrate beyond the surface of things accessible to outward senses and see *something of the realm of beyond which remained hidden from everybody*. His eyes shone with some inner light and looked straight into the soul."

"Without being an ascetic, he had an emaciated appearance and looked like a living relic. His thick curly hair, coming down to his shoulders, made him resemble an ikon. Characteristically enough, he was often taken for a priest: 'What, you are here, Father!'—people used to address him. Little children, catching him by the flaps of his fur coat would exclaim: 'That's Jesus Christ!' His ascetic appearance was in sharp contrast with his loud sonorous voice: it struck one by its mystical force and depth coming—no one knew from where."[16]

Strossmayer said of him: "*Soloviev anima candida, pia ac vere sancta est.*"

Soloviev's emaciated appearance was due to his extremely irregular way of life. Having no family, he had no permanent abode, no fixed hours for meals, for sleep or for work. Constantly on the move, he stayed now at some hotel in St. Petersburg or Moscow, now at the country estate of some friends, now at some boarding house on the shores of Imatra or Saima Lake in Finland.

"Spiritually he resembled the type of the pilgrim, created by wandering Russia, who, in his search of heavenly Jerusalem, spends his life in wandering across the whole measureless expanse of earth, visits and adores all sacred objects of reverence, but does not stay for long in any *earthly* abode."[17]

About his homeless condition he wrote to the Jesuit Paul Pierling

---

16. E. Trubetskoy, *The Philosophy of V. Soloviev*, I, 3, 18.
17. *Ibid.*, I, 33.

"Why do you not admit the idea that though I am not a monk, I have no 'abiding city here,' like yourself?" (5/17, II, 1890.)[18]

Soloviev had no opportunity of creating a family life for himself. When he was eighteen, he fell in love with his cousin E. K. Romanova. For several years they considered themselves engaged, but in 1875 Romanova rejected him. In T. L. Sukhotin's confidential album, answering the question: "Have you been in love, and how many times?" Soloviev wrote: "Seriously—once; otherwise—27 times." It is difficult to say what he means by "seriously": was it his love for E. K. Romanova, for E. M. Polivanova, S. P. Khitrovo or S. M. Martynova?[19]

More than once Soloviev considered entering monastic life. In 1886, after his visit to the Troytzky-Serguiyevsky Abbey, he wrote Canon M. Rachky: "The Archimandrit and the monks are most attentive toward me, wishing me to join them, but I will think this over carefully before making such a decision."[20] A year later he wrote Archimandrit Anthonius: "I would be now very much inclined to become a monk. But for the present this is impossible. I am by no means in favor of *unconditional freedom,* but believe that between such freedom and *unconditional slavery,* there must be an intermediate way, that is *freedom conditioned by sincere submission to that which is holy and legitimate.*" "However, will such freedom be accepted in our midst? Will they not *demand everything* without discrimination, no matter whether holy and legitimate or not."[21]

In the following poem Soloviev depicts his life path:

Once in the misty dawn with timid foot
Towards a mysterious strand I walked alone;
    The stars were paling in the eastern light,
    My soul engaged the host of dreams in fight
And prayed to gods unknown.

Now in the cold hard light I tread as then
A lonely path, beside an unknown stream;
    The mists are fled, and clearly shows by day
    How rough the mountain track, how far away
The haven of my dream:

But till the midnight hour with fearless foot
I travel to the goal of my desires;
    Where on the summit, 'neath an alien star,
    Along the sacred roof will gleam afar
The line of victory fires.

18. Stremooukhov, 309.
19. *Letters*, additional volume, 239.
20. *Letters*, I, 171.
21. *Ibid.*, III, 191.

Careless of the material side of life, Soloviev was always penniless, for he freely gave away the money he earned to everybody who asked him for it. When he was short of money he gave away his things. "I remember," says Trubetskoy, "once late in autumn I found him in Moscow suffering from cold. His entire wardrobe consisted at the time of a light alpaca suit and a still lighter grey cape; being without money, he had just given away to someone all the warm things he had; he counted on earning enough by the winter to buy himself a fur coat."[22]

Not only men, but animals too, enjoyed his generosity and seemed to feel his love for every living thing. Barely had he time to arrive at the hotel where he often stayed in St. Petersburg, when a flight of pigeons would appear on the window sill of his room.[23]

Soloviev had intimate friends and acquaintances among all sorts of people. The profundity of his thoughts, the wide range of his interests, his vast erudition and especially his wit attracted to him people of all classes. "Feasts with him," says E. Trubetskoy, "were truly Platonic feasts; his animation communicated itself to the others: who of his friends does not remember those inspired talks, that wealth of charming and infectious hilarity!" During friendly conversations he was fond of drinking wine. "Wine," he used to say to E. Trubetskoy, "is an excellent test, it reveals the whole man: a beast becomes in wine an absolute brute; a man becomes something more than a man."[24]

In his preface to Soloviev's letters, his friend E. L. Radlov writes that he possessed a "childlike gaiety." His letters and poems are full of puns, good-natured jokes and mocking remarks addressed to "friends and to himself." In the dedication to his play *The White Lilie,* he well defined the role played by laughter in his own life:

> Out of sonorous laughter and muffled sobs
> The harmony of the world is created.
> Resound then laughter, like a free wave,
> And muffle the sobs, were it only for a second.
> And thou, poor muse! above the darkened path
> Appear, were it but once, with youthful smile
> And for a fleeting moment, with kind mockery
> Disarm and tame the wickedness of life.
>
> *Letters,* I.

I have already mentioned Soloviev's visions in connection with his threefold vision of Sophia. He looked on dreams, as he himself put

22. E. Trubetskoy, I, 12.
23. Lukyanov, III, 134.
24. E. Trubetskoy, I, 17.

it, as upon "a window as it were into another world: in   he often conversed with the dead, or saw visions, sometimes pro   ic, sometimes queer, fantastic." Even in his waking moments he sometimes sensed what was happening at a distance. In a letter to Stassiulevitch he wrote: "Thursday of Holy Week, around eight o'clock in the evening, while dining with you, I experienced for no apparent reason a deathly melancholy, of which I told you both (Stassiulevitch and his wife); I expressed my conviction that at that very moment a misfortune had taken place in connection with someone dear to me. Imagine, that actually at that time, around eight o'clock on Good Thursday evening, one of my childhood friends, Lopatin (brother of the Moscow professor) suffered a stroke after which the doctor declared that he was afflicted with progressive paralysis of the brain."[25]

His attitude toward visions that are of the nature of hallucinations and his peculiar theory of such visions may be seen from the following story told by E. Trubetskoy: Once "early in the morning, soon after he woke up, he had a vision of an Oriental man wearing a turban. He uttered some very silly words about Soloviev's quite recent article on Japan ("drove along the road, read about Buddhism, there you are with your Buddhism") and thrust an extremely long umbrella into his stomach. The vision vanished, but Soloviev felt an acute pain in his liver which lasted afterwards for three days. . . . He nearly always had after his visions such painful sensations and other morbid phenomena. Once I said to him in this connection: 'Your visions are simply the hallucinations of your distress.' He at once agreed with me. But one must not interpret his agreement in the sense of his denying the reality of his visions. In his mouth these words meant that a disease makes our mind sensitive to the influences of the spiritual world to which people enjoying good health remain quite insensible. Therefore he did not deny the necessity of medical treatment in such cases. He admitted hallucinations to be phenomena of subjective and morbid imagination. But this did not prevent him believing in the objective cause of hallucinations which is *imaged* in us and *embodied* through the medium of subjective imagination, and in the external reality." (I, 20 ff.)

His nephew (S. M. Soloviev) says that after 1889, in the period of his doubts as to the possibility of the reunion of Churches and of his seeming loss of interest in Church problems "the bright visions of his youth (Sophia) and of his mature age (hermits) give place to frequent visions of the devil in different shapes. I have myself heard V. S. Soloviev tell of such visions."

The thoughts about the evil principle which found such a masterful

25. *Letters*, additional volume, 64.

expression in *Three Conversations,* seemed to disturb Soloviev and make him particularly sensitive to it. Professor A. V. Kartashev tells of the following remarkable story which he heard in 1910 from General Veliaminov, professor of the Military Medical Academy, at the house of Baroness V. I. Uexküll: "Although he was a man in his sixties, a positivist, even a materialist, he yet kept on friendly terms with V. S. Soloviev. In his old age, Veliaminov, the cultured skeptic, felt obviously disturbed by the mystery of the spiritual world. He was interested in me as a religious philosopher and one day told me the following story:

"Once in summer, at the summer residence of Varvara Ivanovna near Moscow, the 'eternal wanderer,' V. Soloviev, who was staying there, was somehow in a state of particular tension and told us many interesting things about the devil. It was a late summer evening. After a long-drawn five-o'clock tea we were three of us sitting on the summer veranda; its floor was of simple wooden boards with rifts. Soloviev sat frowning in an armchair and I now walked and now stood, still slightly provoking him with my questions. Soloviev was talking about the devil more and more concretely and definitely, making us too catch his peculiar mood. Suddenly, from one of the rifts almost in the middle of the floor there rose up with a slight noise, reaching almost to the ceiling, a column of fairly thick brownish smoke or vapor. 'There he is, there he is!' shouted V. S., pointing to it with his finger. Then he got up and fell into silence, looking grave and tired as if he had gone through some ordeal. We were nonplussed too. The smoke quickly disappeared, leaving no trace, no smell behind. A minute after we began looking for an explanation. I had been smoking, perhaps I had dropped a burning match and set something on fire under the floor. But what? And why such an explosion? And why no smell of burning? The investigation made by the dog and the servants under the veranda led to nothing. We had to fall silent too and were left puzzled for the rest of our lives."

"Of course," added the proud skeptic to his puzzling story, "I do not draw any conclusions from this even now and merely state the fact."

In his youth Soloviev was keen on spiritism, thinking that spiritistic phenomena could be used for metaphysical purposes. Yet, after having attended in 1875 several spiritist seances in London, he became disappointed. In his letter to Prince D. Tsertelev he tells of a seance given by the famous Williams and says that the latter "is rather an insolent than a skillful trickster. He did produce the Egyptian darkness, but did not show any other miracles. When the bell flying round the room in the darkness descended on my head I caught with it a muscular hand whose owner did not proclaim himself to be a spirit. After this the remaining details are of little interest."[26]

The principal philosophical works of V. Soloviev are the following (in Russian):

The Crisis of Western Philosophy (Against the Positivists), 1874.
The Philosophical Principles of Integral Knowledge, 1877.
The Critique of Abstract Principles, 1877–80.
Lectures on Godmanhood, 1877–81.
Three Discourses in Memory of Dostoevsky, 1881–83.
The Spiritual Foundations of Life, 1882–84.
The Great Controversy and the Christian Policy, 1883.
The History and the Future of Theocracy, 1885–87.
La Russie et l'Eglise Universelle, 1889.
The Meaning of Love, 1892–94.
The Justification of the Good, 1895.
Theoretical Philosophy, 1897–99.
Three Conversations, 1899–1900.
Collected Works, 9 vols.; *Letters,* 4 vols.

Of Soloviev's numerous writings on political-philosophical questions I will mention only the following:

The National Problem in Russia, 2 parts, 1883–91.
China and Europe, 1890.

Soloviev's poems are rather important for the characteristic and understanding of his work. Some of them express in a beautiful form his profound philosophical ideas.

Translated works: *Three Conversations,* 1915; *The Justification of the Good,* translated by N. Duddington, 1818; *Lectures on God-manhood,* with an introduction by P. Zouboff, New York, 1944; *The Meaning of Love,* New York, 1947; *Ausgewählte Werke,* 2 vols., E. Diederichs, 1914. *Die Deutsche Gesamtausgabe in 8 Bänden,* translated by W. Szylkarski. Erich Wevel Verlag, Krailing vor München, 1950–1953.

The principal works on Vladimir Soloviev are:

Prince E. Trubetskoy, *The Philosophy of Vladimir Soloviev,* 2 vols., 1913; C. Mochulsky, *Vladimir Soloviev,* YMCA Press, Paris 1936; D. Stremoukhoff, *Vladimir Soloviev, La mission et son oeuvre,* Paris 1935; M. Herbigny, *Vladimir Soloviev, a Russian Newman,* London 1918; W. Dunphy, *The Religious Philosophy of Vladimir Soloviev,* 1939;

26. *Letters,* II, 228.

Friedrich Muckermann, *Vladimir Soloviev*, Verlag Otto Walter, Switzerland 1945.

Having outgrown his youthful religious crisis, V. Soloviev, as early as 1873, came to think that the truth of Christ alone is capable of regenerating humanity, of overcoming the coarse ignorance of masses, the moral devastation of the upper classes, the brute force of the state (letter to Mme. E. V. Romanov of July 25, 1873).

He explained "the estrangement of the contemporary mind from Christianity" by the fact that up to now, Christianity had "had an inadequate irrational form." Today, when through the development of science and philosophy, Christianity has been destroyed in its false form, the time has come to re-establish true "Christianity, to bring its eternal contents into" a new, adequate, that is entirely rational form. If "a certain—and were it only a small—part of mankind fulfills actually and seriously, with a conscious and strong conviction, the teaching of absolute love and self-sacrifice, will untruth and evil be able to persist long in the world? But this practical fulfillment of Christianity in life is still a long way ahead. For the present, we must still work at the theoretical aspect, at theological teaching. This is my true mission." When he entered the school of Theology, he did not want to become a monk: "The time has come not to run away from the world, but to go into the world, in order to reform it."[27] And at the end of his life, Soloviev realized that the fundamental issue of culture was "to place humanity before the dilemma: to accept or to reject truth, after having known it, that is truth correctly stated and clearly grasped." By stating Christian truth with precision, thus doing away with theoretical misunderstandings, the decision to go with Christ or to reject Christ becomes a pure act of the will, it is the decision to be "absolutely moral or absolutely immoral."[28]

And indeed it became the work of his life to build up a Christian Orthodox philosophy revealing the wealth and the living efficacy of the principal dogmas of Christianity which in many minds had been turned into dead formulae, severed from life and philosophy. Soloviev showed what importance they have as a philosophical basis for a scientific study of nature, as guidance for the moral life of an individual and as a starting point for working out an ideal of Christian politics.

Soloviev's entire literary work reveals his activism: his theoretical search of truth always aims at the practical goal of reforming the world, conquering selfishness, achieving the Christian ideal of love of our neighbor and of all absolute values. Prince E. Trubetzkoy and D. N.

27. *Letters*, III, 88.
28. *Letters*, additional volume, "To Tavernier, May 1896," 220 C.

Stremooukhoff divide Soloviev's works into three periods, taking into account precisely the different phases of his activism. Stremooukhoff describes these three periods as Soloviev's interest in the field of theosophy, that is Christian teaching, then in the field of theocracy, and finally in theurgy.[29]

During the first period, Soloviev hoped that the incarnation in the world of Sophia, Wisdom of God, can be achieved through Christian *theosophy*, that is through the knowledge of God and of his relation to the world. Soloviev's major writings belonging to that period are *Lectures on Godmanhood* and *Spiritual Foundations of Life*. During the second period, after 1882, Soloviev placed his hopes in the transformation of mankind through *theocracy*, that is through the creation of a just state and a just social order, which realizes Christian politics. His major works belonging to that period are: *The Great Quarrel and Christian Politics, The History and Future of Theocracy, La Russie et l'Eglise Universelle* and *The National Problem and Russia*. Finally, during the third period starting about 1890, Soloviev was absorbed in the problem of *theurgy*, that is mystical art, creating a new life according to Divine Truth. His major works of that period are the *Meaning of Love* and *The Justification of the Good*. Soloviev's last work, *The Three Conversations* expresses the end of his utopian hopes in the achievement of good in man's terrestrial life.

The characteristic features of Russian philosophical thought—the search for an exhaustive knowledge of reality as a whole and the concreteness of metaphysical conceptions—find a particularly clear expression in Soloviev's work and are quite definitely formulated even in his early books, *The Crisis in Western Philosophy; The Philosophical Principles of Integral Knowledge;* and *The Critique of Abstract Principles.*

The empirical theory, according to which all we can know consists of mere sense-data or appearances, does not satisfy Soloviev, since no appearances can exist or be known apart from their necessary relations with other appearances and with that which appears. These relations can only be cognized by means of thought, which reveal to us the general significance or reason of things (*ratio rerum*) as consisting precisely in the relatedness of everything to the whole—the whole being understood not as a chaotic multiplicity but as a systematic pan-unity. The rational character of the contents of knowledge "is not given in experience, since in experience we are always concerned with the particular and multiple reality, and never find either the 'all' or the 'unity.' The

---

29. Prince E. Trubetzkoy, *Soloviev's World Conception*, I, chaps. 2 and 10; Stremooukhoff, 8 c.

reason or meaning of the things we know can only be grasped by the knowing subject's reason; the relation of a given object to all can only exist for us in so far as we ourselves contain the principle of pan-unity, namely, reason." We can thus understand how the theory of rationalism has arisen. "The criterion of truth is transferred from the external world into the knowing subject: human reason and not the nature of things or events is declared to be the basis of truth." Reason, however, as the principle of the correlation of all in unity is only the *form* of truth; every variety of rationalism proves thus to be abstract in character and, therefore, invalid. Dogmatic rationalism cannot explain how our subjective thinking can inform us of the existence of the transsubjective world. The critical rationalism of Kant gets over the difficulty by depreciating the value of reason and maintaining that its a priori truths are the necessary forms of the phenomenal but not of the true being. This, however, leads to a fresh difficulty: if all knowledge be reduced to a combination of the a priori forms of reason with the empirical material of sense, and if these two factors be regarded as mutually independent, their synthesis can not be explained without reference to some third principle—and yet, according to Kant, no third principle is accessible to our knowledge. If reason and sensibility are the only recognized factors, it will have to be admitted that the whole content of knowledge depends upon its form and is entirely determined by the categories of reason. This is the line of thought developed in the absolute rationalism of Hegel. But since the form of reason, like every other form, is nothing apart from the corresponding content, absolute rationalism sets itself the impossible task of deducing everything from nothing.

The final results of empiricism and of rationalism are somewhat similar: empiricism leaves us with nothing but appearances, without an object of which they are appearances and without a subject to whom they appear; rationalism ends with pure thought; i.e., "thought without a thinker and without anything to think of." Neither in experience nor in thought does man transcend his subjective relation to the object and become aware of the object as an existent, that is, as something which is more than his sensation or his thought. Neither experience nor thought can, then, lead to truth, since truth means that which is—i.e., existence. "But only the whole exists. Truth, then, is the whole. And if truth be the whole, then that which is not the whole—i.e., every particular thing, being or event taken separately from the whole—is not truth, because in its separateness it does not even exist: it exists with all and in all. Truth then is all in its unity or as one." "The complete definition of truth thus finds expression in three predicates: is, one, all" (II, 281). To put it shortly "truth is the existent unity of all;" that is—not an abstract idea contained in all, but a concrete principle containing all in itself (I, 27).

For Soloviev, then, truth is an absolute value belonging to the pan-unity itself and not to our judgments or inferences. To understand truth means to transcend the limits of subjective thought and enter the domain of the existent unity of all that is; i.e., of the Absolute. Is man capable of doing this? The question contains the beginning of its own answer. The Absolute "as the pan-unity cannot be wholly external to the knowing subject: there must be an inner connection between them, by virtue of which the Absolute can be known to the subject and the subject can be inwardly connected with all that exists in the Absolute and actually know this All. It is only in connection with that which truly is, as with the unconditionally real and unconditionally universal, that the facts of our experience acquire true reality, and the concepts of our thought—true, positive universality. Taken in the abstract, both these factors of our knowledge are in themselves completely indifferent to truth and derive their true significance from a third, a religious principle."

Both empirical and rational knowledge is relative, for it is the result of communicating with the object from without, from the side of our phenomenal separateness; it is supplemented by knowledge "from within, from the side of our absolute being which is inwardly connected with the being of the object known." Such knowledge is *mystical* and absolute. We find in it something more than our thought; namely, an objective reality independent of us. Soloviev calls this third kind of knowledge *faith*, understanding by this term, like Jacobi, not a subjective conviction of the existence of a reality independent of us, but *intuition*; i.e., immediate contemplation of an essence distinct from our own.

True knowledge, then, is the result of empirical, rational and mystical cognition in their right interconnection. The rational form of knowledge is not lost but merely supplemented by the addition of the life principle. A philosophy constructed on this plan "seeks to combine with the logical perfection of the Western form the fullness of the spiritual intuitions of the East" (I, 143); its purpose is to realize the universal synthesis of science, philosophy and religion. The objective significance of knowledge, its logical necessity and coherence are only possible if the Absolute principle—God, as the pan-unity—gives the world the character of a complete organic system. The same intimate connection between God and the world is to be found in all other *positive* manifestations of existence. A complete knowledge of reality as a whole inevitably leads not merely to a religious but to a Christian world conception which centers round the doctrine of the God-man, that is, of Godhead and Manhood being joined together in Christ "not by confusion of substance but by unity of person."

It has already been said that the Absolute is the unity of all that is. As the absolute first principle, it transcends real content and rational form. Conditioning both content and form and binding them together by an inner tie, it stands above all determination and all existence, since determinate existence is always relative. It has the *power* of existence and may on that ground be said to exist, though it would be more correct to say that as the first principle in the strict sense it is above existence and above power. As incommensurable with any determinations it is Nothing (the positive nothing, the Ain-Soph of the Kabbala); but the Absolute is both ἕν and ἕν καὶ πᾶν.. "The Absolute is all and nothing: nothing, in so far as it is not any one thing; and all, in so far as it cannot be lacking in anything." All existence being relative and therefore plural is, in relation to the Absolute, *its other*. But the Absolute would not be itself if it excluded its 'other;' if it did, that 'other' would be the boundary of the Absolute and, consequently, the Absolute would be 'limited, exclusive and not free;' that is, it would not be absolute. The Absolute, therefore, is the unity of itself and its opposite. In so far as it is the denial of itself and the affirmation of its other, it is love (I, 321).

Thus, two poles may be distinguished within it: first, the principle of absolute unity and freedom from all determinate being; secondly the principle of existence, that is, of the multiplicity of forms. The first pole—the Absolute in itself or as such—transcends existence and is, therefore, the *positive* potentiality of being; the second pole is the striving for existence, the felt absence of existence, and is, therefore, the *negative* potentiality of being, ὕλη or *materia prima*.

It should be noted that the second pole can be regarded as the *materia prima*, or the negative principle, only when taken "in itself and in its potential separateness." As actually existing, it is determined by the positive principle and is the bearer of its manifestations, its eternal image or idea. The interconnection between first matter and the Absolute in its positive aspect brings about the world of existence or actuality—the world of many determinate beings each of which has a natural and an ideal aspect. Every entity is, on the one hand, a force; that is, an independent center of activity and, on the other, the bearer of the idea of the divine pan-unity in some particular aspect of it. It thus acquires an individual character, and its activity is directed to a rational purpose.

Man may be taken as an instance of such an entity. Human personality is negatively absolute: "It cannot and will not be satisfied with any relative, limited content;" it is convinced that "it can attain positive absoluteness" and "possess the complete fullness of being."[30] Man cannot, of course, by himself create absolute fullness of being; it can only be reached through a perfect mutual interpenetration of all creatures united in love with each other and with God. As a final aim, it is contained in the idea of every entity, but its realization cannot be secured mechanically; it must be a free act, based upon love for God and for all beings. In seeking to attain it, the world-manifold gradually becomes one whole, i.e., the Absolute. Thus, the world is the Absolute that *becomes,* while God is the Absolute that *is.*[31]

The beings of this world can only rise up to God if they have perfect love, that is, if they renounce their exclusive self-assertion. Such renunciation leads not to the loss of individuality, but, on the contrary, to finding one's true self and to a perfect life in God. A being that chooses the opposite path of hatred of God—of rivalry with Him, enters the realm of satanic being. The realm of the earthly life with which we are familiar stands midway between these two poles. It consists of beings who do not struggle against the supreme goal of their existence—the participation in the divine perfection—but try to attain it without feeling a perfect love for God, without making their will a mere instrument of the Divine providence; they retain, if only to a small extent, self-will and the egoistic exclusiveness of selfhood. This leads to disastrous consequences, as we know from the history of the Fall. Rejecting voluntary obedience to God, man becomes the slave of nature, which also undergoes a deep change. Beings that preserve egoistic exclusiveness become impenetrable to one another; i.e., they acquire corporeality in the form of coarse matter which admits of external relations only and not of inward unity. The life of beings thus separated from one another inevitably ends in death; the relations between them are almost entirely confined to the struggle for existence which necessarily involves suffering and can never lead to satisfaction, since the fullness of being is not to be found on this path.[32]

What is then this coarse impenetrable matter which sprang up as a result of the original sin? Soloviev gives an answer to that question by developing a dynamic theory of the atom; namely, he understands the impenetrable matter as a manifestation of the interaction of the

30. *Lectures on God-manhood,* II.
31. *The Critique of Absolute Principles,* II, 305.
32. *Lectures on God-manhood,* III.

forces of repulsion and attraction; and these forces themselves he conceives as manifestations of *monads*.

"Hardness and spaciousness forming matter," writes Soloviev, "exist only in the *interaction* of atoms; the atoms themselves must, in accordance with this be defined as the actual cause of such an action; but the actual cause of action is that which we call *energy*." "It is not energy which is the attribute of matter, as must be presupposed by mechanistic materialism, but on the contrary, matter is only the result of energies, or more correctly speaking, the general limit of their interaction." The atoms are "immaterial dynamic entities existing in themselves, they are *living energies* or *monads* existing in themselves and acting out of themselves."[33]

Soloviev's dynamistic teaching concerning matter is confirmed by the development of modern physics; in order to be convinced of this, it is sufficient to replace in his text the word atom by the words electron, proton, etc.

The task of man as a self-conscious being is to overcome all forms of evil and imperfection, deriving from the Fall and connected with the impenetrable corporeality; man has to further the process of the reunion of all creatures with one another and with God. To do this he must sacrifice himself for the love of God and of the whole world. But the great purpose of making the world divine cannot be accomplished by man alone, since the positive potency of being belongs to God and not to man.

God has so far been spoken of only as the positive Nothing, transcending all form and content. If the sphere of the Absolute were limited to this Nothing, there could obviously be no question of its love for, or reunion with, the world. The Christian doctrine based upon *revelation* speaks of God as a person, as a Trinity of God the Father, God the Son, and God the Holy Ghost. In his attempt to interpret the data of revelation, Soloviev points out that they became intelligible to us in connection with the philosophical conception of God as the positive Nothing. God as the Absolute is superpersonal, and for this very reason the realm of personal being is open to Him, though it does not limit Him. Entering it He still, on the one hand, transcends existence as the positive Nothing, while on the other He exists as three Persons which form a perfect unity. Each aspect of this unity is of absolute value both in itself and for the cosmos (VIII, 19).

Soloviev bases his interpretation of the Three Hypostases upon the idea of the self-manifestation of the Absolute, which necessarily involves the following three moments: "(1) that which is manifested in

---

[33]. *Collected Works*, II, *Critique of Abstract Principles*, chap. 33.

and for itself, (2) manifestation as such; i.e., the positing of oneself in or for another. The expression or determination of the manifesting essence, its Word or Logos; (3) the return of that which is manifested to itself, or its rediscovery of itself in the manifestation." The first of these principles is the *spirit* as the subject of will and the bearer of goodness, and therefore also the subject of truth and of the feeling of beauty; the second is Reason (Logos), as the subject and the bearer of truth, and therefore also the subject of the will for goodness and of the feeling of beauty;" the third is the *soul* "as the subject of feeling and the bearer of beauty and therefore, and in so far only, capable of will for goodness and the thought of truth."[34] Thus, three absolute values—goodness, truth and beauty—correspond to the three persons of the Holy Trinity.

The values of which these persons are the bearers are simply various forms of *love* if by love be meant "every kind of inward unity of many beings." Thus, "goodness is the unity of all or of everything—that is, love, as the object of desire;" it is a *substantial* unity. "Truth is also love—i.e., the unity of all—as objective thought; it is an *ideal* unity. Finally, beauty is love too (i.e., the unity of all) as sensed or manifested; it is a *real* unity."

Each of the three persons of the Holy Trinity possesses the power of exclusive self-assertion, but freely renounces it and remains in complete unity with the other two, thus realizing goodness, truth and beauty in their primary form. "Primary goodness is the moral harmony of the three ultimate subjects or their union in one single will; primary truth is their intellectual harmony or their unity in one single presentation; primary beauty is their sensuous or aesthetic harmony—their union in one feeling." "Thus the Absolute realizes goodness through truth and beauty."[35]

The Holy Trinity is the realized ideal of consubstantiality on the basis of perfect love. It was this conception of it that led St. Sergius of Radonezh to dedicate the church in his monastery to the Holy Trinity so that the monks, contemplating the truth of the Divine tri-unity, should do their utmost to embody it in life.

God is love both within the limits of the Holy Trinity and in relation to the world. The calling forth of the world-manifold is in itself an act of love; moreover, Divine love participates in all the positive expression of cosmic existence. The multitude of creatures can only attain fullness of being by forming one single whole, one living universal organism. The wholeness of all which ideally forever abides in God "reveals itself as the all-pervading rationality of the world, so that this

---

34. *The Philosophical Principles of Integral Knowledge*, I, 338.
35. *Lectures on God-manhood*, VII.

rationality is the direct expression or Word (*Logos*) of the Deity, the manifested and active God."[36] Even in a world that has fallen away from God, rational meaning is preserved, at any rate in so far as all beings have a vague instinctive longing for an all-embracing unity; this "longing, common to all" transcends the limits of each separate personality and as the universal inner life of all that exists, may be called the World-Soul. Thus, even in a state of separation from God, the world-manifold is a single organism, though an imperfect one. At the beginning its parts are held together by means of an external law, and only, as the result of a slow historical process, do they gradually come to form "a new positive combination of elements in the form of an absolute organism or of an inward pan-unity." The absolute form of that unity, the eternal divine idea of it, Sophia, is from all eternity contained in the divine Logos. The Logos is thus "the eternal spiritual center of the cosmic organism." The birth of the incarnated Sophia or of the absolute organism can only take place "through the concerted action of the divine principle and the World-Soul." The process of birth is slow and difficult, because it requires a free act of love for God. "Through a free act of the World-Soul, the world which it animates fell away from God and broke up into a number of hostile elements; through a long series of free acts the rebellious multitude must be reconciled to itself and to God, becoming regenerated in the form of an absolute organism."[37]

In order to further this process the Divine Logos, whose love never forsakes the world, descends into the stream of events, and incarnating itself in the person of Jesus Christ, "from being the center of eternity becomes the center of history." This act of love resulting in a perfect union of God and man cannot be a mere return to the primeval immediate unity with God, characteristic of man at the stage of innocence. After the Fall the new unity has to be striven for, and can only be won by free activity and sacrifice—sacrifice both on the part of God and of man. In assuming the limited human consciousness the Divine principle "comes down, humbles itself, taking upon itself the form of a servant." It does not wholly confine itself to the limits of the natural consciousness—this would be impossible—but it actually feels them as its own limits at the moment. This self-limitation of the Deity in Christ liberates His manhood, enabling His natural will freely to renounce itself for the sake of the divine principle, not as of an external force (such self-renunciation would not be free) but as of an inward good, and thus really to attain that good." We have then before us one divinely human personality, combining in itself two natures and possessing two wills.

36. *The Spiritual Foundations of Life*, III, 323.
37. *Lectures on God-manhood*, IX.

This personality "as God, freely renounces divine glory and, by that very act, as man, acquires the possibility of attaining it. On the path to this attainment the human nature and will of the Saviour inevitably meets with the temptation of evil." The act of spiritual heroism in overcoming temptation inwardly is followed by the act of physical heroism and the overthrow of physical nature in the form of death and suffering; the end is resurrection in the flesh, freed from material weight and impenetrability, transfigured and capable of serving "as the direct expression and instrument of the Divine spirit, as the true spiritual body of the resurrected God-man."[38] The normal relation between the divine, the human and the natural principles, disturbed by the Fall, is re-established in the risen Christ, in whom dwelleth all "the fullness of Godhead bodily." Redemption from evil accomplished by the God-man means the salvation both of the soul and of the physical nature. Transfigured matter becomes holy flesh, divine matter, obedient to the demands of the Spirit.

Soloviev's philosophy is anthropocentric: man is the highest stage of creation; the regeneration of the world is accomplished by God in conjunction with man adequately expressing the divine idea of humanity. Such an ideally perfect man is the supreme expression of Sophia, the Divine Wisdom. But the perfect man appeared in Christ. Therefore the God-Man Jesus Christ is a combination of Logos and Sophia.[39] In the divine being of Christ the primary or the generating unity is, properly speaking, the Deity-God as active force or Logos, and in this primary unity we have Christ as strictly speaking a divine being, but the second generated unity to which we gave the mystical name of Sophia, is the principle of humanity, is the ideal or normal man. Participating through this unity in the human principle, Christ is man, or, according to the Scriptures, the second Adam."[40]

Such principle as Sophia has an all-pervading meaning for the world and can receive various definitions from different points of view. Sophia as a relatively passive principle, devoted to God and receiving from Him its form, is the eternal Feminine. "For God," says Soloviev, "His *other* (i.e., the universe) has from all eternity the image of perfect femininity, but He wants this image to be not only for Him, but to be realized and embodied for each particular being capable of uniting with Him. The eternal Feminine itself which is not a mere inactive image in God's mind, but a living spiritual being, possessing all the fullness of forces and activities, strives for the same realization and

38. *The Spiritual Foundations of Life*, III, 337, 341.
39. *Lectures on God-manhood*, VII.
40. *Ibid.*, VIII.

embodiment. The entire cosmic and historical process is a process of its realization and embodiment in the great variety of forms and degrees."

As a single center of the accomplishment of the Divine idea of the world, Sophia is the soul of the world and in relation to Logos she is Christ's body. But Christ's body in its universal aspect is the Church. Therefore, Sophia is the Church, the bride of the Divine Logos. And as a feminine individual personality she is also the Holy Virgin Mary.[41]

The doctrine of the God-man as a source of regeneration of the world is used by Soloviev for his interpretation of the history of mankind and for a theory of social life. Indeed, the God-man is an individual and yet *universal* being, for it embraces "the whole regenerated spiritual humanity" and is present in every cosmic realm in so far as unity, goodness, truth and beauty are realized in it.[42] Even the evolution of the world before man, that is the *evolution of nature* is already a process gradually leading toward the unity of the world, which is indispensable for the achievement of absolute perfection. Therefore, Soloviev's teaching concerning the evolution of nature must be stated as premise to the expounding of his ethics, his social philosophy and his philosophy of history.

According to Soloviev's teaching, the Absolute is the pan-unity which *is*, and the world is the pan-unity in the state of becoming. The world contains the divine element, all-oneness, as a potentiality, an idea; but it also contains the nondivine, natural, material element, the dispersed, the multiplex of the particular which is not all-oneness. However, every particular being tends to become all-oneness and gradually moves toward that goal, uniting oneself with God (II, 301). The process of establishing all-oneness in the world is the *development* of the world.

Multiplex being in its *dispersion* denies pan-unity. However, the divine principle, as idea, acts in all creatures through the blind, unconscious tendency of each being to widen its sphere; it places a limit to disintegration and dispersion first in the form of *outward law*, re-establishing the oneness necessary for the fullness of life; then, on a comparatively high degree of development, following the rise of consciousness, outward unity in man is transformed into *inner all-oneness*, on the basis of *ethical principles*.[43]

Thus we must distinguish two degrees in the development of the world: before man, development is achieved under the form of *the*

---

41. *The Meaning of Love*, VI, 405; *Lectures on God-manhood*, VIII; *La Russie et l'Eglise Universelle*, 258–262; *The Idea of Humanity in Auguste Comte*, VIII, 240; *The History and the Future of Theocracy*, IV, 231.
42. *The Spiritual Foundations of Life*, III, 271.
43. *Collected Works*, I, 228, 263; II, 303; III, 134; IV, 305.

evolution of nature, while in human activities it is achieved under the form of *history.* In its final issue, the development of the world is the establishment of the Kingdom of God, "the reality of absolute ethical order, or—and this is the same thing—general resurrection and reestablishment of all."[44]

The lowest degree of this process, the evolution of nature, is the creation of preliminary stages and conditions for the oneness of the world. There are five of these stages: "the *mineral kingdom* (or the nonorganic), the *vegetable kingdom,* the *animal kingdom,* the *kingdom of man,* and the *kingdom of God.*" These degrees "represent the most clearly defined and characteristic steps of ascension of *being* from the point of view of ethical meaning, achieved in the divino-material process." In reality, the characteristic traits of these kingdoms are as follows: the minerals represent the category of *being* as inert self-assertion; the plants emerge from this inertia, as representing *life,* which "unconsciously tends toward light, warmth and moisture. The animals, through the media of their *senses* and free *movements,* seek the fullness of sensual being: the satisfaction of hunger, the fulfillment of sexual life, the joy of existing (play and song). Natural man, in addition to all this tends rationally through science, the arts and social organization toward the improvement of his life; he actually achieves this improvement under various aspects and finally ascends to the *idea* of absolute perfection. Spiritual mankind, or mankind born from God, not only grasps with the mind, but also accepts with the heart and through action this absolute perfection as *the actual beginning of that which must be in everything,* and tends to achieve it fully or to incarnate it in the life of the entire world." "Every new type presents a *new condition,* necessary for the achievement of the highest and final goal—the true coming into the world of the perfect ethical order of the kingdom of God or the revelation of the freedom and glory of the sons of God." Indeed, "in order to achieve his highest goal, or to manifest his absolute significance, the being must first of all *be,* then it must be *alive,* then *conscious,* then *rational,* and finally *perfect*" (239, 247 c).

Every preceding kingdom serves as material for the next one: it evolves the instruments and organs on which the next, higher kingdom will lean in order to achieve a superior, more valuable, more abundant activity: nonorganic matter is the foundation of vegetable functions; vegetable functions are the foundation of animal functions; animal functions are the basis of the mind's activity.

Inasmuch as the lower level is not lost, but *unites* with the more perfect activity, evolution "is not only a process of development and

---

44. *The Justification of the Good,* 249.

improvement, it is also *a process of unifying the universe"*: plants physiologically absorb the *milieu;* animals psychologically embrace in their consciousness and through the senses a still wider sphere of phenomena; man "includes in himself through reason more distant spheres of being which are not directly perceived by the senses; he can embrace all in one, or understand the significance of all; finally, the God-man, or the Logos, not only understands in the abstract, but actually achieves the significance of everything, in other words, the perfect moral order, embracing and linking all through the force of living personal love" (248).

Up to this point, Soloviev's evolutionism differs from naturalistic evolutionism mainly by the fact that the naturalist studies the *factual* composition of being, while ignoring the objective values and meanings (or even rejecting them); Soloviev, on the contrary, is interested in the entire evolutionary process only inasmuch as one can find in it the realization of objective and even absolute values and meanings.

This difference of the two viewpoints was immediately and inevitably to become even more complex. The naturalist who beholds in the world only the blind interplay of mechanical forces, believes that every successive type of natural being is entirely the product of the preceding types. The philosopher, recognizing the reasonable character of evolution and seeing in it the increasing incarnation of values and meanings, cannot admit that such a process should be *determined solely* by blind factors inferior in value. "The fact that higher forms and types are manifested or revealed following the inferior ones," says Soloviev "by no means proves that they are the product or creation of the inferior realm. The order of being is not identical to the order of phenomena. The higher, more positive and fuller types and conditions of being exist (metaphysically) before the inferior ones, though they manifest and reveal themselves after them. This does not mean a denial of evolution; evolution is a fact. But to assert that evolution creates higher forms entirely out of inferior ones—that is finally out of nothing—means to found a fact on a logical absurdity. The evolution of inferior types of being cannot by itself alone create superior types, but it does create material conditions and offer the necessary milieu for the manifestation or revelation of the superior. Thus every manifestation of a new type of being is in a certain sense a *new creation,* but a creation which can least of all be designated as a creation out of nothing; for firstly, the natural basis for the birth of the new type is offered by the former one; and secondly, the superior type's own positive contents does not arise out of non-being, but exists from all times. It only enters (at a certain point of the process) into another sphere of phenomena. The conditions of the phenomenon depend on natural evolution; that which is revealed depends on God" (245).

The project of a supranaturalistic theory of evolution put down by Soloviev in its general outlines is by no means a negation of naturalist research applied to the evolutionary process. Soloviev's supranaturalism is able to include in its structure and to appreciate all facts and laws of nature's development established by the naturalist. Indeed, Soloviev's theory does not reject the *actual* conditions of evolutionism, but it adds to them the latter's *ideal* foundations; further, this theory borrows from the natural sciences all the factual aspect of evolution, but in addition to the facts it studies the aspects of value and meaning attached to them.[45]

In other words, this theory not only fully utilizes the natural sciences but adds to them a great deal, thus placing everything in an original and clear perspective.

Soloviev's project is one of the attempts of ideal-realistic religious philosophy to evolve a full world conception which contains the synthesis of science, philosophy and religion. Encountering apparent contradictions between facts discovered by natural science (or more correctly speaking by the *theories* of naturalists) and religious conceptions concerning the world, most people do not even attempt to overcome these discrepancies and prefer to restrict their own spiritual nature: some grow indifferent to religion and, plunging into natural-science research applied to the world, lose the vision of the higher aspects of life. Others, devoting themselves entirely to religious interests grow indifferent to positive scientific knowledge. The great merit of systems like that of Soloviev's philosophy consists in the following fact: even if they do not offer a final solution of the secret of the universe, they at least clearly and plainly demonstrate that the human mind has ways and means for working out fruitfully the problem of combining the doctrines concerning the superior and the inferior aspects of the world into a unified whole.

The evolution of nature creates conditions for the development of a higher aspect of the world; this aspect is expressed in the history of mankind, in mankind's ethical behavior and aspiration to improve social life. Soloviev devoted a great deal of thought to the study of the problems of ethics and social philosophy in the spirit of a Christian world conception.

He considered ethics as an autonomous science independent of "positive religions," epistemology and metaphysics, as well as of this

---

45. Concerning the meaning of evolution, see N. Lossky's article: "The Limits of Evolution," *Journal of Philosophical Studies*, II, October 1927.

or that solution applied to the problem of free will. "In creating moral philosophy," says Soloviev, "reason only develops, on the basis of experience, the idea of the Good primarily inherent in it (or, and this is the same thing) the primary fact of moral consciousness, and thereby does not transgress the limits of its own field."[46]

Soloviev is right in the sense that whatever the religious, epistemological or metaphysical ideas embraced by man are, his conscience increasingly claims the realization of absolute good and under its guidance, reason can evolve a conceptual system concerning these claims. But as soon as reason advances further and aims at proving the *possibility of fulfilling* these demands and consequently their *rational character*, it must necessarily link the teaching of the Good and of man's consequent behavior with the complex system of metaphysics, in which the problem of free will is solved in a positive way. Moreover, reason must epistemologically justify metaphysics, and the system of these metaphysics must necessarily be Christian: Christianity alone can explain the possibility of attaining absolute good through the teaching of the Kingdom of God. All fundamental philosophical sciences are organically linked to each other. Ethics are also inevitably linked with metaphysics, epistemology and religious philosophy. Soloviev's moral philosophy obviously contains this link as we shall soon see.

The evolution of nature, according to Soloviev, is the gradual development of the world's unity, indispensable for the achievement of Divine Good. A still higher degree of world unity is reached in man's life especially in the history of mankind.

This close union of God with the world and the establishment in the world of a perfect harmony is only possible on the basis of *mutual love* between God and beings that are capable of voluntary union with Him and are therefore free, rational and eager for perfection. Man is such a being when he "voluntarily submits to the action of God as to a supreme *power*, consciously accepts the Divine action as true *authority* and, finally, independently participates in the action of God or enters into a living *counsel* with Him."[47]

In so far as man enters upon this path, he shares in the work of the God-man Christ, for "the combination of the three principles that have found individual realization in the person of the spiritual man Jesus Christ, must find collective realization in humanity spiritualized by Him." It is only collectively that finite creatures can attain the fullness of being in the Kingdom of Heaven, where the perfect unity of all in God is realized; and on earth the way to that Kingdom is paved not only

46. *The Justification of the Good,* Introduction.
47. *History and the Future of Theocracy,* IV, 302.

by the single-handed efforts made by each individual at his own risk and responsibility, but also by the collective activity of men as members of rightly organized society. Soloviev represents the ideal of such a society as a free theocracy in which moral *authority* belongs *to the Church* and its supreme representative, the high-priest; *power*, to the King; and living *counsel* with God, to prophets "who have the keys of the future" (IV, 582). The characteristic feature of this social order is free submission of the State to the authority of the Church. The leading part thus assigned to the Church finds explanation in Soloviev's theory of its true nature. The visible Church is "an actual and objective form of the Kingdom of God;" it is "the living body of the Divine Logos" containing humanity, in so far as it is "united with its divine principle in Christ."[48]

As a part of the organic unity of the Church, man rises to a higher stage of being than in his isolated solitary existence. "Confessing the faith established by the ecumenical councils," says Soloviev, "we accept a truth independent of the human mind; admitting the divine authority of the apostolic hierarchy, we submit to a social form which is not subject to human arbitrary will—we submit to God's truth; finally, receiving the holy sacraments, we find a source, unpolluted by our body of sin, and an immortal seed of new and perfect life." Indeed, "in order to rule rationally over the material nature, transforming it into a living medium of higher forces, spiritual and divine—into God's body, man must already possess in him the embryo of that God's body, the seed of the new, higher nature and life (spiritual body). That seed of purity and light, the absolute form of the transfigured matter, is contained only in Christ's body, and it is only by communing with it sacramentally that we can receive this embryo of the new life, in which we too are given Christ's power over all flesh."[49]

In his youth (in 1873) Soloviev in a conversation with his friends thus expressed this idea: Man has a "sideric body" which becomes atrophied when one does not go to Communion for a long time.[50]

As is always the case when the object is perfect unity in God, this unity can only be based on a *free* submission of the members to the whole. Therefore true theocracy can only be free: it is a free realization of the unity "without division or confusion" of two powers, the spiritual and the temporal. In such a social organization Christianity aims at achieving not only "personal saintliness, but also social justice."[51]

48. *The Spiritual Foundations of Life*, III, 347.
49. *Ibid.*, III, 350.
50. Lukianov, *Journal of the Ministry of Education*, 19, June 1917.
51. *The Russian National Ideal*, V, 384.

Soloviev devoted a great deal of study to the problems of Christian social organization, and especially to the problem of the nation; but before we become familiar with his *social* philosophy, let us examine his teaching concerning morals in the individual relations of men among themselves. Already in his *Lectures on God-manhood,* Soloviev stated that the human person is negatively unconditioned: "He does not and cannot be satisfied with any conditional limited contents;" and this is not all: the human person is convinced that he can achieve also a positive unconditionality," i.e., that "he can possess the fullness of being" (III, 23). This fullness of being is the Absolute Good; it is conditioned by nothing outside itself, that is by nothing imperfect; on the contrary, "it conditions everything and is achieved through everything. The fact that it is conditioned by nothing ensures its *purity;* the fact that it conditions everything ensures its *fullness;* and the fact that it is achieved through everything ensures its *strength* or active character." The moral significance of life consists in serving this "Good, pure, all-embracing and all-powerful."[52]

Perfect moral good leads to absolute perfection in which we find indivisibly linked: good, welfare and beatitude. Indeed, perfect moral good for a person achieving it in all its fullness is "necessarily also welfare;" and all welfare, whichever one desires, must "in order not to be imaginary and illusory be conditioned by good; this means by the fulfillment of moral claims" (chap. VII, 200 c). So as to achieve such all-embracing good, man must rise to a level "of full being." This is possible for man only "through inner union with that which essentially is all," i.e., with God (195). Without this union with God, without God's creative act, which theology calls "grace," man cannot rise to such a level of perfection as to deserve deification and to become a member of the Kingdom of God (IX, 249).

So as to contribute to the perfection of man, God himself has entered the terrestrial historic process in the person of the God-man, Jesus Christ. "Through his teaching and his life, beginning from His victory over all the temptations of *moral* evil and ending with his Resurrection, that is the victory over *physical* evil, over the law of death and corruption, the true God-man opened the Kingdom of God to mankind." But the God-man is an *individual* manifestation of the Kingdom of God, whereas the goal of world history is a *universal* manifestation of this Kingdom, "in the collective entirety of mankind." It must be achieved freely "through mankind's own experience and for this was needed a new process of the development of the Christian world, a world baptized, but not having as yet *put on* Christ" (253).

52. *The Justification of the Good,* 2nd ed., 18.

Beside grace, beside supernatural Divine help offered to the perfecting process of man, the latter is aided by three primary moral attributes of human nature: *shame, pity and reverence*. Man is ashamed of his animality, he manifests sexual shame. The feeling of pity and sympathy is felt by man toward living beings, "thus manifesting his solidarity with them," a solidarity which is the indispensable condition of social life. The feeling of reverence expresses man's proper attitude toward the superior principle and forms "the individual psychical root of religion" (chap. I). In these three feelings of shame, pity and reverence we find manifested man's proper attitude toward that which is below him, on his own level and above him. The basis of these three feelings, of all morals, are one: they consist in the tendency to attain the *totality* of man's being, disrupted by the division of the sexes, by the separation of mankind into a multitude of hostile, selfish entities, and by the estrangement from the absolute center of the universe," i.e., from God (chap. VII).

Soloviev expressed a number of original ideas concerning sexual love. He discovered the significance of sexual love not in the multiplication of the species, since the preservation of the species can be attained and is actually ensured in the vegetable and animal kingdom through sexless reproduction.[53]

Soloviev believes that childbirth is the "process of evicting one generation by another . . . the descendants live at the expense of the ancestors, they live by the ancestors' death." Moral evil is contained "in the very act, the carnal act, through which we assert by our own consent the dark way of nature, *shameful* for us because of its blindness, *pitiless* toward the departing generation, and *impious*, because the departing generation is that of our fathers." But in this evil there is also to be found an element of good: the children we have born, will perhaps "not be like ourselves, they will be better than we."[54]

Our offsprings may rise to that level of perfection, where multiplication of the species will become unnecessary, because they will be immortal and the preservation of the species will thus be ensured. In man, sexual love has a far higher significance than giving birth to children. It bears the character of the individual love of two persons of opposite sex, equal in respect to each other as persons, but possessed with attributes entirely different and at the same time completing each other.[55]

This love starts with the vision "of the ideal image" of the beloved

53. *The Meaning of Love*, VI, 364.
54. *The Justification of the Good*, chap. VII, 5 f.
55. *The Meaning of Love*, 379.

face, and its further perfect development can produce "a blending of two given organic persons which would create out of them one absolute ideal person. . . . The free unity of the masculine and the feminine principles, each preserving its own particular form, but having surmounted their essential estrangement and disintegration—precisely this is the true, immediate *aim* of love" (384). The solution of this problem is "the *justification and salvation of individuality* through the sacrifice of selfishness" (376). Selfishness consists in the fact that the subject "justly ascribing to itself absolute significance, unjustly refuses to recognize this significance in another." But man can realize his potential absolute "only by removing from his consciousness and from his life the inner limits which separate him from another man" (377). This means freeing himself from egoism. The force leading toward that goal is "love, and especially sexual love" (378). Speaking of sexual love and of its true significance, Soloviev does not mean "the physiological union" which leads to childbirth and "cannot truly re-establish the totality of man's being" (393). He means "union in God" (398), that is Platonic "spiritual love," which transforms man and woman who love each other into one true person (382), attaining "victory over death;" for the true spirituality of such a person having re-established his totality is at the same time "transformation, salvation, resurrection" of the body as well (400). "The image and semblance of God, that which must be re-established, does not belong to half-man, to sex, but to entire man, that is to the positive union of the masculine and feminine principle; this is true androgynism, without the confusion of outward form, which is a monstrosity, and without inner division, which is imperfection and the beginning of death."[56]

The perfect good, toward which we must tend, is good not for one separate person alone, but for the whole of humanity; it is attained through the *historic* process of perfecting. "The spirit of God in mankind, in other words, the Kingdom of God, demands for its true manifestation the most perfect social organization, which is precisely evolved by world history."[57]

Society, according to Soloviev "is a completed or enlarged person, and the person is a restricted or concentrated society." Therefore, "every degree of moral consciousness inevitably tends toward its personal and social realization; consequently, society can become a "full and all-embracing realization of ethics." The State "in its aspect of moral significance" is "collectively organized pity" (550). Law, according to Soloviev, is the "lowest degree, or the determined minimum of morality" (460).

56. *Plato's Life Drama,* VIII, 224.
57. *The Justification of the Good,* chap. VIII, 224.

"Law is the enforced demand of the realization of a determined minimum good and order, which does not permit certain manifestations of evil." The ideal of perfect good is revealed by Christianity: the goal of the historical process consists in the task of contributing to the transformation "of our entire personal and social milieu in the spirit of Christ" (312).

The problem of the relation of the separate person to society is solved by Soloviev through choosing as premise the goal of the historical process taken as the collective realization of the good. "The degree of submission of the person to society, he declares, *must correspond to the degree of submission of society itself to the moral good;* without this, the social environment exercises no rights whatever on the individual person" (XII, 328). Every man is a "moral being or person; he possesses independently from his social usefulness an absolute dignity and the absolute right to existence and to the free development of his positive forces. Every person is something unique and inimitable, and must therefore be a goal in himself, and not a means or instrument only; essentially, this right of the person is *absolute*" (333). The free development of man is so essential a condition of the perfecting process, that law "permits men to be wicked; it does not interfere with their free choice between good and evil; all it does, in the interest of the common good, is to forbid a wicked man to become an *evildoer,* dangerous to the existence of society itself."

A Christian state must have *a Christian policy:* in international relations its object is "the peaceful rapprochement of the peoples." The formula laid down by Soloviev for the relations between nations contains an absolutely perfect solution of the problem. And no wonder, for it is a direct application of Christ's commandment of love for another man to the mutual relations between peoples: "Love all other nations as you do your own."[58]

Soloviev explains that this demand "does not at all imply a *psychological sameness* of feeling, but only the *ethical equality* of the volitional attitude: I must wish the real good of all the other peoples just as I wish that of my own: this "love of good will is the same for the simple reason that real good is one and indivisible. Of course, this ethical love is also bound up with the psychological understanding and approval of the positive peculiarities of all foreign nations; having overcome by our moral will the senseless and ignorant national animosity, we learn to know and appreciate other nations, we begin to *like* them. . . . When such an attitude becomes an actual rule, national *distinctions* will be preserved and even increased, they will become more pronounced, and

---

58. *The Justification of the Good,* VII, 374.

only national *differences* and offences, which constitute the principal obstacle to the moral organization of mankind, will disappear."

Christ's commandment of love toward our neighbor could be extended by Soloviev to the relations of peoples to each other; for he considered every people "as only a particular form of the universal contents, *living in* that contents, filling with it and incarnating it, not only for this given people, but *for all*" (362). Soloviev corroborated this thesis with excellent examples borrowed from the history of most European nations (chap. XIV).

Christian policy must also be realized within every nation. Its object in the domain of economic relations must be to do away with economic slavery and exploitation of man by man, to achieve a fair organization of labor and distribution, etc.; in combating crime it must seek to reform the criminal and to create adequate penitentiary institutions, etc.[59]

In order to create Christian culture and a free theocracy an organic combination of the positive spiritual principles of the East and of the West is needed. The first step in this direction must be the reunion of the Eastern Church, possessing the wealth of mystical contemplation, with the Western which has created a supernational spiritual power independent of the State. The reunion of the Church with the political power of a State, obeying the moral authority of the Church, would lay down the basis of universal theocracy.

The relation between free theocracy and the past history of mankind can be established if we examine the "three fundamental forces" which govern human evolution. One of these forces is *centripetal:* its purpose is to subordinate humanity to one supreme principle, to do away with all the manifoldness of particular forms, suppressing the freedom of personal life. The second force is *centrifugal;* it denies the importance of general unifying principles. The result of the exclusive action of the first force would be "one master and a dead multitude of slaves;" the extreme expression of the second force would be, on the contrary, "general egoism and anarchy, a multitude of separate units without any inner bond." The third force "lends the positive content to the first two, relieves them of their exclusiveness, reconciles the unity of the supreme principle with the free multiplicity of particular forms and elements and thus creates the wholeness of the universal human organism giving it a peaceful inner life."[60]

"The third force, which is called upon to give the human evolution its absolute content, can only be a revelation of the higher divine world; the nation, which is to manifest this force, must only serve as an *inter-*

---

59. *The Justification of the Good,* chaps. XV, XVI, XIX.
60. *Three Forces* (address of 1877), I, 214.

mediary between mankind and the world and be its free and conscious instrument. Such a nation must not have any specific limited task; it is not called upon to work out the forms and elements of human existence, but only to impart a living soul, to give life and wholeness to disrupted and benumbed humanity through its union with the eternal divine principle. Such a people has no need for any special prerogatives, any particular powers or outward gifts, for it does not act of its own accord, it does not fulfill a task of its own. All that is required of the people which is the bearer of the third divine force is that it should be free from limitedness and one-sidedness, should elevate itself over the narrow specialized interests, that it should not assert itself with an exclusive energy in some particular lower sphere of activity and knowledge, that it should be indifferent to the whole of this life with its petty interests. It must wholly believe in the positive reality of the higher world and be submissive to it. These qualities undoubtedly belong to the racial character of the Slavs, and in particular to the national character of the Russian people."[61]

Soloviev hopes, therefore, that the Slavs and especially Russia, will lay the foundations of a free theocracy. He also tries to prove this by the following arguments of a less general nature. "Our people's outer form of a servant, Russia's miserable position in the economic and other respects, so far from being an argument against her calling, actually confirms it. For the supreme power to which the Russian people has to introduce mankind is not of this world, and external wealth and order are of no moment for it. Russia's great historical mission, from which alone her immediate tasks derive importance, is a religious mission in the highest sense of this word."[62]

Indeed, the ideal of the Russian people is of *religious* nature, it finds its expression in the idea of "Holy Russia;" the capacity of the Russian people to combine Eastern and Western principles has been historically proved by the success of Peter the Great's reforms; the capacity of national self-renunciation, necessary for the recognition of the Pope as the Primate of the Universal Church, is inherent in the Russian people, as may be seen, among other things, from the calling in of the Varangians. Soloviev himself gave expression to this characteristic of the Russian people when he said that it was "better to give up patriotism than conscience," and taught that the cultural mission of a great nation is not a *privilege:* it must not dominate, but *serve* other peoples and all mankind.[63]

61. *Three Forces,* I, 224; *The Philosophical Principles of Integral Knowledge,* I, 259.
62. *Ibid.,* 225.   63. *Christian Policy,* IV, 3.

Soloviev's Slavophil messianism never degenerated into a narrow nationalism. In the nineties he was looked upon as having joined the camp of the Westernizers. In a series of articles he violently denounced the epigons of Slavophilism who had perverted its original conception. In the article "Idols and Ideals," written in 1891, he speaks of "the transformation of the lofty and all-embracing Christian ideals into the coarse and limited idols of our modern paganism. . . . National messianism was the main idea of the old Slavophils; this idea, in some form or other, was shared by many peoples; it assumed a pre-eminently religious and mystical character with the Poles (Towianski) and with some French dreamers of the thirties and forties (Michel, Ventra, etc.). What is the relation of such national messianism to the true Christian idea? We will not say that there is a contradiction of principle between them. The true Christian ideal can assume this national messianic form, but it becomes then very *easily pervertible* (to use an expression of ecclesiastical writers); i.e., it can easily change into the corresponding idol of anti-Christian nationalism, which did happen in fact."[64]

In the same article, while advocating freedom of conscience and freedom of thought—the two principles which, for the older Slavophils were "a characteristic sign of the Orthodox faith"—Soloviev speaks of Tiutchev's poem in which the latter "addresses himself with the following thundering accusation to the Popery in the person of Pius IX:

> His undoing will not be the earthly sword
> Which he possessed for so many years,
> But the fatal saying that
> "Freedom of conscience is a delirium."[65]

Soloviev struggled in his works against every distortion of the Christian ideal of general harmony; he also struggled against all the attempts made by man to satisfy his selfishness under the false pretense of serving a noble cause. Such are for instance the aims of chauvinistic nationalism. Many persons believe, Soloviev tells us, that in order to serve the imaginary interests of their people, "everything is permitted, the aim justifies the means, black turns to white, lies are preferable to truth and violence is glorified and considered as valor. . . . This is first of all an insult to that very nationality which we desire to serve." In reality, "peoples flourished and were exalted only when they did not serve their own interests as a goal in itself, but pursued higher, *general* ideal goods."[66] Trusting the highly sensitive conscience of the Russian people, Soloviev

64. *Ibid.*, V, 357.
65. *Ibid.*, V, 368.
66. *The Justification of the Good*, 351.

wrote in his article "What Is Demanded of a Russian Party?" "If instead of doping themselves with Indian opium, our Chinese neighbors suddenly took a liking to the poisonous mushrooms which abound in the Siberian woods, we would be sure to find Russian jingos, who in their ardent interest in Russian trade, would want Russia to induce the Chinese government to permit the free entry of poisonous mushrooms into the Celestial empire. . . . Nevertheless, every plain Russian will say that no matter how vital may an interest be, Russia's honor is also worth something; and, according to Russian standards, this honor definitely forbids a shady deal to become an issue of national politics."[67]

Like Tiutchev, Soloviev dreamed of Russia becoming a Christian world monarchy; yet he wrote in a tone full of anxiety: "Russia's life has not yet determined itself completely, it is still torn by the struggle between the principle of light and that of darkness. Let Russia become a Christian realm, even without Constantinople, a Christian realm in the full sense of the word, that is one of justice and mercy, and all the rest will be surely added unto this."[68]

Soloviev saw with a pang that in his time the principle of darkness was active both in practice and in the ideological field. In practice this was reflected in the Russian government's program of forced russification applied in the borderlands. In the ideological field, the principle of darkness was expressed in N. J. Danilevsky's book *Russia and Europe*. Danilevsky anticipated Spengler; he rejected the unity of mankind, and evolved the theory of the cultural-historical types of humanity, so deeply differentiated that the principle of culture of one type cannot be transmitted to another. Soloviev declared that such a theory leads to the "degradation of the moral demands placed before peoples by Christian universalism. According to the latter, every people must serve the whole of mankind." In order to defend Christian universalism, Soloviev submitted Danilevsky's book to shattering criticism stated in a number of articles.[69]

The Epigons of Slavophilism turned out to be the champions of national egoism and Soloviev criticized this movement in a number of articles. His criticism was most strongly reflected in one of these articles entitled "Slavophilism and Its Degeneration." He pointed out that the founders of Slavophilism—Kireyevsky, Khomiakov, K. Aksakov—waged a "progressive-liberal struggle against the actual evils existing in the Russia of their time;" they defended the "principle of human rights,

---

67. *The National Problem and Russia*, I, V, 69 c.
68. *T. I. Tiutchev's Poetry*, VI, 479 c.
69. See *"Russia and Europe;"* "The German Original and the Russian Copy," etc., *Collected Works*, V.

of the absolute moral value of the autonomous person, which is a Christian principle," and "in its historical development a mainly West-European idea" (163). Khomiakov evolved a theory concerning the order of religious life which he expressed in the following formula: "The Church as synthesis of unity and freedom in love." But unfortunately he opposed his idealistic conception to Catholicism and Protestantism, and did this in such a way as if his ideal had already been achieved in Russia; whereas in reality, the Russian Church had been brought down to the level of "a function of State organization" (170). The essential defect of Slavophilism consists precisely in the fact that it placed at the basis of its teaching not an ideal to be attained in the future, but the idealization of the past, of ancient Russia, of the Moscovite State. The latter was defined by Soloviev as of Tataro-Byzantine essence (194 c). This error of Slavophilism was the cause of its degeneration, which took place during the period of its ultimate extension. Soloviev recognizes three successive phases in the history of Slavophilism: (1) "The cult of the Russian people as of the main bearer of universal truth" (the elder Slavophiles); (2) "The cult of the people as of the bearer of an elemental force, independent of universal truth" (Katkov); and finally: (3) "The cult of national peculiarities and historical anomalies which separate the Russian people from cultured mankind, that is the cult of the Russian people founded on direct negation of the very idea of universal truth" (Yarosh, etc.) (V, 206 c).

In one of his letters to Stassiulevitch, Soloviev characterized in the following words the disintegration of Slavophilism: "I believe old Slavophilism was a mixture of several heterogenous elements, and more specially of these three: Byzantinism, liberalism and belly-patriotism. In our present-day quasi Slavophilism, each of these elements has emerged separately and roams about by itself, like Major Kovalov's nose. The Byzantine element has found its preachers in T. Filipov, K. Leontiev; the liberal trend has its champions in O. Miller, and especially in Professor Lamansky, who has retained from Slavophilism only its name. As to belly-patriotism, freed from all ideological admixture, it has widely spread among our lowest levels; and it is individually represented by such writers as my friend Strakhov, whose mind belongs entirely to the rotten West, and who places his belly alone on the fatherland's altar."[70]

Soloviev dreamed that the historical process would finally lead to the creation of ideal human civilization—a free world theocracy. This dream was inspired by Soloviev's social optimism. In *The Justification of the Good* he depicts the historical process as if he believed in direct

70. *Letters*, additional volume, 40.

moral and social progress. He wrote: "From the day when men of various nationalities and classes were spiritually united in venerating an *alien* Galilean beggar, executed like a *criminal* in the name of national and caste interests—from that day on, international wars, social lawlessness and the execution of criminals were *inwardly* undermined." From the fifteenth century and especially from the end of the eighteenth, Soloviev points to "a rapid and decisive progress along the path traced by Christianity."

Soloviev was acutely conscious of every distortion of Divine truth, and this awareness is most vividly reflected in the passages of his articles and books devoted to man's or mankind's history from the angle of their attitude toward absolute good. And these works of Soloviev should be read most attentively. Here, I can only briefly mention some of them. In *Plato's Life Drama,* Soloviev shows in short and vivid formulae the greatness of Socrates and the influence exercised by the death of the just on Plato's life. Soloviev also shows that Plato did not succeed in solving the problem of absolute good. Elsewhere, Soloviev speaks of Spain's historical destiny; he explains the decline of Spanish power by that country's threefold betrayal to Christianity: after having defeated the Moors, Spain was filled with hatred toward the "Infidels," puffed up with national pride and chose as highest goal the attainment of national unity and power.[71]

In his speech dedicated to the jubilee of Mitzkevitch, Soloviev described the noble quality of the great Polish poet's spiritual development. Most remarkable are also Soloviev's articles on "Pushkin's Destiny" and on Lermontov; in the latter writing, he speaks of that great and unfortunate poet's struggle against God.

In his article entitled "The Russian National Ideal," Soloviev expressed a series of most interesting ideas concerning Dostoevsky: "In his moments of inspiration," writes Soloviev, "Dostoevsky really beheld the all-human ideal of our people" (V, 381). In Dostoevsky's Pushkin-speech, "the formula of an all-embracing, all-uniting and all-reconciling Russian and Christian ideal was proclaimed with the greatest solemnity." But Soloviev cannot agree with "Dostoevsky's attacks on Jews, Poles, Frenchmen, Germans, on all Europe and on all other religions." Soloviev explains this duality of Dostoevsky's conceptions by the fact that "in the realm of ideas, he was a visionary and an artist, rather than a logical thinker, consequent with himself" (382).

According to Soloviev, all peoples and all races are organs of Godmanhood; each people serves in his own way the goal of the Christian

71. "Nemesis," VIII, 125.

faith "to unite the entire world into one living body, the perfect organism of God-manhood."[72]

From this point of view, Soloviev took a special interest in the character and the destiny of the Jewish people. Why was the God-man Jesus Christ incarnated in a Jew? Soloviev answers this question as follows: "The national character of the Jews presents a wholeness and inner unity;" however, three of their typical traits seems at first glance incompatible with each other: "First of all, Jews possess a deep religious feeling, a devotion to their God, entailing complete self-sacrifice. Secondly, the Jews possess an extremely developed self-consciousness, self-awareness, and a spirit of independent, autonomous action. Every Jew has an acute feeling and consciousness of his national ego, his family ego and his personal ego. Finally, the third characteristic trait of the Jews is their extreme materialism in the widest sense of this word," meaning the sensuous character of their world conception.[73]

Where is the link between Israel's religious idea, the human and autonomous activism of Judaism and Jewish materialism? "God," according to the Jewish conception, is "the perfect person or the absolute Ego, and religion is not the cult of blind demonic forces; it is a personal interaction of God and man, an alliance or a pact as of two beings; these beings are not equal, but *of the same essence morally*" (394). "The only true divine-human, Judaeo-Christian religion leads along the direct royal road, running between the two extreme errors of paganism: pagan man is either absorbed by God (India) or else God is turned into his shadow (Greece and Rome)." God who is strong and holy "chooses a strong man who is able to struggle with him. God who is holy unites Himself only with the man who possesses holiness and who is capable of *active* moral action;" only such a man can become "a friend of God" (395). Beholding in God the ideal of all perfection, the Jew "demands that this ideal should be incarnated on earth." In the Easter chant, telling of the coming of the Messiah, the Jews pray: "God-Almighty, now build your temple near and soon, soon in our days, the nearest possible, now build, now build, now build, now build your temple near." "In this impatience to incarnate the divine on earth we discover the guiding thread for the understanding of Jewish materialism. We must distinguish three kinds of materialism: practical, scientific-philosophical and religious." Practical materialism is the result of "the domination in certain individuals of the lower aspect of human nature, of sensuous interests, over the spiritual ones." When the negation of spiritual being is turned into a principle, "practical materialism becomes theoretical,

---

72. "Nationality and Russia's National Affairs," V, 25.
73. *The History and the Future of Theocracy*, IV, 392.

that is scientific-philosophical" (397). Both these aspects of materialism are to be found in all peoples. "But another, special type of materialism was ever inherent" to the national spirit of the Jews—"a materialism radically differing from the first two types, and which I shall roughly and not quite accurately call *religious* materialism." It consists in the fact that "for every idea and every ideal, the Jew demands a visible and tangible incarnation, and he expects from it useful and beneficent results." The Jew "believes in the spirit, but only in a spirit which penetrates all that is material, which uses matter as its envelope and as its instrument" (398). "The Jews' entire religious history was directed toward the aim of preparing not only holy souls, but also holy bodies for the God of Israel" (399). "This is why the Jewish people are God's people, this is why Christ was born in Judea" (400). "In spite of the serpent-like materialism of its nature, in spite of the leprous formalism of its mind, the Jewish people still remain God's people; for in the depth of its soul this people desires more strongly and more fully than any other people the fullest incarnation of the Divine idea" (391). Therefore, "in the future *realization* of Christianity, too, a special, outstanding role will belong to the Jews, according to Saint Paul" (IV, 15).

In anti-Semitic writings we find many allusions to the immoral rules of conduct prescribed by the Talmud. Soloviev wrote an article entitled "The Talmud and Contemporary Polemics in Austria and Germany," which showed how unfounded are such accusations (VI). We Christians should remember that the two fundamental commandments in which Christ summed up His entire teaching—Love God more than thyself, and thy neighbor as thyself—are taken from the Old Testament.

Certain Christians assert that after the crucifixion of Christ the Jews no longer worshipped God but Satan. These Christians forget that Christ Himself said: "Whosoever shall speak a word against the Son of man, shall be forgiven him: but he that shall speak against the holy Ghost, it shall not be forgiven him, neither in this world nor in the world to come" (Matt. 12, 32). I believe that the unfounded suspicion concerning other men's prayer is a sin against the Holy Ghost.

Alluding to his own passionate desire not only theoretically to discover divine truth, but also to contribute to its incarnation on earth, Soloviev often called himself a Jew. Thus, he wrote to Strakhov: "Our common culture, a purely Russian one (because of our ecclesiastical origins), does not prevent you from being a Chinaman, and me—a Jew."[74] Before his death, Soloviev prayed for the Jewish people.

Having evolved a system of ethics, Soloviev intended to work out

---

74. *Letters*, I, 60.

a system of aesthetics and an epistemology, but death prevented him from fulfilling his project. However some time earlier he had the opportunity of expressing his fundamental ideas concerning the beautiful. He did this mainly in two articles, "The Beautiful in Nature," and "The general Significance of Art." He conceived the beautiful as an absolute value of being, and precisely beheld in it "the incarnation of the idea."[75] Now the idea or the "noble aspect of being" is "the full freedom of the composite parts in the absolute oneness of the whole" (40). "The idea really conceived in the sensuous being is the beautiful" (41); in other words, the beautiful is the Good, and it is Truth, sensuously incarnated in material being. The highest goal of art is *theurgy,* that is creation according to God's will, which is precisely "the creation of a universal spiritual organism"[76] in which absolute good, truth and beauty are realized.

Soloviev started evolving his epistemology in 1897–99; but he had only time to write three articles, which were published in the eighth volume of his *Collected Works*. These articles appeared under the title, *Theoretical Philosophy*. In this work, Soloviev denied the substantiality of the individual *ego;* in the last part of *Theoretical Philosophy*, he spoke of the thinking *ego* which conceives truth as of a superindividual subject (213). In my own article, "The Epistemology of Intuitivism," I submit to criticism Soloviev's idea concerning substantiality.

Soloviev's conception of religion proves that he was neither an Orthodox nor a Catholic, nor a Protestant: he stood above the limitations of these various denominations and strove to be a true universal Christian. "As long as we assert our religion, *first of all* in its denominational particularity, and only *after this* as ecumenical Christianity," Soloviev tells us, "we take away from religion not only its sane logic, but moreover its moral significance; we thus transform it into an obstacle on the path of man's spiritual regeneration."[77] He conceives union between the Catholic and the Orthodox Church, not as the absorption of one Church by the other, but as a "combination, in which each Church will preserve its formative principle and its particularities, dismissing only hostility and exclusiveness."[78]

In the *Three Conversations*, Soloviev already describes the union of the Catholic, Orthodox and Protestant Churches as of three branches of the one Church, all three enjoying equal privileges. In 1892, he wrote to Rozanov: "I am as far removed from Latin limitations as I am from

---

75. "The Beautiful in Nature," VI, 39.
76. "The General Significance of Art," VI.
77. *The Justification of the Good*, 344.
78. *The Slavonic Problem*, V, 67, 1884.

Byzantine limitations, or the Augsburg or Geneva ones. The religion of the Holy Ghost which I profess is wider and of a fuller content than all separate religions: it is neither the sum total nor the extract of its separate organs."[79]

Soloviev does not consider Divine Revelation as something which has once for all been given and completed in the past of the Hebrew and Christian Churches. Revelation continues to take place and to be developed, because God educates mankind in view of its gradual acceptance of revealed Truth. "God can lead only those who have spiritually come of age into the perfect counsel of His love; and He acts necessarily on spiritual childhood as force and power; on spiritual adolescence as law and authority."[80]

The law, "thou shalt not adore idols," has been often violated by man, without his even being aware that he is worshipping not the Lord, but a created being or even some material object or some system of ideas. For certain people faith in dogma becomes such an idol. Such a faith is usually linked with denominational vanity, that is one of the aspects of refined egoism. Soloviev defines this distortion of Christianity, as a "monstrous teaching which asserts that the only path to salvation is faith in dogma, and that it is impossible to be saved without it."[81] If love of God and neighbor are replaced by love of dogmatic teaching, this substitution usually leads to cruel and unjust oppression, and to religious persecution. Speaking of the fanatical patriot of the *Moscow News* and of the laws they suggested regarding Russia's non-Orthodox populations, Soloviev describes their Orthodoxy as a "Sphinx with a woman's face and the claws of a beast."[82]

Evolving his Christian world conception, Soloviev insisted most of all on the necessity of building the entire culture, as well as the whole of political and social life on the basis of the principles of Christianity. "No sanctity can be only personal," he said, "sanctity is necessarily the love of *others*, and in the conditions of terrestrial reality, this love is mostly *compassion*. . . . We have moralists, who openly declare that the Russian people's ideal demands personal sanctity, and not social justice. Personal sanctity, of course, is used here only as a red herring, the true aim being to get rid somehow or other of social justice."[83]

Soloviev observes with bitterness that the social progress which has marked preceding centuries, such as the suppression of torture and

---

79. *Letters*, II, 43.
80. *The History and Future of Theocracy*, IV, 387.
81. Quoted from article "The Jews" (VI, 354), written by Soloviev in answer to Diminsky's book on the Jews.
82. "A Historical Sphinx," *Problems of Culture*, V, 450.
83. *The Russian National Ideal*, V, 384.

ruthless executions, the end of persecution of religious denominations and heretics, the abolition of serfdom—all these reforms were achieved in most cases by unbelievers. "Those who will be shocked by the thought that the spirit of Christ acts through those who do not believe in him will be wrong even from the point of view of their own dogma. . . . If the spirit of Christ can act through an unbelieving priest in the sacraments of the church, why can it not act in history through an unbelieving social or political leader, especially if believers cast it out? The Spirit breathes where it wills."[84]

In the last period of his philosophical activity Soloviev came to doubt whether theocracy in the form of a Christian State was the way to the Kingdom of God. In his remarkable book *Three Conversations,* and in the story of the Antichrist appended to it, he represents, in an artistic form "the last act of the historical tragedy" as an epoch of religious impostors "when the name of Christ will be appropriated by such forces in humanity as in their nature and activity are foreign and even hostile to Christ and His work." He describes the social organization of that period as a world empire, at the head of which stands a thinker of genius; he is a social reformer, an ascetic and a philanthropist, but the true motive of his actions is vanity and not love; he tempts mankind by the ideal of a social order which will abundantly secure to everyone *panem et circenses*. Only a small number of people remain true to the Christian ideal of overcoming earthly limitations for the sake of the Kingdom of God; they retire into the desert, bring about the union of the Churches and go forth to meet the second advent of Jesus Christ.

In his life, as well as in his philosophical creation, Soloviev was the bold champion of the absolute Good, to be achieved in the Kingdom of God. He sternly condemned every attempt to justify selfishness by clothing it in worthy purposes: thus for instance he criticized egoism in national life when it pretended to serve the people's interests, and in religious life when it asserted that one faith alone could lead to salvation. Such an assertion was considered by Soloviev as the manifestation of confessional vanity. His attacks and criticisms led to sharp controversies, in which Soloviev often exercised a remarkable sense of humor and a biting wit. His humor is manifest in such articles as "The Quarrel About Justice" and "The End of the Quarrel" (V), directed against L. Tikhomirov and V. V. Rozanov. And we find an example of Soloviev's sarcastic strain in his article "Porfiry Golovlev on Freedom and Faith," in which he compares Rozanov to Stchedrin's famous character Yudushka Golovlev. "The article entitled 'Freedom and Faith' is not signed by

84. *The Decline of the Medieval World Conception,* VI, 357 c.

Golovlev [writes Soloviev], but all its inner symptoms eliminate all possible doubts as to its author: to whom, if not to Yudushka, could we attribute this peculiar, unctious and at the same time cynical babble?" Further, Soloviev condemns the "systematically dishonest attitude adopted toward the written word by Yudushka-Rozanov" (V). No wonder that Soloviev had many enemies in literary circles. Blinded by hatred, they spread calumnies and accusations, branding him with defects incompatible with each other. Thus, in his article "The End of the Quarrel," Soloviev quotes the words used by Rozanov in his controversy; Rozanov calls Soloviev: "a corps-de-ballet dancer," "a pianist strumming on a broken key-board," "a harlot, cynically playing with theology," "a thief, having stealthily crept into a church," "a man guilty of sacrilege," "a man born blind," and "a stick thrown from hand to hand" (V, 509). Some religious publications considered Soloviev as a convert to Catholicism, at the same time denouncing him as a "Protestant rationalist, mystic, nihilist, old-believer, and finally a Jew."[85]

Let us now ask ourselves what is the essence of Soloviev's work, what are the qualities and the defects of his system?

In our enlightened age there are to be found in all Christian Churches ministers and theologians who are ashamed of the "unscientific" stories of miracles, of faith in the transmuting power of sacraments, of hope in the resurrection of the body, and so on; their philosophical education compels them to give up the dogma of the incarnation of the Logos in Jesus Christ, which is essential to Orthodox Christianity. For such persons the Christian religion becomes mainly a moral doctrine and the sacraments are reduced to merely symbolic acts. Such adaptation of religion to modern science and philosophy is the death not only of Christianity, but of morality itself. The moral ideal of Christianity is an absolute, all-embracing love, creating a realm of being in which there is no struggle for existence, no trace of any kind of violence. Now this ideal can only have meaning if the laws of physics and physiology—the laws of our limited earthly existence—are relative, if love is not merely an individual mental state but a metaphysical principle that actively transforms the world, creating a new heaven and a new earth—a city of God in which, through a mutual interpenetration of all beings, each one of them is freed from the limitations of the binding natural necessity. In his philosophy Vladimir Soloviev sets himself the task of bringing to light the spiritual foundations of our life on earth which in their further development lead to the Kingdom of God, that is, to "a complete realization of the divine and the human nature through the God-

---

85. "A New Defense of Old Slavophilism," V, 242.

man, Christ, or in other words, to the fullness of the natural human life united through Christ with the fullness of God" (VI, 30).

Modern Western-European philosophy, which has developed out of the Kantian, the neo-Fichtean and the neo-Hegelian systems, is also concerned with the study of the spiritual principles of reality. It, too, designates them by the term Logos, but it understands by that term the totality of abstract ideal principles, of mathematical principles and categorial forms that lie at the basis of the world, dismissing as a mere myth the belief in the Logos as a living personal God incarnated in the Man Jesus Christ. Russian philosophy, on the other hand, as represented by Soloviev and his successors, attaches particular value to the conception of the concretely ideal living principles (such as Logos, Sophia, Adam Kadmon and each individual human soul) and their incarnation. Abstract ideal principles are, as such, incapable of giving to the world unity and definiteness; existence can be made to conform to abstract ideas only through the instrumentality of living agents, of concretely ideal principles (the "concrete universals" of the English philosophy), of persons acting in conformity with the ideal forms. Moreover, abstract ideal principles condition only the *kingdom of law; the kingdom of grace* is the domain of the concrete, individual manifestations of love; and consequently the uniting principle which makes it into a rational cosmos must be a concretely ideal being and not an abstract idea.

The problem of the incarnation of these principles makes it imperative for a Christian metaphysics to work out a doctrine of the *transfiguration of the body*, of holy corporeality. For if the existence of dense matter, necessarily connected with the struggle for existence, be alone recognized, consistently demands that we should either strictly condemn all bodily life and preach the religion of death, or accept bodily being without any transfiguration of it, substituting for the Christian ideal the task of ordering the earthly life on the basis of calculating sagacity and profitable good will.

Vladimir Soloviev and his successors take Christianity to be a religion of life and of the absolute fullness of being, both spiritual and bodily. Soloviev devotes, therefore, much attention to the doctrine of the transfiguration of the flesh—of spiritualized deified matter and of resurrection of the body. He interprets the sacraments of the Church as the means of leading man out of the state of separateness and "connecting him, both physically and morally, with *all;* thus reinstating the complete wholeness of the true life in God." In the sacrament of the Eucharist "through partaking bodily and substantially of the all-embracing body of Christ (in whom dwells all the fullness of Godhead) and being physically, though invisibly, united with it, man actually participates in the divinely human and the spiritually corporeal, universal wholeness." The rudiments of the complete life received by man through sacraments increase under the guidance of the Church, if man has love for God and his creatures, and "will eventually lead to the bestowal of immortal life upon nature as a whole, which is now in a state of death and disruption. Nature must be united to man as his living body."[86]

Such transfigured nature will lovingly submit to man instead of hindering and limiting his activity. The doctrine, proclaimed by Romantic philosophy, of nature's obedience to the perfect man (the ethical idealism of Fichte, the magic idealism of Novalis) thus finds a place in the Christian philosophy of Vladimir Soloviev. It has been worked out by him on a much wider basis, namely in the form not of idealism, but of ideal-realism; that is, a doctrine which, thanks to its realistic aspect, is much more capable than Fichte's system, of realizing the synthesis of religiously philosophical teachings with science.

The main influences under which Soloviev's philosophy took shape were the Christian platonism of his master, Professor Yurkevich (of the University of Moscow), Schelling's doctrine of the relationship between the Absolute and the world stated in his *Philosophy of Mythology and Revelation*, as well as Schelling's natural-philosophical doctrine of the evolution of nature toward the creation of an absolute organism. Soloviev's search for concrete principles and conditions of complete knowledge is, no doubt, connected with the ideas of the Slavophils Kireyevsky and Khomiakov.

The great merits of Soloviev in working out a Christian metaphysics —e.g., his doctrine of transfigured corporeality as the necessary condition of the realization of the absolute moral ideal, his conception of evolution, of the meaning of historical process, etc.—are beyond doubt. Unfortunately, however, two extremely important doctrines of his, namely those which deal with Sophia and the connection between the Absolute and the world, have been given a form incompatible with Christian religion. At the same time, his view of the Absolute is not sufficiently justified logically and his view of Sophia is inconsistent. Indeed, conceiving the world as the second Absolute, namely the Absolute in becoming, Soloviev contends that this *becoming* Absolute is *indispensable* for the first Absolute which, as absolute pan-unity, must be "the unity of itself and its other."[87]

This doctrine of the necessity of the world and man for God introduces a pantheistic current into Soloviev's system. It is logically not

---

86. *The Spiritual Foundations of Life*, III, 345, 364.
87. *The Philosophical Principles of Integral Knowledge*, I, 321.

justified, for God, being more than an Absolute, namely the Super-absolute divine Nothing, has no need for man and the world.

God and the world he has created differ so profoundly the one from the other, that we do not find between them the rational relation, according to which two objects differing from each other, still present necessarily some similar aspect. If such a rational (logical) difference existed between God and the world, then God and the world would have belonged together to one and the same system, and would have mutually depended on each other. But the doctrine concerning God as the object of negative theology, obliges us to recognize God as the *metalogical*, suprarational principle. This recognition leads us to the teaching that God is the creator of the world, and that the world is the being which He has created, and which is absolutely incommensurable with Him. Between God and the world there is no relation of identity in none of their aspects whatsoever: they are divided by an ontological abyss. The difference which separates God from the world is a "metalogical otherness."[88]

The world's being is something existing entirely outside God's essence; consequently God is not pan-unity. This does not mean at all that God is a limited being. The relation of limitation is only possible between two objects belonging to the same species, as pointed out by Spinoza.

The problem of connection between God and the world is solved consistently only by the Christian doctrine of God creating the world out of nothing: according to this doctrine God created the world, both in form and in substance, as something entirely new, different from Himself, without using for this creation any material either in Himself or outside.

Other defects of Soloviev's system also are linked to his teaching concerning the Absolute as pan-unity, a teaching which lends to Soloviev's metaphysics a pantheistic flavor. In his explanation of the world, Soloviev gives a secondary place to the conception of God as the creator of world-being; instead, he advances the conception of God only as the source of the *idea* of Divine all-oneness, which invests with a positive significance the world's "attraction or tendency toward being."[89]

Thus the multiplicity of beings in the world remains unexplained. Apparently, like Schopenhauer, Soloviev is inclined toward thinking that the world's "thirst for being" is one, and the multiplicity of beings is something derivative. In *The Justification of the Good* he writes:

---

88. Concerning the conception of metalogical otherness, see S. Frank's book *The Object of Knowledge* (in French *La connaissance et l'être*).

89. *The Philosophical Principles of Integral Knowledge*, I, 352.

the attainment of "complete fullness, of which chastity is only the starting point ... is slowed down, not checked by the multiplying of man. Thanks to this new condition, creating *man-society,* the abiding fullness of his being is manifested no more in chastity alone, which preserves him from his natural breaking up into separate parts; it also manifests itself in social solidarity, which re-establishes through the feeling of pity the moral unity of man physically broken up" (chap. VII, 198). Soloviev reasons in such a way as if the multiplicity of individual human egos is not created by God, but has sprung as the result of sin. This *idea* can only be formed in the mind of a philosopher who denies the substantiality of the individual human ego, the supratemporal nature of the person's ontological center. Indeed, in his article "Theoretical Philosophy," Soloviev resolutely rejects the ego's supratemporal nature, for which Leo Lopatin had offered a convincing proof. Soloviev erroneously believes that the flow of the time process would have been slowed down by the substances' supratemporal nature. In one of his humorous poems, directed against Leo Lopatin's teaching, he wrote:

> But the fearless Leo threatens me
> To take the dynamic substances in a sack
> Down to the river, and with its mass invisible
> To dam in the flow of Heracleitus' stream.[90]
> And sensing from afar the sea and freedom,
> I quietly utter: *panta reï.*

Prince E. N. Trubetzkoy, in his book *Soloviev's World Conception,* expounds this controversy concerning the ego's substantiality, and sides with Soloviev. He says that true religious feeling "wants to possess *nothing of its own outside of God. God is felt like an all:* this is the fundamental trait of religious experience." In his *Lectures on God-manhood* (Lecture VIII), Soloviev recognized the substantiality of the human person and the latter's pre-existence before birth. Later, however, according to Trubetzkoy, Soloviev freed himself from this "error of his youth, inspired by Origen;" he now envisaged the person not as a substance, but as "hypostasis," that is as a "support." Trubetzkoy explains as follows the difference between the "hypostasis" and "substance": substance is "supratemporal, eternal being, possessing an unchanging, constant content," which cannot under any circumstances be carried away by "the river of time." The becoming hypostases, on the contrary, precisely lack this attribute of the constant and the unchanging nature of being completed in itself above time; for their eternal contents is

---

[90]. By "Heracleitus' stream," Soloviev meant this philosopher's theory that "everything flows" (panta reï).

not given them, but only offered as a task to be pursued; "it depends on the hypostasis, on the latter's freedom to choose the way of good or evil, to fulfill its mission, to establish itself in the eternal, the divine, or to remain in the earthly and the temporal."[91]

The fact of replacing the conception of substance by that of hypostasis is due to the erroneous interpretation of the word "substance." The idea of substance has a fundamental significance for our entire world conception and even in every act of knowing any concrete object. The history of the development of the conception of substance is extremely complex and the meaning with which various philosophers invested this word is extremely different. The teaching offered by Leibniz is the most fruitful and confirmed by experience: Leibniz understood substance as being, *creating* its manifestations in time and space. In order to stress this dynamic significance of substance, I prefer using the expression: substantival agent. Experience proves convincingly that the substantival agent is *supratemporal and supraspacial* being, creating its manifestations and lending them the form of temporality (psychical and psychoid processes) or the form of spacio-temporality (material processes). Lopatin cited many a proof in favor of the fact that the human ego is a supratemporal being. To this we must add that the creative force of substantival agents is *supraqualitative*. The agent creates its manifestations, lending them a qualitative determination, but the agent itself stands above the limitation inherent to every quality: each substantival agent is a *metalogical* being, standing above the laws of identity, contradiction and the excluded middle to which all qualities and quantities are submitted. It is precisely as the carrier of a supraqualitative creative force that the substantival agent is a free being: it determines its definite qualitative manifestations, but is determined itself by no one and nothing.

If understood in the spirit of the above-stated considerations, substance is the condition of the free creation of temporal processes, and not a dam, checking the process of transformations in time. As we see from his article "Theoretical Philosophy," Soloviev, at the end of his life found in the composition of the individual ego nothing supratemporal; consequently, the "hypostasis," which by nature is not eternal, but can only merit eternal being, represents a temporal process; but in such a case, the eternity which it acquires, is also not the supratemporal; it is but the eternal continuation of the process of life in time. Hence we see, that during the ultimate period of his philosopher's task, Soloviev did not discover *ideal* being in the composition of the world. And this

---

91. E. Troubetzkoy, II, 250 cc.

is not surprising, since during all the preceding periods of his philosophizing, he had no clearly evolved teaching concerning ideas.

Without the recognition of ideal being, and especially without the recognition of the supratemporality of the ego, it is impossible to evolve a teaching concerning free will. And indeed, to the very end of his life, Soloviev had no time to do anything in defense of indeterminism, though his entire system, as Christian philosophy in general, demands the recognition of free will.

In Soloviev's doctrine of Sophia there is vagueness and inconsistency: he now speaks of Sophia as of a being eternally perfect and invariably obeying God's will, now as of the world soul temporarily fallen away from God and then reuniting with Him in the slow process of creating the "absolute organism."[92]

Investigating the sources of that doctrine Prince E. Trubetskoy points out, as Soloviev's predecessors, Jacob Boehme and Baader; Stremooukhov mentions the influence of Cabbala, but Soloviev's own mystical experience, of course, is even more important.

The worship of Sophia as the Eternal Feminine can easily lead to heresies and moral perversions. V. Soloviev was aware of these pitfalls of Sophianism and himself mentioned them in the preface of his collected poems. "Is not the feminine principle being introduced here into Deity as such? Without discussing this theosophical problem on its merits, I must, in order to preserve the readers from temptation and myself from gratuitous reproaches, state the following: (1) the transposition of carnal, animally human relations into the realm of superhuman is a greatest *abomination* and the cause of utter ruin (the Flood, Sodom and Gomorra, the "satanic depths" of the latest period); (2) the worship of the feminine nature as such—i.e., of the principle of ambiguity and indifference, sensitive to lie and evil in no lesser degree than to truth and good—is a great madness and the main reason of the now-prevailing sloppiness and weakness; (3) the true adoration of the eternal femininity as having from all eternity accepted the power of Godhead and truly embodied the fullness of good and truth and, through them, the undying glory of beauty, has nothing to do with this foolishness, nor with that abomination."

"But the more perfect and intimate is the revelation of true beauty which clothes Godhead and by His power leads us to salvation from suffering and death, the narrower is the boundary which separates it from its false image, from that delusive and impotent beauty which

---

92. Some valuable considerations about other important drawbacks of Soloviev's doctrine of Sophia may be found in the work of Prince E. Trubetskoy, *The Philosophy of V. Soloviev*, I, chap. IX.

merely perpetuates the realm of suffering and death. All this has been predicted, and the end has been predicted: in the end the eternal Beauty will bear fruit, and from her will come the salvation of the world, when her illusory images will have vanished as that sea foam from which the earthly Aphrodite was born. Not a single word of my poems is meant to serve *this one* and therein lies the sole indisputable merit which I may and must recognize in them."

Certain Russians who want to be more Orthodox than the Orthodox themselves (just as there are people more royalist than the king), regard Soloviev's mystical experience with suspicion; they believe that his visions of Saint Sophia were "seductions," that is manifestations of the evil spirit, having put on a saintly mask. These persons should recall Soloviev's own words quoted above, for he was well aware of the spiritual dangers of mystical experience. It suffices to take into consideration his acute moral consciousness of every attempt of the evil power to draw man away from the right path through a subtle mixture of good and evil; and we shall reject as completely improbable the idea that while evolving his teaching of the sacred-feminine, he should have yielded to "seduction." Indeed, there have been among Russian poets, in particular during their youthful years, examples of yielding to such a "seduction"; they fell into the abyss of blasphemous erotism, as A. Biely tells us in his recollections concerning Block. But Soloviev is in no way responsible for this distortion of the idea. All that is great suffers distortions on earth, in the mind or conduct of certain persons; the blame is incurred by those who have allowed such distortions, and not by the principle which they have distorted.

Soloviev's social philosophy at the time of his interest in the idea of free theocracy, and even as expressed in his book *The Justification of the Good*, strikes us as a philosophy of extreme optimism. He often depicts the moral progress, attained in mankind's history, as if society on earth could become the incarnation of absolute good. P. I. Novgorodzev writes in his book, *The Social Ideal* (3rd ed., 140), that such teachings "can only be applied to the suprahistoric, transcendent ideal, that is to the Kingdom of God;" it is completely erroneous to apply them to concrete historical reality." True, Soloviev himself clearly realized this at the end of his activity.

Pondering on the historic mission of Russia as the conciliating and unifying factor of entire mankind, Soloviev believed that the Russian people does not possess special gifts; if they can become "the mediators" between the will of God and the world, it is only because they are "free from all limitations and all onesidedness" (see above the quotation from the article "Three Forces"). In a letter to Father Pierling,

Soloviev quotes the following words from the first part of his book *Russia and the Universal Church:* "There is no reason to believe in Russia's great future in the purely worldly (*humaine*) sphere of culture, public institutions, sciences, philosophy, art, literature."[93]

In reality it had already become obvious at the time that the Russian people possess moreover a number of special gifts and have begun evolving a first-rate culture. Such are for example Russian music, Russian literature, the Russian theater, the Russian form of Orthodoxy, the Russian literary tongue; such are in the sphere of public institutions, the Russian courts, the Zemstvos (rural and municipal self-governments). And after Soloviev's death, the Russian people proved that they are also capable of remarkable creations in the sphere of science and philosophy.

There are many shortcomings in the life work of V. Soloviev, and a great deal has been left to his successors, but in any case he was the first to create an original Russian system of philosophy and to lay the foundations of a whole school of Russian religious and philosophical thought which is still growing and developing.

93. *Letters* (November 6, 1887), III, 158.

Chapter 9

EPISTEMOLOGY, LOGIC AND METAPHYSICS IN THE LAST QUARTER OF THE NINETEENTH CENTURY

1. B. N. CHICHERIN

We have seen in the preceding chapters how great was the influence of Hegel's philosophy both among the Slavophiles and among the Westernizers, and even among the writers who from Hegelianism turned to materialism and positivism. We can find in D. I. Chizhevsky's *Hegel in Russia*, which is a book worthy of great appreciation, many details concerning Hegel's influence on authors not mentioned here by us, and who are not closely linked with philosophy.[1]

We must add to the already mentioned writers the names of two professors who during their entire university career were faithful to Hegel's philosophy: P. T. Redkin (1808–1891), a philosopher and a jurist, professor at the Moscow University, and S. S. Gogotsky (1813–1889), professor at the Kiev University. Gogotsky gave his own interpretation of Hegelianism, rejecting Hegel's pantheism and defending the teaching concerning the individual immortality of the human person.

The present chapter will be devoted to Russian thinkers who, starting with Hegel's philosophy, submitted it to a complex and original transformation. One of these thinkers, meriting special attention, is Boris Nikolaievitch Chicherin who evolved an entire system of philosophy.

B. N. Chicherin (1828–1903) was the son of a rich landowner of noble and ancient stock; he studied at the law school of the Moscow University. A pupil of Professor Redkin and Professor Granovsky, he became familiar with Hegel's philosophy in his youth. In 1861 he was appointed professor of the Moscow University, but resigned in 1868 in protest against the government violating the autonomy of the university.

---

1. See also in the book, *Hegel bei den Slaven* (Reichenberg, 1934) the section dealing with Hegel in Russia, written by Chizhevsky.

In 1881, Chicherin was elected mayor of Moscow, but two years later he had to retire at the desire of Alexander III, because he had made a speech in which he stressed the necessity of "crowning the edifice" of rural and municipal self-government with popular representation. The finest Russian scholars and writers such as I. Kireyevsky, Khomiakov and Chicherin awakened the mistrust of the government which feared all those who defended freedom of thought and who showed a spirit of independence. And yet many of these men, as for instance Chicherin, would have been able to form a party of moderate and liberal conservatism; such a conservative party, defending freedom in the framework fixed by law, could have realized the necessary reforms when their time would have been ripe. Instead of this enlightened conservatism, it was an absurd and brutal conservatism which triumphed in Russia under the name of "the black hundred."

Chicherin's main works in the field of philosophy are: *The History of Political Doctrines*, in five volumes, 1877; *Science and Religion*, 1879; *Mysticism in Science*, 1880; *Positive Philosophy and the Unity of Science*, 1892; *The Foundations of Logic and Metaphysics*, 1894; *The Philosophy of Law*, 1900; *Problems of Philosophy and Psychology*, 1904.

Chicherin wrote memoirs of great interest in three volumes. *Positive Philosophy* and *The Foundations of Logic and Metaphysics* have been translated into German. These translations were published in Heidelberg under the title *Philosophische Forschungen*, 1899.

Like Hegel, Chicherin links metaphysics with logic; this logic is not formal but dialectical. Formal logic studies the fundamental abstract laws of thought, while metaphysics is concrete dialectical logic, that is precisely the passing from one determination of thought to another. Metaphysics represents a system of categories, that is of logic laws, given not in experience, but in "pure thought," in speculation. This unity of dialectical logic and metaphysics is explained by the fact that the laws of reason are identical with the laws of being.[2] Therefore reason knows objects according to its own laws. However, the laws of reason, known through speculation, give only the form of being; beside form, there is also content, known through experience. Consequently, the fullness of knowledge is attained through the combination of speculation and experience. Chicherin distinguishes his system from two other one-sided tendencies, from rationalism and empiricism, and he calls his own teaching universalism.[3] Making a parody of Kant, who said that pure concepts of reason are empty, and that experience is blind, Chicherin declares that metaphysics without experience is empty, and experience

2. *The Foundations of Logic and Metaphysics*, 218.
3. *Ibid.*, 356.

without metaphysics blind: in the first case we have the form without content, and in the second case, the contents without understanding. Metaphysics and mathematics are constructed through pure speculation, but natural science is founded on experience combined with mathematical speculation, while humanities are founded on experience combined with metaphysical speculations.[4]

Chicherin considers Hegel's logic as the basis for the further development in philosophy; however, he conceives this development not only as an addition but also as an improvement. While evolving his logic and metaphysics, Chicherin, like Hegel, starts with the concept of being and goes on to that of nonbeing, then to becoming, as a synthesis of being and nonbeing, and after having gone through a series of categories, he reaches the concept of causality, and finally raises himself up to the concept of the Primary Cause of all that is, as of an Absolute power, an absolute potential energy;[5] this energy being absolute, is not determined for action from outside, it is determined by itself, that is it places itself in relation to itself, and that is self-consciousness. Being which knows itself and determines itself is absolute Reason in two contrary definitions inherent to reason—as subject and as object. As subject, this Reason is absolute Power, containing everything in itself as a possibility; as object, Reason is absolute activity, the reality of power, that is absolute fullness of being, as final goal, as Absolute Spirit. And so Chicherin discovers in the Absolute the triune oneness of Power, Reason and Spirit. In regard to the world this is the triune oneness of the producing cause, that is of Absolute Power, of formal cause, that is of Absolute Reason, the Logos, and of final cause, that is the Absolute fullness of being, of Absolute Spirit (341). In the Christian religion this triune oneness is God-the-Father, God-the-Word-Reason and God the Holy Spirit.

What and how does the primary Cause produce? The final goal of creation is fullness of being. But beside *formal cause,* the fullness of being presupposes moreover *material* cause, that is being in regard to another. What is not Absolute is nonbeing; ancient philosophy conceived this nonbeing as matter. The relation of being to nonbeing is a process, a becoming, that is the putting down of restricting determinations, containing being and nonbeing (342). Restricted determinations can only be multiple; they represent a multitude of units with contrary definitions; those units in which there is a preponderance of relation to oneself are thinking substances, while those in which there is a preponderance of relation to the other, are material substances. Thus,

---

4. *Positive Philosophy and the Unity of Science,* 251, 316.
5. *The Foundations of Logic and Metaphysics,* 271.

Chicherin conceives the creative process as an apportionment of contraries (343), but the creation of the world does not stop at this apportionment: since the producing cause is at the same time also the final cause, the apportioned contraries face the problem of combining and forming a new perfect unity, and this is attained by way of evolution, by way of development, as perfecting process. The substance which serves as the combining principle between two contrary forces, between reason and matter, is the soul, a substance acting purposively, that is reasonably, though unconsciously; it acts unconsciously like matter and purposively like reason. The soul organizes matter, it transforms it into organized bodies, for instance vegetable and animal (276, 344). Thus Chicherin reinstates the ancient teaching concerning the vegetable soul.

The process of development leads to the agreement between contraries and to the submission of all to the unique goal of attaining the fullness of being. The supreme spiritual principle of this process is love (280). The beginning, middle and end of the world are under the guidance of the Absolute, which is the Father, the Word-Reason and the Holy Spirit (344). In its entirety, the system conceived by Chicherin contains two contraries crossing each other vertically and horizontally:

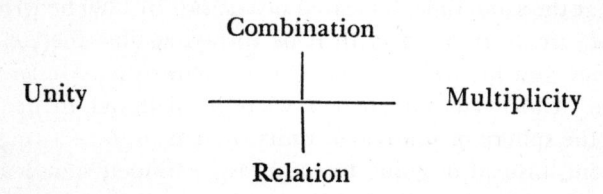

$$\begin{array}{c} \text{Combination} \\ | \\ \text{Unity} \quad \text{———|———} \quad \text{Multiplicity} \\ | \\ \text{Relation} \end{array}$$

In the beginning there is undivided unity; in the end divided multiplicity, brought back to unity; in the middle there are the two contraries opposed to each other, matter and reason. In all the spheres of the world, in all the objects of research, Chicherin seeks and finds the scheme, according to which there are everywhere three steps, and the intermediary step contains two one-sided contraries. The difference between this scheme and the scheme of Hegel's three-membered dialectics, formed of the thesis, the antithesis and the synthesis, consists in the fact that in Chicherin's system the intermediary link consists of two members opposed to each other.

In the entirety of the world, man occupies an exalted place: as a real subject, he is plunged into a relative being, but his consciousness raises him to the Absolute, and places him into a living, conscious interaction with the Absolute, an interaction which is expressed in religion (348). Thanks to the fact that he is raised to the consciousness of the

Absolute, man is able to emerge from the sphere of the relative and to attain freedom. Chicherin borrows from Hegel his teaching concerning free will. This teaching consists in the following: the reasonable subject is able to abstract himself from all relative determinations, that is he can attain complete indetermination; he is further able to place determinations, that is to pass from indetermination to self-determination; and he is at the same time able to remain himself, that is he preserves the ability to pass from each determination back to complete indetermination.[6]

The reasonable attributes of reasonable subjects, as for instance, freedom, are metaphysical principles, revealed through speculation. The life of a reasonable subject contains obvious manifestations of metaphysical principles. Therefore the science devoted to these reasonable subjects and to the relations they have with each other—in other words, sociology—cannot possibly do without metaphysics.

After having briefly surveyed the basis of Chicherin's metaphysics, we must examine one of their chief defects. While criticizing various philosophical tendencies, Chicherin struggled on two fronts: on the one hand, he despised positivism and submitted it to a brilliant criticism in his book *Positive Philosophy and the Unity of Science*. On the other hand and at the same time, he feared mysticism. In 1880 he wrote a book entitled *Mysticism in Science*. In it he turned against the young Vladimir Soloviev and his *Criticism of Abstract Principles*. Under the word "mysticism" Chicherin understood what he believed to be a call to return to the sphere of undivided unity, that is to the starting point of development, instead of going forward (as he himself sounded the call) toward the final ideal of divided harmonious unity in all its pluralism. It seemed to him that Soloviev's fervent belief in the idea of "wholeness" contains this danger of turning back. "This confusing expression," he writes, "never serves any other purpose but the one of obscuring the concepts" (13). Thus Chicherin's philosophy lacks the category of wholeness as such an organic unity as would be based on a suprarational *metalogic* principle, not submitted to the law of restricted determinations, that is to the law of identity, contradiction and the excluded middle. Therefore, in his system, there is no teaching concerning God as object of negative theology, a God who can be expressed in no concept borrowed from the sphere of earthly being. This teaching, placed at the basis of the Christian doctrine by Pseudo-Dionysius the Areopagyte, was largely applied after Soloviev by Russian religious philosophy in its ulterior development. Every individual person created by God, also

---

6. Chicherin, *Mysticism in Science*, 51; Hegel, *Philosophie des Rechtes*, chaps. 5–7.

has at his basis the metalogical principle standing above restricted determinations. Hegel's and Chicherin's teaching concerning free will cannot be clearly stated without referring to this principle.

Using merely the rationalists' discursive concepts, Chicherin cannot imagine any such intimate unity of the world's elements as could offer a condition for the possibility of intuition. He therefore explains speculation not as the subject's contemplation of the ideal reasonable structure of the world in the original; he interprets it as a psychical process of thought of the subject-individual copying in his mind the order of the world. Such epistemology is taught by Descartes and Leibniz. After Kant, this method of establishing the right to pursue metaphysics can no longer be accepted. The philosophers who live after Kant face the dilemma: either intuition does not exist and therefore metaphysics as a science of objects in themselves is impossible; or else metaphysics as a science of objects in themselves is possible, but in that case one must prove that man has the faculty of intuition. Overcoming Kant's criticism, Hegel saw this, and his system of metaphysics is epistemologically justified: conceiving the world in the spirit of pantheism, as undivided unity of the Absolute idea, he considered thought and being identical. The highest level of thought, concrete speculation, is in Hegel's mind intuition containing in itself the depth-metaphysical being in the original. Thus in the system of Hegel whom Chicherin considered as the most perfect representative of rationalism, there is an aspect of mysticism; this aspect is linked to the recognition of metalogical principles, and Hegel is aware of this mysticism of his, and speaks of it himself. In his little "Logic" his most perfect work and a masterpiece of the world's philosophical writings (forming the first part of his *Encyclopaedia of Philosophical Sciences*), Hegel says: "Reason does not grasp life, but suprasensual intellectual intuition (39), . . . concrete speculation (157) grasps life and attains truth, which cannot be expressed in judgements: such concepts, for instance as the whole and the part are of no avail for the understanding of a living organism (267); such a vision of the speculative whole is mysticism (159)." Chicherin himself comes very close to suprarational principles: for instance, in his teaching about substance he starts by saying that substance is unity of symptoms, but as a true metaphysician, he does not stop at that; going deeper, he says that substance is the *source* of principles.[7] Hence, it is logically necessary to come to the conclusion that substance is a principle standing above a logically determined being of qualities; i.e., that substance is metalogical being; however, Chicherin does not draw

---

7. *The Foundations of Logic and Metaphysics*, 70.

this conclusion. Another time, he comes even closer to this principle, adhering to Hegel's idea of freedom as of the subject rising to complete indetermination, that is to its foundation standing above the three laws of formal logic.

It is remarkable, that Vladimir Soloviev, who conceived parts of the world standing above formally logical determinations and beholding the wholeness of the world, the understanding of which Hegel himself calls mystical, actually stands closer to Hegel than Chicherin; but he is not aware of being so close to Hegel, because he interprets him incorrectly as a representative of abstract panlogism. On the contrary, Chicherin, who considers himself close to Hegel is far removed from Hegel by the very spirit of his system: he wrongly considers Hegel as the typical representative of rationalism and ignores the mystical elements of Hegel's system. Rejecting rationalism's one-sidedness, Chicherin completes the world's rational elements by adding to them the irrational contents of experience, that is the irrational standing below the *ratio* and receives its form from the *ratio*. He is not aware that this is not enough, that outside the rational and the irrational there is the suprarational; only by taking the suprarational into account are we saved from the narrowness of rationalism. Thus, in its entire structure and spirit, Chicherin's system is finally very close to the pre-Kantian rationalism of Descartes and Leibniz, and fairly distant from Hegel's post-Kantian suprarationalism.

Both in the case of Chicherin and in that of Soloviev, their incorrect appreciation of their own approach to Hegel is due to the following mistake inherent in both of them: not only in Russian, but also in German philosophical writings, Hegel's system was widely considered as abstract panlogism. Our times have freed themselves of this mistake. A more correct interpretation of Hegel's system is founded on such works as I. A. Ilyin's book *Hegel's Teaching Concerning God and Man, As a Concrete Philosophy*. As to the development of epistemology after Kant, a development necessary for the overcoming of Kant's criticism and for the justification of metaphysics as a science, it is precisely to this problem that N. Lossky devotes a chapter of his book *The Foundation of Intuitivism*. This chapter, entitled "The Teaching Concerning the Perception of the Transsubjective World in Nineteenth-Century Philosophy," examines various types of doctrines concerning direct contemplation of the outer world by the knowing subject.[8]

It must, however, be noted that having known the idea of the organic wholeness of the world-being, Hegel understood it in the spirit

---

8. See also N. Lossky's article "Hegel as an Intuitivist," *loc. cit.*

of pantheism. He therefore submerged in the wholeness of the developing Absolute idea the individual personal being of man and deprived it of its independence. Having evolved a remarkable teaching about the freedom of the person, Hegel at the same time degraded the very owner of that freedom, that is precisely the human person, transforming it into the mere means of the whole. Let us here recall Bielinsky's passionate tirade against Hegel's All-oneness (*Allgemeinheit*) as a Moloch. We find something different in Chicherin's philosophy: he placed man's individual personal being on the heights which it deserves, recognizing him as an eternal and free creator. However, we find neither in Hegel's nor in Chicherin's theory a liberation from the one-sidedness of universalism and individualism. In Hegel, due to his pantheism and his exaggeration of the wholeness of the world linked with it, there is a preponderance of universalism. On the contrary, in Chicherin, who was not sufficiently aware of the world's organic wholeness, we find an exaggeration of individualism, as shown by G. D. Gurvich in his article on Chicherin, published in *Philosophie und Recht*, II, 1922. Gurvich opposes Chicherin to Soloviev and finds in Soloviev a higher level of the synthesis of universal and individual principles than in Chicherin. The difference between Chicherin and Soloviev is most clearly manifest in the field of ethics reflected in the polemics which arose between them concerning Soloviev's work *The Justification of the Good*. Discussing the problem of social ethics, Soloviev attacked two extremes: on the one hand he fought against *moral subjectivism* which asserts that in the realization of good, the individual, moral will of separate persons alone is important; on the other hand, he expressed himself against *social realism* which asserts that social institutions alone are of essential importance, while individual moral will is only of secondary value (chap. XIII). According to Soloviev, individual, moral will is necessary for the realization of good; but it is also necessary to perfect social life in such a way that society should become "organized ethics." One of the goals of such a development of society is to "ensure to each and all a certain *minimum* of well-being, such as would be precisely necessary for the sustenance of human life and dignity." Chicherin interpreted Soloviev's doctrines concerning society as a tendency to "bring the Kingdom of God through compulsory measures, through the action of the government, and this leads to the complete negation of human freedom."[9]

According to Chicherin, this way logically leads to the imitation of Torquemade, to the burning of heretics for the salvation of their

9. Chicherin, "The Principles of Ethics," *Problems of Philosophy and Psychology*, 640, 1897.

soul. "It would be interesting to know," he said, carrying to the absurd the idea of his opponent, "whether the resurrection of the dead itself should be carried out by government orders" (644). Here Chicherin probably had in mind the teaching of Fedorov, who asserted that the chief moral goal of the descendants is to resurrect the ancestors.

In our days it is of particular interest to read Chicherin's speculations on the problem how to preserve man's freedom in the system of social life. Under our very eyes a totalitarian social order has come to life which has assumed the responsibility for all the aspects of the life of the citizen, but which in reality destroys all persons considered unadaptable or disobedient regarding the organs of the state. However, the moral necessity of ensuring every person's welfare is today recognized by all. The problem of our time consists in evolving a system in which each person's welfare is ensured, while at the same time freedom is preserved.

The mistakes of Chicherin's metaphysics did not prevent him from producing in detail extremely valuable applications of the speculative method in all the fields of knowledge. In his book *Positive Philosophy and the Unity of Science*, Chicherin submitted Comte's positivism to profound criticism. He showed that speculation in natural sciences is a precondition to the understanding of nature's process. The necessity of speculation in psychology is proved by Chicherin through the analysis of associationism. No less valuable are Chicherin's ideas in the sphere of the philosophy of nature. In 1892, founding himself on Mendeleyev's periodic law, Chicherin evolved a theory concerning the complexity of the atom and the fact that the structure of the atom is similar to that of the solar system.[10] In the field of the philosophy of biology, Chicherin is the author of a remarkable work entitled *An Experiment in Animal Classification*, which he wrote in 1883, and which was published in 1892. This work is based on a careful study of factual material. In it, Chicherin expresses himself against Darwinism, inasmuch as this doctrine seeks to explain the origin of the higher complex organisms springing from the lower ones by means of the struggle for life. Chicherin points out that the lower organisms are more fertile; the lower simple organisms are less demanding and therefore better adapted to environment. Lower organisms are not destroyed by the higher ones, as should occur according to the doctrine of the struggle for life; they continue to live next to those higher organisms. Hence, Chicherin concludes, the growing complexity of organisms is not due to struggle for life, but arises in spite of it. Chance, insignificant transformations, he tells us, are not useful for

---

10. *Positive Philosophy*, 120.

the struggle for life and cannot create the systematic unity of a new organ necessary for this struggle; finally, the struggle for life and natural selection do not produce anything by themselves; they only consolidate that which is created by some other factor. This creating factor cannot be chance, it can only be an inner force inherent to nature. This creative force leads to the harmonious perfectioning of organisms; it determines a passing from undivided unity to divided multiplicity, brought back to unity. In the details of his classification, Chicherin attempts to show that the scheme of the evolution of the entire world—as it is worked out by him—can also be applied to the evolution of animal organisms. Thirty years after Chicherin, Berg, professor of zoology at the Petrograd University, worked out a doctrine concerning the evolution of plants and animals based on an inner law. The book containing this doctrine is entitled *Nomogenesis* (1922).

In conclusion we must still point out a conception cherished by Chicherin. Being a master of speculative research he is well aware of what is "pure thought," and often uses this term. I recall that around 1910, Professor A. I. Vvedensky developed in his *Psychology* a theory concerning pure thought—true, in a Kantian and not Hegelian form. This teaching was mocked at by Petersburg experimental psychologists-sensualists. But only a few years elapsed, and experimental psychology itself, as represented by the Würzburg school, established the existence of nonsensory thought.

While surveying Chicherin's entire philosophical works, we cannot help admitting that he was an eminent thinker, not sufficiently appreciated in his time of philosophical activity. As a specialist on constitutional law, he was of course highly respected. In 1897, irritated by his polemics with Soloviev, whose sharp response had been, we must admit, provoked by Chicherin himself, he wrote that standing on the brink of his grave, he felt he had the right to declare: "I worked according to my strength and ability, I used as I knew best the gift granted me by God, and calmly offer Him my soul."[11]

Doubtlessly, Chicherin had the right to pass into eternity with this majestic calm.

2. N. DEBOLSKY

Nicholai Gavrilovich Debolsky (1842–1918) was trained as a mathematician. In his work *The Dialectical Method* he makes a distinction between the formal logical method which is concerned with concepts,

---

11. "A Few Words Concerning Mr. Soloviev's Answer," *Problems of Philosophy and Psychology*, 778, 1897.

and the dialectic method, which operates with ideas. He considers all concepts inwardly contradictory. Rising from the concept to the idea, the thinker enters the sphere of the infinite which permits contradictions, being a method of an infinite series of syntheses. Debolsky's major work is entitled *The Philosophy of Phenomenal Formalism*. In it he makes a distinction between the Divine Absolute Mind and man's finite mind. The Absolute mind, which knows both form and content of being, knows objects in themselves. To man's finite mind is accessible only the formal aspect of Absolute mind applied by him for the understanding of phenomena. Being closely acquainted with Hegel's philosophy, Debolsky made an excellent Russian translation of Hegel's *Science of Logic* (3 vols., 1916). In his articles devoted to aesthetics Debolsky is close to Hegel's aesthetics. He perceives the beautiful as a "suprasensual wholeness expressed in a sensual image."

At the end of his life, Debolsky wrote an article entitled "unconditional Skepticism as a Means of Improving Philosophy."[1] The progress of philosophy, Debolsky declares, is checked by its deep-rooted dogmatism, that is by the stating "as axioms of certain propositions recognized as self-obvious truths" (91). "Unconditional skepticism, which doubts everything including one's own doubt, is consequently a means of unconditional liberation of thought from all dogmatic ties." In particular, it is a liberation from the "nightmare of new philosophy," that is from accepting as axiom the proposition that "knowledge as an act of consciousness can have as object only states of consciousness" (109). In his article, Debolsky, among other things, advances a number of arguments against intuitivism.[2]

3. P. BAKUNIN

Pavel Alexandrovich Bakunin (1820–1900) was the brother of the famous anarchist Michael Bakunin. He was a fine representative of the idealism of the eighteen forties. During his entire life, Bakunin philosophized, and his attractive personality influenced all those who came into contact with him. But it was only in his old age that he published his philosophic findings in two books: *A Tardy Echo of the Forties; Concerning the Feminist Problem*, 1881, and *The Foundations of Faith and Knowledge*, 1886.

1. *Journal of the Ministry of Public Education*, November 1914.
2. Debolsky's works: *The Dialectic Method*, 1872; *The Philosophy of the Future*, 1880; *The Highest Good or the Supreme Goal of Moral Activity*, 1886; *The Philosophy of Phenomenal Formalism*, I, 1892; II, 1895; "The Concept of the Beautiful," *Journal of the Ministry of Public Education*, VIII; "The Aesthetic Ideal," *Problems of Philosophy and Psychology*, LV, 1900.

According to Bakunin's teaching, God is a living and eternal mind, the principle and the foundation of all that can be grasped, so that authentic understanding and knowledge are possible only in God and through God. Thought and being, faith and knowledge are indivisible. "Life is life only while it breathes the air of eternity," that is while it is rooted in God. Hence arises Bakunin's teaching concerning immortality. "Man," he says, "is from the beginning and in his very essence the truly existing general being." When man dies, he only returns to himself through the generalizing of death. With man's natural, empiric death, only that dies in him which has not yet been accomplished in him, which should still be accomplished, which is imperfect; it is only his empiric definite existence which passes away or dies, it is only his sensual envelope which is destroyed. Pavel Bakunin realized his unwavering faith in individual personal immortality, when calmly lying on his deathbed, he gaily talked to his doctor and took leave of his wife.[1]

4. M. KARINSKY

Michael Ivanovich Karinsky (1840–1917), Professor at the Theological Academy of Saint Petersburg, devoted his main research to the theory of knowledge and to logic.[1]

In his valuable work, *The Classification of Inferences*, Karinsky resolutely opposed logic's tendency to mould all inferences into the form of syllogism. He demonstrates that such inferences as "$A = B$, $B = C$, therefore $A = C$" can be artificially transformed into the mood Barbara, if we add to them, as major premise, the formula of inference, in the given example, the axiom "two quantities separately equal to a third, are equal to each other." But he points out that there exist a number of inferences having such a nonsyllogistic structure, and the addition to them of the formula of inference does not increase their certitude, and must therefore be considered superfluous.

Karinsky understands inference as the solution of the problem concerning the right to transfer the element from one proposition to another on the basis of the identity or the contradiction between the separate elements of the propositions. He establishes the fundamental classes of inferences: the first fundamental class of inferences consists in

---

1. Concerning Bakunin's time and surroundings, in which lived all the idealists of the eighteen forties, see the books by A. Kornilov *The Youthful Years of Michael Bakunin*, 1915 and *The Years of Michael Bakunin's Wanderings*, 1925.

---

1. Karinsky's main works: *A Critical Survey of the Most Recent Period of German Philosophy*; *The Classification of Inferences*, 1880; *Self-Evident Truths*; *The Discord Among the Schools of New Empiricism Concerning Self-Evident Truths*, 1914. E. Radlov, *M. I. Karinsky: The creator of Russian critical philosophy*. 1917.

the comparison of the subjects of two propositions, in the establishment of identity between them and consequently the transference of the predicate from one subject to another. The second fundamental class of inferences rests on the comparison of the predicates of two propositions: if the predicates contradict each other, we must consider the subjects as also contradicting each other; if the predicates are identical, then we have the right at least to a hypothetical positive inference concerning the relation of the subjects toward each other. Karinsky further subdivides, especially the first class, into inferences from singular objects to singular ones, inferences from singular objects to a group of objects (the logic group or aggregate) and inferences from the group of objects (logic or aggregate) to singular objects.

In the system of knowledge, all propositions cannot be proved by means of inferences. This system must be based on propositions having the character of self-evident truths and serving as axioms. The problem of self-evident truths was the main object of Karinsky's research. He did not give a positive solution of this problem, and mainly undertook the criticism of the theories of other philosophers.

In his book *Self-Evident Truths*, he made a fundamental study of Kant's epistemology, seeking to show that Kant did not prove that the propositions he calls a priori are universal and necessary. Alexander I. Vvedensky, professor at the Petersburg University took the defense of Kant and wrote an article entitled "The Imaginary and the True Kant" (*Problems of Philosophy and Psychology*, XXV).

In his book *The Discord Among the Schools of New Empiricism Concerning Self-Evident Truths*, Karinsky criticized the empiricism of John Stuart Mill and Spencer.[2] The fundamental distinction between the above philosophers and Hume, Karinsky states, consists in the fact that even mathematics is considered by them as a science founded on experience, and not on speculation, that is not on the taking into account of an evident link between the subject and the predicate of the proposition. They assert that every proposition is exclusively determined by the observation of singular facts and that the link between the subject and the predicate of every proposition is only the association of representations.

Mill believes that the highest premises of knowledge are established by means of induction *per enumerationem simplicem, ubi non reperitur instantia contradictoria*. Such an induction is an imperfect method, but it can be trusted when its inference is confirmed at all times, in all

---

2. This book was published in the *Journal of the Ministry of Public Education* from 1901 to 1914, and in 1914 appeared in a separate edition. I will quote it according to the *Journal of the Ministry of Public Education*.

places, under all circumstances, so that the number of confirmations is too large to be ascribed to mere chance. Mill admits, however, that even the law of causality, thus established, cannot be considered as a truth for every time and place: it is possible that events are not subject to this law in far distant regions of the universe or that it will lose its significance in a distant future.

Even the formulae of inferences, for instance in the syllogism, are considered by Mill and Spencer as founded on experience, and not on the evident link between the premises and the inference, that is on speculation. But Karinsky points out that it is impossible to prove by means of experience the adequacy of the formulae of inferences, because in such a proof the formula of inference should have to serve as premise to the proof of itself. Consequently, these formulae, through the consequent development of associanist empiricism, must be considered only as the *condition* of *faith* in the truth of the inferences, and not as a logically justified thesis.[3]

Evolving his epistemology, Spencer founds it on his teaching that life is an adaptation of inner to outward relations. Because of the uniformity of nature, indissoluble associations of representations arise in our consciousness. The fact that the negation of such an association of representations is impossible, is considered by Spencer as a criterion of truth. He believes that in the process of evolution, indissoluble associations are transmitted by heredity, so that a-posteriori propositions of the ancestors become a-priori propositions of the descendants. Hence, the impossibility of the negation of any proposition is the consequence of an infinite number of experiences of many generations of a multitude of beings, and therefore such propositions can be considered as the expression of truth, whereas induction described by Mill, rests on a far smaller number of instances. However, Spencer admits, as stated by Karinsky, that the correlation of indissoluble associations with the laws of nature improves through evolution and it fully corresponds to the laws of nature only by means of the perfect intellect. From this Karinsky draws the conclusion that indissoluble associations in the mind of man are not absolutely sure guarantees of truth.[4] Mill, criticizing Spencer's teaching, points to instances of impossible negation, which for the next human generation become possible. Exponing these considerations as expressed by Mill, Karinsky points out that Mill does not always make a distinction between the concept of the unthinkable and the concept of

3. *Journal of the Ministry of Public Education*, 326 ff., August 1901; 101–108, September 1901.
4. *Ibid.*, 2, July 1903.

the unimaginable as applies to negation. Concerning the unimaginable, Karinsky proves that much that is unimaginable is thinkable.[5]

Speaking of mathematical axioms as of generalizations obtained by means of induction, Mill asserts that in order to establish them, one can use not only perceptions but also imagined ideas, because mathematical ideas are entirely exact. Karinsky states that by admitting such means of establishing mathematical axioms, Mill is unaware of the fact that he is referring to the unthinkableness of the negation of the axiom —in other words, he expresses the same teaching as Spencer.[6]

Having established that not only Spencer, but finally also Mill, uses the unthinkableness of negation as a criterion of truth, Karinsky shows how untrustworthy is such a criterion. When an indissoluble association has arisen in our mind, contradictory instances do not immediately destroy it. Moreover, it often happens that these contradictory to the indissoluble association are established by indirect means, for instance the teaching that the earth is not motionless but that it moves around its axis, is proved by indirect means. Therefore, in addition to the unthinkableness of negation, a methodical research is also needed.

However, a logically evolved associationist empiricism must, according to Karinsky, reach the conclusion that even after such a methodical research, we do not attain a full certainty in the general truth of judgement; this is due to the fact that first experience is always limited, and secondly that even if the law of nature is discovered, the unchanging character of nature is not established.[7]

Thus, according to Karinsky, a logically evolved associationist empiricism, denying the existence of speculative evidence, must lead to skepticism; however, this skepticism can be tempered by pointing out that man is not only a knowing, but also an active being.[8] In practical life all men use scientific and even practical knowledge in order to satisfy their needs. Such a faith in scientific theses is practically justified and psychologically compulsory—in other words it has the nature of an instinct, as was stated by Hume.[9]

Karinsky winds up his research by analyzing Mill's teaching concerning the law of contradiction. According to Mill, the law of contradiction is not a speculative truth; it is a generalization drawn from experience. Karinsky clearly demonstrates that Mill is wrong, and that the law of contradiction is a speculative truth: this law is "a self-evident truth, resting on the direct grasping by thought of the relation between

---

5. *Ibid.*, September–December 1905.
6. *Ibid.*, 324, May–August 1901; 200 f., November 1903.
7. *Ibid.*, August 1903; September 1905.
8. *Ibid.*, May 1906.
9. *Ibid.*, August 1908.

the meanings of the terms which form it;"[10] to speak about A which is not A, means to lose the object of thought, to let consciousness face a void.

Unfortunately Karinsky did not evolve his own theory of knowledge, but his achievement consists in having produced a strict proof of the fact that associationist empiricism, which denies speculation, cannot prove the existence of a logically justified knowledge and inevitably leads to skepticism. By fully analyzing the theories of knowledge evolved by Mill and Spencer, he reveals a number of inconsistencies and contradictions these theories contain. He sees the fundamental error of associationist empiricism in the negation of every speculative evidence.[11]

Unfortunately both of Karinsky's books concerning self-evident truths are written in an extremely clumsy style, with lengthy sentences, which sometimes run to as many as fifteen lines; to read these pages involves painful labor.

5. N. GROT

Nicholai Yakovlevich Grot (1852–1899) was a professor at the Moscow University. In his article "Three Characteristics," Soloviev states that Grot was first a positivist in the spirit of Spencer, later attracted by the philosophy of Giordano Bruno, and ended by being drawn by Platonism. Thus, in his philosophical development, he rose to the heights and plunged into the depths. Grot attempted to evolve a teaching concerning the interaction of psychic and material processes. He believed that next to such types of energy as mechanical, thermal, electromagnetic energies, there is also a psychic energy. Thus, Grot believed, the interaction of material and psychic processes does not violate the law of the preservation of energy: the physical process with energy A generates a psychical process which sooner or later leads to the rise of a physical process with a reserve of energy A. This theory is somewhat similar to V. Ostwald's energitism. Professor Vvedensky expressed himself against Grot's teaching, pointing out that psychical processes have no spacious forms; therefore the concept of energy in the physical sense (the overcoming of resistance in a given space) has no meaning when applied to these psychical processes. Physical models of spacious energic processes explain more or less the transformation of one energy into another one; but we could not understand how spacious energy could be transformed into nonspacious energy.[1]

10. *Ibid.*, 141, November 1914.   11. *Ibid.*, 146, November 1914.

1. Grot's works: *The Psychology of Feelings*, 1880; *Concerning the Problem of the Reform of Logic*, 1882; articles in *Problems of Philosophy and Psychology*, of which Grot was editor.

Chapter 10

PRINCES S. N. AND E. N. TRUBETSKOY

Prince Sergey Nikolaevich Trubetskoy and his brother Prince Evgeny were intimate friends of Soloviev despite the fact that they were respectively ten and eleven years younger than he (S. Trubetskoy was born in 1862, and E. Trubetskoy in 1863). They both carried on Soloviev's work—the working out of an Orthodox religiously philosophical conception of the world.

The conditions under which they developed in their youth are vividly described in the *Memoirs*[1] of Prince Evgeny Trubetskoy and, being highly characteristic of the Russian spiritual culture, are worth dwelling upon.

Studying at a classical gymnasium in Moscow and living in a highly cultured environment, both brothers, since the age of twelve, conceived a strong passion for music, especially for classical music—Haydn, Mozart, Beethoven, and later on also the Russian composers Borodin, Mussorgsky, Rimsky-Korsakov and others. In 1877 the Russo-Turkish war broke out. The Russian public looked upon it as a crusade undertaken with the object of liberating their Orthodox kinsmen, the Bulgarians and the Serbs, from the Turkish yoke. The brothers Trubetskoy, who at the time were passionately keen on the idea of Russia as a great nation, shared in the patriotic enthusiasm which had seized the whole Russian society.

Soon after, however, when they were in the sixth form at school, both brothers, like Soloviev and so many other Russian youths of their time, went through a spiritual crisis involving the negation of all the old traditions. They lost their religious faith and became keen on H. Spencer's and J. S. Mill's positivism. The critical attitude to the social and political regime prevailing in Russia led not only to the condemnation of autocracy but to a repudiation, purely nihilist in spirit, of other values. Although there was a strict control of the pupils' political opinions on the part of the school authorities, the two boys, both of

---

1. Sofia, Russo-Bulgarian Publishing Co., 1921.

whom were bright and clever, did not mince matters when it came to expressing them. The elder, Sergey, would jokingly say to his French master, a Swiss: "Fedor Fedorovich, what have you got your Mont Blanc there for, it merely bars the way, no one can go or ride across it, isn't it a shame! That's what the Republican regime leads to! It's a different matter with us: had there been such a Mont Blanc somewhere in Russia at once either the police captain or the Governor would give instructions for it to be put out of the way—and there would be no Mont Blanc!"

When, later on, the two brothers began studying philosophy in earnest they soon came to the conclusion that Mill's empiricism had long before been refuted by Leibniz in his controversy with Locke, and that Spencer had failed to understand Kant's profound doctrine of the a priori bases of knowledge. Having got rid of positivism Evgeny Trubetskoy came to profess a skepticism which became a source of torture to him; he clearly realized, for instance, that dishonesty was something inadmissible and yet he saw that his reason was unable to formulate any conclusive proof in favor of the necessity of disinterested conduct.

He found a way out of this crisis when, becoming eagerly interested in Schopenhauer's philosophy, he came to realize that pessimism was an indispensable consequence of the repudiation of the absolutely perfect principle ruling the world. He was faced with the alternative, "Either God does exist or life is not worth living" (60 ff.). Just at this time two works were in the course of publication in the review *Russky Vestnik*— Dostoevsky's novel *Brothers Karamazov* and V. Soloviev's thesis *The Critique of Abstract Principles*. In one of them the same dilemma is treated artistically, in the other philosophically, and both arrive at an affirmative solution. About the same time the brothers Trubetskoy took to reading Homyakov's booklets in which he sets forth his doctrine of the Church as Christ's body. On outgrowing the state of duality between his will which yearned for God and his mind which denied Him, Evgeny Trubetskoy felt, as he puts it, "the joy of being healed in the literal sense of the word," because he "felt the reinstatement of the destroyed *wholeness* of his human being" (67). Brothers Trubetskoy went back to the Orthodox faith and once more became interested in the problems of Russian national genius. In 1886 they met Vladimir Soloviev, and this meeting resulted in a friendship.

The final affirmation of the religious conception of the world in the mind of Prince Evgeny Trubetskoy dates from a profound religious experience through which he went during a performance of Beethoven's Ninth Symphony conducted by Anton Rubinstein. "Listening to the first movement of the Symphony," he says, "I felt as if in the presence of some cosmic storm; lightnings flashed before my eyes, one could hear a dull underground thunder and rumbling which made the foundations of the Universe shake. My mind was seeking in vain a relief from the anxiety which had seized it. This anxiety caused by the hopeless universal suffering and confusion goes right through the first three movements, growing, increasing. In the wonderful scherzo with its thrice-repeated, cruel, harsh strokes, the soul tries to escape from this thickening darkness: from somewhere comes the trivial melody of discreet bourgeois merry-making, and suddenly again the same three dry, harsh strokes interrupt and dismiss it: away with the insipid, imaginary relief, there is no room in the soul for the Philistine satisfaction, for the prosaic melody, for the everyday joy! All this discord and chaos, all this cosmic struggle in sounds, filling one's soul with despair and terror, demand a different, a higher climax. And all of a sudden, when you feel yourself to be on the very edge of a dark abyss into which the world is about to tumble, you hear the harsh sound of the trumpets, some accords widening the world, an imperious call from the altitudes beyond, from another plane of being. From infinitely far away comes *pianissimo* a hitherto unheard melody of joy; the orchestra whispers to you some new and solemn sounds. But here they grow, they expand, they draw nearer. It is no longer a presentiment, an allusion to a different future; the human voices which come in one after another, the powerful chorus which takes up the victorious hymn of joy—this is already something genuine, it is the present. And instantly you feel yourself lifted up to the heights above the stars, above the world, above mankind, above all the sorrows of existence.

> *Embrace ye, all nations,*
> *Millions, fall on your knees."*

In Beethoven's symphony E. Trubetskoy perceived the same dilemma which had been tormenting him for a long time: "either God does exist, and in Him is the fullness of life *above the world,* or life is not worth living at all." But in the Symphony there is also "something infinitely greater than the putting of that dilemma, there is in it a *living experience* of the beyond, a *real sensation of dynamic peace.* Your thought takes in the whole cosmic drama from that height of eternity where all the confusion and horror are miraculously transfigured into joy and peace. And you feel that the eternal peace which descends on earth from above is not the negation but the fullness of life. No other great artist or philosopher in the world has felt or revealed this to the same extent as did Beethoven" (96–98).

In 1900, S. N. Trubetskoy became Professor of Philosophy at the University of Moscow. E. N. Trubetskoy was Professor of Philosophy of Law, first in Kiev and then in Moscow. Both brothers played a prominent part in the Russian Liberal movement, championing the idea of limiting the autocracy. On June 6, 1905, S. Trubetskoy, as a member of the delegation of the zemstvo and municipal self-government bodies, held a speech on the necessity of reforms before the Emperor Nicholas II. E. N. Trubetskoy as a philosopher of law was an active publicist and pronounced himself in favor of the independence of Church from the State. In politics he fought both the reactionary forces which were out to "freeze" Russia, and the revolutionary which aimed at setting everything in Russia topsy-turvy. In his pamphlet *Two Beasts* he represents these two forces as two apocalyptic beasts and shows that the jaws of the Red Beast and the claws of the Black Beast are equally dangerous.

S. N. Trubetskoy died suddenly in 1905, of internal hemorrhage, in the office of the Minister of Education—he had come to St. Petersburg, in his capacity as the Rector of the Moscow University, to defend University autonomy.

E. N. Trubetskoy, after the Bolshevik revolution, took part in the civil war against the Bolsheviks and died, in 1920, in Novorossiysk, of typhus.

S. N. Trubetskoy who was engaged in professorial work and died early, had no time or opportunity of working out in full his own philosophy. The most important of his works are two researches on the history of philosophy: *Metaphysics of Ancient Greece* and *The Doctrine of the Logos,* 1900; and three works in which his own views are stated: *On the Nature of Human Consciousness, The Foundations of Idealism* and *The Belief in Immortality.*

Dealing with the conditions that determine the logical character of knowledge and the objectivity of external reality, Prince Sergey Trubetskoy maintains that consciousness is *superhuman*—not in the sense of being an impersonal, epistemological self, but a superpersonal, collective unity of the World Soul. In this connection he works out the doctrine of a universal sensibility, of which space and time are the forms; such contents of it as color, sound, etc., are independent of the individual human consciousness. The condition of the logical coherence of knowledge is the universal Reason; the latter being understood in its original source not as a complex of abstract ideas, forms, categories, etc., but as a concrete subject, the living Logos, the second person of the Holy Trinity. He therefore calls his philosophy *concrete* idealism. Like Soloviev, he explains the knowledge of objective reality, irreducible to sensations and concepts, by the inner connection between all beings. In so doing he takes as his starting point the law of universal correlation which he applies to the structure of consciousness as well. "Our consciousness," he says, "is determined by the inner correlatedness of things, based upon the all-embracing unity of the Absolute." The Absolute Being itself transcends relatedness, is *superrelative* existence, not merely existing in Itself and for Itself, but also revealing its hidden substance in existence for another, in love for the world. He justifies the belief in immortality by the following reasoning. Having established the *supertemporal* character of the *ideal* aspect of thought, feeling and conduct (i.e., the supertemporal character of truth, meaning, etc.), he maintains that the spiritual growth of personality involves an increasing knowledge of the timelessness of the abstract ideal principles and a growing faith in the personal, individual immortality of the subject as the bearer of these principles. This is due to the development of *intuition* in and through which we become aware not of the separate functions, but of the whole indivisible being of man as an individuality of absolute value, characterized by ideal attributes, both moral and aesthetic. This faith receives its supreme justification on the basis of the Christian religion which teaches us to see in our neighbors "the image of Christ."

In its foundations S. Trubetskoy's doctrine is connected with the system of V. Soloviev which he, however, subjects to a thorough revision in the light of the criticism of knowledge carried out by Kant and of the post-Kantian metaphysical idealism, especially that of Hegel. Thus, e.g., the doctrine of universal sensibility represents an attempt at deepening the Kantian conception of sensibility.

Prince Evgeny Trubetskoy had the opportunity of setting forth his ideas at greater length than did his brother, especially in his book on Soloviev where, criticizing the main points of his friend's system, he gives also an idea of his own conception of the world. His principal works are the following: *The Philosophy of St. Augustine*, 1892; *The Idea of God's Kingdom in Gregory VII and the Publicists of His Time*, 1897; *The Philosophy of V. Soloviev*, 1912; *The Metaphysical Assumptions of Knowledge*, 1917; *The Meaning of Life*, 1918. It is also necessary to mention his two remarkable booklets on Russian ikonography —*Two Worlds in the Ancient Russian Ikonography* and *Intellectual Intuition in Color*.

In his book, *The Metaphysical Assumptions of Knowledge* E. Trubetskoy set himself the task of refuting Kant's theory of knowledge by the doctrine of the dependence of Truth upon the Absolute; he worked it out in greater detail than did his brother in investigating the nature of human consciousness. Knowledge can be absolutely trustworthy, maintains E. Trubetskoy, only if its basis is *superhuman*. The judgment that "two plus two equals four" as an absolutely true judgment about everything presupposes that everything actual and conceivable is subordinate to a certain unity, or, in other words, it presupposes that there is a pan-unity, an absolute consciousness in which everything knowable is timelessly determined by thought, so that every truth is eternal.

Singular judgments about fleeting events such as "Brutus killed Caesar" are no exception to this. The paradox of the eternal consciousness of the temporal is explained by the circumstance that absolute consciousness is the eternal contemplation of the past and the future as such; it is a concrete intuition, a synthesis of eternal memory and absolute pre-vision. Our knowledge is only possible because of our participation in the absolute consciousness—because the human and the absolute thought are one and indivisible, though distinct from one another. Since this participation is imperfect and incomplete, we have to make use of abstraction in order to arrive at the absolute truth. Without abstraction we could not get rid of the subjective and accidental arrangement of the immediate data of experience and "re-instate their absolute synthesis," i.e., "the necessary and objective order which binds them in truth." Abstraction is thus merely a means and an intermediate step in knowledge, the purpose of which is the concrete unity of all. This unity includes the sensuous contents of perception which both Sergey and Evgeny Trubetskoy take to be transsubjective.

Prince Evgeny Trubetskoy expounds his doctrine of the relation between the Absolute and the world in a work of two volumes, entitled *The Philosophy of Vladimir Soloviev*. In the course of a critical examination of Soloviev's metaphysics, Trubetskoy introduces several important modifications into it, consistent with the spirit of Orthodox Christianity. Soloviev's cosmogony is akin to that of Schelling in the doctrine of the first matter which lies at the basis of the world, and is at the same time "the first substratum" of the Absolute—just as with Schelling the basis of the world is "nature in God." Hence, quite contrary both to Schelling's and to Soloviev's intentions, their theories have a pantheistic coloring: God and the world prove to be interdependent, and therefore the doctrine of free will cannot be consistently worked out. Evgeny Trubetskoy avoids these defects of Soloviev's theory by insisting that the creation of the world "is an absolutely free act—creation out of nothing." At the same time, his conception of Sophia as the unity of the Divine Ideas acquires a different character. Soloviev maintains that the essence of the individual is his Idea; Trubetskoy points out that he, therefore, sometimes interprets "the relation of God's eternal Wisdom to our changing reality as the relation of essence to appearance." If, however, the Divine principle be thus closely connected with the world, no explanation can be given of individual freedom and of the origin of evil. Consequently, Trubetskoy contends that, although Sophia is a principle real in God from all eternity, for earthly humanity and for "all God's sheep," she is not an essence, but only a norm, an ideal image. The individual is outside of the Divine life and is free to accept or to reject the ideal end thus set before him. If he accepts it, he gives realization to God's image in himself, and if he rejects it he becomes "a blasphemous parody or caricature of it."[2] The fact that God's creatures are external to Him "does not limit the Absolute, for in themselves, apart from a positive or a negative relation to it, they are nothing." According to this view, God is free from the world and the world is comparatively independent of God: without such freedom on both sides the relation between God and the world could not have the character of love, or, on the part of man, of hostility.

These conceptions are further developed by Evgeny Trubetskoy in his book, *The Meaning of Life* (published in Moscow in 1918); they enable him to interpret Christianity as the only religion "in which neither the human element is absorbed by the Divine nor the Divine by the human, but each remaining what it is abides in unity with the other in all its fullness and wholeness." Their union removes the opposition between this world and the world beyond: the process of earthly evolution "is felt to be a transition to a different, to a higher plane." The horizontal and the vertical lines of life are combined in the one "life-giving cross." The upward process which requires victory of selfhood is impossible without suffering, but for the absolute consciousness contemplating reality as a completed whole, the bliss of the fullness of being that concludes the temporal series exists from all eternity. Even man is capable of participating in the timeless splendor of this truth, and then "the sense of the nearness of what is far off fills the soul with joy, the contradictions that have been troubling our hearts and minds are at once removed by the joyful cry 'Christ is risen.'" It is with good reason that for an Orthodox Russian Easter is "the feast of feasts," filling the soul with gladness and setting it free, if only for a moment, from the fetters of the limited earthly existence.

Transfigured bodily life plays an important part in the divine fullness of being. Light and sound are a perfect means for the expression of the spiritual meaning and force of life. "The true source of life will one day clothe itself with the sun; then our relation to the sun will change from an external to an internal one; life itself will become sunny throughout, like Christ's raiment on Mount Thabor—and it is this that justifies the joy of the woods and the fields at the sunshine. Our present

---

2. *The Meaning of Life.*

world contains numberless indications of the symphony of light and sound in the world to come," says Trubetskoy. Each creature, in his view, wears the image of day or of night: "the metallic clang of the owl, the sepulchral howl of the wolf," etc., "sound as the very voice of darkness," while "the sunny hymn of the lark expresses the complete victory of the midday sun and the dazzling radiance of the heavenly orb."

Recent discoveries have shown that the ancient Russian art of ikon painting, with its wealth of color, was keenly alive to the connection between the material and the spiritual reality. "Sophia, the Divine Wisdom, is painted against the dark blue background of the starry sky. The reason is clear: Sophia is precisely that which divides light from darkness, day from night, "The roseate face of the creating Sophia stands out like God's dawn in the midst of the dark starlit sky. And above it the final victory of light is symbolized by the midday sunlike face of the creating Christ. Thus all the three moments—the dark blue of the night, the rosy glow of the dawn, and the clear gold of a sunny day—which are for us distinct experiences separated by time, and in so far incompatible, are represented in the ikon painting as eternally coexisting and making up one indivisible harmonious whole. The idea of universal harmony and of the incarnation of the God of Love in His loving creatures is realized in the threefold triumph of light, sound and consciousness. Perfect love reveals itself not only in the fullness of glory, but also in perfect beauty. This is why the whole idea of the eternal Sophia is presented in the Scriptures in an artistic form."[3]

Examining the problem of Russia's part in the history of mankind, E. N. Trubetskoy in his young years, just as Soloviev in his early writings, shared the Slavophil exaggeration of Russia's mission and dreamed of a universal theocratic Empire which Russia would found. "Later on," he says in his *Memoirs*, "I became convinced that in the New Testament *all nations,* and not any one particular nation *as distinct from the others,* are called upon to be the bearers of God; that the proud dream about Russia as a chosen nation of God, which is clearly at variance with certain passages of St. Paul's Epistle to the Romans, must be given up as incompatible with the spirit of New-Testamental Revelation" (69).

3. The artistic and mystical wealth of Russian ikon painting has become more or less accessible to all nations thanks to the publications of the *Seminarium Kondakovianum* founded in exile, in Prague, by the disciples of the remarkable Russian historian, N. P. Kondakov. This subject is discussed more fully in Prince E. Trubetskoy's remarkable pamphlets: *Two Worlds in Russian Ikonography and Intellectual Intuition in Color.*

Chapter 11

THE RUSSIAN PERSONALISTS

1. A. KOZLOV

The philosophical teachings of A. A. Kozlov, L. Lopatin, N. Bugayev, E. Bobrov, Astafiev, Alexeiev (Askoldov) and N. O. Lossky present the character of personalism. All of them are more or less strongly influenced by the monadology of Leibniz.

Alexei Alexandrovich Kozlov (1831–1901) was the illegitimate son of the landowner Pushkin and of his serf girl. He was educated at the Moscow University in 1850–56. As a young man he was attracted by the socialism of Fourier and Leroux, and sympathized with this movement to the end of his life. He was first a materialist with a positivist tendency and had no interest in philosophy. While managing the estate of his father-in-law, at the age of forty, he happened to read Frauenstädt's book on Schopenhauer; this philosopher as well as E. Hartmann awakened so great an interest in him that he began studying philosophy. He published philosophical works and became in 1876–86 professor of the Kiev University. Having suffered a cerebral hemorrhage and stricken with paralysis, he was forced to resign and made his home in Petersburg, where he pursued his philosophical work. The system of his philosophy is close to that of the Leibnizian Teichmüller (1832–1888), formerly a professor at the Dorpat University.

The main work of Kozlov, *One's Own Word,* consists of five issues (1888–1898). The author makes a distinction between the concepts consciousness and knowledge. For instance the perception of the red color, as long as it is not yet connected with anything, and cannot be consequently expressed in words, belongs to the sphere of consciousness. It becomes knowledge after it has been juxtaposed with other contents of consciousness and distinguished from them. Kozlov establishes the concept of being on the basis of self-observation and defines it in the following manner: it consists "in knowledge concerning our substance, its activities and the contents of these activities in their unity and their relation to each other" (53). This being is spiritual substance. The analogy between our representation of our body and our representation of other bodies permits us to believe that other bodies are symbols of other spiritual substances. Material processes exist only as our representations, arising in us as a result of interaction with other spiritual substances. Due to this teaching concerning matter, Kozlov calls his system *panpsychism*.

Being consists of three aspects: substance, its activities and the contents of its activities. In the history of philosophy, Kozlov declares, onesided movements, which did not consider the three aspects of being, were widespread. Thus for instance, Parmenid's philosophy considers substance alone; Fichte considers only activity; Greek idealism considers only the contents of activities, ideas; while Hegel considers activity in connection with ideas, but without substance.

Like Teichmüller, Kozlov rejected the objective reality of time. He considered being timeless: the geological periods, the entire history of humanity coexist as an accomplished whole. But God's infinite consciousness alone contemplates this system as timeless. Due to our narrow consciousness we evolve a representation of peculiar means of coordination of world phenomena corresponding to the idea of the order "formerly, now, after." In this system the past and the future are mutually adapted: the future depends on the past, but the past also is dependent on the future, so that the causal and teleological understanding of these links complete each other. Time is conceived by us as an infinite and as an infinitely divisible. Precisely because of this one cannot consider it objectively real; if, for instance, one minute were objectively real, then, being infinitely divisible, it would contain a given, realized infinite, that is a calculated infinite, and this is a contradiction. Kozlov criticizes Zeno's paradoxes, founding himself on his own teaching concerning time. In the same way, space is considered by Kozlov not an objectively real, but a subjective representation of the order of our interactions with other spiritual substances—e.g., when we speak of our transfer from Moscow to Petersburg.

The image of our body is a representation of the intimate interaction we exercise regarding other spiritual substances, monads, less developed than our *ego*, and which serve us as organs. Death is the suspension of our interaction regarding these monads, but probably after death, our *ego* enters into interaction with other spiritual substances and builds itself a new body, corresponding to the degree of its development. This teaching concerning reincarnation is explained in the fifth volume of *One's Own Word* (132).

The world order is a system of growing complexity and intensity of the interaction of spiritual substances, which infinitely draw closer to God, the supreme substance, whose body is the entire world.

Extremely interesting is Kozlov's article "The Consciousness of God and the Knowledge of God" (*Problems of Philosophy and Psychology*, XXIX and XXX). In this article Kozlov asserts that God is a being which we are conscious of as directly as of our own *ego*. But, founding oneself on this consciousness of God, it is not easy to reach a correct knowledge of God, expressed in concepts. Along this path, humanity commits all kinds of errors, for instance, being conscious of force as of one of God's attributes, man divinizes the crocodile.

Observing the various currents of Russian social life, Kozlov mocked at the sentimental attitude of the populists regarding the peasants.[1]

2. L. LOPATIN

Lev Mikhailovich Lopatin (1855–1920) was professor at the Moscow University, and after Grot's death, became the editor of the review *Problems of Philosophy and Psychology*. In his basic work, *The Positive Problems of Philosophy*, and in a series of articles, Lopatin evolves extremely interesting ideas concerning the substantiality of the conscious *ego* and the concept of causality. He understands the world as a single organism, at the center of which is the One Absolute, God, creating the multiplicity of world beings. For the knowledge of the nature of world beings, Lopatin turns to man's inner experience. His speculations concerning this matter are presented in the most concentrated and satisfactory form in his article "The Concept of the Soul According to the Data of Inner Experience."[1] The manifestations of psychical life, Lopatin tells us, vary every second: all that takes place in time, presents the character of "uninterrupted disappearance" (270). But the *ego*, which experiences psychic processes, remains identical to itself: it is *supratemporal substance*. If there were no substances, the world would be split into a number of momentary worlds, not linked to each other. Thanks to the fact that substance is at the basis of phenomenas, the latter do not disappear, and pass into further processes, they are linked by real ties, as for instance, causal dependence, which Lopatin understands as the creation of phenomena by supratemporal subjects. Most interesting are Lopatin's ideas concerning the fact that "the consciousness of the reality of time is the most evident, the most precise, the most indisputable proof of the supratemporal nature of our ego . . . time

---

1. Kozlov's main works (apart from those which have been mentioned above): *Philosophical Studies*, 1876; *Philosophy as a Science*, 1887. Askoldov, A. A. Kozlov, 1912.

---

1. *Problems of Philosophy and Psychology*, XXXII, 1896.

cannot be observed and understood by that which is itself temporal . . . the consciousness of time is the substantial function of the soul" (288).

It is difficult to observe one's *ego* as a substance separate from psychical processes. Lopatin helps to evolve in oneself the ability to make these observations, pointing out, for instance, such processes as the comparison of two objects; this comparison would be impossible without the *ego* standing above the two perceptions and juxtaposing them. Lopatin considered that Soloviev was mistaken when he rejected data in the experience of the *ego,* and believed that this mistake was due to the fact that such philosophers as Soloviev imagine that substance is transcendental to the processes. However, in reality, the substance and the process it creates are indivisibly welded together, they form a single whole, in which one aspect is supratemporal substance, and the other aspect a temporal process. Substance stands above time, consequently it is eternal: the destruction of substance is unthinkable, because destruction is suspension of existence in time.

On the basis of the above-mentioned considerations it is clear, that temporal processes are possible only as the creation of supratemporal substance. Therefore, observing material processes in the outer world, we must admit that supratemporal substances are at their basis. Moreover, Lopatin believes, we must admit that beside material exterior manifestations these substances have an inner, that is psychical life; they are the monads of Leibniz.[2]

In the lithographed publication containing Lopatin's lectures on "Psychology" we find the supposition, stated independently from Bergson, that the excitation of the sensory organs is not the cause, determining the contents of perception, but only the condition for becoming conscious of the object. This idea was long ago expressed by Schelling in his "System des transcendentalen Idealismus," *Collected Works*, III, 497.[3]

3. N. BUGAYEV—P. ASTAFIEV—E. BOBROV

N. V. Bugayev (1837–1902) was professor of mathematics at the Moscow University; he was the father of the poet Andrei Biely.

Bugayev wrote an article, "Basic Principles of Evolutionary Monadology."[1] According to his teaching, "the past does not vanish, but ac-

---

2. One of Lopatin's articles is entitled "Spiritualism as a Logical Hypothesis," *ibid.*, XXXVIII, 1897.
3. Lopatin's major works: *Positive Problems of Philosophy*, I, 1886; 2nd ed., 1911; II, 1891. *Collection of Articles in Lopatin's Honor*, 1911.

---

1. *Problems of Philosophy and Psychology*, 1893.

cumulates;" therefore the perfection of every monad and of the entire world increases; it consists in the growing complexity of spiritual life and the development of the world's harmony. "The foundation of life and of the monad's activity is ethical: to perfect oneself and to perfect others" (36 c). The final goal of the monads' activity is to "transform the world" into an edifice of art (41).

P. Astafiev (1846–1893) and E. A. Bobrov (1867–1933) were the champions of the teaching of being as monad, that is, as spiritual substance.[2]

2. P. Astafiev, *Faith and Knowledge in Unity of World Conception,* Moscow 1893. E. Bobrov, *The Concept of Being,* Kazan 1898.

We shall analyze S. A. Alexeiev (Askoldov) and N. O. Lossky when speaking of Twentieth Century religious philosophy.

Chapter 12

THE RUSSIAN NEO-KANTIANS

1. A. I. VVEDENSKY

Western Europeans sometimes state that Russian philosophical thought did not go through the test of Kant's criticism and is not consequently on the level of European philosophy. As in many other cases, these Western minds prove their ignorance as to Russia. Kant entered the field of Russian culture no less than his influence exercised itself on English and French philosophies.

The Critique of Pure Reason exists in three Russian translations. The first of these translations was done by Professor Michael Ivanovich Vladislavlev (1840–1890) of the Petersburg University. Vladislavlev is the author of the work entitled *The Philosophy of Plotinus*. Another of his books, *Logic*, offers an interesting survey of the history of this science. The translation of *The Critique of Pure Reason,* which he undertook in 1867, is quite satisfactory, except that his style is as cumbersome as that of Kant himself in the original German. The second translation was done by N. Sokolov in 1897. Unfortunately this translation is full of mistakes, because the translator did not possess a thorough knowledge of philosophy nor of the German language. The third translation was done by N. Lossky, and the first edition of this work was published in 1907.

We are able to trace throughout the entire nineteenth century a number of Russian philosophic writings which show a knowledge of Kant's criticism and offer a serious critique of his epistemology. Thus for instance, Radlov states that in the early nineteenth century, Professor Ossipovsky pointed out that Kant's dynamistic theory of matter cannot be conciliated with his teaching on the subjectivity of space and time.[1]

As already stated, Russian society in the first half of the nineteenth century was attracted not by Kant, but by the metaphysical idealism of Fichte, Schelling and Hegel, who overcame Kant's phenomenalism. They had achieved this through the teaching according to which the

[1]. E. Radlov, *Outline of the History of Russian Philosophy,* 2nd ed., 14, 1920.

knowing subject is organically included in the supraindividual world unity; thanks to this the identity of thought and being is possible. At the end of the nineteenth century and in the twentieth century, the Russian religious philosophers, starting with Soloviev, evolved, as we shall see, a system of Christian metaphysics; this system does not ignore Kant's epistemology, it overcomes this epistemology creatively through various types of teachings on intuition, that is on man's immediate contemplation of the world's authentic essence.

Apart from this struggle against Kant, there arose in Russia during the last quarter of the nineteenth century, quite a number of champions of neokantism. The chief representative of this movement is Alexander Ivanovich Vvedensky (1856–1925), who was professor at the Petersburg University from 1890 to the end of his life. All of Vvedensky's works and all his courses, devoted to logic, psychology and the history of philosophy, definitely reflect a philosophical thought based on Kant's criticism. Vvedensky did not only possess a precise and clear mind, he was also endowed with exceptional gifts as a teacher. Many thousands of students attended his classes at the University, The Higher Women's Courses and at the Military Law Academy, and he inspired them with his ideas with extraordinary strength. Basing himself on *The Critique of Pure Reason*, Vvedensky became a representative of a specific form of neokantism, which he called *logicism*. He founded epistemology, as the science of the limits of human reason, on logic, by means of a theory concerning inferences and the methods of proving general synthetic judgements.

The direct setting of the data of experience, Vvedensky declares, can justify only singular or private judgements. Consequently the justification of general synthetic judgement is only possible by means of inference; but inference, which proves a general synthetic judgement, must already contain at least one general synthetic judgement among its premises: even in inductive inferences the conclusion derives not directly from separate observations but from their combination with the principle of the uniformity of nature. Hence, it is clear that the system of knowledge containing general synthetic judgements, can be erected and developed only if it has at its base several general synthetic judgements a priori; that is, not proved and unable to be proved, but accepted as part of knowledge, because they can serve as the supreme foundation of scientific knowledge. In combination with definitions (which Vvedensky as a follower of Kant considers as analytical judgements) and the data of experience, judgements a priori serve as a foundation for inferences which offer in their conclusions new synthetic judgements.

What are the objects concerning which we acquire knowledge by means of these inferences? Vvedensky answers this question, basing himself on his teaching on the logical bond and the theory of inferences built on it. The logical bond (the bond between the subject and the predicate of the analytical judgement, as well as the bond between the premises and the conclusion of the inference), Vvedensky tells us, is the bond requested by the laws of contradiction and of the excluded middle. Thanks to this bond we are obliged, inasmuch as we accept the premises of a correct inference, to accept also the conclusion, for in the opposite case we would enter into a contradiction with the premises. Thus for instance, having admitted that "all liquids are elastic" and that "mercury is a liquid," we cannot say that "mercury is not elastic," for this would mean that "there are nonelastic liquids." I call this theory *analytical*, because it regards inference as a system similar to analytical judgement; from this theory it follows that inferences are possible only regarding objects, submitted to the law of contradiction. And such, according to Vvedensky, are our representations alone; as to thought, it is not submitted to the law of contradiction: we can, for instance think of a round square, etc. Therefore, inferences are possible only concerning representations, concerning *apparent* being, (that is being as it appears to us); as to the world of authentic being (i.e., things in themselves), we do not know whether it is submitted to the law of contradiction, and therefore inferences concerning it are impossible. And so metaphysics as a science cannot be realized. Mathematics and natural science, on the other hand, can be considered as sciences only if their object is being as a phenomenon (representation). And Vvedensky adds that we must come to the same conclusion if we base ourselves on the considerations which guided Kant in *The Critique of Pure Reason;* the proof of general synthetic judgements can be made only with the help of a-priori principles, but a-priori principles, which can be proved by no experience, are the thoughts of the knowing subject; therefore they can submit to themselves not authentic being, but being as it appears to the subject.

In Vvedensky's logicism there is an element of perennial value; that is the teaching according to which, in the system of knowledge, there must exist truths, bearing the character of general and necessary synthetic judgements, incapable of being proved either inductively or deductively. Kant gave a complicated and insufficiently clear proof of this thesis in his transcendental deduction of the fundamental judgements of pure understanding. Vvedensky proved this thesis very simply in a system of formal logic, in a theory concerning the conditions of the proof of general synthetic judgements. For one separate case Vvedensky gave a special proof of this thesis. In the preface to his book *The Theory of Matter, Built on the Principle of Critical Philosophy*, 1888, he proved with great clarity that the law of causality cannot be founded inductively: one cannot find a single case of a causal bond, without using the causal bond as premise to research.

The existence of truths, bearing the character of general and necessary synthetic judgements, unable to be proved either inductively or deductively, does not necessarily lead to Kant's apriorism: it can be established also by a different means, for instance, on the basis of intuitivism, as this is proved in N. Lossky's *Logic* (73-78).

Vvedensky is also a follower of Kant in the sphere of ethics. He admits that beside the knowledge of phenomena, evolved by theoretical reason, *faith* in this or that structure of the world of "things in themselves" is possible. The man who recognizes the unconditional obligations of moral law (the categorical imperative), naturally attains through practical reason a faith in the existence of God, the immortality of the soul and free will. However, according to Vvedensky, the three postulates of practical reason established by Kant are not sufficient for the full understanding of moral behavior. It is moreover necessary to raise the question of the animateness of others. In his treatise *The Limits and Symptoms of the Animation of Others*, 1893, Vvedensky solves the problem in the spirit of orthodox Kantism; he demonstrates that the observation of bodily processes does not offer a proof of the animation of others. Mystical feeling, that is intuition, directly contemplating the psychical processes of others, is impossible, according to Vvedensky: in such an intuition he believes, the other would exist in my consciousness as not another, and this is a contradiction. Thus, Vvedensky comes to the conclusion that to the three postulates of practical reason should be added a fourth postulate—the belief in the existence of other *egos*, as a morally established faith.[2]

2. I. I. LAPSHIN

Ivan Ivanovich Lapshin was born in Moscow in 1870. He graduated at the University of St. Petersburg in the Faculty of Arts in 1893, and was sent abroad to continue his studies. He worked at the British Museum specializing in Kantianism as reflected in the English philosophical literature. In 1913 he was appointed professor of philosophy at the Petersburg University. In 1922 he was exiled from Russia by the Soviet Government and since then has been living in Prague.

2. Works by Vvedensky in addition to those mentioned above: *Logic As Part of the Theory of Knowledge*, 3rd ed. 1917; *Psychology Without Any Metaphysics*.

Lapshin's chief work, *The Laws of Thought and the Forms of Knowledge,* was published in 1906. He champions the critical philosophy of Kant and introduces an original interpretation of it. Lapshin argues that space and time are not forms of sensuous intuition but concepts or categories. Further, in contradistinction to Kant he regards all data of experience, including the data of inner sense—e.g., those that form part of emotions—as having a spatial form. Logical knowledge depends upon the applicability of the law of contradiction to objects that are being cognized. That law, Lapshin points out, is necessarily connected with the form of time and space: the object can have contradictory properties at different times, but not at one and the same time, not in coexistence; the present, i.e., coexistence, is "two expressions of one and the same content, one from the temporal and the other from the spatial point of view;" thus the applicability of the law of contradiction depends upon the spatial synthesis or the spatial coexistence (109–112). It follows from this that only objects with a sensuous content and having the temporal, spatial, and other categorial forms; i.e., only phenomena given in experience are knowable; as to "things in themselves," i.e., things as they exist independently of our experience, we do not know whether they are temporal or spatial, or whether the law of contradiction is applicable to them, and therefore we know nothing whatever about them; we do not even know whether they exist; in other words, metaphysics is impossible as a science; thus Lapshin adds a fresh argument in support of Kant's contention.

Lapshin added as an appendix to his book two remarkable essays, brilliant in form and extremely interesting in content: "On Cowardice In Thinking" (an essay on the psychology of metaphysical thinking), and "On Mystical Knowledge and Cosmic Feeling." By intellectual cowardice Lapshin means inconsistency of thought, arising not through fear of persecution, but through fear of losing spiritual values—such as faith in God—in consequence of renouncing metaphysics. In the article "On Mystical Knowledge and Cosmic Feeling" Lapshin compares mystical ecstasies, interpreted as union with God, to experiences in which the subject is conscious of himself as being merged with nature and the world as a whole. Having described various types of "cosmic feeling" Lapshin tries to prove that those experiences must be interpreted in the spirit of critical philosophy as something taking place merely within the subject; i.e., as a totality of *subjective* presentations permeated by particularly deep and intense emotions and wrongly taken by the mystics for an intuition embracing the whole world.

Lapshin's further work in philosophy, especially during his life in Prague, is concerned with the problems of creativeness in the domains of philosophy, of science, and particularly of art. Inquiry into these problems is an inquiry into the mental life of others. But according to the critical theory we know the external world only as the totality of events in our own minds; hence it is clear that the question as to the existence of other selves, of other mental lives is an insoluble problem. Professor Vvedensky, who taught philosophy both to Lapshin and me and who was a Kantian, wrote a remarkable treatise "On the Limits and Expressions of Mentality;" there he cleverly shows that the Kantian theory of knowledge cannot scientifically prove the presence of mental life in others. He comes to the conclusion that the recognition of it is an act of *faith* demanded by our moral consciousness.

It will readily be seen that the problem of our knowledge of other mental lives must be a source of serious perplexity to Lapshin. In 1910 he wrote a book *The Problem of Other Selves In Modern Philosophy*, giving the history of the subject, and in 1924 an article *"The Refutation of Solipsism,"*[1] containing his own answer to it. His theory, briefly, is as follows: The expression of the human face consists of a number of sensory qualities, plus another important experience—the total expression, *Gestaltqualität* (Ehrenfels); "in virtue of former experiences it is involuntarily associated in me with moods similar to the mental states of the person I am observing;" and the total impression has come to be "so intimately interwoven with bodily manifestations that we project this additional psychical process into another person's body; we see, as it were, a *sad* smile, a *happy* expression of the eyes, a *tender* look, a *malicious* jeer; we objectify total impressions," although in fact they have a subjective source (52); in this way there arises an illusion, says Lapshin, that there is such a thing as immediate intuitive apprehension of the mental lives of others. In fact, however, the transcendental reality of another self cannot be proved (53), though we have a right to speak of its *immanent reality:* my fellow-man speaks "as though he were animated; I distinguish his words from the manifestations of the unreal animation ascribed by me to a doll, a tree, etc." Just as in the physical world I fill up the blanks by presentations that come from within me, or are beyond my field of vision, so in the psychic world I fill up the directly unperceivable mental states of others by this "as if." I need nothing but this "as if" for cognizing "another self." "Another self is a *hypothetical construction* which has the same significance for sciences belonging to the spiritual order as the atomic theory has for physics" (60). Lapshin ends his article by the following assertion: "Replacing the transcendental 'another self' by the immanent presentation

---

1. *Uchoniya Zapiski*, I, 1.

of a *plurality* of minds and the co-ordination of all spiritual centers in the world under *one* epistemological subject creates so deep and living a sense of the intimate bond between the microcosmos and the macrocosmos as no metaphysical system can give" (66 f.).

An epistemological justification of the inquiry into the mental life of others is essential to Lapshin because he is particularly interested in the study of creativeness in the various spheres of human activity. His large work in two volumes *The Philosophy of Inventiveness and Invention in Philosophy*[2] is devoted to the consideration of the general features of the subject. Lapshin inquires both into the external and the inner conditions of creativeness. As to the latter, he rejects the simplified explanations of discoveries and inventions by reference to a mere association of ideas, to happy coincidences and other factors of a mechanical character. He quotes Lagrange's words "In great discoveries chance favors only those who deserve it." Lapshin quotes a number of instances showing that the chance observation which gives rise to a theory comes to a scientist or inventor whose whole apperceptive system is already *prepared* in a certain way, who has a *rich and well-organized memory* and whose attention is *keyed up* to a particular problem. In addition to his main book Lapshin has written a number of valuable articles: "The Schematism of Creative Imagination in Science," "The Unconscious in Scientific Creativeness," "The Genesis of the Creative Guess," etc.

Lapshin has given special attention to artistic creativeness in general, and musical creativeness in particular. In 1922 his book *Artistic Creativeness* was published in Petrograd; it is a collection of articles of which the following deserve special notice: "The Power of Transmutations in Artistic Creativeness," "On Musical Creativeness," "Pushkin and the Russian Composers," "Modest Petrovitch Mussorgsky," "Philosophical Motives in Rimsky-Korsakov's Music," "Scriabin's Cherished Ideas." Those articles contain many valuable remarks and observations; thus for instance Lapshin speaks of the *communal* mind of the Russian composers (using Prince S. N. Trubetskoy's term *sobornost*).

Another contribution made by Lapshin to the study of the Russian culture are his essays on the aesthetic methods of Pushkin, Gogol, Turgenev, Dostoevsky, Tolstoy. He has also analyzed certain *aspects of beauty* in the works of the great Russian poets and writers: "The Tragic Element in Pushkin's Works," the comic in the works of Pushkin, Dostoevsky, Tolstoy.

Lapshin is also interested in the study of Russian dramatic art; he has made use of numerous memoirs of Russian actors and written "An

2. Petrograd 1922; 2nd ed., Prague 1924.

Essay on the Russian Actor," containing valuable observations of the methods by which an actor enters into his part.

The pamphlet *La synergie spirituelle* is concerned with the problem of supreme values; Lapshin examines in it the correlation between the three absolute values—truth, goodness and beauty—proving that in spite of the difference between them they are organically interconnected.

In two pamphlets *La phénomenologie de la conscience religieuse dans la litterature russe* Lapshin shows, among other things, that such men as Tchernyshevsky, Dobrolyubov and even the most fanatical representative of nihilism, Pisarev, were deeply religious in youth.

While living in Czechoslovakia Lapshin has been studying not only the Russian but also the Czech culture. He has written articles about the composers Smetana and Suk, "On the Spirit of Czechoslovak Art" and about the greatest of the Czech philosophers, Amos Komensky. In recent years Lapshin has been widening his subjects of study and even using a new form of exposition—the dialogue. Thus, at the Russian Philosophical Society in Prague he read three dialogues: "Modern Discussions on Freedom of Will;" "Do We Cognize Nature as a Copy or in the Original?" "The Problem of Death."

In 1948 Lapshin's new book, *Russian Music (Ruska hudba)*, has appeared in a Czech translation in Prague. Lapshin's mother, an English Swiss, was a teacher of music and singing, and Lapshin acquired from her a good knowledge of music, both Russian and Western European. Moreover, he has been for years a friend of N. A. Rimsky-Korsakov. His book is very readable, well illustrated and full of musical quotations. In sending it to me he said "almost all that I write about I have not only heard, but seen, played, and sung."

The Russian adherents of the school of transcendental logical idealism which arose in Germany as a result of a thorough revision of the criticism of Kant, will be discussed later, because their views have been subject to the influence of the Russian religious philosophy of the twentieth century.

Chapter 13

THE CHANGING MENTALITY OF RUSSIAN INTELLECTUALS IN THE BEGINNING OF THE TWENTIETH CENTURY

Russian philosophy could not develop freely during the first half of the nineteenth century because the government, fearing that its influence might be dangerous, persecuted it in all kinds of ways. In 1850 the Minister of Public Education, Prince Shirinsky Shihmatov declared, "it has not been proved that philosophy can be useful, but it may be harmful," and abolished the chair of philosophy in universities; only the teaching of logic and empirical psychology was permitted, on condition that these subjects should be taught by professors of theology. It was only in 1860 that philosophy was again introduced into the university curriculum.

When the Emperor Alexander II came to the throne there followed the period of great reforms introduced by him; in conditions of far greater freedom than ever before the Russian philosophy developed rapidly and soon reached the level of the Western-European thought. It is sufficient to recall the names of Chicherin, Debolsky, Karinsky, Lopatin, and A. I. Vvedensky. In the domain of religious philosophy Vladimir Soloviev's brilliant name was prominent. In his lifetime, however, religious problems had but little interest for the Russian intelligentsia. One part of it was morbidly preoccupied with the problem of abolishing autocracy, and the other was equally one-sidedly engrossed in social and economic questions and the problem of introducing socialism. It was not till the end of the nineteenth and the beginning of the twentieth century that a considerable section of the Russian intelligentsia freed itself from this morbid monoideism. Wide circles of the public began to show interest in religion, in metaphysical and ethical idealism, in aesthetics, in the idea of the nation and in spiritual values in general.

In 1901 there were organized in Petersburg "Religious-philosophical

Meetings" attended both by the laity and the clergy. The president was Bishop Sergius (Stargorodsky), the future Patriarch. The subjects of discussion included Christianity in public life, the possibility of a "new Revelation," "the holy flesh" (D. S. Merezhkovsky, Rosanov, Minsky). In Moscow too similar discussion meetings were held.

In literature the "decadent" and "symbolist" poets—Alexandr Blok, Andrey Belyi, Viacheslav Ivanov, D. S. Merezhkovsky, Zinaida Gippius, V. Bryusov—not only created artistic values but expressed through them religious and philosophical ideas. In 1906 the editorship of the monthly magazine *Russkaya Mysl* was taken over by the economist P. B. Struve, a man of great learning in every domain of culture. Under his guidance the magazine fully reflected the wealth of spiritual interests of the Russian public in the twentieth century. The change that took place at that time in the intellectuals' mentality found expression in two volumes of essays—in the book *The Problems of Idealism* in 1903 and *Signposts* (Vehi) in 1909. The first appeared when the so-called "liberation movement" was at its height. The whole of the Russian people from top to bottom were engaged in the struggle against autocracy that culminated in the revolution of 1905 after the disasters of the Russo-Japanese war. In the nineteenth century the struggle for political freedom and social justice was waged chiefly in connection with the ideology of materialism, positivism, nihilism and marxism. The authors of the books mentioned above, while upholding the liberation movement, championed ethical idealism against materialism, positivism and marxism. I will name those of them who played a part in the development of Russian philosophy: P. I. Novgorodtsev, philosopher of jurisprudence, Princes S. N. and E. N. Trubetskoy, S. N. Bulgakov, N. A. Berdyaev, S. A. Askoldov (Alexeiev), S. L. Frank.

The government suppressed the revolution of 1905 after making a concession to the popular movement and agreeing to limit the autocracy of the Tsar. The constitution drawn up by the government was, in the words of Maklakov, cleverly worked out by the Russian bureaucracy. V. A. Maklakov, the defense attorney, was a member of the Constitutional Democratic party; in his book *The Government and Society During the Decline of the Old Russia* he writes: "At that time there were two forces in Russia. There was the historically formed power of the government, rich in knowledge and experience but no longer capable of ruling alone. There was the educated class which was full of good intentions and had a right understanding of many things but did not know how to rule anything, not even itself. Russia could only be saved by the union and reconciliation of these two forces, by their harmoniously working together" (585).

THE CHANGING MENTALITY IN THE EARLY 20TH CENTURY 173

Unfortunately, the Russian society was politically completely inexperienced; consequently, the first two Dumas proved incapable of co-operation with the government and were dissolved. The worst thing was that the revolutionary parties continued their fierce struggle against the government. In 1907 the terrorists assassinated 2543 government agents[1] while the Government in that same year executed 782 revolutionaries.[2] The same lack of political experience made many people imagine that "the revolution had been a failure" and the limitation of the Tsar's autocracy had not produced the expected results. In 1909 a group of prominent thinkers brought out a collection of essays under the title *Signposts*, denouncing the defects of the Russian intelligentsia which hindered the normal development of the Russian state and society. Among the authors of the symposium were N. A. Berdyaev, S. N. Bulgakov, Gershenson (a historian of Russian literature), A. S. Izgoev, a publicist, B. A. Kistiakovsky, professor of political economy, P. B. Struve and S. L. Frank.

In his article "Philosophical Truth and Intelligentsia's Righteousness," Berdyaev said that the Russian intellectuals' love of the people and of the proletariate had become a kind of idolatry. They had no love of truth: in discussing an idea they asked not whether it was true, but only whether it furthered the theories of socialism, the interests of the proletariate, the struggle against autocracy, etc. Bulgakov's article "Heroism and Spiritual Achievement." denounced the defects of the Russian intelligentsia and pointed out its good qualities. It will be discussed in dealing with Bulgakov's transition from marxism to idealism and then to Orthodoxy. Kistiakovsky, in his article "In Defence of Legal Justice," accused the Russian intelligentsia and the Russian people of depreciating the significance of law and order. He quoted Almazov's humorous verses on the attitude of the Slavophil K. S. Aksakov toward the machinery of the state:

> We are devoid by nature
> Of juridical commonsense—
> That progeny of Satan.
> The Russian soul is much too great
> To fit its ideal of what is right
> Into the trim and narrow form
> Of legal justice, legal norm.

1. This figure is quoted by Maklakov in his book *The Second Duma* (18) who takes it from official data published by the Bolsheviks in the *Krasny Arhiv* (Red Archives).
2. G. Vernadsky, *A History of Russia*, 194, 1944.

Struve in his article "The Intelligentsia and the Revolution" spoke of the intellectuals having no conception of statesmanship and of their nonreligious maximalism. S. L. Frank in his article "The Ethics of Nihilism" described the intellectual standpoint of the Russian intellectuals as nonreligious moralism which denied absolute values and led to nihilism. The religion of serving earthly needs replaced for them the religion of serving ideal values. This led to destruction and hatred and not to creativeness. The Russian intellectual, said Frank, is "a militant monk of the nihilistic religion of earthly well-being."

In answer to the *Signposts* there appeared a number of articles in newspapers and magazines and many collections of essays. The authors of a symposium entitled *Intelligentsia in Russia*[3] were liberal intellectuals, inclined to positivism. They included the leaders of the constitutional democrats, I. I. Petrunkevitch and P. N. Milyukov, professors N. A. Gredeskul and M. M. Kovalevsky, the economist M. I. Tugan-Baranovsky, and others. In answer to Bulgakov's contention that the revolution had failed and had neither strengthened the state nor improved national economy, Gredeskul rightly observed that the revolution which brought about the limitation of autocracy could not bear fruit the very next day. Milyukov argued that the intelligentsia as a whole could not be accused of being irreligious, anti-state and cosmopolitan. He admitted, however, that being prevented by the government from taking part in political life, the intelligentsia developed certain defects; namely, "too great a love for abstractions, uncompromising radicalism in tactics, sectarian intolerance towards their opponents and ascetic strictness in censoring their own morals" (158).

Essays on national questions were collected and reprinted in a symposium *Along the Signposts*, devoted chiefly to the discussion of the intellectuals' and of Russian people's attitude to the Jews.

The authors of the *Signposts* were right in what they said of the defects of the Russian intelligentsia but mistaken in thinking that the revolution of 1905 was a failure. Soon after it, when the government had suppressed the extreme revolutionary tendencies, there was a marked progress in every domain of life in Russia. Count V. N. Kokovtsev, who was for years Minister of Finance and between 1911–1914 President of the Council of Ministers, speaks in his Memoirs[4] of "the continuous and considerable increase in national wealth in all its aspects" between 1904 and 1913. The growth of industry, he writes, was remarkable; there was reason to hope that in a few decades Russia would overtake the U.S.A. Particular importance attaches to Count Kokovtsev's statement

3. St. Petersburg 1910, publ. by Zemlia.
4. *From My Past*, 2 vols., Paris 1933.

that the third and the fourth Duma were increasingly co-operative with the government for instance with regard to national defence, to the plan of introducing compulsory elementary education, and so on.

As already pointed out, many gifted representatives of the intelligentsia got rid of their former one-sidedness with regard to spiritual problems. In philosophy there appeared many highly complex tendencies. Soloviev's influence made itself strongly felt and gave rise to a school of religious thinkers who began as his followers but gradually developed their own theories. During the revolutionary years when it was difficult to study peacefully in Russia, many students went to Germany and worked in the seminars of philosophers representing the Freiburg and Marburg schools of transcendental idealism. On returning home they founded the Russian section of the periodical *Logos*. Even some of the marxists came under the influence of Mach and Avenarius and began to understand that materialism was untenable.

All this free blossoming of the life of the spirit was crushed by the bolshevik revolution. Since then Russian philosophy has been developing in two sharply opposed directions. In Soviet Russia every philosopher and indeed every scientist and every teacher has to be an adherent of dialectical materialism. On the other hand, thinkers who emigrated or were banished from Russia cultivate for the most part a religious philosophy.

Chapter 14

FATHER PAVEL FLORENSKY

The work of Vladimir Soloviev has laid the foundations of an original school of Russian religious philosophy. It includes a number of thinkers endowed with most varied gifts and often possessing a vast erudition. One of the foremost places in this movement belongs to Father Pavel Florensky.

Pavel Alexandrovich Florensky was born in 1882. He studied mathematics and philosophy at the University of Moscow, and then at the Moscow Theological Academy. In 1908 he was appointed to the chair of History of Philosophy in that same Academy. Priesthood attracted him not less than the academic work and he took Holy Orders in 1911. After the Bolshevik revolution, when theological academies were closed down, Florensky took to work in the technical domain and obtained a post in the "Glavelectro" (Head Office of Electrical Industry) where he was engaged in the study of electric fields and dielectrics. Father Pavel Florensky's personality strikes one by the multiplicity of his gifts. During the German occupation of Pskov V. Filistinsky published an article about him in the Pskov paper *Za rodinu (For Fatherland)* under the title "A Russian Leonardo da Vinci In a Concentration Camp." I will quote a few passages from it. "I recall the striking figure of a Moscow priest, Pavel Alexandrovich Florensky: a man of medium height, in a linen, rather crumpled cassock, with an Armenian type of face.[1] One wondered when he found time to sleep or rest, with the amount of intellectual work he did. He was professor at the Moscow Theological Academy; author of the much-talked-of book *The Pillar and Foundation of Truth* and a number of religious-philosophical articles; a poet-symbolist, whose works appeared in *Vesy (The Balance)* and as a separate volume; a gifted astronomer, defending a geocentric conception of the world; a remarkable mathematician, author of *Fictions in Geometry* and a number of mathematical monographs; an authority on physics,

---

1. My impression of Father Florensky's face was different: it vaguely reminded me of Spinoza's face.

author of the standard book *The Doctrine of Dielectrics;* a scholar in the history of art and author of several monographs, especially on wood carving; a notable electrical engineer, who occupied one of the chief posts in the Commission for Electrification and went to the Supreme Soviet for National Economy in a cassock and priest's cap; professor of perspectival painting in the Moscow Soviet Arts School; a fine musician and discerning admirer of Bach and the polyphonic music, of Beethoven and his contemporaries, thoroughly acquainted with their work; a polyglot knowing to perfection Latin and Greek, most of the modern European languages, and also the languages of the Caucasus, Iran and India. . . . In 1927 he invented some quite extraordinary noncoagulating machine oil which the Bolsheviks called 'dekanite' in honor of the tenth anniversary of the Soviet revolution . . . I only twice succeeded in meeting Father Pavel. The first occasion was in 1928 or 1929 when he read a paper on some highly technical subject at a closed meeting of a group of Leningrad engineers. A friend brought me there. I did not of course understand a word of the paper, but I was deeply impressed by the sense of creative power and the thorough mastery of his subject conveyed by that slender cassocked man who spoke with such power and confidence before the venerable old academicians and professors of technical sciences. Yes, Father Pavel was obviously conscious of his superiority, and the one Christian virtue that seemed lacking in him was humility. But one could not help sympathizing with his involuntary pride! A new Leonardo da Vinci was standing before us—and we all were conscious of it. . . . Many times the Bolsheviks imprisoned Florensky, sent him to the Solovki concentration camp, demanding that he should cease to be a priest and renounce holy orders. But Father Pavel remained true to the Church. In 1934 or 1935, however, the Soviets' patience gave way and they rewarded the great scholar and scientist by condemning him to ten years servitude in a concentration camp." In 1946 a rumor reached the Russian emigrés that Father Pavel Florensky died there.

I should like to add a few personal reminiscences to B. Filistinsky's article. In November 1913 Father Pavel sent me his book *The Pillar and Foundation of Truth*. That book furthered my gradual return to the Church, which finally took place in 1918. Naturally I was very eager to meet Florensky. Unexpected meetings between people, remarkable coincidences, and, speaking generally, the intersection in time and space between two mutually independent series of events regarded as accidental, are not really fortuitous. They are purposeful combinations arising under the guidance of a higher power that holds together distant sectors of reality. Men of high spirituality, considerably advanced on the path toward the absolute good, enter into communion with other men unintentionally and unwittingly at the very moment when they can be of the greatest assistance to them. It is as though they were directed by a higher beneficent power. Two incidents in Florensky's life suggest that he acted precisely as such an intermediary for the divine power. This was how I met Father Pavel. I believe it was in 1915. Returning home from the University I got into the lift to go to our flat on the third floor. That lift was rather primitive: it was set going by the hall porter pulling at a cable, and stopped by his ceasing to pull. In war time (during the war of 1914–1918) the worn cable could not be repaired; it had grown too long and the porter could not stop the lift exactly opposite the landing. On the third floor the lift stopped much lower than it should. I had great difficulty in placing my right foot on the landing and was just going to climb out when the porter began to pull the lift down; the top of the lift was already pressing on my right shoulder and in another moment I would have been crushed to death. At that instant I just managed to extricate myself and jumped out on to the landing. Going into my study I took several turns round the room thinking with agitation of my narrow escape. Just then the front door bell rang, and Father Pavel Florensky walked into the room. He was going through Petersburg on his way to the front where he wanted to be an army chaplain. He stayed no more than half an hour with me; we spent the time in animated conversation and he engaged my attention so completely that when he had gone, I recalled with perfect equanimity the danger I had been through. The fear I had experienced, preserved in my subconscious, might have given rise later to some neurosis, but Father Pavel's arrival dismissed it to the domain of the comparatively unimportant, and cured me.

Another incident relating to Florensky is this. In 1922 our family was spending the summer at Tsarskoe Selo, in the same town with S. Lukyanov, professor of pathology and former Procurator of the Holy Synod. He devoted many years of his life to writing a voluminous biography of Vladimir Soloviev and was collecting materials about him from everyone who had met Soloviev. He invited me too for this purpose. In the course of conversation he told me that the horrible crimes of the Bolshevik revolution had destroyed his love of life. One day he began a letter to Florensky saying that he no longer cared to live; he did not finish that letter and never sent it. But a short time afterwards he received a letter from Florensky who began by admonishing him not to lose the will to live—as though in some supersensory way Father Pavel had come to know of his mood.

Florensky's principal works are: *The Pillar and Foundation of*

Truth, 1913 (there is a German translation of it); *The Meaning of Idealism,* 1915; article on Khomiakov in the *Bogoslovsky Vestnik* (Theological Review) for July and August 1916.

The book *The Pillar and Foundation of Truth* is remarkable for its subject, its form, and its outer appearance. The author displays in it an almost superhuman erudition: he is thoroughly at home in the domain of philosophy, theology, philology and mathematics, and he also supports his philosophizing by arguments borrowed from medicine, psychopathology, folklore, and particularly linguistics. He likes to compare the derivation, in the different languages, of such terms as "truth," "faith," "heart," etc. He points out for instance that the Russian word for truth, *istina* is, according to linguists, to be derived from the verb to be (*est* = is, *istina* = *estina* = that which is), and indicates "the ontological aspect of the idea." The Greek word ἀλήθεια draws attention to the aspect of unforgettableness or indelibility of truth; Latin *veritas* has the same root as the Russian verb *verit*, to believe; the ancient Hebrew word *emet* emphasizes the aspect of trustworthiness or security. Florensky frequently appeals to the most abstract sciences—mathematics and mathematical logic. The notes at the end of his book take up two hundred pages. They contain many interesting and valuable remarks as well as a rich bibliography.

Florensky wants to base his theodicy upon "the living religious experience as the only legitimate method of cognizing dogmas." His book therefore naturally takes the form of letters to a friend. The exposition of theological and philosophical problems is sometimes interrupted by descriptions of nature or of moods inspired by it. And yet that book is a dissertation submitted for his doctorate!

The exterior of the book is no less striking. The colors of the cover imitate "the basic colors of the ancient Sophian ikons of the Novgorod school." Each letter is preceded by a symbolic vignette from Ambodic's book *Symbola et Emblemata selecta*. The book is dedicated "to the all-fragrant and all-pure Name of the Virgin and Mother." The frontispiece is taken from *Amoris Divini Emblemata, studio et aere Othonis Vaeni concinnate.* Antverpiae 1660. It represents two angels on one pedestal with the inscription *finis amoris ut duo unum fiant* (the end of love is that two should become one). That symbol expresses the main idea of Florensky's metaphysics, namely his contention that all created personalities forming part of the world are *consubstantial* with one another. In a remarkable way Florensky connects the initial problem of philosophy —the problem of truth and of its discovery, i.e., the epistemological enquiry—with the trinitarian dogma and the idea of consubstantiality. Truth, he says, is the Absolute reality, superrational wholeness; there is no place in it for the rational law of identity "*A* is *A*." The formula of the law of identity, Florensky thinks, stands for deathlike immobility, static isolation, but Truth as a living wholeness must contain the transition from *A* to non-*A*. In Truth "the other" is at the same time "not the other," *sub specie aeternitatis:* "*A* is *A* because, being eternally non-*A*, it finds in that non-*A* its own affirmation as *A*." Do we find such Truth not as an abstract formula but as a living reality? We do, Florensky answers: we have it in the religious experience which testifies that God is one in essence but tripersonal. In that experience we learn that *love* is the basis of the living reality and truth, because love means that an entity passes from the isolated separateness of *A* into the other, non-*A*, establishes its consubstantiality with it and consequently finds itself, i.e., *A*, in it. It is only possible to discover this structure of being and of Truth if knowledge is directed upon the living reality as such and its transition from one to the "other": what enters consciousness is not a subjective copy of the object or a construct of the understanding, as Kant thought, but the actual object of the external world. In other words, Florensky maintains that perception of objects is *intuition* in Lossky's sense of the term—i.e., direct contemplation of the living reality as it is in itself.[2]

Florensky describes as follows the difference between irrationalistic intuitivism and the Russian intuitivism which places great value upon the rational, systematic aspect of the world. Truth is cognized neither through a *blind* intuition directed upon disconnected empirical facts nor through discursive reason which tries to build up the whole from the parts by adding one element to another; Truth can only enter consciousness through a *rational* intuition which combines discursive differentiation *ad infinitum* with intuitive integration to the point of unity. "If Truth *is*, it is real rationality and rational reality, the Infinite conceived as an integral Unity." Rational intuition works from above downwards, from the whole to the infinite multiplicity of subordinate parts. But such single Truth is possible "only there, in heaven," while "here there are a number of truths, of fragments of truth." The fragmentariness of our knowledge is not so bad in itself, but the worst of it is that the integral Divine Truth, transcending the law of contradiction, reconciles *A* and non-*A*, while when broken up it results in a number of truths that contradict one another and are inevitably antinomic. Thus, for instance, there are many dogmatic antinomies: Divine Oneness and Trinity, predestination and free will, etc. "Only at moments of

---

2. In a note on page 644 Florensky mentions a number of Russian thinkers who regarded knowledge as an act of "inner unification between the knower and the known."

illumination by grace are those contradictions reconciled in the mind, not rationally but in a superrational way" (159).

Inquiring into the relation between created personalities, Father Pavel makes use of the idea of consubstantiality in order to make clear the nature of love.

Victory over the law of identity, a creative transition from one's self-containedness into the realm of "the other" and a real discovery of oneself in that other is a fundamental truth expressed in the dogma of consubstantiality (*homoousia*). The conception of consubstantiality must guide us both in considering the relation between the Three Persons of the Holy Trinity and the relations between earthly creatures in so far as they are individual and seek to realize the Christian ideal of mutual love. "The end of love is that two should become one" (*finis amoris ut duo unum fiant*). Such *homoousian* philosophy of personality and of its creative work is the Christian spiritual philosophy; its opposite is the *homoiousian* philosophy of rationalism which admits generic likeness only and not numerical identity. "It is the philosophy of *things* and of lifeless immovability."

The love that leads to the identification of two beings is not, of course, a subjective mental process, but a "substantial act which passes from the subject to the object and has a basis in the object," *ontologically* transforming the beings that love one another. This is true of perfect friendship that leads to the complete unanimity of two beings, making them into a new spiritual essence capable of knowing the mysteries of the Kingdom of God and of performing miracles. Our Lord Jesus Christ himself said that "if two of you shall agree on earth as touching anything that they shall ask, it shall be done for them of my Father which is in Heaven." Why is this? Because two people can be in absolute agreement with each other only if they follow the will of God; "such agreement between them is co-ascension into the mysterious spiritual atmosphere of Christ, participation in His gracious power; it transmutes them into a new spiritual entity, making of the two a particle of Christ's Body, a living incarnation of the Church." Such absolute friendship is "the contemplation of oneself through the friend in God."

Not only friendship between two individuals, but all true love is impossible without the participation of the Divine power: "in loving we love in and through God, since love necessarily demands that we should overcome the limits of selfhood and enter a new realm of being, which bears throughout the stamp of beauty. Indeed, true love creates a reality in which three absolute values are realized: in love God enters the lover's self and there is knowledge of God as Absolute Truth which is Love; in relation to the other, to 'Thou,' that love is Goodness; as objectively contemplated by a third, the love for another is Beauty. Truth, Goodness and Beauty—this metaphysical triad is not three different principles, but one. It is one and the same spiritual life considered from different points of view." In speaking of the beauty of the world revealed to the man freed from the isolation of selfhood through love Florensky bases his argument on the works of great ascetics such as Macarius the Great, Isaac the Syrian and others, the testimony of pilgrims, and fine literature. "The holy and eternal aspect of every creature is revealed to the inner vision of one who strives after holiness;" he apprehends all creation "in its primordial, triumphant beauty;" his feeling for nature becomes more acute. "All my surroundings appeared to me entrancing: the trees, the grass, the birds, the earth, the light, the air;" says a pilgrim "all seemed to tell me that it exists for man's sake, bears witness to God's love for man, and all was praying and proclaiming the glory of God." According to Florensky "asceticism produces not a *good* but a *beautiful* personality: the characteristic peculiarity of great saints is not the goodness of heart which is common among the carnal and even very sinful men, but spiritual beauty, the dazzling beauty of radiant, light-giving personality, unattainable by the carnal man weighed down by the flesh."

Spiritual beauty is accompanied by a holiness of the body, a radiance which suffuses the flesh with light. Florensky is keenly interested in the stories about the light that issues from the bodies of saints; sweetness, warmth, fragrance, musical harmony, and, above all, radiant light are the characteristic marks of flesh permeated by the Holy Spirit.

Cosmic reality as a whole, welded together by the love of God and illumined by the beauty of the Holy Spirit, is Sophia—the most difficult subject of theological speculation. Florensky regards it as "the fourth hypostasis" possessing many aspects and therefore interpreted by mystics and theologians in a number of different ways. He speaks of Sophia as "the great root of the created world in its wholeness and unity," as "the original substance of creatures, the creative Love of God in them. In relation to the created world Sophia is its Guardian Angel, its ideal personality." Regarded from three points of view with reference to the three divine hypostases Sophia is (1) the ideal *substance* of the created world; (2) the *reason* of the created world, that is, its truth or meaning; (3) the *spirituality* of the created world, its holiness, purity, sinlessness, that is, its beauty. Further, in relation to the structure of the world Sophia has a number of other aspects: as "the beginning and the center of the redeemed creation, she is the Body of our Lord Jesus Christ, i.e., the substance of the created world assumed by the divine Logos." The only way in which man can receive from the Holy Spirit freedom and mysterious purification is by participating in the Body of Christ; in this sense Sophia is the Church, first in its heavenly and then in its earthly aspect, in so far as the Church includes all persons who have already begun the work of regeneration. Since regeneration by the Holy Spirit means purity and humble virtue, Sophia is *Virginity;* "and the incarnation of Virginity—the Virgin in the proper and exclusive sense of the term—is Mary, the Blessed Virgin, filled with the grace and the gifts of the Holy Spirit." Florensky arranges the aspects of Sophia as it were in a hierarchical order. Thus he says: "If Sophia is the whole creation, then the soul and the conscience of creation—humanity—is Sophia pre-eminently. If Sophia is humanity as a whole, then the soul and the conscience of humanity—the Church—is Sophia pre-eminently. If Sophia is the Church, then the soul and the conscience of the Church—the Church of the Saints—is Sophia pre-eminently. If Sophia is the Church of the Saints, then the soul and the conscience of that Church is the Mother of God, the Defender of the creatures, interceding for them before the Word of God. What has been said of the many-sidedness of Sophia clearly applies also to the Mother of God. That is why there exist many greatly revered and miraculous ikons of Our Lady with many significant names attached to them, for instance "Sudden Joy," "Melting of Heart," "Joy of All the Sorrowful," "Seeking Those Who Are Lost," "Quick to Hear," "Steadfast Wall." "Each legitimate 'revealed' ikon of the Mother of God—that is, each ikon signalized by miracles and so to speak approved and confirmed by the Virgin Mother Herself who testifies to its spiritual veracity, is the reflection of *one* of Her aspects, a patch of light on earth from *one* of Her rays, *one* of Her pictorial names. Hence the existence of many such 'revealed' ikons, hence the desire to worship *different* ikons. The names of some of them partially express their spiritual essence." This is the profound explanation given by Father Pavel to the desire to worship different ikons, which seems like idolatry to persons without the religious experience of Orthodoxy.

The characteristic capacity of the Russian philosophers to perceive the concretely ideal principles underlying the world has been strikingly revealed in the philosophy of Vladimir Soloviev. He left unexplored, however, many important aspects of the theory of concretely ideal being. Valuable additions to his doctrine have been made by Florensky. In his treatise *The Meaning of Idealism* (1915) he asks what "seeing an idea" means to Plato, and in his answer quotes Plato as saying in his dialogue *Philebus* that it means seeing that "many are one and one is many" or in other words seeing the union of "infinity with determinateness" (49). In an idea *"unum"* turns toward the other, toward *alia*—say the Scholastics; *unum versus alia* is precisely, according to their etymology, *universale*—singular and general at once" (11).

The most obvious manifestation of an idea is a living being as an undoubted unity in manifold (31). When an artist attempts to re-create it in its ideal essence, by the aid of colors in painting, or of marble or bronze in sculpture, he does not reproduce a momentary position as does the momentary photography which gives a dead, unnatural, even though exact, reproduction: he creates something that is the opposite of photography, namely he blends into a single whole what belongs to different periods and yet forms a unity. Florensky cites Broder Christiansen who in his *Philosophy of Art* points out that the portraits of great Dutch, German and Italian masters contain a synthesis of different expressions harmoniously blended into a unity, e.g., the lines of the mouth show "the excitement and tension of the will," and the eyes "the final calm of the intellect" (38). The famous sculptor Rodin in his talks on art says the same thing of the statues which breathe of truth—they are a combination of movements different in time (32). In contemplating such a work, says Florensky, we have a "synthetic perception," something like the perception of a three-dimensional body from a four-dimensional space, its vision being possible at once from outside and from inside in a four-dimensional contemplation. Picasso in his pictures —e.g., in *Nature Morte*—tries to present a violin from different points of view, from all sides, in order to disclose "more plastically the inner life of the violin, its rhythm and dynamics" (45).

The synthetic vision, necessary in order to see as a whole even such a comparatively simple thing as a human face, is imperfectly developed in us. Still less developed is it in regard to entities of a higher order such as a People, a Nation, or Mankind. For our three-dimensional mind the idea of man is only a general notion, only a class, and our three-dimensional eyes perceive only the disjointed specimen of that class. Yet Man as an idea is a living whole in which individual men play the part of organs. It is the "Heavenly Man" as he is present in the religious consciousness of the Mystics, the "Body of Christ" as it is described by Swedenborg in his treatise *On Heaven, on the World of Spirits, and on Hell* (52).

Many religions, maintains Florensky, attempt to express such ideal wholes symbolically: the mystical tree of life (*der heilige Baum, der Lebensbaum,* also *l'Arbre du Monde*) is the "synthesis of plants revered in the country, the image of life in its wholeness, or, in other words, the *idea of life*" (56 ff.), the *élan vital* not yet broken up into individual specimens or species. Florensky takes the same view of the summarized (composite) animals such as the Egyptian sphinxes, the Assyrian kirubi (winged lions or bulls), the Jewish Cherubs. According to the explanation of the Rabbis, the Cherubs supporting the throne of God's Glory in the vision of the prophet Ezekiel and represented on the Ark of the Covenant, as well as on the curtain of the temple, embody in themselves all created life—the reason of man, the strength of the bull, the courage of the lion and the heavenward aspiration of the eagle (58). Of similar nature is the tetramorphon (the six-winged Angel combining the same four aspects of created life) of the Christian ikonography.

The "idea" in the above instances is embodied in, or immanent to, the phenomena, but Plato speaks of ideas transcendental to the phenomena. Dealing with this distinction Florensky takes the edge off it by pointing out that transcendentality and immanence are relative and interdependent (85): they are two aspects of the idea. The idea in its transcendental aspect is "the heavenly entity forming the earthly" (94). Many religious and philosophical doctrines admit of such principles, of *personal ideas* and not impersonal forces determining from above our earthly existence—"here belongs for instance the Hindu doctrine of Gandharvas or Gandhabbas, which closely resembles Leibniz's doctrine of the central part of the organism outliving death" (92). The same is the meaning of the *feruera* or *fravashi* of parsism, of the genii of persons, places and events of the ancient Romans, as well as the *spermatic logos* of the ancient Greek philosophy, especially as conceived by Plutarch of Cheroneia. In this higher supraterrestrial aspect ideas are not abstract rules, but "concrete fullness of perfection and supreme reality" (73). The perfection of this higher reality is manifested most clearly in the beauty which belongs to it as a concrete living being.

At the opposite pole from the holiness, beauty and blissful rest of the reality that is complete in God lies the domain of sin, in which selfhood, enclosed in the identity of $I = I$, out of relation to its "other," that is, to God and all creation, remains in darkness ("light is the appearance of the real and darkness is invisibility to each other") and instead of possessing the fullness of being, finds itself in a state of dissolution that approaches metaphysical annihilation. Florensky describes this condition from personal experience: "Once in a dream I experienced it with an extraordinary vividness. There were no images, only purely inward experiences. A darkness without a ray of light, almost palpably dense, surrounded me. Some force was dragging me to the brink; I felt that this was the limit of God's being and that beyond it was absolute nothingness. I wanted to cry out and could not. I knew that in another moment I should be thrust into outer darkness. Darkness began to fill my whole being. I almost lost consciousness of myself and I knew that this was absolute metaphysical annihilation. In utter despair I cried out in a voice unlike my own: 'Out of the deep have I cried unto Thee. Oh Lord, hear my prayer!' My whole soul was poured out in these words. Some powerful hands seized me just as I was sinking and threw me far away from the abyss. The shock was sudden and violent. All at once I found myself in my usual surroundings, in my own room; it was as though from mystical nonbeing I was transferred to ordinary everyday existence. Then suddenly I felt that I was before the face of God and woke up, bathed in a cold sweat."

Selfish absorption in one's own selfhood leads, paradoxically enough, not to a greater integration of personality but, on the contrary, to its dissolution. "Without love," writes Florensky, "—and for love it is necessary in the first instance to have love of God—without love the personality is broken up into a multiplicity of fragmentary psychological moments and elements. The love of God is that which holds personality together." When love is absent, the vision of the organic and substantival unity of the self is lost. The organism, both the bodily and the mental, ceases to be an integral and harmonious *instrument* or organ of personality and becomes a haphazard conglomeration of self-acting mechanisms that do not fit in with one another. In short, everything in me and outside of me becomes free—everything except myself. If modern psychology insists that it knows nothing about the soul as a substance, this is a very bad reflection on the moral condition of the psychologists themselves who evidently are, for the most part, 'lost men.' In such cases, indeed, it is not I who do things but 'things are done to me;' I do not *live* but 'things are happening to me.'"

A further degree of self-absorption leads to certain neurotic states: to the experiences of darkness, isolation and remoteness from reality. The Moscow psychiatrist Nicolay Evgrafovitch Osipov (who died as an emigré in Prague in 1934) liked to point out in his lectures the attempts made in psychological literature to trace in the last resort all mental diseases to moral defects of the patient; Florensky emphatically adopts this view.

Disintegration of personality may go still further than it does in certain psychoses, and reach the point described in mystical literature as the second death. The first death consists in the separation of the soul from the body; the second death is, according to Florensky, the separation of the soul from the spirit, the isolation of the selfhood that has become definitely satanical from the man himself, i.e., from the original substantival image of God. Deprived of its substantival basis, "selfhood" loses its creative power, and all its further destiny is determined by the fixed idea of its own sin and the burning agony of Truth. "Eternal bliss of the self and eternal torment of selfhood are the two inseparable antinomies of the final, the Third Covenant. If then you ask me 'will there be eternal torments,' I will say 'yes.' But if you ask me 'will there be eternal restoration and bliss?' I will again say 'yes.' One and the other: thesis and antithesis."

Sinful selfhood is partially annihilated in a healing, salutary way through the sacrament of penance, in which the sinful past, definitely condemned by the penitent is, so to speak, cut away from the soul by the power of grace, is expelled from it, and ceases to affect man's subsequent conduct.

Father Pavel published an article on Zavitnevich's book *A. S. Khomiakov* in the *Bogoslovsky Vestnik* (Theological Review) for July–August 1916. In this article he criticized Khomiakov's theology. He rejected Khomiakov's doctrine of *sobornost* (togetherness) as the principle of Church organization. Father Florensky interpreted as altruism the love which Khomiakov had introduced into his definition of *sobornost*. Therefore he said that according to Khomiakov, Church unity was based "on the immanent powers of men" (539). In reality Khomiakov's *sobornost* is a free union of the members of the Church based upon their unanimous "love for Christ and Divine righteousness." This type of love is, of course, supported by the grace of Christ and of the Holy Spirit, which guides the Church. Berdyaev sharply criticized Florensky's paper in an article entitled "Khomiakov and the Priest P. A. Florensky."[3] Berdyaev says that Florensky regards Khomiakov as an adherent of the "immanent" philosophy of the German type, with Protestant leanings. According to Florensky, Khomiakov "rejected the authority of the Church," "the principle of fear, of authority and of the binding character of canonical institutions," and preached "man's free self-affirmation; he valued above all man's immanent being expressing itself in the organization of love." But in Florensky's view "the essence of Orthodoxy is ontologism—the acceptance of reality from God, given by Him and not created by man—humility and gratitude."

Berdyaev writes: "We have already renounced Vladimir Soloviev, and now it is Khomiakov's turn: for both of them, as for Dostoevsky in the *Legend of the Grand Inquisitor*, Christianity was "a religion of love and freedom," but for Florensky it is "a religion of obedience and not of love." In his philosophy of history Khomiakov interprets the historical process as the struggle of the free creative spirit of the "Iranians" with the materialism of the "Cushites" who denied freedom. Florensky suspects that Khomiakov's "Iranian" philosophy has a tendency toward "immanentism." Berdyaev points out, however, that Khomiakov com-

---

3. *Russkaya Mysl*, February 1917.

bined traditional Orthodoxy with ideal spiritual strivings, whereas Florensky replaced the living, everyday Orthodoxy by the worship of established fact. He "wants to be more Orthodox than Orthodoxy itself" being a *parvenu* in Orthodoxy. Berdyaev accuses him of "decadence" and "aesthetically mystical *gourmandise*."

One could have expected from Florensky many fruitful and original thoughts had he lived not in Soviet Russia, but in a country where there is freedom of thought and of the press. A good instance of the way Christian thought is being passed over in silence is afforded by the Soviet edition of the *Granat Encyclopaedia* (7th edition). We read there that according to Florensky the principal law of the world is the principle of thermodynamics, the law of entropy, i.e., of universal leveling (chaos). The world is confronted with the law of ectropy (Logos). "Culture means struggle against universal leveling (death). Culture (from "cult") is an organically connected system of means toward the realization and revelation of a certain value which is taken as absolute and is therefore an object of faith. Faith determines cult, and cult determines a world conception from which culture subsequently ensues. The fact that the universe is determined by laws means the presence of functional dependence conceived as relational discontinuity and discreteness in relation to the reality itself. This interruptedness and separateness in the world leads to the Pythagorean affirmation of number as form and to an attempt at interpreting Plato's 'ideas' as prototypes." Florensky's Christian philosophy is expounded in such a way as almost to give it the appearance of agnostic naturalism.

What valuable additions has Father Pavel Florensky made to a Christian world conception? His chief merit is that he deliberately made use of the idea of consubstantiality not only in trinitarian theology but in metaphysics; namely, in his doctrine of the structure of created personalities. He divides all philosophical systems into two classes according to whether they recognize consubstantiality or merely similarity. A *homoiousian* philosophy which recognizes merely generic likeness and not numerical identity is rationalistic: it is "the philosophy of concepts and of the understanding, of things and lifeless immobility." The *homoousian* philosophy which recognizes consubstantiality is "the philosophy of ideas and of reason, the philosophy of personality and of creative achievement."

There is indeed a profound difference between these two types of philosophy. The philosophy of mere similarity takes the world to consist of entities whose being is wholly external to one another. They can therefore be bound together only by external relations. The philosophy of consubstantiality affirms on the contrary that ontologically all entities are closely welded together from within. This point of view makes it possible for the first time to give a satisfactory solution of many problems—for instance, to understand the nature of truth, to interpret the world as an organic whole, to establish the existence of absolute values, and so on. The philosophy of consubstantiality existed of course long before Christianity, and later on outside of it. The principle of consubstantiality lies at the basis of the teachings of Plato, Aristotle and Plotinus, of Patristic philosophy and many medieval systems of thought; in the nineteenth century we find it in Fichte, Schelling and Hegel, and in Russia in the philosophy of Vladimir Soloviev and his successors. Florensky's merit is to have consciously introduced this principle into the metaphysics of created being, and thus laid the foundation for a conscious use of it in other philosophical disciplines. Florensky himself applied it with singular success to his *ontological*—as opposed to the popular *psychologistic*—theory of love.

Florensky's teaching that the Ideas of Plato are living concrete personalities and not abstract notions is also highly valuable. He has chiefly in view in this connection personalities of higher order than the human self; e.g., the Race, the Nation, Humanity, and so on. He justly points out that in many religions such "personal ideas" are recognized —for instance the genii of events and places among the Romans, symbolic syntheses of plants and animals, etc. In the New Testament such character attaches to the angels or genii of the local churches. Philosophy is confronted with the vitally important task of developing a theory about such superhuman personalities at all stages of cosmic being, and in the Kingdom of God. Christian philosophy appears to be suspicious of such theories, perhaps because they have been discredited by the fantastic teachings of anthroposophists, theosophists and occultists, who furthermore often manifest a morbid interest in superhuman beings belonging to our sinful realm and perhaps even to the realm of Lucifer. Father Pavel Florensky has mainly in view members of the Kingdom of God and especially Saint Sophia as the Mother of God—an absolutely perfect cosmic entity fulfilling the Divine will as the World Soul. His teaching is free from the defects of Soloviev's theory which actually admitted the Fall of Sophia.

According to Father Pavel the ideal of the Christian life is not a stern contempt for the world, but a joyful acceptance of it, making the world richer through raising it to a higher level. Writing of St. Cyril who christianized the Slavs he says: "All his life is penetrated with Sophian rays. Unlike the desert saints of Egypt or Palestine who find salvation through self-exhaustion, he is a man of royal wealth and splendor whose whole life bestows blessing not upon the cutting off, but upon the transfiguration of the fullness of being. What is characteristic of St. Cyril's achievement is not a sharp turn from sin to purity, but gracious continuity of development."

Under the influence of Kant, many Russian philosophers in dealing with the essential problems of world interpretation like to have recourse to antinomies; i.e., like to express the truth by means of two mutually contradictory judgements, and then seek ways of reconciling the contradiction. Both those antinomies and their supposed solution often prove artificial. A characteristic instance of this is Florensky's contention that all will be saved and attain eternal bliss, but at the same time some will experience eternal torments. Florensky's solution of this antinomy is obviously invalid. He says that when "selfhood" becomes definitely satanical "it is cut off from the substantival basis of personality as originally created, and therefore, being deprived of creative power, is tortured forever by the fixed idea of its sin and the fiery agony of Truth." But to undergo eternal torments—even uncreatively—is an *experience* and therefore belongs to some self who is conscious of it. One is thus driven to suppose that according to Florensky human personality consists of two selves which may be separated from each other, so that one will be living in eternal torments and the other in eternal bliss—which is utterly impossible.

Florensky's criticism of Khomiakov is, apparently, unjustified. Khomiakov says that the Church must be built upon the principle of *sobornost*, "togetherness." He means by that term the free unity of the members of the Church in their communal understanding of Truth and communal salvation based upon their love for Christ and the Divine rightcousness. Khomiakov attaches special value to every manifestation of love, and Christianity is for him indeed the religion of love and therefore of freedom. This does not in the least imply that he denies the authority of the Church, the binding character of its canonical structure or the principle of reverent obedience. The whole of Khomiakov's behavior testifies to his being a faithful son of the Church. The principle of *sobornost* does not by any means lead to canonical anarchy or prevent the excommunication of persons who reject the fundamental doctrines of the Church, thus themselves abandoning the unity of the communal love of it. But of course if our conduct, in accordance with Christ's commandment, is based upon love for every person, excommunication must be a mere statement that so and so no longer belongs to the Church, and involve no hatred or persecution.

Father George Florovsky in his book *The Ways of Russian Theology* sharply criticizes Florensky's book *The Pillar and Foundation of Truth* and his way of thinking. His reason, Florovsky says, "escapes from doubts through the knowledge of the Holy Trinity. Florensky speaks of this with great enthusiasm and reveals the speculative significance of the Trinitarian dogma as a rational truth. But strangely enough he somehow bypasses the Incarnation, and after the chapters on the Trinity goes on straight to the doctrine about the Holy Spirit. Florensky's book has simply no christological chapters. Florensky is not rooted in the Orthodox depths. He remains a stranger to the Orthodox world. In its meaning his book is essentially Western. It is the book of a Westernizer who dreamily and aesthetically seeks salvation in the East. It is highly characteristic that in his work he seems to step back, beyond Christianity, into Platonism and the ancient religions, or to swerve aside into the realm of occultism and magic. The subjects he set to his students for their theses were of that nature (on K. Du-Prel, on Dionysos, on Russian folklore). And he himself had intended to present as his thesis for Master of Divinity his translation of Iamblichus with notes" (495).

Stern critical remarks and valuations contained in Father George Florovsky's remarkable book usually contain at least a fraction of truth; but in defence of Father Paul Florensky the following considerations should be taken into account. The diseases of modern civilization—the loss of the idea of absolute value of personality, of the idea of state based upon justice, of the ideal of free spiritual creativeness—are due in the first instance to the fact that the intellectuals, and, following them, the masses, have forsaken Christianity and become non-religious. The main task of our epoch is to bring, first, the intellectuals and through them, the masses, back to Christianity and consequently to Christian humanism. That purpose may be particularly well served by religiously philosophic works, written in the new, more or less secular style, connecting religious problems with modern science and metaphysical investigations of the higher realms of being which transcend the human world. Florensky's works belong to this category and therefore are highly valuable, whatever defects they may have from the point of view of the traditional style and content of Orthodox theological literature.

Chapter 15

FATHER SERGIUS BULGAKOV

For the last twenty years Father Sergius Bulgakov occupied a foremost place among Russian theologians and philosophers.

Sergei Nikolaevich Bulgakov was born in 1871 in Livny, in the province of Orel, in the family of a priest. After a course of studies at the Faculty of Law at the University of Moscow, he became, in 1901, Professor of Political Economy at the Polytechnic Institute at Kiev, and in 1906, Lecturer at the University of Moscow. In 1911, together with many other professors and lecturers of the University, he resigned as a protest against the violation of the University autonomy on the part of the Government.

In his youth Bulgakov was a Marxist, but afterwards, like many other gifted Russian economists and journalists (P. Struve, Tugan-Baranovsky, Berdyaev, S. Frank) he adopted a more profound world conception. As early as 1900, in his book *Capitalism and Agriculture*, he contended that the law of the concentration of production could not apply to agriculture, for which decentralizing tendencies are characteristic. Under the influence of Kant's philosophy, Bulgakov came to the conclusion that the fundamental principles of social and individual life must be established in connection with a theory of the absolute value of goodness, truth and beauty. Severing all connection with Marxism he published, in 1904, a book entitled *From Marxism to Idealism*. In 1904 S. N. Bulgakov and N. A. Berdyaev decided to have their own magazine. At first they acquired the *Novy Put* ("The New Way"), and later founded *Voprosy Zhizni* ("The Problems of Life"). At this time Bulgakov was undergoing a further evolution from idealistic philosophy to the ideal-realism of the Orthodox Church. At first he became interested in Soloviev's philosophy, then began to work out his own philosophical and theological system. In 1918 Bulgakov was ordained priest. In 1922, when the Soviet Government banished from Russia over a hundred scholars, writers and politicians, accusing them of ir-

beauty of the first creation. But there were no words, no Name, there was no 'Christ has risen' sung to the world and to the heavenly altitudes. And that moment of meeting did not die in my soul, that apocalypse, that wedding feast, the first encounter with Sophia. That of which the mountains spoke to me in their solemn brilliance, I soon recognized once more in the shy and gentle girlish look, on different shores and under different mountains. The same light shone in the trustful, half-childish eyes, frightened and meek, full of the sanctity of suffering. The revelation of love told me of another world, a world I had lost . . .

"There came a fresh wave of intoxication with the world. Along with 'personal happiness' came the first encounter with the 'West,' and the first ecstasies: 'civilization,' comfort, social democracy . . . And suddenly an unexpected, marvelous encounter—the Sixtine Madonna in Dresden. Thou hast Thyself touched my heart and it fluttered at Thy call. There the eyes of the Heavenly Queen, walking in the clouds with the pre-eternal Child, looked into my soul. There was in them an immense *power of purity* and of *prophetic self-sacrifice*—the knowledge of suffering and the readiness for free suffering, and the same prophetic readiness for sacrifice was to be seen in the unchildishly wise eyes of the Child. They know what awaits Them, what They are doomed to, and they go freely to give themselves up, to fulfill the will of the Sender—She to receive the weapon into her heart; He, to the Calvary . . . I could not restrain myself, my head was dizzy, my eyes shed joyful and yet bitter tears, and with them the ice melted in my heart, and some vital knot was being untied. It was not an aesthetic emotion, nay, it was an *encounter*, a new knowledge, a *miracle* . . . I (then a Marxist!) involuntarily called that contemplation—*prayer*.

"I returned home from my travels abroad having lost the ground under my feet, and with my faith in my ideals already shattered. In my soul there grew a 'will to faith,' a determination to make the final jump to the opposite shore, foolish from the standpoint of the wisdom of this world—from Marxism and various other 'isms' that followed it, to the Orthodox faith. Yet, years went by and I was still yearning outside the pale and had not the strength to make the decisive step, to go to confession and to take the sacrament for which my soul longed ever more and more. I remember how one day, on Maundy Thursday, entering a church, I (then a Deputy of the Duma) saw people receiving Holy Communion to the accompaniment of the moving sounds of the Eucharistic hymn . . . I rushed out of the church in tears and crying walked along the streets of Moscow, exhausted with my own impotence and unworthiness. And so it went on till a firm hand lifted me up . . .

"Autumn. A solitary hermitage lost in the forest. A sunny day and the familiar northern landscape. My heart was still prey to confusion and impotence. I seized an opportunity of coming here in the secret hope of encountering God. But here my determination left me completely... I stood during the Evensong, insensible and cold, and after it, when the prayers 'preparatory to confession' began, I nearly ran out of the church, went out, weeping bitterly. I walked, full of anguish, without seeing anything around me, toward the hostel, and came to my senses... in the old hermit's cell. I was *drawn* thither: I had taken the wrong direction owing to my usual absent-mindedness which was now still increased by depression, but in reality—I knew it for sure—a miracle happened to me... The hermit, on seeing the prodigal son approach, once more hurried out to meet him. From him I learned that all human sins were like a drop in the ocean of God's mercy. I left him forgiven and reconciled, trembling and in tears, feeling as if I were carried on wings inside the church gate. In the doorway I met my companion who had just before seen me leave the church in dismay—he was surprised and overjoyed. He became an involuntary witness of that which happened to me—'the Lord has passed,' he used to say feelingly afterwards.

"It was evening again, and sunset, no longer the southern, but the northern. The Church domes were sharply outlined in the transparent air, and the long rows of the autumn monastery flowers showed white in the dusk. The forest receded into the bluish distance. Suddenly, amid that silence, somewhere from above, as if from Heaven, came a stroke of the church bell, then all was still, and only somewhat later it began to peal regularly and ceaselessly. They were ringing for Evensong. As if for the first time, like one newly born, did I listen to the church bells, feeling, with my heart aflutter, that it called me, too, to the church of the faithful. And on the evening of that blessed day, and still more the next day at the liturgy I looked at everything with new eyes, for I knew that I too was called, that I too was actually taking part in it all, that for me and for my sake, too, our Lord had hung on the Cross and shed His sacred blood, for me, too, the holiest meal was being prepared here by the hands of the priest, and the Gospel story of the supper at the house of Simon the Leper and of the pardoning of the woman sinner who had loved much, concerned me too, and I was given to partake of the sacred Body and Blood of my Lord...

"Thus, at the basis of religion lies a personally experienced encounter with the Deity, and therein is the only source of its autonomy. However the wisdom of this age may boast, incapable as it is of understanding religion owing to lack of necessary experience and to religious ineptitude and lifelessness, those who have once contemplated God in their heart, possess an absolutely sure knowledge of religion, know its essence."[1]

While lecturing on political economy Bulgakov was gradually veering round from marxism to idealism and then to Orthodoxy. Up to 1911 he wrote several essays on the meaning of history, on the shortcomings of the "scientific" atheistic socialism, on the character of Russian intelligentsia, on the early centuries of Christianity and its victory over paganism. Between 1911 and 1916 he wrote his chief religiously philosophic work *The Unfading Light*. Something should first be said about the preceding essays, collected in the two volumes entitled, respectively, *From Marxism to Idealism* (Petersburg 1904) and *Two Cities* (Moscow 1911). Bulgakov formulates the conclusions arrived at in the first volume as follows: "I began simply as a writer on social questions, but in investigating the basis of social ideals, I discovered that that basis is to be found in religion. Is there Goodness? Is there Truth? In other words, is there God?"[2]

"There are two main paths of religious self-determination," says Bulgakov: "Theism culminating in Christianity, and pantheism culminating in the worship of man and anti-Christianity" (*Two Cities*, p. IX). Corresponding to these two paths the historical process is the expression of the free activity of the human spirit, and is a struggle between the two Cities—of the other—worldly Kingdom of Christ and the earthly, this world's kingdom of the antichrist. In the passionately religious Russian soul, lacking in cultural self-discipline, the conflict between those two principles is particularly violent and destructive, giving rise on the one hand to dark, reactionary fanaticism, which mistakes itself for Christianity, and on the other to equally fanatical self-deification of man" (p. XVIII).

At our epoch the chief expression of the self-deification of man is the socialism of Marx. Having emancipated himself from Marxism Bulgakov analyzed its religiously philosophical basis, derived by Marx from Feuerbach. In his article "Feuerbach's Religion of Man-Worship" he unfolds and criticizes Feuerbach's main idea expressed in the formula *homo homini Deus est,* meaning that "mankind is the god of the individual man" (17). The analysis is continued in the article "Karl Marx as a Religious Thinker." In speaking of Marx's personal character, Bulgakov vividly describes Marx's will to power and shows that his prevalent feature was hatred rather than love. Following Annenkov he calls Marx a "democratic dictator" and notes his "unceremonious atti-

---

1. Bulgakov, *The Unfading Light,* 7–11; see also 12–14; see further *Jacob's Ladder,* 21, 31 ff.
2. The Author's foreword to the *Two Cities,* p. VII.

tude to the human individuality." "From Marx's point of view men fall into sociological groups, and those groups in an orderly and well-regulated fashion form geometrical patterns, as though human history contained nothing but this measured movement of sociological elements. This abolition of the problem of personality and of the care for it, this extreme abstraction is the fundamental feature of Marxism" (75). Marx "is not troubled by the fate of the individual," he values in man that only "which is common to all individuals and therefore is not individual in them" (76). Marx says that in a socialistic society "man will become a generic being (*Gattungswesen*) and then he will emancipate himself from religion" (93 f.). Marx is bitterly hostile to religion, especially to Christianity. Bulgakov explains this by the fact that "Christianity awakens personality, makes man conscious of his immortal spirit; it individualizes man, pointing out to him the goal of inner development and the way to it; socialism depersonalizes man in so far as it is concerned not with the human soul but with its social exterior, and reduces the actual content of personality to social reflexes" (II, 30). Militant atheism is one of the means of destroying individuality and transforming human society "into an ant heap or a beehive" (I, 94). The attempt to put man in the place of God and to glorify him as a man-god may easily lead, says Bulgakov, to transforming him into a man-beast (173).

In 1873 Marx declared himself to be a disciple of Hegel. Bulgakov proves that "there is no link of succession between German classical idealism and Marxism. Marx's Hegelianism goes no further than verbal imitation of Hegel's peculiar style." In Bulgakov's opinion it was a kind of caprice or perhaps coquetry on Marx's part to regard himself as a disciple of Hegel. In his articles "Primitive Christianity and Modern Socialism" (1909) and "Apocalyptics and Socialism" (1910) Bulgakov compares Marx's socialism with the Jewish chiliastic utopia (chiliasm is the name of the millennium utopia—the thousand years of the reign of saints upon the earth). Confusion between the two planes, the eschatological and the chiliastic, says Bulgakov, imparted to the apocalyptic doctrine "the specific character that made it so fatal in the history of the Jewish people, blunting their sense of actuality and historical realism, blinding them with utopias, developing in them an adventuresome attitude to religion and a tendency to clamor for miracles" (II, 79). Belief in progress has a chiliastic character and "for many people plays the part of an immanent religion," especially at our time (76). That is true of Marx's socialism. Bulgakov says that "socialism is a rationalistic adaptation of Jewish chiliasm, translated from the language of theology and cosmology into that of political economy, and all its *dramatis per-*

sonae are therefore interpreted in terms of economics. The chosen people—the bearer of the messianic idea—or, as later in the Christian sects, the saints or the elect, are replaced by the proletariat that has a special proletarian soul and a special revolutionary mission. The part of Satan and Belial naturally fell to the lot of capitalists, promoted to the rank of representatives of the metaphysical evil. To the last sorrows and messianic agonies there corresponds the inevitable and ever-increasing impoverishment of the workers and the increasing antagonism between the classes. In keeping with the spirit of the times and its beloved scientific-sounding mythology, the part of *deus ex machina*, facilitating the transition to chiliasm is played in socialism by the 'laws' of social development or of the growth of productive forces which, first, prepare that transition and then, at a certain stage of the process, by virtue of its 'immanent and inevitable dialectics' forcibly bring about the transition to socialism and ordain the jump from the realm of necessity into the realm of freedom" (116–118). The emotional strain in socialism and its eschatology (the jump into the realm of freedom) shows that "socialism has both its apocalypse and its mysticism, familiar to everyone who has lived through it" (39). The religious enthusiasm of Marxism in conjunction with materialism is "utterly self-contradictory: personality is transformed into an impersonal complex of economic relations and at the same time is deified and made into a man-god" (41). "In socialism, and indeed along the whole line of our civilization, struggle is waged between Christ and antichrist" (I, 104).

The success of socialism in our time is, in Bulgakov's opinion, "a punishment for the sins of historical Christianity and a menacing call for repentance" (II, 16). Christians had taken too little care to reform the economic system in the spirit of social justice: practical socialism, Bulgakov wrote in 1909, is "a means of realizing the demands of Christian ethics" (35, 45 f.). This certainly does not imply that in his view socialism would give mankind final satisfaction. "In history there may be progress, growth of civilization, increase in material welfare," he says, "and yet the immanent result of history is not harmony but tragedy, a final segregation of good and of evil and thus a final intensification of the cosmic tragedy" (106). A personality striving for the absolute good can find complete satisfaction only in the Kingdom of God, after the transfiguration of the world, and therefore not in the historical process but in *metahistory* (103).

Having gone through the revolution of 1905 people with a sensitive conscience noticed the satanic aspect of the revolutionary movement and pondered over the part played in it by the intellectuals. Bulgakov wrote a number of essays on the character, the faults and the merits of the Russian intellectuals, reprinted in the second volume of the *Two Cities* under the general title "The Religion of Man-Worship Among the Russian Intelligentsia." The most important of those essays, "Heroism and Asceticism," was first published in the symposium *Vehi* (Signposts). Bulgakov says in it that "not in a single country in Europe are the intellectuals as a body so utterly indifferent to religion as in Russia." They replaced religion by faith in science and by the striving, noted by Dostoevsky, "to settle down without God finally and forever." As a member of the second Duma, Bulgakov watched its political activity and "clearly saw how remote those men were from politics in the proper sense; i.e., from the prosaic everyday work of keeping the machinery of the state oiled and in good repair. Their psychology was not that of politicians, of sound realists and believers in gradual improvement—no, it was the psychology of impatient, ardent visionaries, looking for the realization of the Kingdom of God on earth in the immediate future. They remind one of the anabaptists and other medieval sectarians, awaiting the speedy coming of the millennium and preparing the way for it by the sword, by popular risings, communistic experiments and peasant wars; one thinks of John of Leiden with his retinue of prophets at Münster. Of course the likeness is only in the psychology and not in the ideas. As far as ideas go, Russia reflects the theories and tendencies of the present age even more strongly and uncompromisingly than Western Europe, and it reflects too the cosmic drama of apostasy and struggle against God, which lie at the core of modern history" (135 f.).

External historical conditions developed in the Russian intellectuals "a religious frame of mind, sometimes actually approaching the Christian." Government persecutions made them feel "like martyrs and confessors," and the enforced remoteness from life furthered "dreaminess, utopianism, and altogether an insufficient sense of reality" (180). Bulgakov draws attention to the intelligentsia's dislike of "the petty bourgeois spirit" and to its spiritual traditions inherited from the Church, such as "a certain puritanism, moral strictness, a peculiar kind of asceticism and, generally speaking, the high tenor of personal life," giving as examples the lives of such "leaders of the Russian intelligentsia as Dobrolyubov and Chernyshevsky" (182). "Russian intellectuals, especially of the former generations, had also a sense of guilt towards the peasants" (182). A Russian intellectual dreams to be "a saviour of humanity or at any rate of the Russian people. What is necessary to him (in his dreams, that is) is not a safe minimum but a heroic maximum. Maximalism is an inalienable feature of the intellectuals' heroism which is somewhat akin to autosuggestion and to being possessed by an idea, and leads to enslavement of thought and to fanaticism deaf to the voice of life;" accordingly "it was the most extreme tendencies that triumphed in the revolution" (191 f.).

In its further development atheistic humanism degenerates and leads to self-deification, to "putting oneself in the place of God and Providence—not only in respect of plans and ends but also of the ways and means of their realization. I am realizing my idea and for its sake set myself free from the fetters of customary morality, I give myself the right not merely to the property but to the life and death of others, should that be required by my idea." The next stage of self-deification is that the heroic "all things are permissible is imperceptibly replaced by simple absence of any principles of conduct in all that concerns personal life" (198).

Leaving aside the extreme perversions of the religion of manworship Bulgakov sums up as follows his evaluation of the Russian intelligentsia: "Side by side with the antichrist element there live in it the highest religious possibilities. That intense seeking for the City of God, the striving to carry out God's will on earth as in heaven, are profoundly different from the pursuit of stable earthly welfare characteristic of the bourgeois culture. The absurd maximalism of the intelligentsia utterly inapplicable in practice, is a consequence of religious perversion, but it may be overcome through religious recovery." The suffering image of the Russian intelligentsia "bears traces of spiritual beauty which liken it to some quite special, tender and precious flower grown by our gloomy history" (221).

This judgement of Bulgakov's will be resolutely opposed by Russians whose spirit has been so deeply wounded by the Bolshevik revolution that they came to hate the intelligentsia and can see nothing but its defects. The extreme injustice of their attitude will be obvious to all who know that Russian culture at the end of the nineteenth and the beginning of the twentieth centuries was very high indeed and that its great attainments were due precisely to the intelligentsia. Everyone knows of the greatness of the Russian literature, music and theatrical art, and I am not speaking of that; I am referring to the aspects of Russian culture unknown to the Western world. Russian municipal and rural self-government was developing rapidly and along original lines; the law courts after the reform of Alexander II were better than the Western European and the American; the gifted and self-sacrificing work of the Russian doctors is gratefully remembered by the older generations; mention should also be made of the educational movement on which Russian intellectuals were very keen and which led to the formation of many private schools with the most advanced methods of teaching and training; the Russian universities, especially those of Moscow and Petersburg were on the level of the best universities of Western Europe. Those who know and remember this will agree that the Russian intelligentsia was indeed "a precious and tender flower."

Believing as he does in the providential significance of every historical process, Bulgakov tries to find the meaning of European culture passing through a period of man-worship. He finds it in the fact that the Christian religion must be freely and consciously adopted by the human mind. "History comes to real fruition only in the free triumph of the divine principle in free human creativeness; this is implied by the divinely human character of the historical process" (I, 176).

In his articles about Christianity written at that period of his activity, Bulgakov says a great deal about the relation of Christianity to social problems and about the historical significance of Christianity for the development of culture and economics. He particularly insists that in our time too the Church must take a creative part in every domain of cultural life. Bulgakov compares the attitude of church people in our "nonecclesiastical and even antiecclesiastical humanistic age" to the attitude of the prodigal son's brother in the parable "who met his younger brother with distinct hostility. Though strict and faithful in their service they have adopted a haughtily distrustful and pharisaically formal attitude to their younger brother who in spite of 'having sinned before heaven and before the Father' during his wanderings preserved a warm and open heart. That comparison will probably offend many church people of the old style," Bulgakov goes on. "They conceive the Church as the complete fullness of gracious gifts which must merely be preserved in accordance with tradition, so that it is out of place in their opinion to speak of any new creativeness. We are opposed to this interpretation, according to which the function of the Church is merely to guard and preserve the tradition, the ideal of a creative, growing, developing Church" (306 f.). In Bulgakov's view, even the formulation of dogmas must continue till the end of history (I, 271). The Head of the Church, the God-man Christ is not subject to the historical process of development, but earthly humanity, which forms part of the Church, rises only gradually through a process of development "to the sphere of God's Kingdom" (II, 309). In the course of that ascent toward perfection there must be worked out "a truly Christian, ecclesiastical culture" embracing all aspects of life, science, philosophy, art, social organization. "If social life were at last made to conform to the Christian Church ideal, socialism would lose its present deadly character, conditioned by its narrow class basis; it would be a living embodiment of the universal Christian love and would no longer lead to the spiritual devastation which the narrowness of its doctrine brings about in the hearts and minds of its adherents" (312). Those ideas are expressed with particular vividness in the article "Church and Culture," a good example of Bulgakov's gifts as a writer.

Bulgakov's main religiously philosophical work, *The Unfading Light*, written before he had taken holy orders, begins with a general consideration of the "nature of the religious consciousness." In the author's view the basic feature of that consciousness is faith. "It is a free, two-sided, divinely human act: on the one hand it is man's subjective striving, his search for God, and on the other, it is God's answer, His *objective revelation*" (29). "The religious truth being objective and *catholic*—i.e., conformable to the whole—is at the same time *communal*. Its communal character means not merely that it is proclaimed by a council, but rather that those who seek God attain unity in the whole and all-embracing truth" (55). The substitution of religious individualism for catholicity is a consequence either of spiritual unripeness or of morbid decadence. "The most difficult thing of all is to believe in truth because it is true; i.e., because it demands humble recognition and self-abnegation; it is far easier to accept that truth as *my opinion* which *I* posit as truth" (54 f.). Religious truth revealed in the mystical experience is "unutterable but that does not mean that it is wordless, alogical or antilogical; on the contrary, it ever seeks utterance, giving rise to verbal symbols for its embodiment." Bulgakov points out the enormous significance "of the ecclesiastical tradition of the *historical* church, expressed in dogmas, cult and ways of living, which, in the name of the mystical church and frequently in the name of its personal mysticism, always moderates unauthorized claims. We find here a certain antinomy: bare historicity, external authority in religion, means so to speak the ossification of the church, while self-willed mysticism means its dissolution; neither is needed, and yet both are needed—both ecclesiastical authority and personal mysticism" (64). "The stern and manly nature of dogmas" makes it possible to preach religion and not only "to grow numb in the sweet langor of mystical experience" (73). But of course, dogmatic formulae made up of concepts never express "the fullness of religious experience" (70) and therefore in the life of the Church new dogmas must always be fashioned to supplement those already formulated.

Criticizing the doctrines of Kant, Fichte, Tolstoy and others who reduce religion to ethics Bulgakov speaks of conscience as of a light proceeding from God for the discrimination between good and evil; he expresses that idea with wonderful force in a kind of prayer or description of mystical experience beginning with the words "Thou seest me always" (46).

Following Florensky, Bulgakov accepts the doctrine of the antinomic character of the religious consciousness and makes use of it in various ways. The first section of his chief work *The Unfading Light* is entitled "The Divine Nothing" and is devoted to a detailed examination of the fundamental antinomy of God's transcendence of, and immanence in, the world. On the one hand the Absolute is the Divine Nothing that transcends the world (hence the "negative" or apophatic theology), on the other hand it "posits itself as God and consequently renders possible the distinction between God and the world, and man in it; the Absolute becomes God for man" and thus "God is born with the world and in the world, *incipit religio*. Hence the possibility of defining God as immanently transcendent, as coming out of His transcendence and absoluteness into immanence and a certain dualism. Hence the possibility of knowing God and communing with Him, of entering the domain of positive theology (cataphatic theology) and the need for dogmas and myths" (102).

"Religious philosophy," says Bulgakov, "has no problem more vital than that of the meaning of the Divine Nothing" (146). He therefore expounds in detail various conceptions of the Divine Nothing, beginning with Plato and Plotinus and going on to the teachings of the Eastern Fathers and of Western philosophy (Eriugena, Nicolas of Cusa, G. Bruno, Eckehart, Jacob Boehme and others). Even in the works of Thomas Aquinas he finds a passage wholly in the spirit of negative theology.

Bulgakov points out the profound difference between the doctrine of the Divine Nothing in the sense of the Greek ἀ *privativum* and in the sense of μή. The first implies the impossibility of definition as a matter of principle; the second indicates a state of potentiality, of being yet unmanifested. The first doctrine leads to an *antinomic* religious philosophy, opposed to pantheism; the second is the dialectic philosophy of evolution, leading to pantheism. In the first case "God as the Absolute is completely free from the world;" in the second He is necessarily connected with the world. According to the first doctrine, "no self-purification or withdrawal into its own depths (Eckehart's *Abgeschiedenheit*) will enable immanent self-consciousness to overcome its relative character and become absolute or find itself in God through drowning itself in Him, so to speak, and getting rid of all Maya." Man and the world become divine not through the power of divinity which they possess as creatures, but through the power of grace that is poured out into the world; man may become god not by virtue of his own nature as a creature, but only god by grace (according to the well-known definition of the Fathers of the Church)" (150). "True religion is based upon revelation; i.e., upon the Deity coming down to the World, voluntarily entering it and approaching man; in other words, it is bound to be the work of grace, of a supernatural or supercosmic activity of God in man" (151). God as a Person "is known only through *meeting* Him, through His living revelation of Himself" in the religious experience. As to the Christian dogma of God as Tripersonal, it can, in the first instance be known only through the Revelation (151 f.).

"It is possible to distinguish three ways of attaining the religious consciousness: the knowledge of God may be gained *more geometrico* or *analytico, more naturali* or *mystico* and *more historico* or *empirico*— i.e., by abstract thought, mystic self-absorption, and religious revelation; the first two ways acquire their rightful significance only in connection with the third and become false if accepted in their separateness" (151). This is the source of such false doctrines as the emanational pantheism of Plotinus, Erigena, Boehme, Eckehart, of the acosmism and anticosmism of the Hindu philosophy and religion, or, in Europe, of the philosophy of Schopenhauer, of the dynamic-pantheism of E. Hartmann and Drews, of the logical pantheism of Hegel, etc. In discussing these theories, Bulgakov remarks that "the Germanic genius seems to be doomed to distort Christianity in the direction of religious monism, pantheism, buddhism, neo-platonism, immanentism" (162).

The only way to avoid the errors of pantheism and religious immanentism, says Bulgakov, is to admit that the transition from the Absolute to the relative is effected by the creation of the world out of nothing. The act of creation "is the transformation of the οὐκ ὄν into the μὴ ὄν. The word οὐκ ὄν means here non-being in the sense of emptiness or absence of being, and μὴ ὄν means being which is as yet completely indefinite. "The transformation of the οὐκ ὄν into the μὴ ὄν is the creation of the universal matter of the cosmos, of the Great Mother of all the natural world. In and through the act of creation God posits being in the non-being, or, in other words, through the same act He posits non-being together with being as its limit, its accompaniment or shadow" (184). This does not imply, however, that the world is entirely new being, alongside and outside of God. Here as elsewhere Bulgakov tries to unite opposites. The world, he says, "is penetrated through and through by divine energies which form the basis of its being" (148). "Creation is emanation, a plus, something new, created by the Divine *fiat*" (178). "By the side of the Absolute which is above existence there appears existence in which the Absolute reveals Itself as Creator, manifesting or realizing Itself in it; the Absolute thus actually takes part in existence, and, in this sense, the world is God as *becoming*. God exists only in and for the world; in the absolute sense one cannot speak of

Him as existing. By the very act of creating the world God throws Himself into it, and as it were, makes Himself a creature" (193). The world is thus both a *theophany* and a *theogony* (192). Bulgakov goes so far as to say that "the creation by the Absolute of the relative is a self-division of the Absolute" (179). In developing this conception Bulgakov, like Vladimir Soloviev, is guided by the conviction that the Absolute must be pan-unity. He believes that being which was external to God, which existed alongside of Him would limit Him (148). He thinks that his doctrine provides a solution of the cosmological antinomy that lies midway between two errors—pantheistic monism and manichean dualism (194).

The antinomic character of the divine and the earthly principles appears to be even more complex when we come to deal with Bulgakov's doctrine of St. Sophia, first as it is expounded in *The Unfading Light*. St. Sophia is the boundary *between* God and the world, between the Creator and the creation, herself being neither the one nor the other. She is the Divine "Idea," the object of God's love, the love of Love. "Sophia is loved and loves in return, and through this reciprocal love she receives all, *is all*" (212)—the *ens realissimum,* Pan-Unity (214). Sophia's love differs profoundly from the love of the divine hypostases: she "merely receives, having nothing to give, she contains only that which she has taken. By giving herself up to the Divine Love she conceives everything in herself. In this sense she is Feminine and receptive; she is the Eternal Feminine" and "may perhaps be said to be a 'goddess,' though certainly not in the pagan sense of the term. As receiving her essence from the Father she is the creature and the daughter of God; as knowing the Divine Logos and known by Him she is the bride of the Son (the Song of Songs) and the spouse of the Lamb (the Gospels, the Apocalypse); as receiving the outpouring of the gifts of the Holy Spirit she is the Church and at the same time the Mother of the Son who incarnates by the Holy Ghost of Mary, the Heart of the Church; and she is also the ideal Soul of creation—Beauty. All this together—the Daughter and the Bride, the Wife, and the Mother, the triunity of goodness, truth and beauty, the Holy Trinity in the world—is the divine Sophia" (213c.). Being above creation she is the Fourth Hypostasis, but since she does not take part in the intradivine life, the Trinity does not become a quaternity (212).

In relation to the world-manifold Sophia is the organic unity of the Ideas of all creatures. Every being has its Idea, which is both its basis and its norm and entelechy, and Sophia as a whole, "in her cosmic aspect," is the entelechy of the world, the world soul, "*natura naturans* in relation to the *natura naturata*" (213, 223). Every creature on its positive side may therefore be called Sophian; but creatures have another, a negative side, a lower "substratum," namely, *matter* as *nothing*, as blank, empty non-being. That is not the nothing which we know as an aspect of being or even as its shadow. No, what is meant here is the complete nothing which God called into being. "How light came to shine in this outer and total darkness, how being was sown in the absolute nothing, is the unfathomable act of God's wisdom and omnipotence —of His creative fiat" (234).

As already said, the universal matter of the world is the οὐκ ὄν transformed into the μὴ ὄν (184). Material being in which non-being is present is characterized by mutual limitation and division; it is "individual in the bad sense: the basis of individualism here is dividedness, fragmentariness;" it is the negative sense of individuality. "The ideal, Sophian world remains on the other side of such being-non-being; in other words there is no place in it for matter-as-nothing" (237); "it contains all *principia individuationis* in the *positive* sense, as unique principles of being, rays in the spectrum of the Sophian pleroma. But as they enter the world of being-non-being, the *kenoma* of materiality, they become associated with *principia individuationis* in the negative sense" (238). "The act of the world creation is realized through the making of heaven and earth in the Beginning, through the formation of two centers in Sophia" (239). The Earth created by God is not the "matter" of Greek philosophy, but it is "nothing which has already received the outpouring of Sophian-ness and is therefore a potential Sophia. The nothing has received actual being and has become Chaos, a real ἄπειρον spoken of in the Greek, Babylonian and other mythologies. That is 'the native Chaos,' in the words of the poet 'stirring' under the surface of being and sometimes breaking through as a destructive power. The creation of the earth lies *outside* the six days of creation and is its ontological *prius*." The separation of light from darkness, the appearance of the heavenly bodies, plants, animals—"all that is the work of God's creative word and is called forth not out of nothing but out of the earth, as a gradual unfolding of its Sophian content, of its ideal fullness. That 'earth' is therefore, as it were, 'a cosmic Sophia' (239 f.), the feminine principle of the created world. She is the Great Mother piously worshipped of old by the Gentiles: Demeter, Isis, Cybile, Ishtar. And that earth is potentially divine, that mother at its very creation contains within its depths the future Mother of God, the womb of the divine incarnation" (245).

The creation of the world in Sophia is *"the separation of Sophia's potentiality from her eternal actuality,* which gives rise to time and the temporal process; the actualization of Sophian potentiality forms the content of that process" (223). The cosmic process takes place by virtue of "the earth's eros for heaven. All creature is longing for liberation from bondage of corruption, for the radiance of Sophian light, for beauty and transfiguration" (242). That purpose is achieved under the guidance of Sophia as the World Soul. "She is the universal, instinctively unconscious or superconscious soul of the world, *anima mundi*, manifesting itself in the wonderful purposiveness of the structure of organisms and the unconscious functions and instincts of generic origin" (223). The world is animated throughout and is "a great hierarchy of ideal entities, an ideal organism, and the great merit of occultism (including under that heading fairy tales, legends, folklore, beliefs and superstitions) is its apprehension of the Sophian nature of the 'lifeless world,' akin to the poetic apprehension of nature in general. The same may be said to a certain extent of naturalistic pagan politheism which is so to speak a religious paraphrase of the doctrine of the Sophian nature of the world and of all creation being animate" (230). "Platonic ideas-qualities are known to the people's mythological consciousness and are reflected in its sagas, fairy tales, folklore: that lies at the root of charms, incantations, spells, of totems and other animal symbolism which plays such an important part in all religions including Judaeo-Christianity" (230).

In speaking of Ideas Bulgakov like Florensky dwells upon the difference between ideas and concepts. "In an idea both the general and the individual exist as a simple whole: the individual entity's generic personality and the collective individuality of the genus are united in it. In its *idea* the genus exists both as a unity and as the fullness of all its individual members in their uniqueness, and that unity exists not only *in abstracto*, but *in concreto*." This is particularly applicable to man. "Mankind is truly a single Adam, the old and the new, the first-created and the regenerated in Christ; and the words of Lord Jesus that He is Himself present in the hungry and the thirsty and the prisoners and in the whole of the suffering humanity must be accepted in their full significance. But at the same time, equal reality attaches to individualization, to the contrast between separate human beings as individuals and the Christ-humanity in them" (231).

The theory that there exist two Sophias, the Divine and the created, is hinted at in the *Unfading Light* and is expounded at length in the *Agnus Dei, The Comforter* and *The Bride of the Lamb*. Bulgakov bases his doctrine of the Divine Sophia on the difference between the conceptions of the Divine personality and Divine nature (*ousia*). He says "spirit has personality and nature;" the Divine spirit "has a triune personality and one nature which may be called *ousia* or Deity. The divine nature is the Divine life, *ens realissimum;* i.e., positive pan-unity including within itself "all, for no limitations of any kind are befitting with regard to Deity." That "all-qualitative All-in-unity is God in His self-revelation, is that which in the Scriptures is called the Wisdom of God, Sophia" *(Agnus Dei,* 124 f.).

The Divine Sophia has significance not only for God as His life but for man too, and through him for all creation as his archetype: "man is created by God in God's image, and that image is *ens realissimum* in man, who becomes through it a created God" (135). "Divine Sophia as the panorganism of Ideas is the eternal humanity in God, as the Divine archetype and basis of man's being." There exists a certain "analogical identity" between God and man, archetype and image. The Logos in Whom the Divine Sophia is hypostasied is the eternal Man, the Heavenly Man, the Son of God and the Son of Man (136 f.). Sophia as Deity in God is "the Image of God in God Himself, the realized divine idea, the idea of all ideas realized as beauty" (126). God's relation to the Divine Sophia is love: "in Sophia God loves Himself in His self-revelation, and Sophia loves the personal God Who is Love with a reciprocal love" (127). "She is a live and living entity, though not a *personal* one" (128). The Divine Sophia is not a person and yet she is not outside personality: her hypostasis is the Logos Who reveals the Father as a demiurgic hypostasis (136). The Logos in Whom the Divine Sophia is hypostacized is the Eternal man, the Heavenly man, the Son of God and the Son of Man" (137).

The created Sophia is an entity closely akin to the Divine Sophia. "Everything in the Divine and the created world, in the Divine and the created Sophia is identical in content (though not in the manner of being)" writes Father Sergius Bulgakov. "One and the same Sophia is revealed both in God and in creation. The negative statement that God created the world out of nothing does away with the conception of any nondivine or extradivine principle in creation; but its positive implication can only be that God created the world through Himself out of His nature. Metaphysically the creation of the world consists in God's positing His own divine world not as eternally being but as becoming. In that sense He diluted it with nothing, by plunging it into becoming. The Divine Sophia became also the created Sophia. God, so to speak, repeated Himself in creation, mirrored Himself in non-being" (148, 149). "The positive content of cosmic being is as divine as is its basis in God" (148).

Thus, the positive content of the world is not created by God anew: it is identical with the content which is in God already. Besides, the further development of the world is the work of God Himself—the

Holy Spirit: "the power of life and development is the power of the Holy Spirit in nature, the natural grace of life. One must understand and accept this natural grace of creation, inseverable from the natural world, without fearing apparent paganism or pantheism, the alternative to which is, in fact, empty and deadly deism separating the Creator from the creature" (*The Comforter*, 24).

"Every creature must be recognized as Sophian in so far as its positive content or its idea, which is its basis and norm, is concerned; but it should not be forgotten that creatures have another aspect—the lower 'substratum' of the world, matter as 'nothing' raised to the level of the μὴ ὄν and striving to embody the Sophian principle in itself" (*The Unfading Light*, 234, 242).

The conception of incarnation is fundamental for the Christian metaphysics. It necessitates a distinction being drawn between the ideas of materiality and corporeality. In Bulgakov's view the essence of corporeality is "sensibility as a distinct and independent element of life, different from spirit but by no means opposed or alien to it" (249). "It is different from thought and will, does not admit of any logical determinations, and can only be apprehended through sensation. Corporeality is essential to everything that may be called real; even Ideas that belong to the intelligible world of Sophia must be concretely qualified by having a body. There are many species of corporeality, beginning with our coarse, material one and ending with the transfigured spirit-bearing corporeality. There may be bodies of different degrees of refinement, 'astral, mental, etheric,' etc." (251). Once, observing that Father Sergius was not well, I asked him what was ailing him, and he answered "my astral is out of joint."

The high significance of corporeality is manifested in the fact that it is the condition of beauty. "Spiritual sensibility or the perceptible character of Ideas is Beauty. Beauty is as much an absolute principle of the world as the Logos. It is the revelation of the Third Hypostasis, the Holy Spirit" (251). "Beauty is the sinless, the holy sensibility, the perceptibility of Ideas. Beauty cannot be confined to any one sense, such as vision, for instance. All our senses are capable of apprehending beauty—not only vision, but also hearing, smell, taste and touch" (252).

Bulgakov's teaching about Ideas being embodied reflects a characteristic feature of the Russian philosophy—its concreteness, which I already pointed out in dealing with Florensky.

In Father Bulgakov's theological work *Jacob's Ladder* the doctrine of the concreteness of Ideas reaches its consummation. In this work which deals with angelology Bulgakov comes to affirm that angels, in particular the guardian angels of individual people, churches, nations, elements, etc., are members of the Created Sophia and correspond to the principle which Plato designates as the Ideas. "The truth of Platonism," says Bulgakov, "is revealed only in angelology as a doctrine of Heaven and earth in their mutual relationship;" Plato's Ideas "exist not as logical abstractions and schemes of things, but as personal substances, the angels of the Word" (118 ff.).

Bulgakov's doctrine of the angels is a logical consummation of Florensky's ideas as set forth above. Florensky works out his conception of Platonism through philosophical reasoning, while Bulgakov does it on the path of theological investigation, namely by analyzing the texts of the Scriptures, as well as liturgical and ikonographic data. The fact that the same results are arrived at by such different methods shows that "all the roads lead to Rome," that truth can be attained by very different methods. There is nothing surprising in this: Bulgakov's theological method consists in making use of the *religious experience,* and moreover not of the individual but of the collective experience of the Church. In speaking of "truth attained" in this connection, I mean Bulgakov's and Florensky's teaching about the higher beings standing at the head of different departments of the world, and not their interpretation of Plato, which is utterly untenable.

Connected with the same feature of the Russian philosophy—its concreteness—is Bulgakov's defense of the cult of ikons, so essential to Orthodoxy. In his book *The Ikon and its Cult* he demonstrates the difficulty of advocating ikon worship which remains theologically unjustified, for the ikonoclasts proceeded from the obviously right thesis of the imagelessness of Godhead; basing themselves on the dogma that in Christ there was no division of substance or confusion of persons they asserted that an image of His body was not an image of His Godhead and therefore not an ikon of Christ (24). Bulgakov gets over the difficulty by setting up three pairs of antinomies (54)—the *theological* (God is the Divine Nothing, God is the Holy Trinity), the *cosmological* (God in Himself, God in creation), and the *sophiological* (Uncreated Sophia—Deity in God; Created Sophia—Deity outside God, in the world). Bulgakov solves the problem of the ikon by working out the implications of his doctrine of the Uncreated Sophia as God's image which is at the same time the original image of creation; all creatures, and especially man, being created after the image of God, are therefore, in their positive characteristics, a living Ikon of the Deity (83). Consequently, Christ, a new Adam, "in His flesh took on His own image of Heavenly Adam, His ikon" (92). The task of the ikonographer, while representing Christ's body, consists in expressing some of the numberless aspects of God the Word Who is the Image of images and the Idea of ideas (93).

In framing a theory concerning the incarnation of ideal principles, it is essential to give an account of the still more mysterious incarnation of God the Word Himself, the Second Person of the Holy Trinity. Why did it happen, and how is it possible? An answer to that question can be given in connection with the answer to the problem of evil and of liberation from it.

Neither matter nor body as the vehicle of sensibility is evil, and, indeed, as originally created the world contains no evil at all; it is simply in the state of childish incompleteness and there lies before it the task of "making its Sophian character actual" (*The Unfading Light*, 250). Evil is a deviation from this path; it is the result of the self-will of the creatures that use the powers of being in order to make actual the non-being which is the world's substratum; evil is therefore a non-Sophian or an anti-Sophian parasite of being (263). For such "poisoned being" death, i.e., return to the earth with the hope of resurrection and of the life of the world to come is a blessing and not a calamity (262).

The resurrection and transfiguration of all creatures is bound up with the incarnation of God the Word as the man Jesus Christ. Man thus plays a central part in the life of the world. This is due to the fact that man is made in the image of God. He is a personality, a hypostasis, his nature cannot be exhausted by any definition. Man has an aspect of "uncreatedness." "Having created man's body out of the dust of the ground—i.e., having united him to the created nature as man's own world—God "breathed into his nostrils the breath of life; and man became a living soul" (Gen. 2, 7) (*Agnus Dei*, 114 f.). The spirit is uncreated in the two senses of that term: first, as the ray of God's own glory, and secondly as the self-positing ego: "In calling His own breath to personal being and hypostasying the rays of His own glory, God accomplishes it by one eternal act together with the personality itself. God's creative act asks, as it were, the created self whether it is a self, whether it has in it the will to live, and hears the creation's 'yea' in response" (114 f.). "Thus, man is both uncreated and created" (197); he is absolute in the relative and relative in the absolute" (*The Unfading Light*, 278). Man is a microcosm: all the world's elements are to be found in him. "In its psychic pan-organism the human spirit has found and become conscious of all that is living. Contrary to the Darwinian theory, man is not descended from the lower species, but includes them in himself: man is pan-animal, and contains as it were the whole program of creation. There is to be found in him eagle-ness, and lion-ness and other psychic qualities that form the basis of the animal world—that spectrum into which the white light of humanity may be broken up. This is the explanation of the partial truth of totemism and of the combination of the human and animal forms in the images of the Egyptian gods" (286). It is one of the many instances of what Bulgakov calls the mystic clearsightedness of paganism, which sees gods where our "scientific" consciousness can only detect lifeless forces of nature (326). Generally speaking, paganism "may be said to be the cognition of the invisible through the visible, of God through the world, the revelation of the Deity in the creation. It is animated by many motives and is wider in scope than the Old or even the New Testament, which contains the promise of a Comforter who is still to come. Paganism has a living presentiment of 'holy corporeality' and of the revelation of the Holy Spirit" (330). There is religious truth, too, in the pagan worship of divine motherhood. "The similarity between Isis weeping over Osiris and the Mother of God bending over the body of the Saviour" (332) does not disturb Bulgakov; he thinks that the problem of the feminine hypostasis of the Deity is a mystery that has not as yet received sufficient consideration in Christianity (331). But in paganism these glimpses of truth assume the mistaken form of pantheistic naturalism, while in Christianity emphasis is laid on the fundamental antinomy of the religious consciousness, "the inseparable unity of the transcendent and the immanent" (339).

The Christian ideal—the Kingdom of God—cannot be realized within the limits of the earthly life and earthly community. After the fall "man became the prey of the lust for knowledge obtained apart from the love and consciousness of God, the lust of the flesh that seeks bodily pleasures apart from the spirit, the lust for power that seeks might apart from spiritual growth." In his relation to the world "man has succumbed to the temptation of magic, hoping to gain possession of the world by external, unspiritual means" (353). The world resists man's attempts to gain possession of it, and the disharmony between man and the world leads to the necessity for labor and for economic activity, which is of the nature of *grey magic,* "combining in itself the inextricably interwoven elements of the white and the black magic, the powers of light and of darkness, of being and of non-being" (354).

A characteristic peculiarity of this dual world is the antagonism between economic labor and artistic work: "the artist looks down upon the economic activity, despising it for being calculating, utilitarian and lacking in creative inspiration, while the producers take up a condescending attitude towards art because of its dreamy impotence and its inevitably parasitic character from the point of view of economic needs" (356). The ideal unity of these two activities is attained by means of the art of life which transforms the world and creates life in beauty. Vladimir Soloviev was wrong in describing such active art as *theurgy*

—divine activity. In truth it is a combination of theurgy and sophiurgy; i.e., the joined effect of God descending into the world and of man ascending to God.

"Beauty will save the world," said Dostoevsky. This true beauty is the transfiguration of the world, sophiurgy, which can only take place "in the bosom of the Church, under the vivifying influence of the uninterrupted stream of sacramental grace that flows in it, in an atmosphere of devotional inspiration" (388). This consummation of the creative work of God is achieved in a new aeon, and not within the limits of earthly history: "the purpose of history leads beyond history, to the life of the world to come, and the world purpose leads beyond the world, to a new heaven and a new earth" (410). "Historic failures are beneficial because they heal men of the tendency to worship humanity, or the nation, or the world, and to believe in humanitarian progress, the mainspring of which is neither love nor pity but the proud dream of an earthly paradise" (406).

As already said man is "both created and uncreated, absolute in the relative and relative in the absolute." Therefore, not being expressible in any definition, man strives for absolute creativeness after the image of God, but is unable by his own powers to create anything perfect, a *chef d'oeuvre* (279). His created being is made up of being and non-being; hence "man's nature has the characteristics of genius and of insignificance. His lower basis is the other side of being, a fictitious quantity that had reality bestowed upon it. To will one's own exclusive selfhood, to shut oneself up in one's creaturehood as in the absolute means to seek the lower depths and become rooted in them. Therefore the chief character of the lower depths is Satan who loves himself as though he were god, is rooted in his selfhood and imprisoned in his own lower depths. He willed to find the divine all in his own non-being and was forced to shut himself up in the realm of Hades, peopled by shades and ghosts, believing it to be the dwelling place of a god of light. The beauty of Lucifer and the demon that so greatly attracted Byron and Lermontov is merely a pose, merely a cover for deception and tastelessness, like somebody else's fine clothes worn over dirty linen, like luxurious life on borrowed money with no hope of repayment, like pretensions to genius on the part of an artistic nonentity. The demonic cloak hides Hlestakov and Chichikov, and the fairy-like demon becomes a hideous devil with hoofs and a cold in the head. Vulgarity is the hidden underlining of demonism" (182). Freedom from all temptation and from "the anguish of nonabsolute absoluteness can only be found by man through the heroism of humble love" (280), through communion with the Heavenly Man, Adam Cadmon, in whom the union between God and man is realized. The Heavenly Man "embraces in himself all in positive pan-unity. He is the organized all or a pan-organism" (285).

How is the perfect union of God and man in one person possible? The highest task of the Christian world conception is to give a philosophic interpretation of the doctrine of Jesus Christ as a God-man. Therefore, Father S. Bulgakov's christology, soteriology and eschatology developed in his voluminous work *Agnus Dei, The Comforter* and *The Bride of the Lamb* may be regarded as the summit of his theological and philosophical activity. In the book *Agnus Dei* he examines in detail the fundamental antinomy of the religious consciousness, "the indissoluble biunity of the transcendent and the immanent" and seeks to expound the theologically philosophical meaning of the Chalcedon dogma according to which Jesus Christ is perfect God and perfect man. The indissoluble union "without confusion" of the two natures, the Divine and the human, in one Person cannot be interpreted as their alternation or as a mixture and so on (94). The unity of personal life requires the unity of all its manifestations so that each of them is a divinely human, "theo-andric" act: Christ's miracles, His insight, His spiritual power and other expressions of His high perfection must, equally with His bodily weariness, lack of knowledge, the sense of God-forsakenness, and other expressions of His limitations, be interpreted as divinely human. The antinomies of the religious consciousness, says Bulgakov, cannot be solved simply by formulating two sets of judgements logically contradictory of one another (67). We must rise to a level where the opposition between them is somehow removed. That is achieved, according to Bulgakov, by kenotic theology (248) which regards the Incarnation as the self-limitation of the Logos, Who renounces the *glory* of his Godhead to such an extent that His divine nature becomes commensurate to the human nature. That is possible only if, even before the Incarnation, the Person of the Logos was to a certain extent akin to man, and the human personality—akin to the divine. Such "co-respondence between Deity and humanity" (136) exists owing to the Divine Sophia in God and the created Sophia in the world. "The Divine Sophia as the pan-organism of ideas is the eternal Humanity in God—the Divine archetype and basis of man's being" (136). The Divine Sophia is hypostasied in the Logos Who is a demiurgic Hypostasis; hence Logos is the Heavenly Man, the First man, the Son of God and the Son of Man (137). Man is created by God in the image of that Divine archetype. Moreover, as already said, man actually has in him an aspect of "uncreatedness." "The spiritual being which God breathes out of Himself into man's body is rooted in the Divine eternity; the created spirit is, like it, eternal and uncreated and bears in itself the consciousness both of that eternity and the uncreatedness and, altogether, of its divine nature; hence spiritual self-consciousness is, at bottom, awareness of God. Moreover the created spirit is aware of itself as a self-founded, self-posited entity" for it posits itself as a self (115). Thus man is both a created and uncreated being and "this duality of natures in man, his original God-manhood makes possible the deification of life, the communion of both natures in man without division or confusion" (117, 136 f., 160 f.). That explains how the Second Person of the Holy Trinity can, through self-emptying (*kenosis*) bridge the abyss which divides the Divine and the created world, for we have here on the one hand, *natura humana capax divini* and on the other *natura divini capax humani*. Father Sergius's excellent little book *The Miracles of the Gospel* is devoted to the exposition of the lofty qualities of the human nature and especially of the spiritual power of men who fulfill the will of God.

The union between the divine and the human nature is not, however, achieved painlessly. The gulf between the two natures has been made deeper by the Fall of man: "having in himself, as it were, two centers of being, the spiritual and the created one, man made his choice by deviating toward the flesh, by subordinating his spirit to its appeals instead of spiritually mastering it." In consequence nature appeared before him not in its Sophian, but in its created aspect "of the fallen or dark Sophia, in the image of non-being, i.e., of materiality—an undue, abnormal, perverted condition" (168). "The metaphysical nature of creation having non-being for its substratum becomes "the source of undue self-affirmation, of creaturely egoism which is reflected in mutual spatial impenetrability as the force of disintegration and 'wakeful' and restless chaos." Moreover, "a created spirit bears in its secret depths the satanic temptation of selfhood, of recognizing itself as the archetype" (170). Owing to the Fall of man, the incarnation of the Logos is "a cross which He takes upon Himself": being free from sin, He receives of the Virgin Mary through the Holy Spirit flesh burdened with the "consequences of the original sin," weak and obeying the divine nature only after intense and continual struggle (271, 200).

The kenotic descent of God into the world consists in the fact that the Second Person of the Holy Trinity, while retaining the fullness of Godhead in the "immanent" Trinity, puts off His Divine glory in the "economic" Trinity (i.e., Trinity in Its relation to the world) and "for Himself ceases to be God" (253). "The timeless-eternal God makes Himself a *becoming* God in the God-man, denudes Himself of His eternal Godhead in order to come down to human life and, in and through it, to make man receptive of God, living in God, in short, the God-man" (249). He is conscious of Himself as the Son of man and the Son of God, obedient to the Father (292–316). He is the link that unites man to God, for He is consubstantial "with God in Godhead and with us in humanity" (263). His two natures, the Divine and the human, are indivisible "for they are not different but identical in their content, as a noumenon and a phenomenon, as ground and consequence, as principle and its manifestation" (224). But at the same time there is no confusion between them, for one of them is the Divine, and the other the created, Sophia (223); the first is supertemporal, and the second is realized through a temporal process.

From the point of view of this kenotic theology, according to which the Logos puts off His Godhead for Himself, it is understandable that all His manifestations in the earthly life, both the perfect and those marked by human weakness, are equally divinely human and are not alternative manifestations now of the Divine and now of the human element. The miracles worked by Him indicate the norm of the human spirit's mastery of nature; like the saints and the prophets, He often manifests wonderful insight but, having put Himself within the limitations of space and time, He manifests ignorance natural to man; He turns to the Father with prayer for inspiration from above which He needs, having inwardly confined the manifestations of His own Divinity within the range of the human nature. On the other hand, however, He does not renounce His Godhead as such, and that renders intelligible "the most daring christological paradoxes: the Lord asleep in the boat sustains the universe by His word; the Lord hanging on the tree and suffering the agonies of death, is the Creator and Source of life, sustaining by His word all creation; the Lord born in the manger and resting in the sepulchre is the Lord of all creatures and so on" (255). "In the God-man there are no nonhuman manifestations of the divine life, and all that is human is deified, graced, penetrated by the divine light, though not glorified as yet: everything in Him is divinely human" (284). "When the fullness of the time was come, God sent forth His Son, made of a woman, made under the law, to redeem them that were under the law, that we might receive the adoption of sons" (Gal. 4, 4).

The purpose of the Logos's self-renunciation is to regenerate the fallen humanity, to redeem it from sin and reconcile it with God. Moreover, it has a more general purpose, independent of the Fall, namely the deification of man, "so as to unite all things, heavenly and earthly, under one head, Christ." The Incarnation then is not merely a soteriological act (193 ff.). By coming out of eternity into the temporal process God unites Himself with the world "not from outside only, as its

Creator and Providence, but from within." Thus, "the Incarnation is also the inner basis of creation, its final cause" (196).

Having assumed human nature the Lord "became a historical individual," but His individuality "is not bound by any ontological limitations." He had no "individuality in the negative, limiting sense" that was the consequence of the Old Adam's Fall. "He was a Universal man, and His personality contained all human images, was a Pan-Personality. He is *equally* near and accessible to everyone who contemplates Him ... for He is, for everyone and for all, the image that speaks directly to heart and mind and penetrates into the secret depths. That is the basis of the Gospel's catholicity and its universally human appeal. In His human nature Christ adopted into Himself the whole of cosmic existence in so far as man is a microcosm" (229). He is therefore the New Adam, regenerating the whole of humanity which, together with the Old Adam, committed the sin of the Fall. Before the Fall, Adam "was a universal man and in him the whole mankind with all its possible aspects lived in reality. Being a person, Adam had no individuality in the negative, limiting sense resulting from disintegrated pan-unity that becomes the bad infinity of egocentric entities. With the Fall, the image of universal pan-humanity in Adam grew dim and he became merely an individual who could only give birth to other individuals" (230).

Christ redeems the world from sin as the Universal man Who takes upon Himself the sins of the whole world, past, present and future. This is possible owing to "the metaphysical reality of the whole mankind, by virtue of which humanity is bound together by the joint responsibility both for good and for evil—all are responsible not only for themselves, but for all and in all things" (377). "Christ's self-identification with mankind that lies at the basis of the dogma of redemption gives a literal and not a figurative meaning to his words at the Last Judgment: 'Inasmuch as ye have done it unto one of the least of these my brethren, ye have done it unto Me,' and in the negative form 'Inasmuch as ye did it not to one of the least of these, ye did it not to Me' (Matt. 25, 40, 45)" (377). Bearing the sins of the world means not the defilement of the soul by sin, but the fact that Christ experienced, lived through and suffered the whole burden of sin and thus overcame it (380 f.). To begin with, He suffered "from the sins of the world warring against Him from without;" secondly, He bears the sins of the world from within through "compassionate love":[3] on the night of Gethsemane He endured the sins of the world as something "terrible and repulsive which tortured His soul unutterably by its very presence"

---

3. This is pointed out by the Metropolitan Antony.

(389); in the third place, He experienced the consequences that inevitably follow from God's justice, namely, the sense of being forsaken by God: "Divinity is not compatible with sin, It burns it up with Its fire" (381). Those tortures taken together are equivalent to the punishment which would be appropriate to mankind, i.e., to the torments of hell. "Christ's taking upon Himself the sins of the world would be apparent and not real if it were not followed by all the consequences that sin entails, i.e., by the burden of God's wrath and by being cast away from Him. God has mercy on the sinner but hates sin. God's justice is as absolute as His love is infinite. Sin may and must be lived down, rendered powerless and destroyed, for it has no power of life in it, being a wrongful progeny of created freedom: God did not create either sin or death. In the process of getting rid of sin, sin is burnt out by the wrath of God which means suffering or punishment for the subject of sin, for its bearer. If sin must be atoned for by suffering, the God-man who takes sin upon Himself, suffers too. In that sense it may really be said that the God-man suffers the *equivalent* of punishment for the sins of the world, i.e., of the tortures of hell, though in a different way. There can be no question here of commensurability in time, for in any case temporal measurements are not applicable to eternal torments: eternity is a qualitative and not a quantitative conception. But the short hours of the Saviour's agony contained the whole 'eternity' of torments in their full force. And that 'eternity' was such that it could undermine and wipe out the sins of the world. That is the meaning of redemption and reconciliation with God" (390 f.).

The last stage of the agony of overcoming the consequences of sin is the death of Jesus Christ on the cross. The metaphysical Calvary of the Logos voluntarily crucifying Himself through His kenosis inevitably led to the historical Calvary of the God-man being put to death on the cross (260). "The consequences of the Saviour's taking upon Himself the sins of mankind could not be confined to spiritual experiences alone[4] but were bound to extend to the bodily life as well. Together with the sins the Saviour had to take upon Himself bodily sufferings and to taste death, and do so differently from any man who knows only his own sufferings and experiences his own death. It was necessary for the New Adam, the Redeemer of all mankind, bodily to experience the essence of all human suffering and taste the bitterness of all deaths, to accept Death in order to conquer it, destroying death by death—the universal, integral death" (395). "Only the deified human nature of the God-man

---

4. That is the one-sided, and, consequently, mistaken conception of the Metropolitan Antony.

was capable of actually living down the *whole* of human sin" and of all death, "and His divine nature and will fully consented to it. Thus, only the God-man could take upon Himself the sins of all mankind; no man, however holy, could possibly do it. And yet it was done by the powers of His *human* nature, which was in perfect harmony with the divine" (388). "He reinstates in Himself" the normal "correlation between the spirit and the body," lost by the Old Adam, namely the power of the spirit over the body, and yet "it was not an easy victory of the Divine power over human weakness, but was a *human* victory which alone was needed and valuable here, and was accomplished by the God-man" (316).

The Christian doctrine of redemption from sin through the sufferings of Jesus Christ gives rise to perplexity: "How can the sin of one man be forgiven on the ground of sufferings endured by another? What truth and justice is there in such substitution? The very way the question is put," answers Bulgakov, "errs on the side of individualism and legalism, for it takes into consideration only separate, isolated personalities to which the principle of abstract justice is applicable. But the distinction between 'mine' and 'thine' is overcome through love which knows both the difference and the identity between 'I' and 'thou.' In relation to every human being Christ is not 'another,' for the New Adam includes—*naturally* in His manhood and *compassionately* in His love—every individual, and is the universal man. The sin which He takes upon Himself through the power of love, is not alien to Him but His own, though not committed, but only accepted by Him. We have here not a *juridical* but an *ontological* relation, based upon the real unity of human nature in spite of the actual multiplicity of its numberless separate and yet conjoined personal centers. Christ took upon Himself the whole of human nature and therefore He can take upon Himself in and through it the whole sin of all individuals, though personally He has not committed it" (391 f.). "In Christ everyone may find himself and his own sin, and the power of redeeming it, if through his freedom and through his nature of Old Adam he wills to be included in that power; 'believe and be saved' " (387). Man's freedom is not cancelled by Christ's redeeming sacrifice. Every man coming to Christ "with faith, love and repentance" may freely participate in His immeasurable suffering that renders sin powerless, and then it may be said of him "I live and yet not I but Christ liveth in me." Salvation must be objectively realized for everyone through his subjectively receiving (or not receiving) it on the basis of free, personal self-determination (Mark 16, 16). "Grace is a gift and is given freely, but it does not compel (as *insuperabilis* and *indeclinabilis*), it does not transform man into an *object* of creation: it convinces, subdues, regenerates. The path of personal salvation may be complex, interrupted and contradictory. But the Divine love finally overcomes the creature's sin and in the fullness of time, God shall be all in all" (362).

God's whole relation to the world is an expression of His love. The very creation of the world is an act of God's sacrificial love; man's redemption from sin is even more sacrificial, for "the Author of man's being takes upon Himself the consequences of His act of creation—the possibility of sin which has beome an actuality" (393). Together with the incarnate Son of God, the Father suffers too, since in letting the Son die upon the cross the Father endures "not death, of course, but a certain form of spiritual dying together in the sacrifice of love" (344). The Holy Spirit too takes part in that suffering since He is "the actual personal Love of the Father for the Son and of the Son for the Father . . . and not to manifest Itself to the Beloved is a kenosis for personal love" (345 f., 393). This conception of the Holy Trinity as a whole participating in the sufferings of the Incarnation is not heretical, for it is not antitrinitarian (401).

The theological and philosophical doctrine of the Incarnation contains a theodicy. In the Incarnation the Lord "completes His work as Creator and thereby *justifies* the act of creation, for apart from this entrance of the Deity into the created world, the world inevitably remains imperfect, since it has its origin in nothing and, consequently, its created freedom has a limited and changeable character. Though the world is perfect as originally created ("very good") it contains the inevitable ontological imperfection of createdness and the incompleteness that ensues therefrom, and God could not abandon such a world to its own devices (as deists believe). Hence there arises a further task for the Creator—to overcome the very createdness of the world, to raise it above its created nature and deify it." The Divine Incarnation is "the price of creation for God Himself, the sacrifice of God's love in the creation of the world, God so loved the world that He gave His only begotten Son" (375). The final end—the deification of the creature—demands that Christ should be not only prophet and high priest, but king as well. His service as prophet consists in His preaching the divine truth (354) and especially in being what He is as its living incarnation (356); hence miracles and signs also form part of His prophetic work (362). He is high priest not only in so far as He redeems mankind from sin by sacrificing Himself, but in the more general sense of establishing the basis for "the universal deification of the created human essence" (364). That basis is the starting point of Christ's *kingly* service which goes on throughout the tragic course of human history (451). "Christ is the King of the world but He does not reign in it as fully as in the Kingdom of God: He is only *establishing* His kingly power. His kingly service in the world is still going on" and "takes the form of striving for the kingdom, of struggling against the prince of this world and the powers of antichrist." Such struggle is possible because it is not a question of the power of God the Creator over His creation, but of Christ the God-man, whose coming into power is "a tragedy of conflict and of division between light and darkness—the fundamental theme both of St. John's Gospel and of his Revelation" (447). In so far as the arena of that struggle is the human history, the Logos proves to be not only a demiurgic, but also a *historical* hypostasis.

Christ's mysterious presence on earth after His ascension is most really manifested in the eucharistic sacrifice: the supertemporal significance of the one sacrifice on the Calvary is made real upon every altar at every liturgy in a number of different places (435). The final result of this presence of Christ in the world must be the complete victory of the good in virtue of the "Sophian determinism." Such determinism does not violate human freedom and consists in the fact that "Christ upon His Incarnation became the law of being for the natural humanity, its inner natural reality, hidden as yet in the Old Adam, in the old natural and human world" (462). The complete realization of that Sophian nature in the world will complete Christ's work as King and lead beyond the confines of history into the Heavenly Kingdom "that God may be all in all" (447 f.; I Cor. 15, 28).

The doctrine about the Holy Spirit is expounded by Father Sergius in his big work *The Comforter*. The Orthodox Church teaches that the Holy Spirit proceeds from the Father through (διά) the Son; the Roman Catholic Church speaks of the Holy Spirit proceeding from the Father and the Son. The addition to the Creed of the word *filioque*, made by the Western Church without agreement with the Eastern, gave rise to a dispute that has lasted many centuries. Bulgakov says that it cannot be settled so long as the disputants mean by the "birth" of the Son and "procession" of the Holy Spirit *causal* generation of the Second and the Third Persons from the Father (171). In truth the trinity of Persons in the Divine Absolute Subject can only be understood if we start with the conception of the self-revelation of the Absolute Spirit (75). The personal self-consciousness of the Absolute Subject "reveals itself fully not in a self-contained, single 'I' but presupposes 'thou, he, we, you'" (66). "The self-revelation of the Holy Trinity" consists in the fact that "the Son appears to the Father as His Truth and His Word" (76). "But this diadic relation between the Father and the Son cannot possibly exhaust the self-determination of the absolute Spirit, which reveals itself not only as self-consciousness, as being in truth, but also as self-life, as being in beauty, as the experience of its own content. That vital dynamic relation is not merely a *state,* and in that sense an external *datum* of self-determination, which is altogether out of place in the absolute subject, but is also a hypostasis" (77). "The Holy Spirit is the union of love between the Father and the Son" (176). "The union within the Holy Trinity is a union of tri-personal love or of three forms of love." All love contains the sacrificial element of self-renunciation, but the highest aspect of love is "joy, bliss, triumph. That bliss of love in the Holy Trinity, the *solace* of the Comforter, is the Holy Spirit" (79).

If we give up the mistaken idea that the procession of the Holy Spirit means generation, says Bulgakov, we may interpret the relation of the third Hypostasis to the first two in several different ways (181).

In discussing the problem of God-manhood Bulgakov asks whether in addition to the incarnation of the Logos there must also be "a special incarnation of the Third Hypostasis," and answers the question in the negative. "The Incarnation is made up of two acts: the *descent* of the Divine Hypostasis into a human being, and of Its *acceptance* by the latter. The first is the work of the Logos sent into the world by the Father, the second is the work of the Holy Spirit, also sent by the Father on to the Virgin Mary, in whose flesh the divine incarnation takes place." This "must not be understood as a kind of fatherhood on the part of the Holy Spirit making up for the absence of a husband; on the contrary, the Holy Spirit becomes as it were identified to a certain extent with the Virgin Mary in the conception of the Son." Hence "the personal incarnation of the third Hypostasis is completely excluded" (*Agnus Dei,* 200). But the revelation of the Holy Spirit in the Virgin Mary differs profoundly from the incarnation of the Logos, inasmuch as the God-man Jesus Christ has only one Hypostasis, namely that of the Logos, while the Virgin Mary with whom the Holy Spirit after the Annunciation "remains for ever" (*The Comforter,* 285) has a human hypostasis, distinct from the Hypostasis of the Holy Spirit.

Since both the masculine and the feminine principles participate in the Incarnation, Bulgakov detects the presence of both those principles in the Divine Sophia who is "the heavenly archetype of the created humanity." The human spirit is a biunity: "It combines the masculine, solar principle of thought, Logos, with the feminine principle of receptivity, of creative completion, of being enfolded in beauty. Man's Sophian spirit is androgynous. The masculine and the feminine are images of one and the same spiritual principle, Sophia, in the fullness of its self-revelation, after the pattern of the Second and the Third Hypostases" (*Comforter* 218). "This distinction, which is parallel to the masculine and the feminine principles, is reflected in the Incarnation:

Christ incarnates in the image of a man, and the Holy Spirit is revealed most perfectly in the image of the Spirit-bearer Ever-Virgin Mary." In this connection Father Sergius points out that "Church literature gives us glimpses of the Spirit as a feminine hypostasis" and quotes a number of such passages (219).

In his book *The Bride of the Lamb* Father Sergius repeats his sophiological doctrine adding little that is new to it; his new and extremely valuable theological conceptions are developed in the second part of the book and deal with death, the state of the soul after death and universal salvation.

The created Sophia, like the Divine Sophia, is not personal. Hence she is the soul and not the spirit of the world (90). She is personalized in the human personality; accordingly, the cosmos is "cosmo-anthropos" (96). The two aspects of the human being, man and woman, are the image of the Logos and the Holy Spirit (99). In Adam all mankind is one; hence, the Fall of Adam is the fall of each one of us (178), the loss of wholeness[5] and the emergence of plurality (89). But this plurality is not absolute disintegration. The created Sophia acts as the uniting power of wholeness (89); the New Adam, Christ, re-establishes the oneness of mankind; the Mother of God, the Second Eve (100) contains in herself the *nature* of all personalities and is therefore the Mother of mankind (328) and "the manifestation in a human hypostasis of the Holy Spirit" (438).

In speaking of the historical process, Father Sergius says that its subject is mankind as a whole: the transcendental human subject is the pan-human self "in the unity of Adam," in the first instance the transcendental epistemological self, the subject of knowledge. Similarly, the subject acting throughout history, say, the subject of economic activity, is one and the same (343).

The individually qualified human self receives the *theme* of his life from God, but at the same time he posits it for himself freely in the sense that he freely accepts or to a greater or less extent rejects that theme (106). A man's personal theme, set for him by God, is his "thatness," his genius; and a man's talent, his "whatness," consists in the way and the extent to which he accepts his genius (125). Thus, there exist different degrees of sinfulness (127) and different degrees of evil (164–7). Victory over evil means that individuality is extinguished by humble love (109); "individual" being must be overcome (162).

Death is the separation of the spirit and the soul from the body. Therefore man's *post-mortem* existence is spiritually-psychic with no

---

5. The Russian word is *tselomudrie* (lit.: "the wisdom of wholeness") which also means continence or chastity.

admixture of the psychically-bodily life. In that condition man's spiritual experience becomes richer; he sees the whole of his past life as a synthesis and begins to understand its meaning (388), condemns himself and gradually—perhaps in the course of aeons of time—overcomes all evil in himself and is therefore found worthy of entering God's Kingdom. Thus, there is no everlasting hell, there is only "purgatory and a temporary sojourn in it" (391). As to non-Christians, it is possible for them "to receive after death the light of Christ" (462).

If eternal paradise had been prepared for some beings, and eternal hell for others, it would mean that creation of the world was a failure and no theodicy would be possible. Father Sergius calls the doctrine of everlasting torments of hell "penitentiary-criminal code of theology" (513). It is inadmissible that finite and limited sins should be visited with punishment of infinite duration. "The fact that we have been created by omniscient God is so to speak an ontological proof of future salvation" (550, 573).

In conclusion I will summarize the main contentions of Bulgakov's philosophy of language, valuable not only from the linguistic, but from the religiously philosophical point of view. It is expounded in a big volume *The Philosophy of Words*. Father Sergius read his introduction to it in 1924 at the Russian Academic Congress in Prague and it appeared in the *Festschrift T. G. Masaryk zum 80 Geburtstage* (Part I, 1930) under the title *Was ist das Wort?* According to Bulgakov the sound mass is the σῶμα of the word, as the Stoics put it: it is matter idealized by form, which is meaning or idea. A word idea may have various embodiments—sound, gesture, written signs, but just as Beethoven's symphonies are written for the orchestra, so the word idea finds its embodiment pre-eminently in the sounds of the human voice. The connection between an idea and its incarnation is not an external association. Bulgakov flatly rejects all psychologistic theories that reduce meaning to a psychical process in the human mind and regard the word as merely a token, external to the meaning, for communicating this psychic process to other people. At the inception of the word in the cosmic reality, says Bulgakov, a double process, developing in opposite directions, takes place: an idea is liberated out of the complex whole of existence, and creates for itself, in the microcosm of a human individuality, according to man's vocal resources, a new body—the word. The cosmos itself speaks through the microcosm of man in words which are living symbols, active hieroglyphics of things, for the real soul of the word sound is the thing itself; e.g., the soul of the word "sun" is the heavenly orb itself. The plurality of languages does not exclude the unity of the "inner word," just as the same Chinese characters are in different provinces pronounced in a different way (39). The Babel confusion of tongues means the disintegration of the white ray into a plurality of spectral colors, but this does not affect the "inner word"—witness the possibility of translation from one language into another. Considerable value attaches to Bulgakov's theory that the plurality of languages is a consequence of the disintegration of mankind in connection with increasing subjectivism and psychologism; i.e., a morbid concentration of attention on subjective individual peculiarities of speech, and to his reflexions on the attempts of the Kabbalah to regard letters as the original elements of language and at the same time as cosmic forces.

Bulgakov's philosophy of language naturally implies a sympathetic attitude on his part to the so-called *"imiaslavie"* (literally "glorification of the name").[6] In *The Unfading Light* he writes: "The name of God is as it were a point of intersection between two worlds and is the transcendental in the immanent; hence *imiaslavie*, apart from its general theological significance is so to speak a transcendental condition of prayer, rendering religious experience possible." God as it were confirms "His name and recognizes it as His own, not merely answering to it, but being actually present in it" (22).

Father Sergius's work is remarkable for his creative energy, the multiplicity of his subjects and the bold originality of many of his doctrines. Especially valuable at the early stages of his activity was his struggle against man-worship, demonism and other varieties of modern anti-Christianity. In his speculative system his philosophy of language, his theory of beauty and of the cosmos as an animated whole are particularly noteworthy. As to his theology, the greatest value attaches to his arguments in favor of universal salvation, and his teaching that the Incarnation is not only a means of saving mankind from sin, but has a far more fundamental meaning as the necessary condition of the deification of created personalities, and that therefore the Son of God is, in connection with the creation of the world, God-man from all eternity. Equally valuable are Father Sergius's remarks about the "mystical insight" of paganism, about the spiritual power manifested in Christ's miracles and the co-relation between the Holy Spirit and the Mother of God. The centuries' old dispute between the Roman Catholic and the Orthodox Churches about the *filioque* clause is put by Father Sergius on a new basis through his pointing out that the words "born" and "proceeding" used, respectively, of the Son and the Holy Spirit, indicate not their causal connection with God the Father, but the dif-

6. The doctrine that divine grace is actually present in the very name of God.

ferent aspects of the self-revelation of the Absolute personality. If the question is considered from that point of view, the dogmatic conflict between the disputants may become less irreconcilable.

Bulgakov's sophiology and some of his other doctrines have been sharply attacked by the Moscow patriarchate and the emigré Karlovatsky Synod. The Moscow patriarch's condemnation and two replies to it by Bulgakov in which he defends his position have been published in the book *Sophia the Divine Wisdom* (Paris 1935). A criticism of Father Sergius's replies was made by Vladimir N. Lossky in the book *The Dispute About Sophia*. A member of the Karlovatsky synod Archbishop Serafim wrote a large book entitled *A New Doctrine About Sophia, the Divine Wisdom* (Sofia 1935). The fundamental defect of Father Sergius's system is that in his teaching about the Divine Sophia as the nature (*ousia*) of God, he affirms the ontological identity between God and the world. Neither the negative nor the positive theology admits of this. For the negative theology God is the Divine Nothing not expressible by any conceptions borrowed from the realm of cosmic being. God and the world are ontologically sharply divided from each other: it is impossible to find either complete or partial identity between the Divine Nothing and the world. Nor does positive theology fill up the gulf between God and the world. True, religious experience testifies that God is a personal being; moreover, we know from the Revelation that He is a unity of Three Persons. It must be remembered, however, that even as a Person, God still remains the same Divine Nothing. Words which indicate ideas in the earthly realm of being acquire a different sense when applied to God. We make use of them in view of a certain similarity between the world and God as the subject of positive theology. Both the similarity and the difference are, however, *metalogical*.[7] Any two objects that are similar or different in a logical sense are of necessity partially identical or at any rate are necessarily connected with an element of identity; metalogical similarity is not connected with partial identity in any sense of the term. Hence it is clear that if ideas of personality, reason, existence, etc., as applied to God were identical with the corresponding ideas applied to earthly beings, the Divine Nothing would be distinct from the Persons of the Holy Trinity: we should then have to regard It as a higher principle giving rise to the latter as to a lower realm of being, connected, in its turn, with the world by the relation of partial identity.

In rejecting the conception of a higher and a lower God and, consequently, in recognizing that the Divine Nothing coincides with each

7. The conception of metalogical difference is worked out in S. L. Frank's book *The Object of Knowledge*, 237.

Person of the Holy Trinity, it is essential strictly to adhere to the following position: there is an ontological gulf between God and the world; pantheism is logically untenable. Father Sergius denies that position. His contention that in the Divine and in the created world all is "one and identical in content (though not in being)" (Agn. 148), and all his theories connected therewith contain too great an ontological approximation of the world, and especially of man, to God. As already mentioned that is logically incompatible with the teaching about God expounded by the negative theology, even if additions be made to it from the positive theology.

If the logical impossibility of identifying the content of God and of the world be overlooked, this disregard for logical coherence will involve us in hopeless difficulties. To begin with, the doctrine in question minimizes the creative power both of God and of man. It asserts that although in creating the world God does not make use of any material from outside, He borrows the whole of the world's content from Himself; thus there is no real creativeness, but merely a shifting or externalization of contents already present in God. Man does not create any positive new contents, either, but merely repeats in a temporal form the eternal content of the Divine nature. If God and man are brought ontologically too close together, it belittles them both. According to Father Sergius the creatures' activity can be new only in a "modal" sense, i.e., can only transfer the possible into the actual; their inspiration is in itself "incapable of bringing something ontologically new into being, of enriching reality with new themes" (*The Comforter*, 250 f.).

If the positive content of the human nature were identical with the Divine, man would have to be recognized as consubstantial with God. According to the Christian dogma, man draws nearer to God through the Mediator God-man Jesus Christ. Having two profoundly different natures miraculously combined without confusion, the Divine and the human, Jesus Christ is through one of these natures consubstantial to the Father and the Holy Spirit and, through another, consubstantial to us, men. In Father Sergius's view it is not the fact of Christ being made man that brings man nearer to God, but, on the contrary, the consubstantiality between God and man helps the Logos to become man. Consider, too, in this connection his doctrine that man's spirituality is uncreated, but has its origin in God "breathing into" man "the breath of life;" God gives to this "breath," to this outpouring of His own essence, personal being. Does this not imply that man, being uncreated as a person, stands in this respect on the same level as God the Son and the Holy Spirit: the Son is born of the Father and not created; the Spirit proceeds from the Father, and man emanates from

Him? Fortunately, Father Sergius does not go to such extremes, for he considerably modified his doctrine in his later works. In the *Agnus Dei* it was asserted that man at his creation "receives his personality from God breathing into him the Divine spirit and thus becomes 'a living soul,' a living man, a self for which, and in and through which, his humanity lives" (136). In *The Comforter* this doctrine is changed as follows: "Man is a supercreational element in the world having in himself the spirit that came from God, and a personality which though created is in the image of God" (244). These words, apparently, must be interpreted in the sense that the spirit which came direct from God and formed man is spirituality and not man's actual self; as to the actual personal self to which that Divine spirituality is given, it is created by God in His image and partly self-created. Even this conception of man's supercreatedness, however, is of little avail if we recall that according to Father Sergius creation itself and especially creation in the image of God is, in its positive content, mere externalization of the Divine Sophian content. Father Sergius himself, particularly in his book *The Comforter*, often says that his system may appear pantheistic and to a certain extent agrees with this, observing "yes, in a sense it is pantheism too, but quite a pious one, or, as I prefer to put it in order to avoid misunderstanding, it is panentheism." Pantheism, he says, "is a dialectically inevitable aspect of a Sophian cosmology" (232).

Like many other theologians Father Sergius interprets the words "God created the world out of nothing" as though they referred to some "nothing" out of which God made the world. In truth, however, those words express, it seems to me, the following simple thought: the Creator does not need to take any materials either from within or from outside Himself in order to create the world: He creates the world as something new, that has never existed before and is utterly different from Him. Only such appearance of something new is true creativeness. Father Sergius's system does not allow for such creativeness: in his view God creates all the positive content of the world out of Himself; the nondivine aspect of the world proves to be so characterless that his theory really must be regarded as a peculiar variety of pantheism. It is not surprising, therefore, that it exhibits the main defects of pantheism: (1) it is logically unfounded; (2) it cannot explain freedom; (3) it cannot account for the source of evil.

As already pointed out, it is logically impossible to admit any, even partial identity between God and the world, while maintaining that God is the Divine Nothing. Father Sergius fails to see this because he does not fully appreciate the peculiar nature of apophatic theology and thinks of God as the Absolute (407). But in truth God is the Superabsolute: He is not the Absolute as co-relative to the relative. There is also another, positive, reason which leads Father Sergius to the view that God and the world are partly identical. He believes that the Divine nature as the *Ens realissimum* must be a positive unity of all, including everything within itself, for otherwise—i.e., if there existed any positive nondivine content—God's nature would prove to be limited and impoverished. That idea is widely prevalent in philosophy in general, and in Russian philosophy in particular: we find it in Soloviev, Karsavin, Frank. And yet it is erroneous. As Spinoza pointed out long ago, limitation is a mutual relation between two objects of the same nature. But God and the Divine life within the Trinity is something metalogically different in comparison with the created world; hence, the fact that the created world is outside of God does not in any way diminish the fullness of the Divine life.

The two other important defects of panentheism (as well as of panthcism) are its inability to give a reasonable explanation of the presence of evil in the world, and of the freedom of the created agents. Evil is not merely a lack of the fullness of being, i.e., a relative nothing. It has a certain peculiar content which represses other positive contents and thus, in the last resort, leads to decreasing the fullness of life. No doubt, evil is always a parasite of the good and is realized only through utilizing the powers of goodness; but this very inability to do without the good presupposes creative inventiveness on the part of the evil agents and the fact that in their vital manifestations they are free from God in spite of having been created by Him. The agents who have entered upon the path of evil do really bring something new into the world if only in the form of a new combination of the already existing world elements, and that something new is not to be found in the Divine being—which proves that created agents are capable of independent creativeness. Father Sergius cannot explain evil and therefore unquestionably extradivine creative activity, and the creatures' freedom from God, because in creation he finds nothing but the Sophia and the nothing which becomes μή ὄν. But the μή ὄν cannot be a free antidivine agent. Christian experience clearly testifies that the beings who enter upon the path of evil are not some mysterious *meons,* but creatures that assert their self and proudly, or at any rate egoistically oppose their self to God and the world. That fact alone proves that *Ens realissimum* does not include everything and that there is existence not identical with the Divine Sophia in its content. Father Sergius's system is particularly lacking in any explanation of the nondivine aspect of the world; we suddenly find him talking of the "dark image of Sophia"

(*The Comforter*, 234) and even of "the fallen Sophia" (317), but it is scarcely possible to give the name of Sophia to a fallen being.

Sergius, the Metropolitan and later the Patriarch of Moscow, severely criticized Father Sergius Bulgakov's teaching and on the strength of it the Synod of the Moscow Patriarchate pronounced his sophiology to be "a doctrine, alien to the Holy Orthodox Church of Christ" and warned against it "all the Church's faithful servitors and children" (see the book *Sophia, the Divine Wisdom*, 19). When Father Sergius replied to this criticism in a paper submitted by him to the Metropolitan Eulogius in Paris, Vladimir Lossky wrote a book *The Dispute About Sophia* in which he explains the Metropolitan Sergius's criticism, adding his own considerations to it.

In criticizing Bulgakov's doctrine of the Divine Sophia as the "eternal feminine" in God, the Metropolitan Sergius remarks, "in order to be spiritual and all the more to be Divine, love, even if it be feminine and passive love, must be conscious, i.e., belong to a Person" (8). The Divine Sophia interpreted as God's *ousia* would thus be a *fourth hypostasis* in God. The Metropolitan Sergius further objects to distinguishing "within the simple essence of God two principles, masculine and feminine" and also to Bulgakov's connecting "the Divine image in man precisely with the duality of the sexes. This is not far removed from the deification of the sexual life such as we find in some of the Gnostics" (9).

Equally weighty is the accusation that Father Sergius "lays special stress on man's createdness as the cause of his fall, i.e., on the imperfection of the nature given him by the Creator" (16). Vladimir Lossky explains that this idea of Father Sergius arose from his teaching that the creation of the world by God consists in "the mergence of Sophia with nothing. The creation of the world becomes on that interpretation not the making of something new and perfect in its createdness ("very good"), but the warping of the already existing Divine world (Sophia), its deterioration and imperfection, i.e., an evil" (*The Dispute About Sophia*, 55).

The problems discussed by Father Bulgakov are among the most complex and difficult problems in Christian metaphysics. Each of them is open to a number of different solutions, and every solution is so interconnected with numberless other problems that it cannot be final but needs further elucidation, limitation or completion. That can only be done if many persons are able calmly to discuss the subject. Disputes about such matters can only be fruitful in an atmosphere of good will, tolerance, and spiritual discipline that holds passions in check. Most unfortunately, a calm discussion of the sophiological problem has been made almost impossible by the Moscow Patriarchate and the Synod of the Russian Church at Karlovtsi sharply and hastily condemning Father S. Bulgakov's theories before they have been debated in philosophical and theological literature.

Replying to the Metropolitan Sergius's criticism, Father S. Bulgakov said in his report to the Metropolitan Eulogius: "I solemnly declare that as an Orthodox priest I profess all the true dogmas of Orthodoxy. My sophiology has nothing to do with the actual content of those dogmas, but merely with their theological interpretation. It is my personal theological belief to which I have never ascribed the significance of a generally binding church dogma" (51 f.).

Indeed, Father Sergius never opposes the dogmas of the Orthodox Church. The criticisms made by his opponents, e.g., their contention that his doctrine of the Divine Sophis brings in a fourth Hypostasis into God's being, is a deduction from Father Sergius's teaching—a deduction which he never intended to make. Therefore, everyone who values the freedom of theological thought must admit that Father Sergius's doctrines might be criticized or definitely rejected by his opponents, but could not be condemned by the Moscow patriarchate. The friendly attitude to Father Sergius's activity on the part of his bishop, the Metropolitan Eulogius, is therefore highly instructive. At Father Sergius's burial the Metropolitan Eulogius spoke as follows: "Dear Father Sergius! You were a Christian sage, you are a teacher of the Church in the pure and lofty sense of the word. You were enlightened by the Holy Spirit, the Spirit of Wisdom, the Spirit of Reason, the Comforter, to Whom you dedicated your learned work."[8]

The work of every original ecclesiastical thinker calls forth bitter disputes, and only after a certain lapse of time the positive and negative aspects of his theories are sorted out in the life of the Church. The same fate awaits the teaching of Father Sergius Bulgakov who will undoubtedly be recognized as one of the outstanding Russian theologians.

8. See L. A. Zander's booklet *To the Memory of Father Sergius Bulgakov*.

Chapter 16

N. BERDYAEV

Nicolay Alexandrovich Berdyaev, the best-known of modern Russian philosophers, was born in 1874 in the province of Kiev. He studied at the Kiev University in the faculty of Law but did not graduate there, for in 1898 he was arrested for taking part in the socialist movement. In his youth he thought of combining marxism with neo-kantianism, but he soon gave up both those theories, became interested in Vladimir Soloviev's philosophy and then began independently to work out a Christian world conception. A similar evolution took place in the case of Sergey Nikolaevitch Bulgakov who in 1901 was professor of political economy at the Kiev Polytechnical Institute, in 1918 became a priest and in 1925 was appointed professor of dogmatic theology at the Orthodox Institute in Paris. In 1903 Berdyaev and Bulgakov came to Petersburg in order to found a new journal *Voprosi Zhizni* (Problems of Life). They asked me, as one who was less compromised politically than the others, to obtain permission in my name from the Government to publish the journal; I complied, but unfortunately the journal continued for one year only. In 1922 the Soviet Government arrested more than a hundred professors and writers accusing them of being in disagreement with their ideology and exiled them from Russia. Among the philosophers in that group were Berdyaev, Bulgakov, I. Ilyin, Lapshin, S. Frank, Karsavin and myself. At first Berdyaev settled in Berlin and afterwards moved to Paris where he worked chiefly at the Y.M.C.A. From 1926 till the end of 1939 he was the editor of the religious and philosophical journal *Put*. Nicolay Alexandrovich died suddenly, while working at his writing table, on March 24, 1948.

Berdyaev wrote a great many books and articles. Most of them have been translated into many languages. I will mention only some of the most important of his books: *Subjectivism and Idealism in Social Philosophy: A Critical Study of N. K. Mihailovsky*, 1900; *Sub specie aeternitatis*, 1907; *The New Religious Consciousness and Society*, 1907; *The Philosophy of Freedom*, 1911; *The Meaning of Creativeness*, 1916; *Dostoevsky's*

World Conception, 1923; *The Philosophy of Inequality,* 1923; *The Meaning of History,* 1923; *New Medievalism,* 1924; *The Philosophy of the Free Spirit: Christian Problematics and Apologetics,* 2 vols., 1929; *The Destiny of Man, an Essay in Paradoxical Ethics,* 1931; *The Self and the World of Objects,* 1934; *Spirit and Reality, the Foundations of the Divinely Human Reality,* 1937; *Man's Slavery and Freedom, an Essay in Personalistic Philosophy,* 1939; *The Russian Idea: The Main Problems of the Russian Thought of the Nineteenth and Early Twentieth Centuries,* 1946; *An Essay in Eschatological Metaphysics,* 1947.

Berdyaev's principal translated works are the following: *Christianity and Class War,* Sheed and Ward, 1933; *The Bourgeois Mind and Other Essays,* Sheed and Ward, 1934; *Dostoevsky,* Sheed and Ward 1934; *Freedom and the Spirit,* G. Bles, London 1935; *The Meaning of History,* G. Bles 1936; *New Medievalism; Spirit and Reality,* G. Bles 1934; *Solitude and Society,* G. Bles 1938; *K. Leontiev,* G. Bles 1940; *A. Khomiakov; Slavery and Freedom,* Scribner's Sons 1944; *The Russian Idea; An Essay in Eschatological Metaphysics; Autobiography.* Y.M.C.A. Press, Paris 1949 (available in English). O. F. Clarke, *Introduction to Berdyaev,* 1949; Matthew Spinka, *Nicolas Berdyaev: Captive of Freedom,* Westminster Press, Philadelphia 1950.

According to Berdyaev, the fundamental opposition with which we should start in formulating a theory about the world is that between spirit and nature, and not between the psychical and the physical. Spirit is the subject, life, freedom, fire, creative activity; nature is the object, thing, necessity, determinateness, passive endurance, immobility. To the realm of nature belongs all that is objective and substantial (by substance Berdyaev understands unchanging and self-contained being), multiple and divided in time and in space; not only matter but mental life on that view belongs to the realm of nature. The realm of spirit is of a different character: in it division is overcome by love; hence, spirit is neither an objective nor a subjective reality (*Philosophy of the Free Spirit,* chap. I). Knowledge about the spirit is attained not through concepts of reason or logical thought but through living experience. All philosophical systems not based upon spiritual experience are naturalistic; they are expressions of lifeless nature.

God is a spirit. He is really present in the life of the saints, the mystics, men of high spiritual life, and in man's creative activity. Those who have had spiritual experience need no rational proofs of God's existence. In Its deepest essence the Deity is irrational and superrational; attempts to express it through concepts are inevitably antinomic; i.e., the truth about God has to be expressed in pairs of judgments that are contradictory to each other. The Deity transcends the natural world and can only reveal Itself symbolically. Symbols in religious philosophy are necessarily connected with myths, such as the myth of Prometheus, of the Fall, of redemption and the Redeemer. This interpretation of the symbolism of religious truths must not be confounded with modernism according to which symbols are merely subjective expressions of the inmost reality. In Berdyaev's view symbols are the actual natural reality taken in connection with its supernatural significance. Therefore, the birth of the God-man from the Virgin Mary, His life in Palestine and His death on the cross are actual historical facts, and at the same time they are symbols. Thus, Berdyaev's symbolism is not Docetism; it does not lead to iconoclasm or undermine Christianity. It is a *real symbolism*. He calls such events as the birth of the God-man from the Virgin Mary and His death on the cross, "symbols" because they are an expression in the earthly reality of relations between spirit and the nonspiritual principle which subsist in a still deeper and more primary form in the domain of the Divine life itself (*Freedom and the Spirit*, chap. II).

According to Berdyaev, man's spiritual being is closely connected with the Divine spirituality, and he opposes his view to dualistic theism and to pantheism, regarding both those theories as the outcome of a naturalistic religious philosophy. His conception of the relation between God and the world can be gathered from his doctrine of freedom. Berdyaev distinguishes three kinds of freedom: primary irrational freedom, i.e., arbitrariness; rational freedom, i.e., the fulfillment of moral duty; and finally, freedom permeated by the love of God. Man's irrational freedom is rooted in the "nothing" out of which God created the world. That "nothing" is not emptiness; it is a primary principle prior to God and the world, containing no differentiation, i.e., no division into a number of definite elements. Berdyaev borrowed this conception from Jacob Boehme (German mystical philosopher, 1575–1624) who designated this primary principle by the term *Ungrund* (the groundless, the abyss). In Berdyaev's opinion Boehme's *Ungrund* coincides with the conception of the "Divine Nothing" in the negative theology of Dionysius the Areopagite and with the teaching of Meister Eckhardt (1260–1327) who distinguished between *Gottheit* and *Gott*, Godhead and God.[1]

1. The Christian teaching about God falls into two parts: the negative (apothatic) and the positive (cataphatic) theology. In negative theology, based upon the works of Dionysius the Areopagite, all determinations borrowed from the realm of cosmic being are said to be inapplicable to God; God is not a person, is not reason, is not a being, etc. In that sense God is the "Divine Nothing." But that "Nothing" is *above* all determinations: God is superpersonal, superexistent, and so on. Positive theology says of God that He is a Person, that He is Love, Spirit, and so on. The difficult task

Berdyaev says: "Out of the Divine Nothing, or of the *Ungrund*, the Holy Trinity, God the Creator is born." The creation of the world by God the Creator is a secondary act. "From this point of view it may be said that freedom is not created by God: it is rooted in the Nothing, in the *Ungrund* from all eternity. The opposition between God the Creator and freedom is secondary: in the primeval mystery of the Divine Nothing this opposition is transcended, for both God and freedom are manifested out of the *Ungrund*. God the Creator cannot be responsible for freedom which gave rise to evil. Man is the child of God and the child of freedom—of nothing, of non-being, τὸ μὴ ὄν. Meonic freedom consented to God's act of creation; non-being freely accepted being" (*The Destiny of Man*, 34). Hence it follows that God has no power over freedom which is not created by Him: "God the Creator is all-powerful over being, over the created world, but He has no power over non-being, over the uncreated freedom" (*ibid.*). This freedom is prior to good and evil, it conditions the possibility of both good and evil. According to Berdyaev, the actions of a being possessing free will cannot be foreseen even by God, since they are entirely free.

Berdyaev denies God's omnipotence and omniscience and maintains that He does not create the cosmic entities' will, which springs from the *Ungrund,* but merely helps that will to become good; he is led to that conclusion by his conviction that freedom cannot be created and that if it were, God would be responsible for cosmic evil. A theodicy would then be impossible, Berdyaev thinks.

Evil arises when the irrational freedom leads to the violation of the Divine hierarchy of being and to separation from God owing to the pride of the spirit desiring to put itself in the place of God. This results in disintegration, in material and natural being, and in slavery instead of freedom. But in the last resort, the origin of evil remains the greatest and most inexplicable mystery (*An Essay on Eschatological Metaphysics*, 127).

The second freedom, that is, the rational freedom which consists in submission to the moral law, leads to compulsory virtue, i.e., again to slavery. The way out of this tragedy can only be tragic and supernatural: "The myth of the Fall tells of this powerlessness of the Creator to avert the evil resulting from freedom which He has not created. Then comes God's second act in relation to the world and to man: God appears not in the aspect of Creator but of Redeemer and Saviour, in

---

for the Christian teaching is to show that the negative and the positive theology are not contradictory but, strictly speaking, complementary to each other. Thus, God, being One in essence is a Trinity of Persons. Hence it is clear that the conception of personality as applied to God is different from the conception of a created personality and is used in theology simply as an "analogy."

the aspect of the suffering God Who takes upon Himself the sins of the world. God in the aspect of God the Son descends into the abyss, into the *Ungrund,* into the depths of freedom out of which springs evil as well as every kind of good." God the Son "manifests Himself not in power but in sacrifice. The Divine sacrifice, the Divine self-crucification must conquer the evil meonic freedom by enlightening it from within, without forcing it, without depriving the created world of freedom" (*The Destiny of Man,* 34–35).

This doctrine, Berdyaev says, is not pantheism. "Pantheism does contain some truth, and that is the truth of negative theology. But the falsity of pantheism lies in rationalizing the mystery and translating the truth of negative theology into the language of the positive" (*The Destiny of Man,* 35).

Berdyaev is particularly concerned with the problem of personality. Personality, he says, is a spiritual and not a natural category; it is not a part of any whole; it is not a part of society—on the contrary, society is only a part or an aspect of personality. Nor is it a part of the cosmos: on the contrary, the cosmos is a part of man's personality. Personality is not a substance, it is a creative act, it is unchangeable in the process of change. In personality the whole is prior to the parts. Being a spirit, personality is not self-sufficient, not egocentric, it passes into something other than itself, into "thou" and realizes a universal content which is concrete and different from abstract universals. The unconscious elemental ground of human personality is cosmic and tellurgic. The realization of personality means the ascent from the subconscious, through the conscious, to the superconscious. The human body as an eternal aspect of personality is a "form" and not merely a physico-chemical entity, and it must be subordinated to the spirit. Bodily death is necessary for the realization of the fullness of life; that fullness presupposes resurrection in a perfect body. Sex means bi-section; an integrated personality has no sex, it is androgynous. Man's creative activity is complementary to the Divine life; hence it has a theogonic and not merely an anthropological significance. There is eternal humanity in the Deity and that implies that there also is Divinity in man.[2]

Man's essential nature is distorted because he fell away from God; beings separated from God and from one another have no immediate experience of spiritual life; they suffer from the disease of isolation. Instead of the immediate experience which reveals the life of the subject, of the existential self, distorted reason develops a way of cognizing the world in an *objectified* form. Man exteriorizes his subjective sensa-

---

2. These ideas are to be found in the article "The Problem of Man," *Put,* No. 50, 12–26, 1936.

tions, projects them and builds out of them objects which stand over against him, form a system of external reality, forcibly act upon him and enslave him. The world system created by such objectivization is nature as opposed to spirit; it is the world of appearances, of phenomena, while the true, fundamental reality is spirit, the world of *noumena*, i.e., a world cognizable in and through immediate spiritual experience and not through objectivization.[3]

Berdyaev takes it to be a great merit of Kant's to have drawn a distinction between the phenomenal and the noumenal world, but thinks Kant was mistaken in regarding the noumenal world as unknowable; the defect of his philosophy, in Berdyaev's view, is that he failed to explain why man makes use of knowledge in its objectified form. According to Berdyaev this form of knowledge arose as a consequence of the sin of falling away from God which leads also to a mutual severance between persons.

Does nature consisting of objects exist in man's mind only, as Kant thought, or is it a special cosmic realm generated by sin? Berdyaev says "the subject is created by God, the object is created by the subject" (*An Essay on Eschatological Metaphysics*). This does not, however, by any means imply that he, like Kant, regards nature studied by the natural sciences as merely a system of our presentations. To understand Berdyaev's position it is essential to remember that in his view sin leads not merely to objectivization through cognition but actually creates nature as a lower realm of being. "Evil gives rise to a world bound by necessity, in which everything is subject to causal relations" (*Spirit and Reality*). "If the world is in a fallen state, this is not the fault of the mode of cognizing it—as L. Shestov maintained, for instance—the fault lies in the depths of the world's existence. This can be best pictured as a process of splitting up, division and alienation which noumenal subjects undergo. It is a mistake to think that objectivization takes place in the cognitive sphere only: in the first instance it takes place in reality itself. It is produced by the subject not only as a knower but as a living being. The fall into the objective world took place in the primary life itself. But as a result of this we regard as real only that which is secondary, rationalized, objectified, and doubt the reality of the primary, the not-objectified and not-rationalized" (*An Essay on Eschatological Metaphysics*, 77). Nature as a "system of relations between objects" has the following characteristics: (1) the object is alien to the subject; (2) the personal, the unique and individual is submerged by the general, the impersonally-universal; (3) necessity, determination

---

[3]. It is not correct to transcribe the word as *numen:* in Greek it is spelled νοούμενον, so that the *o* should not be omitted.

from without is predominant, freedom is suppressed and hidden; (4) life adapts itself to mass movements in the world and in history, and to the average men; man and his opinions are socialized and that destroys originality. In this world of objects life is lived in a time which is divided into the past and the future, and that leads to death. Instead of "existence" as a unique and individual creative activity of the spirit, we find in nature mere "being" determined by laws. The use of general ideas about this uniformly recurrent being serves as a means of communication between the isolated selves which create social institutions; but in this sociality, subordinated to conventional rules, the subject remains solitary. Fortunately, however, in his "existential depths" man still preserves the communion "with the spiritual world and the whole cosmos" *ibid.,* 61). Man is a "dual entity, living both in the phenomenal and the noumenal world" (*ibid.,* 79). Hence "the noumena can break through into the phenomena, the invisible world into the visible, the world of freedom into the world of necessity" (*ibid.,* 67). That victory of spirit over nature is achieved through sympathy and love overcoming isolation by the communion of the "I" and "thou" in the immediate spiritual experience which is of the nature of intuition and not of objectivization. "This knowledge is 'the conjugal' union of personalities based upon true love" (*Solitude and Society,* 118). There can be no marriage between universals, between "objects": marriage is only possible in respect of "I" and "thou" (*ibid.,* 109). Spiritual knowledge is the meeting between two subjects in the mystical experience in which "all is in me and I am in all" (*ibid.,* 115, 148). Berdyaev designates such direct spiritual communion by the term "communalty." It creates unity on the basis of love. Love is a free manifestation of the spirit. Hence it is a communal, *soborny* unity, to use that term in the sense given to it by Khomiakov. "The free spirit is communal, and not individualistically isolated" (*An Essay on Eschatological Metaphysics,* 21).

Regeneration of the fallen man means his deliverance from nature as created by the objectifying process; it means victory over servitude and death, the realization of personality as a spirit, as an existence which cannot be an object and cannot be expressed by general ideas. Therefore Berdyaev calls his philosophy existential or personalistic. But he thinks that true personalism is to be found not in Heidegger or Jaspers but in St. Augustine who put into the foreground the conception of the "subject."

The society, the nation, the state are not personalities; man as a person has a higher value than they. Hence it is man's right and duty to defend his spiritual freedom against the state and society. In the life of the state, the nation and society we often find a dark, demoniacal force which seeks to subordinate man's personality and make it merely a tool for its own ends (*Solitude and Society*, 177). In social life man's conscience is distorted by the process of objectivization and by conventional rules. The pure, original conscience can only manifest itself in and through personality; everything must be submitted to the judgment of that "existential" conscience, unspoiled by objectivization.

In his ethics Berdyaev struggles against the imperfect good developed in the social life on the basis of objectivization. He expounds it in his book *The Destiny of Man* which he calls "an essay in paradoxical ethics." As an epigraph to this remarkable book Berdyaev chose Gogol's saying "It is sad not to see any good in goodness." The whole of Berdyaev's ethics boldly reveals the sad truth that "there is very little good in goodness, and this is why hell is being prepared on all sides" (*The Destiny of Man*, 358). The fundamental paradox of his ethics is that the very distinction between good and evil is, according to him, a consequence of the Fall which is "a manifestation and trial of man's freedom, of man's creative vocation" (*ibid.*, 362). The experience of good and evil arises when irrational freedom leads to severance from God: "The world proceeds from an original absence of discrimination between good and evil to a sharp distinction between them and then, enriched by that experience, ends by not distinguishing them any more" (*ibid.*, 47); it returns to God and His Kingdom which lies beyond good and evil (*ibid.*, 371). The paradox is this: "It is bad that the distinction between good and evil has arisen, but it is good to make the distinction, once it has arisen; it is bad to have gone through the experience of evil, but it is good to know good and evil as a result of that experience" (*ibid.*, 49).

Berdyaev gives the name of "ethics of law" to ethics which takes cognizance only of the middle part of the course, i.e., only of the distinction between good and evil. In analyzing legalistic ethics and legalistic Christianity Berdyaev shows that they are adapted to the requirements of social everyday life and therefore are full of conventions and lead to hypocrisy and tyranny. He proposes to evaluate the rules of this ordinary morality from the point of view of "pure conscience" and not of man's temporary needs. He wants to create a "Critique of pure Conscience" similar to Kant's "Critique of pure Reason." Berdyaev makes use of the Freudian discoveries to show up the sadistic elements in legalism, and the impure subconscious sources of the rigorous demands made by many champions of "the good;" for instance, he traces all fanaticism, all concern for the "far off" at the expense of the "neighbor," to a lack of real love, namely of the love for the concrete individual person and to replacing it by a love of abstract theories, programmes, etc., backed up by the pride of their authors and champions.

Berdyaev does not by any means propose to cancel the ethics of law or the legal forms of social life. He merely demands tolerance in the struggle with evil and points to a higher stage of moral consciousness than the ethics of law. That higher stage is expressed by the ethics of redemption and the love of God; it is based upon the descent of the God-man into the world and His acceptance of suffering out of love for the fallen. Berdyaev pictures this descent of God as the tragedy of God's love for all creatures. As already mentioned, he maintains that in so far as the world contains irrational freedom, it is not created by God, but is rooted in the *Ungrund,* a potency which is independent of God and is the basis both of God and of the world. In God this irrational freedom is overcome from all eternity; in the world it is not overcome; it plunges the world into evil and makes its history a tragedy. Irrational cosmic freedom is not subject to God. Hence God's love for the creature inevitably acquires a tragic character: the Son of God can only help the world by personally entering the world tragedy so as to realize from within the world the unity of love and freedom which leads to the world's transfiguration and deification. This aspect of God's relation to the world is specially emphasized in Berdyaev's book *Freedom and the Spirit:* the victory of the Logos over darkness, the "nothing" is only possible if the Divine life be a tragedy (I, 240). "God Himself longs to suffer with the world" (251). The coming of Christ and redemption are "a continuation of the creation of the world, the eighth day of creation, a cosmogonic and anthropogonic process" (254). Transfiguration and deification are only possible through ascent to the third kind of freedom penetrated by the love for God. Hence it is clear that they cannot be achieved compulsorily: they presuppose man's *free* love of God. Hence Christianity is the religion of freedom. In all his works Berdyaev fervently and insistently defends man's freedom in matters of faith. Chapters VI–X of *Freedom and the Spirit* are specially devoted to the subject of freedom and free creativeness which God expects of man as His friend. The Church, Berdyaev says, must give a religious sanction not only to the holiness that seeks personal salvation, but also to the genius of poets, artists, philosophers, scientists, social reformers who consecrate themselves to creativeness in God's name (230). "In the salvation of the soul man is still thinking of himself" (64), but creativeness in its inner meaning implies thinking of God, of truth, of beauty, of the higher life of the spirit. In his book *The Destiny of Man* Berdyaev repeats that not only the ethics of redemption, but also the ethics of creativeness is a way to the Kingdom of God.

Social life, Berdyaev maintains, is an organization based to a greater extent upon falsehood than upon truth. Pure truth is often not safe but destructive; it acts as an explosive and leads to judgment being passed on the world, and to the end of the world. Pure truth is existential; in social life, we use objectivized knowledge which arrives at truth which is no longer existential, but is adapted to the needs of millions of men (*Freedom and the Spirit,* 57). In the state and in the church as a social institution we often find not the existential spiritual reality but conventional symbols: "Titles such as Tsar, General, Pope, metropolitan, bishop are all symbols. All hierarchical grades are symbols. In contradistinction to them we have such realities as saint, prophet, creative genius, social reformer. Thus the hierarchy of human qualities is real" (*ibid.,* 64).

The Kingdom of God is permeated with love for all creatures, both holy and sinful. "The morality of the transcendent good does not by any means imply indifference to good and evil or toleration of evil. It demands more and not less;" it aims at "enlightening and liberating the wicked" (*The Destiny of Man,* 372). Hence, true moral consciousness cannot rest content while there exist wicked souls suffering the torments of hell. "Moral consciousness began with God's question: 'Cain, where is thy brother Abel?' It will end with another question on the part of God: 'Abel, where is thy brother Cain?'" (*ibid.,* 351). "Paradise is possible for me if there is no everlasting hell for a single being that has ever lived. One cannot be saved singly, in isolation. Salvation can only be a communal, universal deliverance from torments" (*An Essay on Eschatological Metaphysics,* 205). Berdyaev is convinced that ways of redeeming evil and conquering hell can be found and believes in universal salvation, apocatastasis. He regards the development of creative activity as one of the best ways to combining freedom and love.

In *Freedom and the Spirit* there is a chapter called "Theosophy and Gnosis" in which Berdyaev subjects to a scathing criticism modern "theosophy." He points out that in theosophy there is no God, but only the divine, no freedom, no understanding of evil; it is a species of naturalistic evolutionism. It attracts people by its fictitious gnosis, by its claim to the knowledge of the Divine world. The Church must oppose to it the real gnosis and free itself from antignosticism which has in a sense become identical with agnosticism. With regard to ancient gnosticism the Church feared that it was allied to magic, but the modern man who has passed through all kinds of temptations can no longer be protected against them by artificial barriers. "The method of protecting these little ones from temptation has been grossly abused in the history of Christendom," says Berdyaev, as he calls for free creative development of the human spirit in the name of God.

Berdyaev's social theories are closely connected with his religious philosophy. Many of his works deal with the philosophy of history or with the philosophical aspect of political problems—e.g., *The Meaning of History, The Philosophy of Inequality* and *New Medievalism.* The historical process, according to Berdyaev, consists in the struggle of good against irrational freedom and is "a drama of love and freedom unfolding itself between God and His other self, which He loves and for whose reciprocal love He thirsts" (*The Meaning of History,* 52). "Messianism is the fundamental theme of history—true or false, open or secret messianism" (*An Essay on Eschatological Metaphysics,* 174). The credit for discovering this truth belongs to the Jewish nation. "Three forces operate in world history: God, fate, and human freedom. That is why history is so complex. Fate turns man's personality into the playground of the irrational forces of history. At certain periods of their history nations are particularly subject to the power of fate; human freedom is less active and man feels forsaken by God. That is very noticeable in the fate of the Russian people, and in the fate of the German people. Christianity recognizes that fate can be overcome—but it can only be overcome through Christ."

When irrational freedom gains the upper hand, reality begins to disintegrate and revert to the primeval chaos. This is depicted with the greatest vividness by Dostoevsky, especially in his novel *The Possessed* (see Berdyaev's *Dostoevsky's World Conception,* one of the best things he wrote). In social life revolution is an extreme form of the return to chaos. Berdyaev's works contain many valuable ideas about the nature of revolution and the character of its leaders. "Revolutions," he says, "are preceded by a process of disintegration, a decline of faith, the loss by the people of a unifying spiritual center of life. As a result of it the people lose their spiritual liberty, become possessed by the devil;" the leading part among them is played by the extreme elements, Jacobins, Bolsheviks, men who imagine themselves to be free creators of a new future, but in truth are passive "mediums of formless elements; they are really turned not to the future but to the past, for they are slaves of the past, chained to it by malice, envy and revenge" (*Philosophy of Inequality*). Hence, revolutions can do nothing but destroy; they are never creative. Creativeness begins only in the periods of reaction that come after a revolution: the new forms of life for which the people had been prepared by their past then come to be realized. But even the creative epochs of history have never achieved the ends men had set before themselves. "Not one single project elaborated within the historical process has ever proved successful" (*The Meaning of History*, 237). In the Middle Ages the compulsory Catholic and Byzantine theocracy was a failure. True, it is to the credit of that period that it hardened man's will by the discipline of the monastery and of chivalry; thanks to the medieval Christianity man rose above nature; his bond with the inner life of nature was severed: "The great Pan was dead" for him and man came to look upon nature as a dead mechanism. But he severed himself not only from nature: at the period of the Renaissance and of humanism he also fell away from God. The watchword of our own time is "the liberation of man's creative powers;" the center of gravity is transferred from the Divine depths to the purely human creativeness which seeks to perfect life by subduing nature without God's gracious help. Regarding nature as a dead mechanism, modern man has worked out a positivistic science and technics which interpose machinery between man and nature. The power of machine helps man in his struggle with nature but at the same time it disintegrates him: he begins to lose his individual image, "is depersonalized and submits to the artificial machine-made nature which he himself has called into being." Thus the epoch of extreme individualism ends by the loss of individuality; nonreligious humanism leads to the dehumanization of man. Such an end was to be expected, because man who is severed from the higher principle, who has ceased to strive for the realization of the image of God in himself, is doomed to be the slave of the lower elements. New forms of slavery are threatening man; they are the result of socialism which replaces true "togetherness" (*sobornost*) based upon love and the religious transfiguration of the creature, by the false, based upon the compulsory service of the individual to society for the sake of satisfying its material needs. It is significant that modern socialism has been founded by a Jew, Marx, a representative of the nation which "passionately demanded the fulfillment of truth and happiness on earth" and rejected the true Messiah because he came in the form of a servant and not as an earthly king-liberator. The Jews are still expecting paradise on earth and are wholly turned to the future; hence, they are ready to declare war on all historical and sacred traditions, on all that has been handed down through the ages from one generation to another; a Jew easily becomes a revolutionary and a socialist (*The Meaning of History*, 199).

It must not be imagined, however, that Berdyaev is an anti-Semite. Like Vladimir Soloviev, he thinks very highly of the Jewish people. There is no trace of anti-Semitism or of undue fear of socialism in his teaching. He readily points out the valuable aspects of socialism. He champions a special variety of it which he calls *personalistic* and maintains that socialization of the economic life can only be useful if "the supreme value of the human personality and its right to attain the fullness of life be recognized" ("The Problem of Man," *l.c.*). But the efforts to realize socialism will transform it "into something quite different from the socialist ideal." Socialism will reveal fresh discords in the human life. It will never achieve the liberation of human labor which Marx sought to achieve by binding labor, it will never give man wealth or establish equality, but will merely create new enmity between men, new separateness, and new, unheard of, forms of oppression (*The Meaning of History*). The elimination of hunger and destitution "does not solve the spiritual problem;" man will be "faced as before with the mystery of death, of eternity, of love, knowledge and creativeness. Indeed it may be said that when the social life is more rationally organized, the tragic element in life—the tragic conflict between the individual and society, the person and the cosmos, personality and death, time and eternity—will grow in intensity" (*Spirit and Reality*).

Berdyaev points out, however, much in the same way as Bulgakov, that it is precisely the historical failures which lead to true achievements: the failures rouse the will to a religious transformation of life (*The Meaning of History*, chap. X), to transferring the center of gravity from the disrupted earthly time to the eternal time in the Divine life. In that Divine life universal resurrection is achieved—the necessary condition of solving the moral contradictions of the earthly life. Even man's economic activity must undergo a profound change: basing itself on "the love for nature's inner being" it must become a force that leads to resurrection, whereas the modern technics remain in the realm of death (*Philosophy of Inequality*). "The only kingdom which can be successful is the Kingdom of God" (*An Essay on Eschatological Metaphysics*). That kingdom is not in the historical, but in the existential time. The difference between these two kinds of time is this: the historical time "may be symbolized by a line stretching forward to the future, to the new," but in the existential time "there is no distinction between past and future, beginning and end." Hence life in the Kingdom of God is not a part of history, but is metahistorical. The meaning of history lies "beyond the confines of history," in metahistory. It must not be imagined, however, that history and metahistory are entirely separate: "Metahistory is continually present as the background of history. That which is metahistorical breaks up both the cosmic endless sequence of events and the determinism of the historical process: it disrupts objectivization. Thus, the coming of Jesus Christ is pre-eminently a metahistorical event; it took place in the existential time" (*ibid.*). In the same way all true creative activity on the part of man "takes place in the existential time" and is "divinely human" (*ibid.*). But the realization of the creative impulse in history—i.e., in our objectified world—is always imperfect and always ends in tragic failure. "World history knows the most terrible creative failure—the failure of Christianity, of Christ's work in the world. The history of Christendom has been but too often a crucifixion of Christ." It must not be supposed, however, that human creativeness, distorted by objectivization, is completely wasted. "The Resurrection as the end which includes all individual creative achievements" imparts meaning both to the personal and to the historical existence. That end is the metahistory of the Kingdom of God in which objectivization is overcome, and the opposition between subject and object holds no longer. In our world "the sun is outside of me" and that "indicates my fallen condition" but in the transfigured world "it must be within me and radiate from me" (*ibid.*).

A personality capable of worshiping the Holy and serving it follows the path that leads to the perfection of the Kingdom of God. It develops within a community containing an infinite multiplicity of beings, sharply distinguished from one another in quality and *hierarchically* interrelated. Berdyaev devotes a whole book, *The Philosophy of Inequality*, to proving that the egalitarian strivings of democracy, socialism, internationalism, etc., lead to the destruction of personality and are prompted by the spirit of non-being, of envy, resentment and malice.

All the distortions of personality that take place in our fallen world are overcome through a long process of development in many world aeons. "If we refuse to accept the slavish and terroristic doctrine of everlasting damnation, we must admit the pre-existence of souls on another plane before their earthly birth and their passing through other planes after death. The theory of reincarnation on one plane is incompatible with the wholeness of personality and the unchangeability of the very idea of man, and is untenable; but the idea of reincarnation on many planes, which makes man's destiny dependent upon his existence on planes different from that of the objective phenomenal world, may be accepted. Leibnitz rightly spoke of metamorphosis and not of metempsychosis" (*ibid.*). Final liberation from the distortion of the world of objects will only be reached "at the paracletic aeon and will be the revelation of the Spirit" (*ibid.*).

Berdyaev wrote often and at length about Russia. He says that "as intended by God, Russia is the great integral unity of East and West, but in its actual, empirical condition it is an unsuccessful mixture of East and West." He traces the origin of Russia's ills to the wrong correlation in it of the masculine and the feminine principles. At a certain stage of national development among the Western peoples, in France, England and Germany "the manly spirit rose up and imposed form upon the elemental forces of the people organically and from within" (*Philosophy of Inequality*). There was no such process in Russia, and even the Orthodox religion failed to provide that discipline of the spirit which Catholicism with its firm and clear-cut lines built up in the West. "The Russian soul remained unbounded, it was not conscious of any limits and spread itself out indefinitely. It demands all or nothing, its mood is either apocalyptic or nihilistic and it is therefore incapable of building up the half-way kingdom of culture." In accordance with these national characteristics the Russian thought, too, is directed chiefly "towards the eschatological problem of the end, is apocalyptically colored" and penetrated by a sense of the impending catastrophe (this phrase was originally used by Ern and Prince E. Trubetskoy). The eschatological bent of the Russian mind and its lack of interest for the "half-way kingdom of culture" is fully expounded in Berdyaev's book *The Russian Idea*. He particularly has in mind Dostoevsky, Vladimir Soloviev, K. Leontyev, N. Feodorov, and Prince E. Trubetskoy. Berdyaev himself is one of the most striking representatives of this trend of the Russian thought.

Even Christian-minded philosophers in reflecting on the significance of their own nation in the historical process fall into the temptation of naturalism, in the sense of attaching too high a value to the empirical national character. In his book on *A. S. Khomiakov* Berdyaev notes this defect among the Slavophils in so far as they have a tendency to admire the Russian people's natural characteristics and the historical forms of their national life. Modern Russian philosophers are on their guard against this tendency.

Berdyaev belongs to the group of thinkers who strive to develop a Christian world conception and whose work is the most original expression of Russian philosophical thought. It was begun more than a hundred years ago, with the founders of the Slavophil movement Ivan Kireyevsky and Khomiakov, but came into its own much later, under the influence of Vladimir Soloviev. A whole galaxy of religious philosophers appeared after Soloviev. Among them are Prince S. N. Trubetskoy, Prince E. N. Trubetskoy, N. Feodorov, Father Pavel Florensky, Father Sergius Bulgakov, Ern, Berdyaev, Karsavin, S. L. Frank, S. A. Alexeyev (Askoldov), I. A. Ilyin, Father Vassili Zenkovsky, Father G. Florovsky, Vysheslavtsev, Arsenyev, Novgorodtsev, Spektorsky. Some of those philosophers, for instance Father P. Florensky, Father S. Bulgakov, Berdyaev, Karsavin, Frank, have worked out entire systems of Christian philosophy. Some of their ideas are not in strict conformity with the traditional doctrines of the Orthodox and the Catholic Churches; moreover, it may be said with regard to some of their theories that they disagree with the data of religious experience and intellectual intuition, and should therefore be rejected in the course of further development of the Christian world conception. One of such theories is Berdyaev's teaching about the *Ungrund* as a primordial principle giving rise on the one hand to God and on the other to the will of the cosmic entities.

Berdyaev is wrong in thinking that his *Ungrund* is identical with the "Divine Nothing" of Dionysius the Areopagite. The Divine Nothing in every respect transcends all possible determinations and is so perfect that it cannot be adequately expressed by means of our conceptions. When the Areopagite passes to the positive theology—for instance, when he interprets the Supreme principle as personal and at the same time superpersonal—he does not rationalize it, but still remains true to the negative theology: thus, if the one God is tripersonal, the word "person" can only designate here something that is analogous to the idea of a created personality, but not identical with it. Mystical experience, so admirably described in Otto's book *Das Heilige,* wholly confirms Dionysius the Areopagite's teaching of the "Divine Nothing" as a primordial and absolutely perfect principle.

Neither mystical experience nor intellectual intuition find any evidence of a "nothing" existing independently of God and utilized by Him for the creation of the world. Philosophers and theologians wrongly interpret the statement that "God created the world out of nothing" by supposing that some kind of "nothing" served as material out of which God created the world. That statement has a very simple and at the same time a much more significant meaning: God creates the world without borrowing any material either from within Himself or from without; He creates cosmic entities as something ontologically entirely new as compared with Him. The will of the created beings is also His creation. It is free because in creating a personality God endows it with a superqualitative creative force, giving it no empirical character whatever—neither goodness, nor wickedness, neither courage nor cowardice, and so on. Each personality freely develops its own empirical character, or its essence (*essentia*) and transcends it in the sense that it remains capable of freely working it out afresh. Having created our will as free, God never forces it, because freedom is a necessary condition of the attainment of perfect goodness by the person, but at the same time of course it conditions the possibility of evil.

Freedom of the creatures' will is quite compatible with Divine omniscience. God is a supertemporal being. He therefore is not separated from the future by the relation of precedence; He cognizes the future as well as the present and the past not by means of inference but through contemplation or direct perception. This was pointed out as early as the sixth century A.D. by Boëthius.

During the many years of our friendly intercourse, Berdyaev and I disputed over questions of epistemology. Berdyaev affirms that there are two kinds of knowledge: intuition with regard to spiritual reality and objectivization with regard to nature. I maintain, on the contrary, that both the higher and the lower realms of being are known through intuition, i.e., through direct contemplation (see e.g., my book on *The Sensuous, the Intellectual and the Mystical Intuition*).

As already pointed out, Berdyaev's doctrine of the *Ungrund* and of the creatures' will not being created by God, cannot be accepted as a part of a Christian philosophy. But this by no means implies that the rest of his system must be rejected also; the main content of it is unaffected. The essential theme of Christian philosophy is the doctrine of the absolute good, realizable only in the Kingdom of God, and of the imperfections of our sinful world. Berdyaev's greatest merit lies in showing in a highly original way "how little good there is in our goodness," in our individual, social, and even ecclesiastical life. Like L. Tolstoy he boldly denounces the wrongs of our way of living and teaches us to detect those of them which, through force of habit, we fail to see. He vividly depicts the whole of the historical process as a struggle between good and evil, the end of which can only be attained beyond history. He convincingly shows that everything earthly must perish except the rays of the Kingdom of God which find their way into the historical process because the God-man Jesus Christ does not withhold from us His gracious help.

Highly valuable, too, is Berdyaev's contention that the doctrine of terrible torments of hell, hopeless and lasting for ever, has a sadistic character. No theodicy can be formulated apart from the doctrine of apocatastasis or universal salvation. A noble feature of Berdyaev's philosophy is his defense of the truth that Christianity is a religion of love and therefore of freedom and tolerance. Great credit is due to him also for his criticism of socialism, communism, the bourgeois spirit, and for his struggle against any attempts to make relative values absolute. He criticizes modern class struggle from the point of view of the Christian ideal. As to the principles of social life, Berdyaev champions the traditions of the Western-European and Russian humanism, namely, the absolute value of personality and its inalienable right to spiritual freedom and decent conditions of life. He convincingly shows that those principles can only be consistently substantiated on the basis of a Christian world conception.

There are people who in their wish to be more Orthodox than Orthodoxy itself condemn Berdyaev's work as dangerous to the Church. They forget that the historical life of Christianity, ecclesiastical practice and traditional theological teaching suffer from many defects which have driven wide circles of society away from the Church. In order to bring them back, much work is needed by such laymen as Berdyaev who show that those defects may be removed without damage to the foundations of the Christian Church. By expressing the essential truths of Christianity in new and original terms, different from the style of the traditional theology, such philosophers as Berdyaev awaken an interest in Christianity in many minds that had turned away from it, and may succeed in drawing them back to the Church. Men like Berdyaev lend powerful support to the work of preserving and developing the civilization that defends the absolute value of personality—and for this, all praise and honor to them!

Chapter 17

THE INTUITIVISTS

1. N. LOSSKY

Nicolay Onufrievich Lossky was born in 1870 in the village of Kreslavka in the province of Vitebsk. He graduated both in the faculty of Science and of Arts at the University of St. Petersburg, where subsequently he was professor of philosophy. In 1922 he was exiled from Russia by the Soviet Government and lived in Prague until 1942. From 1942 to 1945 he was professor of philosophy at Bratislava in Czechoslovakia. At the present time Lossky is residing in America and is professor of philosophy at the Russian Theological Academy in New York.

Lossky's chief works are the following: *The Fundamental Doctrines of Psychology From the Point of View of Voluntarism*, 1903; translated into German in 1905 as *Die Grundlehren der Psychologie vom Standpunkt des Voluntarismus; The Foundations of Intuitivism*, 1906; in German *Die Grundlegung des Intuitivismus*, Halle 1908; *The Intuitive Basis of Knowledge* translated by N. Duddington, Macmillan, London 1919; *The World As an Organic Whole*, Moscow 1917, translated into English by N. Duddington, Oxford University Press, 1928; *The Fundamental Problems of Epistemology*, 1919; *Logic*, 1922, translated into German as *Handbuch der Logik*, Teubner, 1927, and also into Serbian; *Freedom of Will*, Y.M.C.A. Press, Paris 1927; translated into English by N. Duddington, William & Norgate, London 1932; *Value and Existence: God and the Kingdom of God As the Basis of Values*, Y.M.C.A. 1931; N. Lossky and John S. Marshall, (translated by Vinokurov); *Value and Existence*, Allen & Unwin 1935; *Types of World Conception*, Y.M.C.A. 1931; *Dialectical Materialism in U.S.S.R.*, Y.M.C.A. 1934; *Sensuous, Intellectual and Mystical Intuition*, Y.M.C.A., 1938; the first part of this book appeared in German in the *Archiv für gesamte Psychologie*, LXXXVII, 1933, under the title "Der Intuitivismus und die Lehre von der Transsubjektivität der sinnlichen Qualitäten," and in English in five booklets published by the Université libre Russe in Prague 1934–1938; *Intuitivism; Transsubjectivity of Sense Qualities; Intellectual In-*

tuition and Ideal Being; Creative Activity, Evolution and Ideal Being; Mystical Intuition; God and World Evil (a theodicy) 1941; *The Conditions of the Absolute Good (ethics)* in Slovak 1944, translated into French by S. Jankélévitch, *Les conditions de la morale absolue,* La Baconnière, Neuchâtel; *Dostoevsky and His Christian World Conception,* in Slovak, 1945; *The World As the Realization of Beauty* (in press). Full bibliography will be found in *Festschrift N. O. Losskij zum 60. Geburtstage,* F. Cohen, Bonn 1932.

Lossky calls his epistemological theory *intuitivism.* He designates by that word the doctrine that the cognized object, even if it forms part of the external world, enters the knowing subject's consciousness directly, so to speak in person, and is therefore apprehended as it exists independently of the act of knowing. Such contemplation of other entities as they are in themselves is possible because the world is an organic whole, and the knowing subject, the individual human self, is a supertemporal and superspatial being, intimately connected with the whole world. The subject's relation to all other entities in the world that renders intuition possible is called by Lossky *epistemological co-ordination.* That relation as such is not knowledge. In order that the object should be not merely connected with the self but also cognized by it, the subject must direct upon it a series of intentional mental acts —of awareness, attention, differentiation, etc.

According to the intuitive theory the objects' sensory qualities— colors, sounds, warmth, etc., are transsubjective; i.e., belong to the actual objects of the external world. They are regarded as mental and subjective by the adherents of the *causal* theory of perception according to which the stimulation of sense organs by the light rays, air waves, etc., is the cause that produces the content of perception. Lossky has worked out a *co-ordinational* theory of perception; he shares the view expressed by Bergson in *Matter and Memory* with regard to the part played by physiological processes in perception. The gist of it is that the stimulation of a particular sense organ and the physiological process in the cortex are not the cause producing the content of perception, but merely a stimulus inciting the knowing self to direct its attention and its acts of discrimination upon the actual object of the external world.

External objects are co-ordinated with the knowing individual in their wholeness, in all the infinite multiplicity of their content, but all that wealth of the object is only connected with the human self subconsciously. We cognize only an infinitesimal part of the object; namely, only those aspects of it which are of interest to us and which we discriminate against the background of the actually present and the remembered contents of being. Human powers are limited and we cannot at once perform an infinite number of acts of discrimination. Therefore our perception as awareness of the object in a discriminated form is only a *selection* from the object; hence, our knowledge is always *fragmentary*. Differences in the perception of one and the same object by different persons are mostly due to the fact that the selection from the whole content of the object of aspects which are raised from the subconsciousness to the realm of consciousness and knowledge is done differently by different people; hence, two observers will often find profoundly different contents in the same object.

Lossky accepts Bergson's theory of dream memory and interprets memory as the immediate contemplation by the subject of his past as such. Illusions and hallucinations may therefore be explained as subjective syntheses of the remembered transsubjective data of past experience.

Lossky gives the name of *ideal being*, in the Platonic sense of the term, to all that has no spatial or temporal character. It includes the contents of general notions, all relations such as the connection between a quality and its bearer, quantitative forms and relations (number, unity, plurality, etc.) and so on. All events—i.e., all that has a temporal or a spatially temporal form—are called by Lossky *real being*. Real being can arise and have a systematic character only on the basis of ideal being. In order to emphasize this aspect of his conception of the world, Lossky calls his theory *ideal realism*. Besides the ideal and the real being, there is also *metalogical* being; i.e., being which transcends the laws of identity, contradiction and excluded middle, for instance, God. Ideal being is the object of *intellectual intuition* (speculation). It is contemplated directly, as it is in itself; hence, discursive thinking is not the opposite of intuition, but a species of it. Metalogical being is the object of *mystical intuition*.

Lossky's intuitivism differs profoundly from that of Bergson. According to Bergson, real being is irrational, whereas Lossky considers the rational and systematic structure of being an essential aspect of reality, observed by means of intellectual intuition.

Cognitive acts are performed by the supertemporal and superspatial agent, the subject. It is not the epistemological self of Rickert's or the transcendental self of Husserl's philosophy but the *individual* human self creating its individual mental acts of attention, remembering, desiring, etc. Being superspatial and supertemporal, the human self is an ideal entity and may be designated by the term substance, or for the sake of greater clarity, by the term *substantival agent*. Not only cognitive acts but all events, all processes—i.e., all real being—are created by substantival agents: the singing of a tune, the experiencing of feelings or desires is the manifestation of some self. Acts of attraction and repulsion and movements in space are produced by human beings and also by electrons, protons, etc., in so far as substantival agents also lie at their basis.

Events that have a temporal but not a spatial form are *psychical* processes. Events that are both spatial and temporal are a *corporeal* reality. If they include processes of repulsion they are *materially* corporeal.

The human self is an agent which produces not only psychical, but material processes of attraction and repulsion and these form its bodily sphere; or, to put it more exactly, the human body is the result of co-operation between the human self and a number of other substantival agents at a lower stage of development. Thus, there is not the slightest need to admit, as Descartes did, two different substances one of which is the cause of mental and the other of material processes. Adopting a *dynamistic* theory of matter—i.e., recognizing that material reality is not a substance but merely a process of creating sense qualities and acts of repulsion and attraction—one can understand and admit that one and the same agent is the source both of a mental process (e.g., disgust at the smell of a decaying plant) and of a material process (repulsing that plant). A substantival agent is an ideal, superspatial and supertemporal entity and as such transcends the distinction between mental and material processes: it is a "metapsychophysical" entity (this term is used by W. Stern in his book *Person und Sache*).

Being supertemporal, a substantival agent can correlate the past, the present and the future; it carries out its activities on the basis of the past it has experienced for the sake of the future it desires; in other words, its actions are *purposive*. The simplest type of an agent's manifestations are the activities of attraction and repulsion which form its *material corporeality*. Activities which are spatially temporal in form can only be realized under the guidance of the same subject's purely temporal activities: at a higher level of development they are the mental processes of striving and effort connected with the ideas of past and future and the emotional experience of values; at the lower stages of development they are psychoid unconscious strivings and efforts. On this view, every material process is *psychomaterial* or at any rate *psychoidly material*. The psychic and the psychoid processes are not a passive superstructure over the material processes but an essential condition of the material processes being possible; they guide it, i.e., determine its direction, composition, and meaning or purpose.

Lossky's doctrine of agents carrying out purposive psychophysical processes resembles Leibniz's theory of monads or W. Stern's conception of personality. A substantival agent always is an actual or at any rate a potential personality. An agent becomes an actual personality when he is sufficiently developed to apprehend absolute values, especially moral values, and recognizes the duty of realizing them in his conduct. Such a theory may be called *personalism*. Lossky's theory differs from the personalism of Leibniz, in the most popular version of it, by the *realistic* (and not subjectivist) interpretation it gives of the material processes. It also differs both from Leibniz's and from Stern's in so far as it denies psychophysical parallelism and recognizes the dependence of material processes upon the psychical. Thirdly, it differs still more profoundly from Leibniz's theory by recognizing the *consubstantiality* of substantival agents.

In creating his manifestations a substantival agent makes them conformable to the principles of the structure of time and of space, to the mathematical laws of functional dependence, and so on. Those principles have an *abstractly ideal* character. The profound difference between substantival agents and those abstract ideas consists in the fact that abstract ideas have a limited content, whereas every substantival agent is infinitely rich in content and cannot be exhausted by any combination of abstract ideas. Substantival agents may therefore be said to be *concretely ideal* entities. Besides, abstract ideas are passive; of themselves they are incapable of imposing form; there must be an agent to impose form on real processes in accordance with abstract ideas. This is precisely what a substantival agent does: being endowed with creative power he produces real processes and informs them in accordance with abstract ideas. Thus, concretely ideal agents are the bearers of *abstractly ideal* forms.

All agents create real processes in accordance with the same ideal forms of time, space, etc., which are not merely qualitatively but *numerically identical*. This implies that in a certain aspect of their being substantival agents are not separate but identical, i.e., *consubstantial*. The fundamental difference between Lossky's personalism and Leibniz's monadology is that Lossky denies the separateness of the agents—denies Leibniz's idea that monads "have neither windows nor doors." As bearers of creative powers substantival agents are distinct and independent, but as bearers of basic abstractly ideal forms they are identical and form one being; therefore even in their independent aspect they are mutually co-ordinated to an extent which ensures the possibility of intuition, love, sympathy (in the true sense worked out by M. Scheler), i.e., of direct intimate communion.

In so far as the agents' identical aspect consists solely in abstractly ideal principles, their consubstantiality may be called *abstract*. In imposing form upon their activities in accordance with identical principles, agents create numerous systems of spatiotemporal relations which do not fall apart into separate worlds, but form one single system of the cosmos. At the head of that system stands a highly developed substantival agent, the World Spirit.

Communion between agents within the framework of the cosmos is subordinated to general forms that condition the possibility of the cosmic process; but the nature of their communion is not predetermined: the agents may combine their powers for living in love and unity or in hostile opposition to one another. The latter course results in various stages of disintegration which do not, however, destroy the general formal framework of cosmic unity determined by the abstract consubstantiality.

Abstract consubstantiality is the condition of the cosmic process having meaning, i.e., of the realization of absolute values in it. The all-embracing absolute value is the absolute fullness of life. It may be attained by agents through their being complementary to one another, through their participating in one another's life, adopting one another's purposes by means of love and intuition and refraining from mutual hostility that limits and impoverishes life. Such unanimous life means *concrete consubstantiality*. The totality of principles that constitute abstract consubstantiality and, when rightly used, lead to concrete consubstantiality may be called the *Abstract Logos* of the World.

The combination of several agents which have adopted at any rate some of one another's strivings in order to realize them together is a means of attaining more complex stages of existence. Remarkable forms of such consubstantiality arise when a group of agents subordinates itself to one agent standing at a higher level of development and becomes its organs. That results in such a hierarchy of unities as an atom, a molecule, a crystal, a unicellular organism, a multicellular organism, a community of organisms like a beehive or a nest of termites; in the sphere of the human life there are nations and mankind as a whole; further, there is our planet, the solar system, the universe. Each subsequent stage of unification possesses higher creative powers than the preceding and is headed by a personality on a higher stage of development. Thus, Lossky's metaphysics, like Leibniz's monadology, is a *hierarchical personalism*.

The group of agents subordinated to a more highly developed agent and serving as organs to it is that agent's body. The agent's separation from his allies is death. Usually, the word "body" has a different connotation and means the spatial system of processes produced by the agent together with his allies. In order to distinguish between these two meanings, one might call the group of agents subordinated to the chief agent by the term "the agent's *allied body*." As to spatial processes, they may be called the agent's *material body*, if they include processes of repulsion which give rise to comparatively impenetrable bulk. In most cases, however, there is no need to use these terms, for it is clear from the context which body is meant.

A world system composed of a number of creatively independent agents welded together by abstract consubstantiality which provides the single framework of the cosmos, cannot be conceived as containing the ground of its own existence. It necessarily points beyond itself to a principle which does not belong to the world system and is not in any sense a system of many elements, because a system of relations would presuppose the existence of another, still higher principle which would be its ground. Thus, the ground of the world system can only be a Principle which is above and beyond the world, and transcends all system. It is incommensurable with the world and therefore in speaking of it one has to characterize it by negative predicates only ("negative theology") or by predicates qualified by the word "above." It is not reason, but is above reason, it is not personal but is above personality, and so on. Even the term Absolute is not applicable to it, for the Absolute is correlative with the relative, i.e., with cosmic being. In other words, it means that the Supracosmic principle is free from the world: there is no necessity whatever for It to be the ground of the world. The world cannot exist without the Supracosmic principle, but the Supracosmic principle could exist without the world. Philosophy discovers It through speculation about the world; i.e., through intellectual intuition directed upon the world and leading to *mystical intuition* directed beyond the world to the Supracosmic metalogical principle.

The Supracosmic principle is incommensurable with the world; therefore It is the Ground of the world, not through dialectical development or emanation or any other species of relation admitted by pantheism, but through absolute creation, i.e., creation out of nothing. This biblical doctrine, grammatically badly expressed, should not be taken to mean that God took some "nothing" as a material out of which He created the world. Those words should be understood more simply: in order to create the world God had no need to take any material either from Himself or from outside; He creates the world as perfectly new being, other than Himself.

This conception of the Supreme principle is purely philosophical. It must be supplemented by the data of religious experience. In intimate and especially in devotional communion that principle reveals itself as the Living God, as a Person. In addition to religious experience, philosophy must also take account of the *Revelation* which tells us that God, being One in substance, is a Trinity of Persons: He is God the Father, God the Son and God the Holy Spirit. Philosophy has a right to make use of the Trinitarian dogma because it imparts a lofty meaning, connectedness and consistency to the rest of our world conception. In the living religious experience, based upon the Revelation, man discovers God as the absolute fullness of life in the Three Persons, concretely consubstantial in their perfect mutual love. All these determinations belong to God as the Divine Transcendence, inexpressible by any words or notions. It should therefore be borne in mind that they are not identical with notions applicable to created beings and are used only as a metalogical analogy. In that case, positive (cataphatic) theology does not contradict the negative (apophatic), but contains it within itself.

In religious experience God reveals Himself not only as the absolute fullness of being, but also as the supreme absolutely perfect value, as the Good itself or rather the Supragood; namely, as Love, Moral goodness, Truth, Freedom, Absolute fullness of life and being, Beauty. The most important aspects of God's perfection are expressed by such attributes as Almighty, All-good, Omniscient, Omnipresent.

God in His Triune life is the absolute fullness of being, the primary and all-embracing intrinsic value. Each personality created by Him is endowed with qualities which, if properly used, enable it to attain the absolute fullness of life. Hence, every created personality is, at any rate potentially, also an all-embracing and absolute—but not primary—intrinsic value. All the necessary aspects of the absolute fullness of being, love, beauty, truth, freedom, etc., are also absolute intrinsic values, but being merely aspects of a whole they are *partial* absolute values. Each of them is *existence in its significance* for the absolute fullness of life. That means that value is not an addition to existence, not a quality which it has alongside of other qualities, but the organic unity of existence and meaning. That theory, Lossky says, is an *ontological* theory of values. Existence that brings us nearer to the absolute fullness of life is a positive value, and that which draws us away from it is a negative value.

The All-good, Almighty and Omniscient God creates the world as a system of entities that has the highest meaning, for it consists of entities capable of creating, with His gracious help, the highest good—the Divine fullness of life. Only personal beings are capable of this: hence, God creates personalities only.

The final end of every personal being's life is the absolute fullness of being. The first and fundamental condition of realizing that end is the participation of the created personality in the perfect fullness of life of the Lord God Himself. To render this possible, the ontological gulf between God and the world has to be bridged: in creating the world and loving His creation God has come down to the world; the Second Person of the Holy Trinity, the Son of God, the Logos, has united human nature to His Divine nature and become the God-man. By the words "human nature" Lossky means the nature of every created personality in general. From all eternity since the creation of the world the Logos exists both as God and as the Heavenly Man; i.e., as ideally perfect man, such as he is in the Kingdom of God. As God the Son He is consubstantial with the Father and the Holy Spirit, and as man He is consubstantial with all created personalities. If we accept the ontological theory of love worked out by Father Pavel Florensky, it follows that a created personality which loves the God-man with a perfect love, i.e., more than itself, becomes concretely consubstantial with the God-man in His human nature; therefore, with the help of the incarnate Concrete Logos it contemplates God "face to face" and is vouchsafed deification by grace. The totality of such deified persons constitutes a special realm of being—the Kingdom of God.

However intimate the communion of the dwellers in heaven with the Lord God may be, passive contemplation of His perfection does not as such mean the living fullness of being for the contemplator. That fullness is attained through participation in the Divine Good by means of the person's own creativeness free from all taint of selfishness, and devoted to producing absolute values—moral goodness, beauty and truth.

Life in God cannot be creativeness isolated from the creativeness of other beings: perfect love for God, Who created the world lovingly, necessarily includes love for all entities created by Him. Hence it follows that the creativeness of all beings that live in God must be completely unanimous, *soborny* (communal). Every member of the Kingdom of God must make his individual, i.e., unique, unrepeatable and unreplaceable contribution to the communal creativeness: only in that case will the members' activity be mutually complementary, creating a single and unique beautiful whole, instead of being a repetition of the same actions. This implies that every created entity, in its ideal essence corresponding to God's will, is an *individual* person, completely unique and unreplaceable by any other created entity.

In the Kingdom of God there is no egoism and consequently there are no acts of repulsion and therefore no material processes. Members of the Kingdom of God have spatial bodies, but they consist solely of light, sound, warmth and other sensory qualities which embody and express absolutely valuable spiritual contents. Such a spiritually bodily whole has the value of absolutely perfect, ideal beauty. The transfigured bodies of the dwellers in heaven are not isolated from one another, but are mutually interpenetrated. As to the "allied" body, each member of the Kingdom of God is connected through perfect love with the whole world and therefore has a *cosmic* body: the whole world serves him as his body. In his article "Resurrection of the Body" (*Anglican Theological Review*, 1949) Lossky tries to show that all the difficulties of the problem of the resurrection in the flesh are solved by this theory of the cosmic body. There is no death in the Kingdom of God because its members are bound together by perfect love and perform no acts of repulsion, so that their transfigured spatial bodies are not accessible to any destructive influences.

The conduct of the dwellers in heaven is morally perfect: it is guided by the love of absolute values in accordance with the hierarchy of values. God is the highest value and therefore He must be loved more than anything in the world. Next in the order of value is every created personality as an individual, unrepeatable as an existent and unreplaceable by any other value if we take into consideration his possible creativeness in the Kingdom of God. Therefore one should love every person as one's own self. Further, we ought to love impersonal absolute values such as truth, moral goodness, freedom, beauty, which are the constituents of the absolute good of the fullness of life, and are subordinate to the value of persons.

Love can only be a *free* expression of personality. Determinists deny freedom of the will on the ground that every event has a cause. They mean by causality the order of temporal sequence of one event after other events and the uniformity of that sequence. Causation, generation, creation and all other dynamic aspects of causality are ruled out. Lossky proves that the will is free, taking as his starting point the law of causality but defending a *dynamistic* interpretation of it. Every event arises not out of itself, but is created by someone; it cannot be created by other events; having a temporal form events fall away every instant into the realm of the past and have no creative power to generate the future. Only supertemporal substantival agents—i.e., actual and potential personalities—are bearers of creative power; they create events as their own vital manifestations. According to the dynamistic interpretation of causality it is necessary to distinguish among the conditions under which an event takes place the *cause* from the *occasion* of its happening. The cause is always the substantival agent himself as the bearer of creative power, and the other circumstances are merely *occasions* for its manifestations, which are neither forced nor predetermined by them. The agents' creative power is *superqualitative* and does not therefore predetermine which particular values an agent will select as his final end. That selection is the agent's free act. Consequently, the temporal order of events is not uniform even in the inorganic nature. It is quite possible that although some two electrons have millions of times repulsed each other, they will not do so the next time. But functional connections between ideal forms conditioning the existence of the world as a *system*—e.g., mathematical principles and the laws of the hierarchy of values and their significance for conduct conditioning the presence of *meaning* in the world—are independent of the agents' will. Violation of these laws is unthinkable, but they do not destroy the agents' freedom: they merely create the possibility of activity as such and of its value. Those laws condition the cosmic structure within the framework of which there is freedom for an infinite variety of activities. The system of spatiotemporal and numerical forms provides room for activities that are opposed to one another in direction, value, and significance for the world.

The absence of rigidly uniform connection between events does not make science impossible. It is sufficient for science that there should be a more or less regular connection between events in time. The lower the agents' stage of development, the more uniform are their manifestations. In those cases there may be *statistical* laws.

Many misunderstandings of the doctrine of free will are disposed of by distinguishing between *formal* and *material* freedom. Formal freedom means that in each given case an agent may refrain from some particular manifestation and replace it by another. That freedom is absolute and cannot be lost under any circumstances. Material freedom means the degree of creative power possessed by an agent, and finds expression in what he is capable of creating. It is unlimited in the Kingdom of God, the members of which unanimously combine their forces for communal creativeness and even derive help from God's omnipotence. But agents outside the Kingdom of God are in a state of spiritual deterioration and have very little material freedom, though their formal freedom is unimpaired.

Life outside of the Kingdom of God is the result of the wrong use of free will. An agent may direct his love upon some value preferring it to all else, regardless of its rank in the hierarchy of values. Thus, while loving the perfection of the absolute fullness of life an agent may strive for it in and for himself, preferring himself to all other beings. This is simply ordinary selfishness. It deserves condemnation, because a selfish love for oneself violates the hierarchy of values indicated by Jesus Christ in the two main commandments: love God more than yourself, and your neighbor as yourself. The failure to fulfill these commandments is the Fall.

There is another kind of selfishness which violates the hierarchy of values much more: some agents who strive for perfection and the absolute fullness of being and even for the good of the whole world are determined to do it in their own way, so that they should occupy the first place and stand higher than all other beings and even the Lord God Himself. Pride is the ruling passion of such beings. They enter into rivalry with God, thinking that they are capable of ordering the world better than its Creator. Pursuing an impossible aim, they suffer defeat at every step and begin to hate God. This is what Satan does.

Selfishness separates us from God in so far as we put before us purposes incompatible with God's will that the world should be perfect. In the same way selfishness separates an agent in a greater or lesser degree from other agents: his aims and actions cannot be harmonized with the actions of other beings and often lead to hostility and mutual opposition. The spatial bodies of selfish beings contain processes of mutual repulsion which create comparatively impenetrable bulk; in other words, they are *material* bodies. Accordingly, the whole cosmic domain to which such agents, including human beings, belong is called by Lossky the psychophysical realm of being. He designates by the terms "psychical" or "mental" such nonspatial processes in and through which relative values are created or assimilated; i.e., values that are good in some respects and evil in others; hence mental processes always have an admixture of selfishness. Lossky gives the name of "spiritual" to nonspatial processes in and through which absolute values are created or assimilated. In the Kingdom of God only spiritual processes and their incarnation in transfigured bodies are to be found; but in the psychophysical realm there are both mental and spiritual processes and their incarnation in material bodies.

The creative capacity of a selfishly-minded substantival agent is diminished, since his powers are not harmoniously combined with the power of God and of other beings. Hence selfishness impoverishes the life both of the agent himself and of other beings in the psychophysical realm. Consequently, selfishness is an evil, and a *primary* evil, giving rise to all kinds of derivative evil necessarily connected with the relative separation of agents from one another and leading to ruptures and dissolution. That is the explanation of disease, monstrosity, death, and also of social conflicts and imperfections. Moreover it is the explanation of natural catastrophes—storms, floods, volcanic eruptions. According to the theory of personalism the whole nature consists of entities which would have been members of the Kingdom of God had they not entered the path of egoism. Owing to this fall and to mutual disconnectedness many of them have become not actual, but merely potential personalities forming the lower kingdom of nature, both organic and inorganic.

The fundamental positions of Lossky's ethics and theodicy are as follows. The primary act of the creation of the world by God, preceding the six days of the world's development and described in the Bible by the phrase "in the beginning God created heaven and earth" consists in God's creating substantival agents and endowing them with the properties of being supertemporal and superspatial, with the principles of Abstract Logos and with superqualitative creative power. Those qualities are the image of God in the creature. God has not given them any empirical character. To work out one's character—i.e., one's type of life—is the task of each entity's creative activity. The agents who at once entered the path of right conduct in accordance with the moral law which demands love for absolute values alone in their hierarchical order, have from the first been found worthy of life in the Kingdom of God and had deification bestowed upon them. They are the "heaven." Beings which entered the path of egoism formed the realm of imperfect being in which they are freed from their defects by means of a slow and more or less painful evolution. In view of this destiny awaiting them, the Bible describes them as "the earth."

Instead of the fullness of life, selfish—i.e., sinful beings create for themselves a limited, impoverished existence; disappointments resulting from selfish activities are the immediate *immanent sanction* of the moral law. Preserving the instinctive striving for the fullness of life, selfish agents continually struggle to work out new types of existence, more complex and occupied with more significant activities. To achieve this, they enter into alliances with one another; they combine their powers, giving up to some extent their exclusive egoism and submitting to some agent who has invented a more complex type of life. They form the "allied" body of this more developed agent and serve him as his organs. This is how there come to be, for instance, atoms—i.e., such types of life as oxigen'eity, phosphor'eity etc.; at a higher stage molecules appear—i.e., such types of life as water, salt, etc. An enormous step towards greater complexity and wealth of life has been taken by agents who invented organic life, vegetable and animal. The further stage of the development of life on earth is the appearance of man. Earthly man is a creature that rises from animality to spirituality. Life of the earthly human type has been invented by agents who on the basis of all their previous experience, first, of the inorganic, and then of the plant or animal life, have risen to the awareness of absolute values and of the duty of creating them in their conduct. At the former stages of their development those agents were only potentially personal; having reached the human stage they became actual persons. The assertion that one and the same agent may evolve from the electron to the human type of life and rise above man, for instance, in the form of a social ego, is nothing other than the doctrine of *reincarnation*.

Lossky champions the doctrine of reincarnation as worked out by Leibniz under the name of metamorphosis.[1] Leibniz considered that doctrine acceptable to Christian theology since he admitted that the transition of the monad (substantival agent) from the animal to the rational human stage is achieved through a complementary creative act of God which he called "transcreation." Such a conception of the origin of man combines the theory of the pre-existence of the soul with that of creationism.

The development of the types of life described in the Bible as the six days of creation takes place through the free creative activity of sinful beings, not quite independently, however, but with the co-operation of the Lord God. All the good that is produced in the world is achieved through the combination of "nature" and Divine "grace."

Lossky says that in the process of reincarnation all agents sooner or later overcome their selfishness and are vouchsafed deification through grace. But since the process of development is carried on by means of free creative acts, it frequently is not a direct ascent to the Kingdom of God, but contains temporary falls and deviations. Lossky gives the name of *normal evolution* to the line of development which leads straight to the threshold of the Kingdom of God.

It is only in the Kingdom of God that a substantival agent fully realizes his individuality as an absolutely valuable element of the world. Since every agent is co-ordinated with the whole world in its present, past and future, an agent's subconsciousness contains the anticipation of his future perfection in the Kingdom of God. That future is for every agent his *individual normative idea*. An agent's conscience is the evaluation by him of his own conduct from the point of view of his normative individual idea. The agent's personal identity is preserved in spite of his numerous reincarnations because even at those stages of development at which he does not remember his past life, he preserves the habits and capacities acquired in it in the form of instinctive sympathies and antipathies, faculties and innate skill. But the point of

---

1. See N. Lossky, "Leibniz's Doctrine of Reincarnation as Metamorphosis" (in Russian), in the Symposium published by the Russian Scientific Institute in Prague V. II 1931; in German, "Leibniz's Lehre von der Reinkarnation als Metamorphose," *Archiv für Geschichte der Philosophie*, XL, 1931.

particular importance is that this whole process of development takes place in connection with one and the same normative individual idea, thanks to which all the stages of an agent's existence form one single individual whole.

Lossky rejects the doctrine that God creates the world in accordance with His Divine ideas which form part of His being, because God and the world are ontologically entirely different from each other and have no identical aspect whatever. Ideas that necessarily enter from the first into the constitution of the world, such as mathematical ideas, are *created being* and not states of God. Lossky considers his conception of God and the world the extreme opposite of pantheism, i.e., the purest form of theism.[2] It preserves the poetical character of pantheism because the ontological gulf between God and the world does not prevent God always and everywhere entering into relation with His creatures as a loving Father. That relation can be particularly intimate because God the Son, the concrete Logos became from the first, at the very creation of the world, the God-man, namely—the Heavenly man, and everything good, especially the absolute perfection of the Kingdom of God is realized only with the gracious co-operation of the God-man.

As the Heavenly man, the God-man is intimately near to the members of the Kingdom of God, but is still little understood by us, sinful men, members of the psychophysical realm of being. Therefore, having in the course of history, prepared for His coming beings that had attained rationality the God-man subjected His heavenly divine-humanity to limitation (Kenosis) and assuming "the form of a servant" realized the second stage of incarnation appearing on our planet as an earthly man Jesus Christ.

Christian conception of the world is anthropocentric because it puts the God-man at the head of the world. In doing so it is generally concerned with the sin-warped nature of the earthly man. Such a conception of the world may therefore be called *micro-anthropocentric*. In Lossky's doctrine of the God-man the primary divine incarnation is understood as the creation and the realization by the Logos of the ideally perfect all-embracing man; such a world conception may be called *macro-anthropocentric*. It is not contradictory of the micro-anthropocentric, but contains it as a part.

The God-man Jesus Christ is intimately near to our psychophysical realm thanks to His earthly life in Palestine. His gracious influence upon us is made much easier when we become His members in the

---

2. See N. Lossky, "The Creation of the World by God," *Put* 1937; "Ueber die Erschaffung der Welt durch Gott," *Schildgenossen* 1939.

Church of which He is the head. We then live under His present influence and take part in His life on earth as vividly depicted in the Gospels and continuing concretely to exist for us in the liturgy.

Jesus Christ's co-workers in guiding our life are the angels and the saints, members of the Kingdom of God. At the head of the whole world, next to Christ as His closest co-worker stands a created being, the World Spirit, St. Sophia. The Virgin Mary is the earthly incarnation of St. Sophia who has thus served the work of the Incarnation of Jesus Christ.

It will be seen that Lossky accepts the sophiology of Russian religious thinkers, but only in so far as it is concerned with the created Sophia standing from all eternity at the head of all creature and having no part in the Fall.

Lossky works out the problems of aesthetics on the same plan as those of axiology and ethics, i.e., taking as his starting point the conception of the Kingdom of God. The first chapter of his aesthetics deals with the problem of ideal beauty realized in the Kingdom of God. By ideal beauty he means perfect spiritual life devoted to creating and assimilating absolute values and having a bodily incarnation so that it can be sensuously apprehended. Starting with this idea, he solves the problems of aesthetics in our realm of being where beauty is always limited: every object in the realm of sinful being has an aspect of beauty and at the same time an aspect of ugliness. That leads to the existence of such an erroneous theory as relativism in aesthetics.

In his books and articles dealing with religious problems, Lossky is less concerned with theology than with the task of working out a system of metaphysics necessary for a Christian interpretation of the world.

2. S. L. FRANK

Semyon Ludwigovich Frank was born in Moscow in 1877, studied at the Moscow University in the Faculty of law and continued his education in Berlin and Heidelberg where he took up philosophy and sociology. He was professor of philosophy at the University of Saratov and subsequently of Moscow. In 1922 he was banished from Soviet Russia and is at present living in England. In his early youth he was a Marxist, then passed on to idealism and eventually to Christian ideal-realism. S. Frank died in London in 1950.

S. L. Frank's chief works are *The Object of Knowledge*, 1915 (translated into French as *La connaissance et l'être*, Aubier 1937); *The Human Soul*, 1917; *The Methodology of Social Sciences*, 1922; *The

Spiritual Foundations of Society, Paris 1930; *The Unfathomable,* Paris 1939; *God With Us* (in English), London 1946.

It is impossible to work out a systematic philosophical world conception, especially of a religious character, apart from a theory of knowledge. Original Russian thinkers from the time of the Slavophils onwards were always inclined to maintain that the knowing subject has a direct apprehension of the transsubjective reality. This theory of direct apprehension has been worked out in detail by N. Lossky who gave it the name of Intuitivism. He called his first work on the subject, "The Intuitive Basis of Knowledge," originally published in the magazine *Voprosi Filosofii* (Problems of Philosophy) in 1904–5, as a *propaedeutic* theory of knowledge. He based his theory solely on the analysis of consciousness and therefore recognized that it required supplementing by a metaphysical conception of the organic unity of the world which would explain the possibility of intuition, i.e., of immediate apprehension. Such a conception would provide the basis for an "ontological theory of knowledge." Lossky worked out such a conception in his book *The World As an Organic Whole* which first appeared in *Voprosi Filosofii* in 1915. At the same time Frank was writing his book *The Object of Knowledge.* In a letter to Lossky Frank said that in the *Intuitive Basis of Knowledge* the fact of intuition is used as a starting point, but the conditions of that fact remain unexplained; the object of his book is to discover the ontological conditions of the possibility of intuition as a direct apprehension of a reality independent of our cognitive acts. Frank explains the possibility of intuition by pointing out that individual being is rooted in the Absolute as "Pan-Unity," in consequence of which every object, *prior to all knowledge of it* is in immediate contact with us, since we are "united with it not by means of consciousness but through our very being" (177). Abstract logical knowledge is only possible because of the intuition of this all-embracing unity. A logically determined object is an object subordinated to the laws of identity, contradiction and excluded middle: it is A in contradistinction to all else, i.e., to *non-A*. Thus the determinateness of A is only thinkable as "forming part of a complex $(A + non\text{-}A)$." Such a correlation can only have its ground in a whole which transcends the determinations A and *non-A,* and consequently is a metalogical unity (237), i.e., a unity not subject to the law of contradiction. It belongs to the realm of the "coincidence of opposites" (*coincidentia oppositorum*) or, rather, *there are no opposites in it at all,* so that "the law of contradiction is not violated, but simply inapplicable to it" (220). Determinations can only be differentiated out of that unity; hence, logical knowledge is only possible on the basis of another, metalogical knowledge, on the basis of "the intuition of integral being" (204, 241). That integral being is absolute unity or pan-unity (239); it is not correlative with plurality, but contains multiplicity within itself; it is therefore the unity of unity and plurality (257, 320).

Logical knowledge deals with elements that have been differentiated out of the whole, and is always *abstract;* it relates to the lower level of being, discrete and having no life in it; it is given through contemplative intuition. All living being, unfolding itself in time as continuous creative becoming, belongs to the realm of the *metalogical;* it is apprehended not through contemplative intuition, not through knowledge as thought, but through living knowledge, or knowledge as life, attained at moments when our self "not merely contemplates an object (i.e., has it supertemporarily) but lives by it" (370–431).

The philosophical basis of psychology is worked out by S. L. Frank in his book *The Human Soul*. He examines in it the realm of *mentality* as existence interpenetrated by subjectivity, and studies the changes that occur in it when it becomes recognized as an object; he draws a distinction between the spiritual and the mental, and through tracing the ways in which our mental life is interrelated with the world as a whole by means of cognitive activity on the one hand, and of superindividual interests on the other, shows that the human soul is a *microcosm.*

Doctrines expounded in the *Object of Knowledge* and *The Human Soul* are further elaborated in *The Unfathomable*. The domain of the fathomable includes all that is rational; i.e., subject to the laws of identity, contradiction and excluded middle, all in which there are identical, recurrent elements belonging to the world familiar to us and expressible in concepts (9). That domain stands over against us as "objective being" (19); our conceptual knowledge of it is abstract (9) and rationalistic (15). Knowledge of objects does not embrace all that reality contains: mystical experience reveals to us a deeper sphere, inexpressible in concepts and "unfathomable;" the only knowledge we can have of it takes the form of *docta ignorantia*, to use Nicolas Cusanus's term. Frank discovers the presence of this sphere "on three levels of being": (1) in objective existence; (2) in our own being as our inner life, both mental and spiritual; (3) "on that level of reality which as the primary basis and all-embracing unity somehow unifies these two heterogenous worlds and provides a basis for them" (19).

Objective existence is not exhausted by successive acts of cognition: there always remains an infinite remainder of the still unknown and inexhaustible because our powers are limited (34). Such a remainder is unfathomable for us. But Frank is concerned with the unfathomable *as such*. The ideal of knowledge is an object as a "sum or system (even if it be an infinite system) of determinations;" what we call the objective world consists of such univocally determined contents (41). Contents of reality as expressed in abstract ideas are not reality itself: they are rooted in that which contains them, in something which may be designated as "fullness," "primary inner unity," "concreteness," "vitality" (42); it cannot be broken up into definite contents and is *transrational and essentially unfathomable* (43). In the *Object of Knowledge* it has already been shown that determinations subject to logical laws presuppose a more fundamental *metalogical* reality (45 f.). In the same way the systematic nature of rational knowledge, i.e., the presence of relations between its different parts, is the result of the analysis of "the integral continuous unity" (45). Thus we have as it were not one, but two kinds of knowledge: secondary, abstract knowledge through judgments and concepts, and "the direct intuition of the object in its metalogical wholeness and continuity" (primary knowledge). There is no logical identity, but only a "metalogical similarity" between the two (47); "the concrete image of existence is translated by us into the language of ideas," somewhat in the same fashion "as a scheme of a material three-dimensional body can be drawn on a flat surface" (48). The determinate is the definite, but the concrete metalogical reality is *transdefinite* (52); it is unique, i.e., individual (54); being greater than any given, i.e., any definite magnitude, it is "transfinite" (58). Every segment and every point of being has at the base of it "the undefinable abyss of the transfinite." This is particularly clear with regard to *becoming*. Conceptual knowledge has in view "nontemporal," "identical," "stable" contents (61). In becoming, however, there is something changing and dynamic; for instance, in movement, every point of space contains neither the being nor the non-being of the moving body (61). Being which contains an element of becoming is *potentiality*, latent power (62). All that is new in it arises not out of a definite ground, which as determinists suppose, necessarily predetermines the future, not out of A, but out of A-X; i.e., out of the transfinite essence of reality in so far as it is partially determined by the presence of A (65). Hence, potentiality always contains an element of indefiniteness and indeterminateness, i.e., of freedom (67). Reality includes the unity of rationality and irrationality, i.e., of necessity and freedom (68). The one-sidedness of the rational knowledge of reality has to be overcome through *dialectical* thought (53).

Objective existence, i.e., the world of fact, combines ideal nontemporal being with the temporal in a way which may be accounted for by the theories of ideal realism (85); but the connection between these two aspects of objective existence presupposes a deeper principle which has just been mentioned—the all-embracing unity as nonobjective, *unconditional being* (86 f.). All determinations spring from this "mysterious and unfathomable maternal womb" (88). "By comparison with every definite 'thing,' it is nothing," an X, a mystery (89). Pervading everything as an all-embracing unity of all, it is "an antinomic coincidence of opposites," not in different respects, but *unconditionally*, for it is a case of "absolute and indivisibly simple being" (90). That explains why *skepticism* is legitimate in reference to all theories and judgments (90 f.).

Absolute being as an all-inclusive pan-unity cannot be contemplated, since "that which is contemplated presupposes outside of itself the act of contemplation and the contemplating subject" (91). The potentiality of thought, knowledge, or consciousness is an element of absolute being not as "given," but as "given to itself," as "possession" (92): "Absolute being is *ipso facto* 'being for itself'" (93). That is the solution of the problem of transcendence: all-embracing being is present in every "I am," and is "with us and for us" and we are conscious of it "through its own self-revelation in us" (93). Frank designates this all-embracing being characterized by its *absoluteness* by the term *"reality."* As the unity of truth and existence it is "immediacy itself" which "silently expresses itself in mute, unutterable experience" (94). It is the primary and inexpressible unity of "I am—there is," the *brahman* and *ahtman* of the Hindu philosophy (95), the concrete fullness, not divided into the outer and the inner world; it is *life in general* (96).

After saying a great deal about the unfathomable, Frank asks how is it that mystics who recognize that God is beyond our knowledge give us nevertheless much information about Him. His answer is as follows. Rational knowledge is attained through distinguishing by means of negation (99). The unfathomable lies beyond negation: it contains the reinforced negation and is the sphere where negation itself is negated or overcome; in the words of Nicolas Cusanus its categorial form is "not-otherness." It cannot be said of the unfathomable that it is "either this or that;" as all-embracing fullness it is "both this and that" —it is the principle of tolerance, of spiritual breadth (101). Though indeed this too is not exact: although pan-unity is the unity of unity and plurality, "the deepest level as primary unity must be something absolutely simple, inwardly one;" consequently, it is "neither this nor that;" it is absolutely detached being, not all-embracing fullness, but rather "nothing," "a still desert," *Abgeschiedenheit* of Master Eckhardt (102). If we stopped at this "nothing" and "the pure ignorance" to which it gives rise, negation would not be overcome but posited in the absolute as "an all-destroying monster" (103); thus, even in a reinforced form negation is not a means of cognizing the superlogical and the transrational (103). In order to cognize it, let us consider what the negation of negation means: its purpose is to do away with the *destructive* effect of ordinary negation, but to preserve its *positive* significance—the connection between distinct, differentiated entities (106), and thus ascend to the universal "yea," to the all-embracing acceptance of being, including the negative relation as well as that which is negated, and perceiving "the relativity of all opposition, of all disharmony" (107); struggle and opposition "can never totally disappear and be replaced by the smooth, conjoint, unquestioning affirmation" (108). To ascend to this transrational principle that conditions all rationality we must turn to transcendental thinking which discovers the general conditions of objectivity and of formal logic (109 ff.). In such thinking knowledge is not judgment, but pure "contemplation through experience" (112), self-revelation of the transrational reality (112). There cannot be in it any judgment or definition; hence, this knowledge is "wise ignorance" (112). This living knowledge may be expressed in judgments by "transposing, as it were, the immediately self-revealing reality into a different key" (114). This is done through "the unity of positive and negative judgments" (115) in antinomic knowledge which is "the logical form of the wise, knowing ignorance." Antinomic knowledge is not a combination of two contradictory judgments (116) or impotent wavering between them but free ascent *"between* or *above* these two logically unconnected and unconnectable judgments" (116). In giving expression to such a pair of judgments we must humbly renounce logical synthesis (116): the supreme truth "speaks of itself in silence" (117). The highest point that can be reached in antinomic knowledge is *antinomic monodualism:* "one thing is not the other, and at the same time it is that other. Thus, reality is always trinitary or triune; but the third, the highest level, the synthesis, is absolutely transrational, inexpressible in any concept or judgment, and is, as it were, the very embodiment of the unfathomable" (119).

The unfathomable has proved to be direct being-for-itself, a reality which reveals itself to itself and to us in so far as we participate in it (121). We know this reality as mental life, and we live in two worlds, "public" objective, and "private" subjective (124). That inner being is the true reality, but in a certain sense it is experienced as "subjective," dreamlike, or "unreal" (125). By the subject in this connection is meant the experiencing self and not the subject of knowledge which, in Frank's opinion, does not coincide with the real self because the cognitive function is "the most impersonal aspect of personal being;" it is the logos, the knowing *light* (126), and our knowledge is a *gift* acquired "through the communion of the personality with the light which is external to it" (127).

Inner being is the unity of the experience and of the experienced, both conscious and subconscious (127); it is life as being-for-itself (128) in the form "I am." Is it the *same* unfathomable, Frank asks, which has revealed itself to us as the all-embracing reality? He answers that the transdefinite essence of the unfathomable "never is the same or self-identical, at every moment and in every one of its concrete manifestations it is something absolutely new, unique and unrepeatable." The form "I am" is one of the modes of being, one of the instances of antinomic monodualism (131): man both "is and is not the absolute reality" (132); "all is in me—and I am in all" (133); selfhood as self-affirmation is opposed to everything else, but in its depth it is "at one with the absolute" (134); and yet, it is not pan-unity in general, but one of such unities (135), unlimited in a limited form, one among many and yet unique and unrepeatable (135), a monad (136). The one all-embracing "consciousness" or "selfhood" *generates* "a number of interconnected particular selfhoods which mutually limit one another." This immediate being-for-itself is "actual potentiality or power" which we have already found at the basis of objective being; in itself that principle is "absence of ground," *Ungrund* (137), Tyutchev's "chaos," blind freedom which leads to slavery in contradistinction to real freedom which is self-determination through self-conquest (139). Without such self-determination immediate being-for-itself is not the fullness of reality (140); it is only "a striving towards being," "subjectivity similar to a dream" (141) that requires completion, that must transcend itself in order to gain its soul through losing it (142). The most general form of such transcendence, the cognitive, is merely *ideal;* there must also be *real* transcendence, a going outwards to "thou" and inwards to the spirit (145).

Immediate being-for-itself, Frank maintains, can only become "my" self as related to a *thou* which really enters into the *me* in the experiences of love, hate, etc., or indeed at the mere encounter between two pairs of eyes (153). Such real interpenetration between the "I" and the "thou" which nevertheless retain their opposition is another instance of antinomic monodualism (167). In love, "two become one" (170) and this is possible because in "their inmost depth," in the pan-unity they are one (171). The unity of "I" and "thou" is "we," a unique aspect of reality (172) which lies at the basis of society and is deeper than the "I" (173 f.). Christianity had this reality in view in accepting St. Paul's conception of the Church as a living body of which human beings are members and Jesus Christ the head (174). Every self is rooted in the pan-unity of "being-for-itself" which is "the kingdom of spirits or of concrete bearers of immediate being-for-itself" (156).

The soul frees itself from self-willed ungrounded "subjectivity" (197) by transcendence inwards, into the depths, toward spirit which is "objective being" not in the sense of being an object, but of being actual, completed, stable *reality* (184) having value in itself and therefore imparting meaning to our mental life as well (188). Personality is "selfhood as confronting higher, spiritual, objectively significant powers, as penetrated by them and as representing them" (198); it is "the image of God (200), the principle of supernatural being manifested in the immediate being-for-itself. It is capable of true freedom which means "being at one's self" (198).[1] It is individual, for it is unique and unreplaceable (201).

In spite of the sharp distinction between objective existence and immediate being-for-itself, both belong to the same world, and there must exist, accordingly, a common source of them, a unity which embraces them both (206). A way of overcoming the opposition between the outer and the inner world is suggested by the perception of beauty as *harmony*, as inner completeness that has absolute value (211). The primary basis of this all-reconciling unity may be found through "going deeper into the realm of the inner life" (220). When we attain the primary basis of all, we transcend the limits of existence, as Plato and Plotinus pointed out (227); that principle is the unity of existence and value (229), the unity of the real and the ideal, more powerful, profound and significant than all actual existence; it combines being and justice, truth-verity and truth-justice (225). As the unity of opposites this superexistential principle is *unfathomable as such* (230). It is best to describe it as The Holy or Deity, reserving the word "God" for a definite form of the revelation of The Holy (232). Our thought can, as it were, only "circle round" this unfathomable principle trying to determine the sense in which it "is," to account for its essential relation to everything else and delineate the forms in which It manifests itself in us and in the objective world. In the usual sense the word "is" is applicable only to particular entities (234); the Deity not *is* but "abides in divinity, hallows and creates being as such" (235). The presence of the Deity is self-evident (236) and therefore cannot be proved either deductively or inductively (237). The ontological proof alone is on the right track if it be understood to mean that the idea of God and the content of that idea are inseparable. The adequate expression of that

---

1. Hegel's *bei-sich-selbst-sein*.

proof "is formulated not by Anselm, but for instance by Bonaventura, Nicolas of Cusa and Malebranche" (236). Nicolas of Cusa shows that "in denying the existence of some particular object we presuppose existence as such from which the object in question is excluded through our negation; hence negation is inapplicable to existence as such." God is "the essential potentiality or power of all that exists or does not exist and therefore it is self-contradictory to think of Him as nonexistent" (238 f.).

The Deity "cannot be separated from the rest of reality, for Its essence consists in being the ground and the source of it" (245); in positing the rest of reality "outside of Itself," the Deity still has it "in and through Itself." The Deity is "God-with-us" (Emmanu-el), the bi-unity of "God and me" without division or confusion (246). "God-with-me" is the primary "thou" (249), the transcendental condition of the form "thou" (248) creating the relation of love which is always *religious:* the love of God is the primary basis of love for one's neighbor (249). My bi-unity with the eternal "thou" of God implies, in the first place, the absolute self-evidence of God which is greater than that of my own existence (St. Augustine) and, secondly, the preservation of my being, my immortality (250 f.).

How is it possible for the Deity which is the Absolute and the First Principle to be a "thou"? Frank answers this question as follows. The Deity is a superpersonal principle, but It turns to me that aspect of Itself in which It is personal as well (259). As love, God infinitely enriches me by His self-surrender and creates life as "being of the self with God," which contradicts all "that is certain for logical thought" (271). In the life of "the self-with-God," the first shall be last (first not only in wealth, power, or fame, but in moral and intellectual attainments and even in right belief), and the last shall be first; to those who have it shall be given, and from those who have not it shall be taken away; strength is weakness, and infirmity is strength; suffering is the joyful way to bliss, and material welfare leads to perdition and so on (273).

As a stream of love, God creates me and provides the ground for me; "He contains me within Himself, as it were from the beginning. Hence the profound idea of the Eternal or Heavenly Man, found in all the deeper religions" (280 f.).

Mystical religious experience interpreted by philosophy is the eternal *universal revelation* of God. It should be distinguished from concretely positive revelation interpreted by theology and consisting in the fact that "God's 'thou' itself enters earthly, temporal being" (254 ff.).

In addition to the problem of "God-and-I" we are faced with the problem "God and the world." The world, says Frank, is a certain "it" (285), actual and impersonal being. Until quite recently it appeared rational in form, but chaotic and meaningless in content (286). Worse still, it is indifferent to good and evil, and indeed rather hostile to the good. It is all the more important, therefore, to solve the question as to the world's ground—not the metaphysical problem of its cause (Frank thinks that problem objectless) but of the sense in which it may be said to arise out of its Primary basis (289 f.). Emanatory theories which presuppose substantial identity between God and the world are untenable, for they "rationalize the transrational." Truth must therefore be sought for in the religious idea of "creation." The doctrine of the creation of the world out of nothing cannot, however, be accepted literally: to begin with, the "nothing" out of which the world is supposed to be created "is simply a word which does not denote anything;" secondly, "the origination of the world already presupposes *time,* but time itself can only be significantly thought of as an element or a dimension of cosmic being." On those grounds Frank comes to the conclusion that God's "calling the world forth into being" consists in bestowing upon it value and meaning: "the world has its real basis and its ideal ground in God—and this is precisely what the createdness of the world means." The world lasts immeasurably in both directions in time, and yet it has an absolute beginning and end, not in time, of course, but in so far as it has an absolute ground and an absolute purpose (290). Thus, the idea of emanation also contains some truth: the relation between God and the world is "the inner unity of both" or "the duality of one. This is applicable both to the world's essence and to its existence." The essence of the world consists in its being a distant likeness of God, and this is felt in the apprehension of its *beauty* (293). The world is a theophany (296), God's self-revelation (294), "the garment" of God or His expression—somewhat after the same fashion as the bodily form is the expression of the spirit (295). Thus, beside the God-manhood there is revealed to us the "theocosmism" of the world (297). But the world as empirically given contains evil as well as good. Hence arises the problem of theodicy (298).

The presence of evil does not affect the truth of God's existence because the reality of God "is more self-evident than the reality of facts" (299); and it is "the reality of God as omnipotent and all-merciful" (300). It follows that the connection between God and the "bad" empirical world is "antinomically transrational, and self-evident only as *unfathomable.*" In other words, "the problem of theodicy is absolutely insoluble rationally, necessarily and essentially insoluble in principle." Indeed, to explain evil would mean to find its ground, its meaning, i.e., to justify it. "But that contradicts the very essence of evil" as of that "which *ought not to be*." Hence, "the only right attitude to evil is to reject it, to banish it, and certainly not to explain it" (300).

It is possible to describe evil, but not to make hypotheses about it. Evil is present wherever reality itself "wants to be groundless and makes itself such, affirming itself in its groundlessness;" it then "falls away from being, and pan-unity becomes a 'split unity'" (301). This implies that reality has immeasurable "depth, inaccessible to us" in which "absolutely *everything* is possible—including the logically and metaphysically *unthinkable*." Such an assertion is "a simple confession of the inability of philosophical thought to decide the problem, it is *docta ignorantia* (312). "The positive, individualizing *not* becomes the excluding, the completely segregating *not—not* as absolute division;" in this way "the paradox of actual, existent non-being is realized;" limitation becomes "a defect, a deficiency." The particular individual entity "mistakes its own inward center in its isolation from all else, for the absolute ground of reality. That is the *perversion* which constitutes the essence of evil as existent non-being" (304). The particular "becomes for itself a fictitious Absolute, a kind of pseudo deity. Not being *all* and needing a great deal, it strives to appropriate everything." Self-assertion and pride are accompanied by insatiable cupidity and lust (304 f.). Hence the struggle of all against all, plunder, murder and suicide—"the hellish torments of earthly existence" (305).

Who is to blame for evil? Frank refuses to explain the origin of evil by the freedom of choice, for choice already presupposes the existence of evil. Besides, we freely strive only toward the good which constitutes "the true inner basis of our being;" as to evil, we are on the contrary, "*involuntarily* drawn to it" (308). There is thus an antinomy between my own responsibility for evil, on the one hand, and the power of evil affecting me, on the other (308).

I am both a tiny particle of the world-whole and its center in which "it is present *as a whole*. Hence, the cosmic fall is *my* fall, and my fall—the fall of the world. I am subject to the world's demonic forces and at the same time all the demonic forces of the world exist in me" (309). Evil, however, "is unable to destroy universal being as such," for since evil means isolation and division "it is always connected with suffering and perdition, not only of the victim but of the *bearer of evil* as well," and that is a proof, as it were, of God's absolute omnipotence." But this truth does not solve the problem of theodicy (311). On the contrary, says Frank, it leads us "to the admission that in some ultimate and profoundest sense evil, or at any rate the primary source of it is hidden in the unfathomable depths of God Himself." Frank points to

Jacob Boehme's and Schelling's intellectual intuition of evil. "The responsibility for evil rests upon that primary element of reality which, though *in God* (for everything without exception is in God) is not God Himself, or is something opposed to Him" (312). "Evil springs from the unutterable *abyss* which lies as it were at the dividing line between God and not-God" (313). Frank evidently has in mind the conception of the *Ungrund* in Jacob Boehme and of "nature in God" in Schelling. In Russian philosophy the same idea is found in Vladimir Soloviev and Berdyaev.

"In living experience," Frank writes, "this abyss is given me 'as *my own self*,' as the bottomless depth which both unites me to God and separates me from Him." That is why I am conscious of being guilty of sin and of evil; that consciousness leads to overcoming and extinguishing evil by reinstating the violated unity with God (313). "Apart from suffering," says Frank, "there is no perfection" (316); there is suffering in God Himself, in the God-man. But "the falling away from being, i.e., from God," and the split in the pan-unity exists "only in our human aspect" (318). In the Divine aspect pan-unity "remains forever unviolate, for all its cracks are immediately filled up by positive being flowing from the Primary Source itself." In the aspect of His eternity God "is all in all. In spite of all the problems of evil the world in its ultimate basis and meaning is transfigured being—the Kingdom of God" (319).

In his book *God With Us* Frank expounds the main basis of Christianity and shows that its essential content rests upon the religious experience, upon "the encounter of the human heart with God" (20) and the living communion with God. He distinguishes between two conceptions of faith—faith as confidence, i.e., as trust in authority, and faith as certainty, i.e., faith as knowledge, and points out that trust in authority presupposes experiences which testify that the authority really does express the truth about God. Hence even faith in authority rests upon faith as knowledge based upon religious experience. In the same way he proves that our confidence in "the positive revelation" is connected with our immediate religious experience (114–119).

God is not our judge but our Saviour. Man passes judgment on himself in his own conscience, but God saves man and shows more love for the sinner than for the righteous because the sinner needs it more (145 ff.). God is "beyond good and evil" (149). God is Love, and Christian religion trains man for sacrificial love and for entering the way of the Cross, in imitation of the God-man Jesus Christ. By eternal torments Frank means not the duration of torments in time but their quality (209).

There is much to be said for the distinction Frank draws between the mystical church which contains the fullness of perfection and is not divided into different denominations and the empirical church which has many defects (244–261). In speaking of our epoch, abounding in deflections from Christianity, Frank says that it is not pagan but *demonical* (282). There must be a reunion of churches if this evil is to be combatted successfully (286).

Frank has written also about the problems of social philosophy. I have chiefly in mind his pamphlet *An Essay on the Methodology of Social Sciences,* his article *I and We* (in the symposium dedicated to P. B. Struve, 1925), and his book *The Spiritual Foundations of Society.* Society is, according to him, a primary whole, a single entity. Starting with his theory of knowledge and his conception of the human soul, he shows that the minds of different individuals are not isolated, but always to a certain extent merged together (e.g., in the perception of one and the same portion of reality) and that communion between them is "a primary quality, a constitutive feature of every consciousness" (e.g., in the experiences of love, friendship, hatred, etc., and in all knowledge of the mental life of others which can only be a direct knowledge). Individual consciousness is not primary, it is but gradually differentiated out of consciousness in general, never severing itself from the whole, so that "the individual is in the fullest and deepest sense derived from society as a whole" (*Essay,* 68). "I" is impossible without opposing it to "thou," but the opposition is overcome in "we" which is the unity of categorically *heterogenous* personal being (*I and We,* 422). Thus, "I" and "we" are the primary categories both of personal and of social being. Since they are correlative, a theoretical knowledge as well as a practical realization of them can only be attained through ascending to a still higher, absolutely primary principle, God, "Who is at one and the same time a unity embracing from outside and determining from within the essence of all being. True 'me,' as well as true 'we'—and therefore their true biunity—are only realized when 'I' give myself, and 'we' give ourselves to the supreme principle—God. That makes clear why and in what sense all social existence must be based upon the *religious* consciousness of its members; the ruin of social and personal existence tossed about between despotism and anarchy is the inevitable result following sooner or later from atheistic, self-assertive interpretation of life" (447).

Arguing against psychologism in social sciences Frank shows that social life cannot be merely the sum of socially psychological events: everything psychical takes place in individual minds, but social phenomena are *superindividual,* both because they exist for many persons at once, and because their duration does not depend upon the duration of human life. "Laws, customs, institutions, etc., as aspects of social existence are distinct from the existence of social feelings, opinions and so on, connected with them" (*Essay*, 47 ff.). Every social phenomenon has an *ideal* aspect (the idea of law, of marriage, etc.) which is normative in character; i.e., it acts upon human will as *the consciousness of the duty to realize the norm* (77). Frank calls such ideality, indissolubly connected with concrete reality, "a living idea" and regards all social phenomena as ideally real (76 ff.). The superindividual character of social phenomena is due precisely to their ideal aspect.

This conception of social philosophy is worked out in detail in Frank's book *The Spiritual Foundations of Society*. Particular value attaches to his analysis of the *dual* character of society, of the presence in it of two layers—the inner and the outer. The inner layer consists in the unity of the "we," and the outer "in that unity being split up into division, opposition and struggle between many selves" (98). Frank describes those two aspects of social being by the terms *sobornost* (togetherness) and "external sociality" (110–119). He deduces from them the inevitable presence in society of *organic* unity on the one hand, and *mechanism*, compulsory external organization on the other, a dualism of morality and legal justice, grace and law, the Church and the world. Moreover, in morality itself and in legal justice, too, Frank discovers the presence of those two aspects, pointing out for instance the difference between the "concrete, individualizing indications of conscience and the stern universality of abstract duty" (172 ff.).

Frank defines the end of social development as "the fullest possible embodiment in communal human life of the fullness of Divine righteousness, the realization of life itself in the all-embracing fullness, depth, harmony and freedom of its divine primary basis" (222). He deduces from this the hierarchical structure of the principles of social life, giving first place to the principles of service, solidarity and individual freedom as man's primary *duty*, for without freedom there can be no service of God (238).

The state, according to him, is "the unity of the systematically organizing, social will" (292). The central power in the state must contain the unity of two principles—supertemporality and temporal development. "The most perfect realization of this concrete biunity is, so far, the dualistic system of constitutional monarchy" (281).

Frank's theory of knowledge is extremely valuable. He proves that consciousness is not the highest conception in epistemology: being does not depend upon consciousness, but on the contrary, consciousness depends upon being. Further, he proves that discursive thinking is always based upon the intuitive contemplation of integral being. It is a prevalent doctrine in modern epistemology that every judgment and every inference is an organic whole: they can be analyzed into their elements, but cannot be built up out of them by adding concepts to one another. Recognizing as he does the close connection between discursive thinking and intuition, Frank works out this view far more perfectly than for instance, Cohen does in his *Logik der reinen Erkenntnis*. Such an interpretation of judgment and inference results in the tendency to deny that there is a difference of kind between analytic and synthetic judgments and to regard both as synthetic systems, not to be explained by mere reference to the law of contradiction. To prove this, it is necessary to show that *definitions* are synthetic judgments. The Marburg School is developing in this direction; thus Kassierer, discussing in his *Substanz und Funktionsbegriff* Leibniz's teaching about genetic definitions, shows that a concept is the *product* of such definitions and not their starting point, ready-made for analysis. But one cannot stop halfway: it is necessary to show that in this respect all definitions are similar to genetic definitions, and that they all are synthetic judgments. The main lines of the argument are set forth in Frank's *The Object of Knowledge* where he proves that the subject of a definition is the object as an intuitively observed part of reality, and the predicate is the totality of the object's characteristics as aspects of the universal whole "through relation to which the place of the *definiendum* is univocally determined within the whole" (273). The relation between the subject and the predicate in such a judgment is that of the whole to its parts; this relation cannot be reduced to partial identity, and therefore a judgment of that type is not analytic.

Such an interpretation of definition presupposes a preliminary inquiry into the conception of whole and part. That inquiry has been carried out by Frank and forms one of the most valuable sections of his book, important not only for epistemology, but also for the solution of all the problems involved in an organic world conception. The merits and defects of Frank's theory of knowledge have been examined in detail in my book *The Fundamental Problems of Epistemology* (225–247, 1919).

Here I will critically examine those theories of Frank which I regard as mistaken and, besides, as leading to conclusions incompatible with a Christian world conception.

According to Frank, all determinateness—i.e., everything subject to the law of identity—is a nontemporal content of knowledge (*The Object of Knowledge*, 244). "All logical determination is something completed, immovable, self-contained" he says (198 f., 364, 366, 405);

all that is subject to the laws of identity and contradiction he takes to consist of *isolated* contents (210); i.e., he apparently regards such contents as discrete (240), because he insists that *continuity* is one of the qualities discoverable by ascending into the sphere of absolute being Hence logical knowledge—i.e., knowledge of contents which are subject to the laws of identity and contradiction—cannot as such inform us about relations, transition, movement, etc., and is altogether impossible apart from intuition which gives us "metalogical knowledge" about "the original unity which is prior to particular determinations" (204).

There is a great deal of vagueness and inconsistency in this view of logical determinateness and of the need for two kinds of knowledge. The first impression it gives one is that Frank, like Bergson, regards logical knowledge as *subjective,* as merely a construct in the subject's mind. But Frank does not really depreciate the value of logical knowledge to that extent. He thinks that abstract knowledge does express the actual content of being, but only of the lower type of being. "There are *levels of reality that have different epistemological and, therefore, different ontological value,* and accordingly it may be said that whatever corresponds to the lower and the less true, does not correspond to the absolute or the highest reality." Consequently, "the system of abstract or self-contained determinations is not a fiction but an adequate representation of reality *in so far as reality is such a system*" (319).

I think Frank's contention could be expressed as follows: the world contains a stratum of life and a stratum of lifeless being; logical knowledge is knowledge about lifeless being. But in that case, why should logical knowledge be inadequate to its object? Surely the inadequacy would arise if we used living knowledge for studying lifeless, determinate being, for in that case we would be attempting to impart life to what in fact is lifeless. Frank anticipates such a question, and answers it by saying that logical knowledge is inadequate in the sense that "truth about secondary or derivative being cannot in any case be a self-contained truth," since "in the last resort all knowledge has only one object—the All-embracing Unity itself" (319). But the objection must still be urged that if there exist two levels of being, the higher, absolute, and the lower, derivative from it, there is not one object of knowledge but at least two, and although the truth about the lower *depends* upon the truth about the higher, it is not submerged by it: if logical determinations are really lifeless, the representation of their lifelessness *is* the truth; if, however, there is in reality no lifeless being, logical knowledge is merely a subjective construct of the human mind. It can be seen how closely Frank comes to this admission from the comparison he draws between rational knowledge and a flat drawing of a three-dimensional body (*The Unfathomable*, 48). He says that there is no relation of logical identity between the primary intuition of reality as continuous, and secondary, abstract knowledge (47).

The very opposition between the subject and the object which lies at the basis of all knowledge about determinate being seems to be regarded by Frank not as the condition of knowledge but as the product of "the essentially primary act of cognition" (*The Object of Knowledge*, 258), namely, of attention. Attention, he says, "may be defined as a state of *directedness*, as the differentiation of consciousness into the subject and the object; all other kind of directedness—through volition, valuation, etc.—is based upon this primary directedness of attention by virtue of which the duality between the subject and the object, and the relation of the former to the latter, is first posited" (259; see also 431 f.). We are thus driven to the conclusion that subject and object are only posited as distinct from one another in knowledge and not in the reality which is prior to it. In Frank's description the individual life approximates so closely to the life of the absolute, that he actually regards it as merely a segment of the absolute's own continuity (176) differentiated from it in inadequate knowledge only. He ventures to say that "we are absolute being itself, but only in a potential, unclarified form" (431). In his book *The Unfathomable* he expresses the same idea: "the ultimate depth of our inner being" is, he says, that which in Hindu thought is called "brahman" and "atman" (95).

Too close an approximation between the world and God is also found in his doctrine that not only the world cannot exist apart from Deity, but Deity is inseparable "from all the rest of reality, in generating the ground of which its own being consists" (245). Accordingly, he sympathetically quotes the lines of Angelus Silesius: "I know that God could not exist without me for one instant: if I perished, God would have to die for need of me" (246).

Frank wrongly interprets the idea that God created the world out of nothing in the absurd sense that God took "nothing" and created the world from it as from some material given to Him. Rejecting such a view, Frank replaces it by a theory which while retaining the words "Creator" and "creation" deprives them of their proper meaning. As already said, when he speaks of the world being called into being by God he means that "God imparts value and meaning to it" (290 f.). My question is, to whom or to what does God impart meaning and value, and where does He find that to which value and meaning are to be imparted? Frank's book contains no answer to that question. We have to surmise that God finds it in Himself as pan-unity and, more precisely, in His *Ungrund*. In that case, God's creation of the world consists merely in demiurgic shaping of the *Ungrund* through bestowing spiritual meaning and value upon it (290). This makes clear why Frank, while rejecting the rationalistic theory of emanation according to which God is partially identical with the world (289), says nevertheless that "a certain amount of truth contained in it" should be taken into account, but interpreted transrationally (293).

The creation of the world out of nothing ought to be understood as meaning that God does not need any material either contained in Himself or given Him from without, since creation consists precisely in producing something completely new, which was neither in the Creator nor outside of Him. Those who adopt this interpretation, sharply distinguish God from the world as Creator from creature and understand the relation between them as a one-sided dependence of the world upon God: the world cannot exist without God, but God does not in the least need the world's existence. He creates the world in His goodness so that there should exist beings capable of actively participating in His perfection. Ontologically He and the world are absolutely different, for the difference between them is not logical, but metalogical. When the difference between two objects is logical, it is always possible to find in them an identical aspect as well, e.g., an elephant and a snail contain an element of identity in so far as both are animals. But if the difference between two objects is metalogical, no identical element can be found in their make-up.

Too great an approximation between God and the world, inevitably involved in the conception of the Absolute as pan-unity, leads to insuperable difficulties with regard to the origin of evil and individual freedom, as is always the case with pantheistically-colored theories. Frank discovers the primary source of evil in the *Ungrund*, in the principle which "in God is not God Himself" (312). No philosopher who recognizes such a principle, says that it has been created by God—nor does Frank. In "living experience" he finds the source of sin and evil in man's own self (313), and that self, he says, is not merely a small particle of the world, but also its center, so that *my* fall is the sin of the whole world, and *vice versa*. Moreover, "my 'self' is the point of intersection between God and the world, the point where God and the world meet" (309). There is only one step from this to admitting that the Deity itself as pan-unity has a part in the origination of evil. Frank does not take that step, but I think a consistent working out of antinomic monodualism should lead to affirming the antinomy: God is *not*, but in a certain sense He also *is*, the source of evil. The Buddhist philosophy, in which there is no conception of God as the Creator of the world, does, strictly speaking, come to this conclusion: regarding all cosmic existence as an evil, it maintains that that existence is the consequence of "agitation," "disturbance" or "clouding" in the Absolute principle.[2]

Through exaggerating the unity between God and the world Frank cannot isolate God from evil, but does not venture to introduce evil into God; he therefore has to maintain that "a theodicy in a rational form is impossible, and the very attempt to build it is not only logically, but morally and spiritually inadmissible" (317). "The first answer, the most general and indefinite," he says, "evidently is that reality has infinite, immeasurable depth" and in that depth "in some sense absolutely *everything* is possible—including the logically and metaphysically *unthinkable*. This is simply seeking refuge in wise ignorance. If one likes to put it so, it is simply an admission that philosophical thought is *incapable* of solving this problem" (312). Frank is aware that in this context he uses *docta ignorantia* in a different meaning than elsewhere: in other passages it meant "rising above" two antinomic positions, and here it consists in simply refusing to tackle the problem.

Through that same overemphasis on unity, individual entities in Frank's system are not delimited from one another, and therefore the fall is not the individual act of every separate self, but the common guilt of the world as a whole. The Christian experience of the Kingdom of God and the experience of personal life compel us to adopt another view, according to which God creates personalities as entities ontologically distinct from Himself and from one another, so that every person is a comparatively independent, free creator of his actions and is solely responsible for them. Therefore it certainly cannot be maintained that all created entities have committed the act of fall. The Kingdom of God consists in the first instance of an innumerable multitude of angels who are its members from everlasting to everlasting without participating in any sin. Frank has no such conception of the Divine Kingdom. That is evident not only from his teaching about "the fall of the whole world" (309) but also from his saying that "apart from suffering there is no perfection" (316). That idea is partly connected with Frank's conception of negation as conditioning the rational determinateness of being and the existence of opposites. Frank says: "Neither the negative judgment, nor the attitude of struggle and counteraction, corresponding as they do to the very structure of being, can ever wholly disappear or be replaced by a smooth, conjoint, finally reconciled affirmation" (108). He confuses here two kinds of opposition, which I carefully distinguish in my book *The World As an Organic Whole* (49)—the *ideal* or the differentiating opposition necessary for the world's richness, complexity and diversity, and the *real* opposition of mutual struggle which hampers

---

2. O. O. Rosenberg, *The Problems of Buddhist Philosophy*, 77.

and impoverishes the life of the struggling entities. It is quite thinkable that real opposition should completely disappear while the ideal distinctions, capable of interpenetrating and completing one another, would be preserved. That is precisely how the structure of the Kingdom of God should be conceived.

The explanation of evil by the misuse of human freedom understood as a power to choose between good and evil does not, in Frank's opinion, go to the root of the matter, since it already presupposes the existence of evil. His criticism would be just if the explanation were really such as he takes it to be. In truth, however, it does not assert that man has to choose between ready-made good and evil, spread out before him, somewhat like pears and apples might be, so that he has only to take the one or the other. Those who uphold the view in question maintain that an entity committing the act of fall creates freely and for the first time good or evil conduct. And even when they speak of free choice, what they mean is choice between the idea of possible good or bad conduct, ending in favor of evil and bringing about its realization which leads to evil becoming for the first time *actual*.

Frank's doctrine of freedom is not satisfactory—owing to the same reason—to too great a unity between God and the world and of all entities with one another. Frank maintains that we never do evil freely: "We are involuntarily drawn to it." He thinks that only the striving toward the good is truly free because the good "coinciding in the depths of reality with existence, forms the true inner basis of our being;" the conception of freedom which "essentially coincides with holiness" as *"free* devotion to the *good only"* (308) does not strike him as absurd. Freedom, just as "being-at-one's-self" is the state when "selfhood *forsakes* itself and becomes rooted in something, other and higher" (199). Hence it is clear that freedom means for him entire dependence of conduct upon the inner basis of personality, and since that basis is reality as the Good, freedom in his view means what is usually called rational freedom. Both these conceptions of freedom are species of determinism. The extent to which Frank approaches determinism can be seen from the fact that, in regarding evil conduct as not free and only good conduct as free, he does not appreciate *formal* freedom; i.e., the creative power of personality which is not predetermined to any *content* of action and therefore conceals in itself the *possibility* both of good and of evil. Even the highest kind of *material* freedom, connected with an unlimited power of creating absolutely valuable being, includes formal freedom as a *possibility* of creating any content of reality. Of course Frank's philosophy cannot sink to the level of real determinism which is only possible for philosophers who reject superrational being and believe that the world wholly consists of "determinations." The true conception of freedom is hinted at in the early part of Frank's book where he speaks of "potentiality" and "dynamism" as freedom (*The Unfathomable*, 67).

The defects of Frank's system, due to connecting too closely God with the world, and the created beings with one another may be remedied, first of all, by renouncing the conception of the Absolute as pan-unity. The supercosmic principle, God, as the metalogical subject of negative theology constitutes quite a special realm standing high above the world. He is the ground of the world in the sense that He *creates* the world as something completely *different* from Himself, new in comparison with Him and *external* to Him—not in the sense of absence of communion, but in the sense of the total *ontological* difference between Him and the world.

Frank may raise the objection that if the Absolute be not conceived as pan-unity, it is put on a level of limited entities *distinct* from it, and itself becomes one of such entities, subject to the law of determinateness. This objection, however, has no force: to have something external to oneself does not, in this case, mean to be limited. Limitations are only possible in the realm of *homogenous*, i.e., of rational being in which difference between any two objects coexists with their likeness in some respect. But difference between God and the world is metalogical and excludes all identity between them.

Among the world's constituents, substantival agents alone, as bearers of superqualitative creative power, belong to the domain of the metalogical and the superrational; all their manifestations in space and time, i.e., the whole of their life, as well as all the abstract ideas belonging to them in accordance with which they act, form part of determinate being subject to the laws of identity, contradiction and excluded middle. Frank has a different conception of the world's structure: he maintains that every manifestation of life, dynamism, becoming, change, movement, being continuous, belong to the domain of the metalogical and unfathomable. He arrives at that conclusion because he regards all being subject to the laws of identity, contradiction and excluded middle as nontemporal, static, discrete, lifeless (*The Object of Knowledge*, 198 f., 210, 240, 244, 364, 366, 405; *The Unfathomable*, 61, 46 f.).

I regard this interpretation of determinateness as erroneous. In order to avoid the error, it is essential in the first instance to be clear about the meaning of the law of identity. The usual formula of it is $A = A$ or A is A. The repetition of A may be a source of misunderstanding. It is necessary to distinguish the law of identity as an ontological law from the law of identity as a law of thought; Frank admits this. As an ontological law, the law of identity refers to the self-identical character of every finite aspect of the world, ideally excluding all the rest of the world's content and therefore being something unique and strictly determinate. It is impossible to find unambiguous abstract term for the exact expression of this highly abstract idea, and so one has to use the symbol A in the formula of the law of identity to illustrate its meaning, and word it as follows: "Every finite element of the world is something determinate, e.g., A" (i.e., it has the character of A'ity, or B'ity, or C'ity). The symbol A in this case ought on no account to be repeated, for what is meant is not the identity of two instances of A (which would be impossible if they are *two*) but of the self-identity of A, i.e., of the self-identity of every determinate content. When, on the basis of this *ontological* law of identity we formulate the *logical* law, concerned with the nature of truth and of judgments expressive of truth, it should be expressed as follows: "In all judgments the objective content A always remains identical with itself as A." In this formulation the symbol A is repeated, but it too, refers not to two instances of A, but to two or many intentional acts of judgment directed upon the one, *literally the same A*. This absolute identity of the object preserved for the conscious mind in spite of the numerous acts of judging about it or of remembering it, and so on, is, on the one hand self-evident and on the other very difficult to explain. Few systems of philosophy can clearly show what structure of the world and of consciousness makes it possible for many different intentional acts (apprehending, remembering, etc.) to be directed upon literally one and the same A.

The self-identity of the determinate content, referred to in the ontological and the logical law does not in the least require nontemporal being: the swiftest change in every phase and in the whole of it is something strictly determinate, i.e., self-identical. Repeated cognitions and recognitions of that change may contain the truth about it only if those numerous mental acts have for their observed object both the dazzling swiftness of the change and its absolute numerical self-identity. How is this possible? The intuitive theory of knowledge gives a very simple answer to the question. Suppose that in recalling the past I say "when my neighbor's house was struck by lightning, it was almost instantly enveloped in flames." As supertemporal I, the knowing subject, can long after apprehending an object direct my acts of remembering many times upon *absolutely the same event* as it was and contemplate it afresh; my acts of apprehension, recognition, etc., are new events, but the *object* of which I am conscious is absolutely the same *unique* event. Philosophical systems unable to account for the possibility of such absolute identity in case of memory, judgment and inference cannot explain the truth of the simplest inferences and judgments—which proves that they are untenable.

Doubts as to the applicability of the laws of identity and contradiction to continuous change in time arise, partly, owing to the following reason. Reflection upon such an event as, e.g., the flight of a cannon ball compels us to admit that at a given *moment* of time the ball occupies a definite position in space and cannot be said to be elsewhere; hence the conclusion is drawn that at one *moment* of time the ball rests in a definite place, at the next moment it is at rest again and so on. By summing up states of rest it is impossible to arrive at motion. And so it is concluded that if motion exists, it is not subject to the law of contradiction: at each moment of time the moving ball both is and is not at a definite point of space.[3]

This argument contains the following error. A moment of time is the *dividing line* between two fractions of time and has no duration; it is quite true that at a moment of time the cannon ball occupies a definite position in space and does not move from it, but that does not mean that it is at rest: rest implies abiding in one and the same place during a fraction of time however short it may be, e.g., during one-thousandth part of a second; in our analysis, however, we were concerned not with a *fraction* but with a *moment* of time, which is an ideal aspect of time. It belongs to its structure being a limit between its parts, but is not itself a *part* of time.[4] It is therefore quite possible that in time a body is in continuous motion, but *in relation to a moment of time* it is at rest; that would not convert movement into a sum of positions at rest, because time is certainly not a sum of its moments. The objection may be urged that we thus ascribe to the moving body both motion and rest. That is true, but there is no contradiction in it, since both movement and rest belong to the body in different respects. There is no more contradiction in this than in saying, as we watch a car rushing alongside a train at the same speed, that the car is at rest in relation to the train, but in motion in relation to the sign posts.

Frank is right in maintaining that continuity of becoming is impossible apart from a metalogical principle; but all it comes to is that the metalogical substantival agent, owing to his supertemporal character, is able to create his manifestations in time not by piecing together their discrete fragments but as a continuous process. But the process as such is wholly determinate, i.e., subject to the laws of identity and contradiction, so that it is only the substantival agent in his inmost supertemporal essence who belongs to the realm of the metalogical.

3. See e.g. Hegel, *Collected Works*, 2nd ed., IV, 67.
4. All these questions are discussed in my *Logic*, 30–36 (on logical laws of thought).

If then only God and supertemporal substantival agents belong to the metalogical realm, while all the cosmic life of the agents taking place in space and time, as well as its abstractly ideal principles, is *determinate*, rational knowledge has the greatest value. It gives us correct information about the world, on condition, of course, that the metalogical sources of the processes in it be pointed out; otherwise, rational knowledge becomes too pretentious and promotes temporal forms of life to the rank of immutable laws of nature.

According to Frank not only the Deity and the inmost essence of personality, but also all continuous processes, all becoming and movement belong to the realm of the unfathomable, the metalogical. Where, then, are we to find what he calls objective being, accessible to rational knowledge? Even that department of nature which is studied by physics and chemistry consists of continuous activities of electrons, protons, atoms, etc., of innumerable movements, i.e., of that which Frank includes in the domain of the metalogical. We are left to suppose that rational knowledge proceeds by singling out of the world discrete, nontemporal fragments and therefore gives us a profoundly erroneous impression of it. Frank must regard such distortion of reality not as an error of this or that particular thinker, but as a necessary characteristic of rational knowledge following from its very nature. And indeed the whole content of his book *The Unfathomable* convinces the reader that not one of the fundamental problems of philosophy can be solved through rational knowledge and even suggests that the truth about any realm of being cannot be expressed in the form of rational knowledge.

The principle which, in *The Unfathomable,* solves the fundamental philosophical problems is that of *antinomic monodualism*. According to Frank the domain of the absolute contains a "coincidence of opposites." Does it mean that the laws of identity and contradiction are violated there? No, Frank himself in his *The Object of Knowledge* says that "the law of contradiction is not violated, but is simply inapplicable here" (220). In *The Unfathomable* too, Frank does not say, when making two antinomic assertions, that superrational truth is a pair of mutually contradictory judgments; he says it is attained by rising *above* both such judgments and lies "in the inexpressible midway between them" (116). As to the continuous temporal processes such as movement, I have shown above that there is no reason to regard them, with Hegel, as an embodied contradiction, or with Frank, as a metalogical supercontradiction: everything temporal belongs to the realm of "determinate" being, accessible to rational knowledge.

Now I want to go further and attempt to show that even problems relating to the Deity cannot be solved by means of antinomic monodualism. The laws of identity and of contradiction, if properly understood, are absolutely inviolable. The law of contradiction would be really violated only if we could discover a definite *A*'ity which, in its very *A*'ity was not *A*'ian, for instance if we could say "the number nine is divisible into three" and add that at the same time, in the same relation and in the same sense "the number nine is not divisible into three." As soon as we try to utter two such judgments, we see that in doing so we *say nothing* about the object. Once we understand this emptiness of two mutually contradictory judgments, we understand that there is no point in "rising above" it; if we dwell upon it, it simply means that we waver between two ideas, and Frank justly rejects such wavering. When two antinomic judgments uttered together do not produce an impression of emptiness, that shows that they both contain truth, but not fully thought out truth, that is, they are concerned with a property which belongs to the object in one respect but not in another; the task of further inquiry is to discover these two different respects. As soon as this is done, the two judgments will prove not to be mutually contradictory at all. This is the case not only with reference to created temporal being, but also to its connection with superrational principles, with God and substantival agents. The superrational is on all sides surrounded by the rational and connected with it by rational relations. Hence, to express an idea in an antinomic form is a clear sign of not having thought it out to the end. That is reflected even in the verbal form of it: Frank generally expresses one of the mutually contradictory antinomic assertions not in a straightforward form, but tones it down by adding "somehow," "in a way," or words to that effect. For instance, in speaking about the distinction between God and the human self and at the same time of their mutual interpenetration, Frank says "my self is somehow rooted in God's own being" (278). We may inquire into that "somehow" and point out in what respect God and the self are absolutely distinct on the one hand, and on the other in what perfectly definite sense they are mutually interpenetrated. In all such cases fully thought-out inquiry results in a complete absence of ambiguity, in a strictly definite "yes" or "no."

In science it is very seldom necessary to reflect upon metalogical principles; violations of the law of identity and contradiction are absolutely unthinkable; hence the assertion that the domain of the metalogical exists and that it transcends identity and contradiction is utterly unintelligible to many minds. To make it more comprehensible I would use the following analogy: mathematical triangles are not subject to the laws of chemistry; that does not mean that they violate chemical laws; they simply contain nothing which may be subject to the laws of chemistry. Similarly, metalogical principles contain nothing which could be subject to the law of contradiction.

It is still more difficult to understand that metalogical principles are independent of the law of identity. Frank tries to make it clearer by saying that the unfathomable, absolute reality "never is *the same,* i.e., unchangeably identical with itself, but on the contrary transcends all identity and therefore at every moment and in its every concrete manifestation is something absolutely new, unique and unrepeatable" (131). Frank speaks here of the absolute reality, consequently of the Deity too, as though It were something temporal, dazzlingly changeable and therefore not subject to the law of identity. I affirm on the contrary that everything temporal, even the most changeable, is always subject to the law of identity and that everything metalogical contains no change whatever, for it is *supertemporal.* Thus, God is a supertemporal principle. It may appear that in that case He is pre-eminently subject to the law of identity in so far as He is eternally and unalterably *stationary.* Such an idea is due, to begin with, to a wrong interpretation of the law of identity and secondly to a confusion between supertemporality and infinite duration in time; it is imagined that the supertemporal is today the same as it was millions of years ago and as it will be millions of years hence. That is an absurd idea, for the supertemporal is not in time and there is for it no "was," "is" or "will be." The independence of metalogical principles from the law of identity should be explained as follows. In order to be subject to the law of identity one must be a finite "this," belonging to a *system* of numerous finite entities mutually interconnected by the relations of sameness and difference; the metalogical is not a member of such a system and therefore is not subject to the law of identity; but it does not violate it, since it has no aspect of finiteness to which the law of identity is applicable.

That which is not subject to the laws of identity and contradiction and yet does not violate them, certainly is unfathomable for logical thought. But it is comparatively seldom that we have to turn to that domain with the purpose of gaining knowledge about it—it has to be done only when we must have to deal with the metalogical as such in its own essence. When we are led up to it by logical necessity we must contemplate it *in silence* and not utter antinomic judgments about it; Frank himself rightly says that the highest truth "speaks of itself in silence, expresses itself and reveals itself" (117). The silent contemplation of that which is unutterable provides us with the ground for numerous logical deductions with regard to the structure and the properties of the logically apprehensible rational existence. It is only occasionally that we ought to have recourse in philosophy to silent, unutterable knowledge, and then immediately return from it to rational speculation which is the true domain of philosophy.

A Christian world conception cannot be worked out without the help of metaphysics as a science. After Kant's *Critique of Pure Reason* metaphysics can only be epistemologically justified on the ground of an intuitive theory of knowledge, i.e., of the doctrine which shows that human knowledge is based upon experience as the direct apprehension of actual reality. Frank's book *The Object of Knowledge* is a highly valuable contribution to the literature on Intuitivism and therefore is a substantial help to the building up of a Christian world conception. Frank himself makes admirable use of it for expounding the fundamental positions of Christianity in his book *God With Us*. A writer of outstanding literary gifts, he presents in it a heartfelt and convincing defense of the Christian religion.

3. A. LOSEV

A. F. Losev (born in 1892), a distinguished philosopher, now living in U.S.S.R. His main works are: *The Ancient Cosmos and Modern Science*, 1927; *The Philosophy of the Name*, 1927; *The Dialectic of Artistic Form*, 1927; *A Logician's Interpretation of Music*, 1927.

Losev is a passionate adherent of the dialectical method which in his works appears as a combination of Hegel's dialectics (concrete speculation) with Husserl's *eidetic* vision (*Wesensschau*). Possessing a great erudition in ancient philosophy, especially in neoplatonism, Losev in his book, *The Ancient Cosmos and Modern Science*, has set out to present in a new light the history of ancient speculative philosophy interpreting it in the spirit of concrete eidetic dialectics. His main object is the study of the "ancient doctrines of cosmos and of the building up of spatial forms in the ancient Greek dialectics." With that object in view he subjects to an analysis chiefly Plato's *Parmenides* and *Timeos*, making especial use of Proclus's works and resorting to various commentators—Simplicius, Damascius, Philopon, etc.

Dialectics is defined by Losev as "logical construction of the eidos," meaning by eidos "the complete logical image of a thing," containing "a fusion of contradictory properties, organically transformed into the living and real organism of the thing." Formal logic dismembers and disjoins all these elements considering each element as something independent and separate from the rest, whence follows its formal nature, though it is not less real than in the eidos. The main law of formal logic, the law of contradiction, does not exist for dialectics which makes use of a diametrically opposite law of *coincidence* of the opposites.

Dialectics explains only the eidetics of the connections between the categorial definitions of a thing; therefore it is not the highest stage of knowledge; above it stands *mythology*, i.e., that "complete and full knowledge which operates with living things and living world, apart from any abstractions."

In the orphic cosmogonies and in Pythagoreanism Losev discovers the dialectics of the "one" and "many;" with Plato it becomes more mature. In his dialogue *Parmenides* the starting point of dialectics is "one." So long as one is conceived only as one it is "neither identical with itself nor with the other, nor different from itself or from the other;" under these conditions it "does not exist," it is above existence, it is a thought about the unthinkable (53 ff.). This superexistent Nothing is that principle which is called the Divine Nothing and serves as the object of the negative (apophatic) theology.

From the superontological One, conceived as inaccessible to thought, Losev passes to its manifestation, to the One as an existent something, and shows that it is thinkable only in connection with the nonexistent, the meon, the formless plurality as the principle of evolution and separateness (60); then he passes to the category of becoming, and so on.

Looking at Plato's speculations in *Parmenides* and at Proclus's speculations from the point of view of the dialectics of the eidos, Losev opens up before his readers a fascinating prospect—of learning to see the structure of spiritual being, to contemplate intuitively the eidos of a thing, its meaning as an organic whole interpenetrated, not only by different, but by opposite categories. Many thorny problems of the history of ancient philosophy are thus presented in a new light: e.g., Plato's doctrine of the soul (in *Timeos*) as a unity of the identical in itself and the other (307); Plato's doctrine of the elements as containing a physico-mathematical, dialectical, mythological, and aesthetic moments (186); the ancient doctrine of the heterogeneous nature of space and time as the basis of astrology, alchemy and magic (229), and the dialectical condition of the modern theory of relativity, etc.

The principal difference between Platonism and Aristotelism is seen by Losev in that the system of Plato is dialectical, and that of Aristotle formally logical. "For Plato the thing and the idea are both different and identical, and their interrelatedness is construed by deducing one conception from the other; that is, for Plato the thing and the idea are dialectical categories. According to Aristotle, the thing and the idea are also both different and identical, but their interrelatedness is construed by deducing the idea from the thing; i.e., the thing and the idea are not dialectical principles. Things are taken as they have been created by the existing reality, which can only be explained by empirical science; the task of logic or philosophy consists merely in the eidetic fixation of things whose origin is unknown, i.e., only empirically known. In Platonism the idea is a self-developing meaning, itself positing its 'other,' i.e., its opposite, within itself, and thus giving origin to all other forms and categories of meaning, including also the category of expression of meaning. In Aristotelianism the idea is an *immovable form of an actually existing thing*, so that the whole mobility of this form consists in the immovably eidetic reflection of the mobile actuality of the thing. In Platonism the idea is throughout an antinomically interpenetrating meaningful play of meanings, so that meaning passes into its 'opposite' and its 'opposite' into it. In Aristotelianism the idea has the static nature of thinghood and in this respect it is absolutely immoveable, and there is no transfusion of meanings; there is a static meaning poised on the immoveable power of facts, so that there is no complete freedom in the dialectical play of meaning with itself" (396 ff.). Plotinus' doctrine is a synthesis of Platonism and Aristotelianism: "Aristotle's dynamism is understood by Plotinus dialectically and para-deugmatically, and Plato's eidology and antinomics—dynamically and energically" (407).

In his book entitled *The Philosophy of the Name* Losev works out a philosophy of language akin to Bulgakov's and representing a sketch of a whole philosophical system, dialectically constructed. The word, according to Losev, is the outward appearance of the eidos of a thing, arising with dialectical necessity in the process of the evolution of being which arrives at *being for itself*, i.e., self-consciousness. Every essence as a definite entity, differing from its "other," from the *meon* (from the principle of indetermination) and consequently containing in itself that other, includes the following three aspects: (1) the *genological* aspect or the aspect of unity which transcends existence and comprises all the existing and the nonexisting, meonic aspects of a thing; (2) the *eidetic* aspect, or the aspect of form, the manifestation of the meaning or idea in a thing; and (3) the *genetic* aspect, or the alogical becoming.

A conception of the world which starts with its apophatic essence is *symbolism*. The revealed eidos of an entity is a symbol: it does not contain all its essence, for it is "more unfathomable and deeper than its appearance," but at the same time "all the essence is wholly present in it, because it is solely owing to this permanent, ubiquitous and whole presence, that the appearance in the form of a *single entity* is possible" (165).

The essence as an eidetic symbol full of meaning is the *inner word of the world*; it is necessarily supplemented by the *outer word*, when it enters into its material "otherness" (meon as matter) and becomes an embodied fact (99); in the body the ultimate realization is attained. The body, says Losev, is "the moving principle of all expression, manifestation, realization." Thus, Losev's ideal-realist symbolism is also *pansomatism,* similar to the one we find in Stoics.[1]

The eidos which has reached expression in corporeal "otherness" is the outer word, the name, which forms the new symbolical moment of the world, symbolical in the sense of the *objectivity of the name* (104). "In the name as a symbol the essence for the first time appears to everything else, for in the symbol flow those very energies which, without leaving the essence, partially reveal it to all which surrounds it" (104). The whole world is, according to this doctrine, a word. "If essence is a name and a word, then this means that the whole world, the universe, is a name and a word, or names and words. The whole being is words, some more living, and some more dead than others. Cosmos is a ladder of different stages of verbality. Man is a word, animal is a word, inanimate object is a word. For all this is meaning and its expression" (166). *"The intelligible name of an object is the object itself in so far as it is manifested and understood"* (172). Yet a word taken isolatedly, even in its "human" stage, is still devoid of ontological fullness: "In my word I know only myself from within and do not know the other; the other I still know only outwardly. And intelligence means awareness of oneself as all and of all as oneself. *It is only in the myth that I begin to know the other as myself,* and then *my word is magic.* I know the other as myself, and can direct and use it. Only such a word, a *mythically magic name,* is the full dwelling of the essence in the other, and only such a word is the summit of all other words" (170 ff.).

The plurality of words as psycho-physio-physical processes for expressing one and the same object (e.g., a Greek calls truth, ἀλήθεια, and a Roman, *veritas*) does not impair this doctrine, but merely shows that now one now another moment can be emphasized in the same cosmic word (the Greek emphasizes the "unforgettableness," the everlastingness of truth, and the Roman the trust in it) (191).

In his book Losev hardly deals with any particular problems of linguistics. But had there been linguists capable of understanding his and Father S. Bulgakov's philosophy of language they would come across some quite new problems and might be able to explain in a new and fruitful way many features in the development of language. Among other things, they would find a way to get rid of associationism and extreme psychologism and physiologism in the theory of language.

[1]. See N. Lossky's article "The Metaphysics of the Stoics as Unconscious Ideal Realism." *Journal of Philosophical Studies,* IV, 1929.

4. D. BOLDYREV—S. LEVITSKY

After N. O. Lossky and S. L. Frank had worked out a system of integral intuitivism, i.e., the doctrine that all species of knowledge are an immediate contemplation of reality by the knowing subject, some of their followers pursued the subject further. Among them D. V. Boldyrev and S. Levitsky should be specially mentioned.

Dmitri Vassilyevich Boldyrev (1885–1920) was a lecturer at the University of Perm. During the civil war he fell into Bolshevik hands and died of typhus in the Irkutsk prison. His chief work, *Knowledge and Existence* remained unfinished and was published by his widow at Harbin in 1935 with an introduction by N. Lossky. In this book Boldyrev develops a highly original conception of "intensive magnitude," i.e., of the degree of an object's reality which varies as the object recedes in time and in space. In other words, Boldyrev maintains the omnipresence of an object-image in space and in time in varying degree and formulates the position that "all exists in everything" which is of fundamental importance for his "objectivism" and intuitivism. The intimate interconnectedness of all objects with one another and the continuous transition from one to another, which lies at the basis of the similarity between them, are made use of by Boldyrev in his original doctrine about fantasy and the nonsubjective character of its images.

While working out his theory of fantasy as the vision of otherworldly objects, Boldyrev spent the summer of 1914 in the Pyrenees with the idea of being near Lourdes in the surroundings in which Bernadette had her vision of Our Lady. He described his impressions in an article "The Bath of Fire" (*Russkaya Mysl,* 1915) which shows that he had a distinct literary gift.[1]

Epistemological inquiry in the spirit of intuitivism was continued even in Soviet Russia in the early days of the Bolshevik regime when its tyranny had not yet completely crushed all philosophic thought that did not conform to the materialistic pattern. In 1926 there was published in Moscow a symposium *The Ways of Realism* by B. Babynin, A. Ognyov, F. Berezhkov and P. Popov. They called their line of thought "intuitive realism" in view of the similarity between Lossky's intuitivism and Anglo-American realism of Alexander, Laird, Montagu and others. Both these theories assert that perceived objects enter the field of the knowing subject's consciousness as they are in themselves and are therefore cognized as they exist independently of the act of cognition.

Sergey Alexandrovitch Levitsky left Russia after the Bolshevik

---

1. See Boldyrev's Obituary in the magazine *Mysl,* No. 1, 1922.

revolution. While studying at the University of Prague he became a follower of Lossky's intuitivism and personalism. He was awarded a doctorate in philosophy on submitting a thesis in which he argued that freedom of will is a necessary condition of the critical attitude to judgment apart from which truth is unattainable. After the Second World War he has been living in Germany as a D. P. but succeeded in writing a book *The Foundations of an Organic World Conception*. He expounds in it in a lively and talented manner the essence of intuitivism, personalism and morally social theories of "solidarism."

5. V. KOZHEVNIKOV

Vladimir Alexandrovich Kozhevnikov (1850–1917) lived and worked in Moscow as an independent scholar and philosopher. He was chiefly interested in problems of religious philosophy and in beauty in nature. In 1873 he published a study of religious teachings in Greek philosophy of the second century A.D. He also wrote *The Philosophy of Feeling and Faith in the Eighteenth Century; Marxism and Christianity* (1907); *Darwinism and Vitalism*, and an extremely valuable work *Buddhism Compared to Christianity*, 2 vols., 1916.

With the help of many quotations from Buddhist literature Kozhevnikov vividly depicts the Buddhist absolute rejection of the world, their teaching that all cosmic being is an evil and that the source of personal existence is self-love. The Buddhist ideal is therefore a complete annihilation of the world and in the first instance of personal being—self-annihilation. Kozhevnikov well describes the exercises worked out by the Buddhists for the destruction of personal being and concludes his book by the following argument. "Neither before nor after the appearance of Buddhism has anyone ventured to take so decisive a step towards utter hopelessness; and this constitutes the tragic grandeur and the educative value of its achievement unsurpassed in history. Perhaps this was its providential mission in the evolution of man's religious experience. One is inclined to believe that in the complex and mysterious plan of Divine world guidance, by the side of so many ways of seeking God, Truth, Righteousness, Bliss and Beauty, of so many hopes that gave wings to the human soul in the strenuous search, it was necessary to show in all its comfortless force another path: the refusal to seek all this because of an utter absence of hope in the triumph of anything positive. More deeply and acutely than anyone else the Buddhists understood the truth of the tragic cry of the suffering man 'I am weak,' and that is the universally historical achievement of Buddhism, the educational, admonishing value of which is not exhausted to the present day. But Buddhism is completely blind to the second truth that directly follows the first; it has not heard or did not want to hear the second call of the human soul—the call of the believers in salvation by the grace of God. In Buddhism the creature has forgotten and rejected its Creator and Provider; having lost faith in the Creator, it lost faith in itself; pride and disbelief prevented it from joining in the third call of the sick soul, needing help and salvation: being Thy creature and work of Thy hand I despair not of my salvation (A prayer of St. Basil the Great). At this point the comforting and healing spiritual force and moral beauty of Christianity stands out clearly in all its grandeur. Having renounced the proud and inconsistent pretensions to self-salvation through self-annihilation, a Christian appeals to God who is Love and who calls us through the Meek and Lowly in heart: 'Come unto Me all ye that labor and are heavy laden ... and ye shall find rest unto your souls'—not the rest of the nirvana or eternal non-being, but of life in God, eternal life" (II, 754–756).

Kozhevnikov wrote about philosophy of feeling and faith because he was in sympathy with Jacobi's theory of knowledge. Jacobi was opposed to Kant's agnosticism and overcame it by the theory that in addition to sense perception and logical thought man also has the faculty of mystical intuition; i.e., of direct contemplation of the reality of the individual being of others. Unfortunately Jacobi inappropriately called this mystical intuition "faith." His theory of knowledge is intuitivism, though not total but partial, somewhat similar to the intuitivism defended by Vladimir Soloviev in his early works on philosophy.

Detailed information about remarkable men like Kozhevnikov will be available when the "iron curtain" is lifted and the activities and libraries of Moscow become accessible. Some data about Kozhevnikov are to be found in N. S. Arseniev's book *Holy Moscow*, p. 137–142, 1940. There is a French and a German translation of this book.

Chapter 18

L. P. KARSAVIN

Lev Platonovich Karsavin was born in 1882. His father was a ballet dancer; his sister is the world-famous ballet dancer Tamara Karsavina; he too, as a child, went to the ballet school. He received higher education at the Petersburg University where he specialized in medieval Western-European history, and eventually occupied the chair of history. In 1922 he was exiled from Russia by the Soviet Government. After that he was professor at the Kovno University in Lithuania, and then at Vilna where he is at present.

Karsavin's main works are the following: *Essays on the Italian Religious Life in Twelfth and Thirteenth Centuries,* 1912; *The Foundations of Medieval Religion in Twelfth and Thirteenth Centuries* (with main reference to Italy), 1915; *Saligia* or a brief and edifying treatise on God, the world, man, evil, and the seven deadly sins, Petrograd 1919; *East, West, and the Russian Idea,* 1922; *Roman Catholicism* 1922; *Medieval Culture; Monasticism in the Middle Ages; Of Doubt, Science and Faith; The Church, the Individual and the State; Dialogues,* 1923; *Giordano Bruno,* 1923; *The Holy Fathers and Teachers of the Church* (the exposition of Orthodoxy in their works) 1926; *The Philosophy of History, Berlin* 1923; *On First Principles, Berlin* 1925; *On Personality,* Kovno 1929; *The Poem of Death.*

Like Frank, Karsavin bases himself on Nicolas of Cusa and builds his philosophical system on the conception of the Absolute as pan-unity and *coincidentia oppositorum.* "Absoluteness," he writes, "transcends our understanding and our conception of the absolute as necessarily opposed to the relative" (*The Philosophy of History,* 72 f.). He lays down "the conception of true absoluteness as the perfect pan-unity of the absoluteness of God—the Creator, the Redeemer and the Perfecter —with the 'other' which is built up by it out of nothing" (351). That "other"—i.e., created being and more particularly, every personality that forms part of it—may be absolutized and become a perfect pan-unity embracing all time and all space, because the Absolute is Absolute

Goodness which gives itself entirely to its creatures. In so far as a creature is deficient in willingness freely to appropriate the Absolute Good, it retains its character of contracted pan-unity, of empirical being, limited in time and in space. The Absolute Goodness does not forsake its creation even in this its pitiable state: "through the Divine Incarnation this self-limitedness of man in his insufficiency becomes an element in the Deity;" it is redeemed and "fulfilled" in the God-man (358). Hence, Karsavin distinguishes between four meanings of pan-unity: "(1) Deity as absolute and perfect pan-unity; (2) perfected or deified (absolutized) pan-unity of creation, different from God, for when it is present, there is no God, and it itself is 'nothing' which has become God; (3) completed or contracted pan-unity of creation striving for perfection as its ideal or absolute aim and, through it, for mergence with God: striving to become God and to disappear in God; (4) the incompleted pan-unity of creation, i.e., comparative plurality and unity which becomes perfect through completion, or pan-unity in its limited aspect" (48 f.).

Karsavin maintains that his religious metaphysics transcends the opposition between theism and pantheism. It differs from pantheism, because he affirms the creation of the world out of nothing and the finite nature of the created entities, as well as the eternal and unchangeable being of God (351). But the creation of the world out of nothing does not mean for Karsavin that God creates anything different from Himself. "It is usually supposed," he says, "that God creates a certain something, a certain reality which, though derivative, is quite other than He, and that that something places itself in harmony or out of harmony with God" (*First Principles*, 37). Karsavin rejects such a positive "something." "Apart from God and without God there is no 'me,' absolutely not" he says. "By myself and in myself I do not exist. But in so far as I think, will, exist—i.e., in so far as I participate in God and become God—I confront Him as another substratum of His Divine content, so inseparable from Him that without Him, apart from Him, in my own self, I am nothing, I do not exist" (37).

According to Karsavin the creation of the world is a theophany or epiphany. In Itself, as an eternal and unchangeable principle, God is unfathomable; in that aspect He is the subject of negative theology, the Divine Nothing inexpressible in ideas; by limiting Himself, He realizes self-creation as Divine Becoming, as a relative something (20) which is realized in a temporal and spatial form and becomes knowable (42). But it should be remembered that, as distinct from God, "this something is nothing" (20).

In his book *First Principles* Karsavin develops his system as follows: the creation of the world is a *theophany;* the Absolute gives the whole of itself to the "other" which is absolute nothing, but in receiving the Divine content becomes "the created something," "a second subject" (45). It must not be imagined, however, that the created subject is endowed with creative power even in the sense of creating his own vital activities. "The creature," Karsavin says, "cannot create out of nothing, and only God Himself creates in it" (39). "Our every thought, feeling, desire, or action is nothing other than God and we cannot see in them anything but God" (20). Although the whole content of the created subject and his whole life are thus asserted to be divine, he cannot be said to be God. Karsavin actually speaks of the free origination of the creature: "God's creation of me out of nothing is at the same time my own free self-generation" (37).

Having created finite subjects the Absolute gives Itself to them. The self-surrender of the Absolute is an expression of Its all-goodness owing to which the finite created world can be made infinite and deified by means of a process that is a kind of Divine circle: "At first (not in a temporal sense) God only, then God narrowing and annihilating Himself in His self-surrender to the creature, God the Creator limited by His creature, and creature becoming God in its self-assertion. Then creature *only* which has wholly become God, All-Goodness and therefore 'again' God *only,* Who has re-established Himself in and through the creature and Who has been re-established by it" (48).

The pantheistic nature of Karsavin's system shows itself in the fact that in it the relation between God and the cosmic process is a kind of game that God plays with Himself: "In so far as creature is also God, God in surrendering Himself to it receives back from it and in it that which He gave it. He fulfills Himself to the extent to which He empties Himself. He actively empties and annihilates Himself as God in the creature; the creature actively re-establishes Him. And since creature is also God, its active rehabilitation of God is also His active self-rehabilitation" (39).

Karsavin distinguishes his system from pantheism by pointing out that in his view every creature is not God, since, having "nothing" as its basis, creatures are finite, temporal and changeable, whereas God, the Absolute, is eternal and unchangeable (*The Philosophy of History,* 351).

It should be remembered, however, that every created entity is a manifestation of God: all created contents come to be through God's self-surrender, so that not only our good thoughts, feelings, desires and actions are divine; "our anger and envy and hatred are divine too; not only bliss, but suffering also is divine. Otherwise God would not be pan-unity and there would exist some other evil deity—which is an absurd and impious supposition" (*First Principles*, 21). Thus, with Karsavin the solution of all problems is dominated by the idea of pan-unity as a principle which is truly all-embracing. Like many other Russian philosophers—Vladimir Soloviev, Father S. Bulgakov, Frank—Karsavin supposes that if something, even a created something, were ontologically external to God, it would limit God. Hence Karsavin staunchly maintains that God is pan-unity, and creature is nothing (7). He foresees the objection that God is not absolute in the sense of being correlative with the relative and therefore of standing in the relation of interdependence with the relative. He knows that there are philosophers who recognize God as Superabsolute and accordingly maintain that nothing external can limit Him. But Karsavin argues that if God be not pan-unity there could exist outside Him another, a third ... a tenth God (8).

Inquiring into the Divine reality and into the domain of the created being Karsavin finds *triunity* everywhere. He bases this conception upon the doctrine of the Absolute as the all-embracing pan-unity: if he discovers a principle involving opposition to another principle, he shows that they enter into the relation of opposition through forsaking the primary unity and severing themselves from one another; the severance leads to a striving for reunion and to establishing the unity of opposites.

Karsavin demonstrates the triunity of God by different methods—by analyzing God as Truth, then as Love and then as All-Goodness. Thus for instance in love he detects the elements of (1) self-assertion that demands complete possession of the beloved (destructive love); (2) self-surrender to him (sacrificial love); and (3) resurrection in him. All these inquiries lead to the investigation of the ultimate and fundamental problem—of the connection between indeterminateness and determinateness. As the First the unfathomable, truly all-embracing pan-unity is Indeterminateness; as the Second, it is Determinateness, opposed to it, and as the Third it is their reunion. Thus, triunity and the Trinitarian dogma proves to be the basic and all-illuminating truth of the Christian world conception.

In Karsavin's book *On Personality* the doctrine of the coincidence of opposites is applied not only to the Divine triunity, but to every personality in so far as it perfects itself and attains deification. According to Karsavin's definition personality is a "concretely spiritual, corporeally spiritual determinate entity, unique, unreplaceable and many-sided" (2). The unity of personality is its spiritual, and the plurality is its corporeal nature. Since the unity of personality is the unity of plurality, personality is "wholly spiritual and wholly corporeal" (143). In its mere corporeality—i.e., in its plurality—it is givenness, necessity, and in its spirituality it is the overcoming of necessity, self-determination, i.e., freedom. The relativity of these definitions shows that personality contains "something higher than its unity, freedom and necessity—namely itself" (4). As such, the principle of personality is indefinable (37), it is *ousia,* essence, in relation to the determinate primary unity, the Father, to the self-dividing unity, the Son, and to the self-reuniting unity, the Holy Spirit. The principle of personality is indefinable, since determination is only possible where there is division; it lies at the basis of a determinate primary unity of personality correlative with its self-division and, further, with its self-unification. Thus, in the Absolute the indefinable primary unity is a triunity; in theological language it is *ousia;* the determinate primary unity is the Father, the self-dividing unity is the Son, the self-reuniting unity is the Holy Spirit, the tripersonal Holy Trinity (39).

The Divine Triunity is, strictly speaking, unique personal being (85); it reveals and determines itself chiefly in the Second Person, the Logos, which as self-division, is the Body of the Holy Trinity (145).

In his book *On First Principles* Karsavin says that the created self is (1) original unity; (2) its division into the subject and the object; and (3) their reunion in consciousness (99). The reunion attained through knowledge is incomplete: in it the unification is *less* than the dividedness. We know about this incompleteness and therefore it seems to us that our being and self-consciousness is "something unreal, a kind of dream" (103). To become aware of this illusoriness of one's being means to define it from the point of view of higher being; it implies that in addition to my lower being I am also a higher being, namely, I am that perfected pan-unity which I possess in the God-man. As soon as we cease to concentrate on our lower being, as soon as we empty ourselves, "become conscious of our nothingness, we see God in our self-consciousness, and the whole of our self-consciousness, the whole of our knowledge becomes a spiritual prayer the sweetness of which increases in proportion to our humility" (108).

In this higher aspect of ourselves we are all-spatial and all-temporal, but in the lower we are reduced to the limited temporal moment that comes into being and perishes, and to a finite position in space (130). The theory that my self has an all-spatial aspect implies that a particle of my body on leaving me and becoming an element in the body of another being does not forsake me altogether: "Stamped by me, it is my own self and in the all-temporal and all-spatial reality remains 'me' forever and everywhere, though it also becomes something else—the world as a whole" (139).

In his book *On Personality* Karsavin elaborates his doctrine about the created self. Strictly speaking, creature is not a personality: it is created by God out of nothing as a free—i.e., self-generated out of nothing—indefinable substratum, and in itself does not constitute anything; in assimilating the Divine "content" it first becomes a personality. In so far as the creature receives all its content through its participation in the Logos, the whole of the created world is a *theophany* (85, 175).

Evil and imperfection of the creature is merely a lack of Goodness in it, incomplete assimilation by it of the Divine content: "Having begun its existence in God and in itself, the creature at once began to center in itself, replaced humility by pride" and desired the impossible —a part of being instead of the fullness of being; but "what is impossible to man is possible to God—God fulfilled the absurd desire of the creature" and, respecting its freedom, gave it the half-being, half non-being it desired, incomplete death and incomplete life, the bad infinity of dying (195 ff.). That incomplete life is a consequence of our sloth and inertia which prevent us assimilating the fullness of the Divine being which God gives us in His sacrificial love. Our repentance for this guilt may correctly be expressed by the words: "I have not sufficiently desired" to accept Divine being into myself. This sinful "weakness" is not a special force; to believe that it was would be Manicheism, says Karsavin; weakness is simply a lack of desire to assimilate God (35 ff.). Evil as guilt is always accompanied by evil as suffering which is both the punishment for the guilt and its redemption (30). Repentance in one's guilt is not, strictly speaking, self-condemnation: it consists in the condemnation of the action by the 'Higher standard' and not by my own self (23). Indeed, in self-condemnation one theophany opposes itself to another, the greater to the lesser, the one that symbolizes the fullness of Godhead to the less full: "We condemn ourselves for not having apprehended God fully" (34 f.).

Every sin, according to Karsavin, is incompleteness of theophany. Thus, pride is an attempt to affirm oneself in one's own self; in so far as it *exists*, it is a theophany (49), because "possession is a reflection of possessing everything in God," but it suffers from incompleteness; a proud man is a foolish thief (51): he wants to possess everything, he is grasping and greedy, but he does not attain to the possessions in God that belong to a self which desires to possess *truly everything*—i.e., "desires that all, including God, should possess the gifts which he possesses" (52).

Karsavin deduces from this conception of evil that the way to perfection lies "not in the struggle with some nonexistent evil, but in the fullness of our love for God and with God" (68). "Judge not," says the Lord (68); do not sever yourself from one another through condemnation and, "in overcoming weakness, you will understand that there is no evil" (69). "Resist not evil, for there is no evil," but "do good," detect in what is called evil "a faint glimmering of good, and fan that small flame till it sets the world on fire" (69). Cognize "good only, for there is no evil" (75).

"May be it shall fall to your lot to defend the weak by violence, to save life by killing the guilty" (70); "I think that God sends such a trial only to men with no understanding" (71). "There is such a thing as righteous killing and a righteous war," Karsavin admits, but in deciding this in actual life one must beware of the voice of the Antichrist (72).

The imperfection of the creature may be such that it will have only embryonically personal being (animals) or even merely potentially personal being (things) (*On Personality*, 127). The perfection of personality depends in its completely assimilating Divine nature, i.e., in its attaining deification. The ontological sequence in the process of God's self-sacrifice for the creature and of the creature's self-sacrifice for God is as follows: "At first—only God alone, then—the dying God and the creature coming into being, then—only creature alone instead of God, then—the dying creature and the rising God; then—again only God alone. But everything 'at first' and 'then' and 'all at once': God is also the God-man" (161).

This unity between God and man in the Divine Hypostasis is rendered possible by the incarnation of the Logos, consisting in the fact that He freely becomes imperfect, having willed not imperfection as such, but only the existential aspect of it, i.e., imperfection as guiltless suffering and death (224). Since Christ's humanity is not external to His Person, but is "within it," Christ's suffering and death are a Divine tragedy in spite of the resurrection; indeed, even patripassionism (the doctrine that the Father suffers as well as the Son) contains a certain element of truth (192).

Creature deified through grace is the true God, but that does not lead to a pantheistic identification of God and the world: there is a most profound ontological difference between "*is not* which comes from *is* and after *is*" and "the *is* which comes after *is not* and from *is not*" (160).

Karsavin has an interesting theory about corporeality which he defines as plurality in a self-dividing personality, conditioning the determinateness of the self. That determinateness necessarily is "the correlatedness of my body with other bodies, not their external co-position or contact, but their interpenetration and intermergence. My body contains corporeality external to it, and external corporeality contains mine. All that I cognize, remember or even imagine is *my* corporeality, though not only mine, but *also* external to me. The whole world, while remaining a corporeality external to me, becomes my corporeality as well" (128).

By means of this theory Karsavin, true to his principle of the coincidence of opposites, overcomes the difference between *phenomenalism* and *intuitivism* (79 f.). For him the whole world external to the individual body of an imperfect personality is to a certain extent its body also, but an "external" one (131 ff.); he tries to make use of this conception for explaining such things as psychometry, exteriorization of sensibility, etc. He explains the presence of sensation in amputated limbs by urging that parts and particles of the body separated from it do not lose all connection with it (130). Karsavin therefore maintains that the method of disposing of the corpse is not a matter of indifference to us. A materialist curses himself in discovering his folly when his body is being burned to ashes in accordance with the last word of technics in a godforsaken crematorium.

The difference between an imperfect and a perfect personality consists in the fact that the first has both an individual and an external body, and for the second the whole of its external body is merged with its individual body (134).

Karsavin's *The Philosophy of History* is a particularly valuable work. In it Karsavin formulates the fundamental principles of historical being and considers "the place and the significance of the historical in the world as a whole and in relation to absolute being" (5). He regards it as "the highest aim of historical thinking to apprehend the whole cosmos, the whole created pan-unity as a single developing subject" (77). History in the narrow sense of the term is concerned with "the development of mankind as a single all-spatial and all-temporal subject" (75). By "development" Karsavin means a process in which some whole (an organism, a mental life) is continually changing, "continually becoming qualitatively different—becoming from within, from out of itself and not through addition of something from outside" (10).

The continuity of development shows that the developing object does not consist of separate parts, of atoms, but forms a *single subject*, who is not distinct from his development, but real in it and therefore all-temporal, all-spatial, all-qualitative, all-embracing (11). (Karsavin rejects the idea of substance as a principle distinct from the process.)

Such a subject is a *personality* potentially all-embracing, and even every qualitative aspect of it is "an contracted pan-unity." The development of the subject is the transition from one of its aspects to another, conditioned by the dialectical nature of the subject himself and not by impacts from without. Karsavin rejects external relations in the domain of historical being. Every historical individual (a person, a family, a nation, etc.) is in his view the world-whole itself in some one of its unique and unrepeatable aspects; thus, the domain of historical being consists of subjects that interpenetrate one another and nevertheless develop freely, since each of them contains everything in an embryonic form, and there are no external relations between them. This leads to conclusions that are of importance for the methodology of history. Thus, Karsavin rejects, in historical research, the conception of causality as an external influence. If two nations affect each other in the course of their development, that is only possible because they are both aspects of a higher subject which embraces them both (culture, mankind, the cosmos), and therefore that which is "alien" to a nation is in a certain sense "its own," so that development takes place continuously and dialectically out of the idea of the nation itself and is not made up like a mosaic from external impacts upon it (64). The influence of nature on the life of a people is not an external influence either, according to Karsavin: the nature of a country like all material elements of existence (e.g., dress, the size of individual allotments, etc.) affects the historical process not as such, not as taken separately, but only in so far as it is reflected in consciousness and transformed into a *socially psychic* element (95-100); this is possible because nature, like humanity is the individualization of a higher subject, the macrocosm; true, it is less complete than humanity, but nevertheless through that higher subject it forms part of man's mentality (347).

Karsavin's argument that "everything new in historical process always springs from non-being—otherwise it would not be new" (237) is also of great importance to the methodology of history. On the strength of it he rejects genetic explanations which reduce the new to recombinations of the old, as is done for instance in the attempt "to deduce" Christianity from the "synthesis of the Jewish and Hellenic culture" (180). The conflict between the individualizing and the generalizing method in history is not irreconcilable for Karsavin, since for him universality means individualization of the higher subject in a plurality of lower subjects; a universal is itself a concrete individual, it is "not abstract, not isolated from its concrete expressions" (191).

Certain historical objects may be definitely placed in a *hierarchical* order in relation to one another: such for instance are the individual, the family, the nation, civilization (Indian, Greek and Roman, European, etc.), mankind, the world. In the empirical development of every historical individuality the following periods may be distinguished according to Karsavin: (1) potential pan-unity of the historical personality —"the transition from non-being to being;" (2) the primarily differentiated unity—i.e., division into elements, decrease in unity, but not a marked one since "the elements easily pass into one another," are interchangeable and in that sense have the character of "superorganic individualities;" (3) organic unity—i.e., the period of functional limitation and comparative stability of individual features; (4) degeneration of the organic unity into *systematic* unity and then its destruction through disintegration (211 ff.).

The purpose of development is the realization of the cosmic pan-unity of creation as the Absolute individuality. We have already seen that in the empirical world that purpose is unattainable; it is realized in superempirical order, in so far as the Absolute as Absolute Goodness gives itself entirely to the world, redeems the world through the Incarnation and makes it perfect. Thus the whole of the historical process is Divinely human. Perfection is not the chronological end of development: from the point of view of the imperfect subject the ideal always stands before him, is eternally realized "in the infinite number of individualizations, but that does not in the least prevent the ideal from being also a reality, higher than the aspect of becoming which it contains or than the empirical historical process." In the pan-unity "at every point of it, becoming and completion, perfecting and perfection, coincide" (86 ff.).

Thus, Karsavin's conception of development differs sharply from the positivist conception of progress. In the pan-unity every moment of development is recognized as qualitatively equivalent to every other and not one is regarded as merely a means or a stage of transition to the final end; empirically, the moments have a different value according to the extent to which the pan-unity is revealed in them. The history of every individual contains a moment of the fullest revelation of pan-unity and that is the *apogee of its development*. The criterion for deciding which moment is the apogee may be found by inquiring into the religious character of the individual in question, meaning by that its "specific relation to the Absolute" (to truth, goodness, beauty). Since historical development as a whole is a Divinely human process, the criterion of its approximation to the ideal is to be found in the personality which most fully expresses the Absolute in the empirical realm —namely, in Jesus. The whole history of mankind is the "empirical becoming and perishing of the earthly Church of Christ" (214). Hence historical science must be religious and, moreover, *orthodox* (175, 356).

Karsavin formulates his theory about the Church in relation to the state in a pamphlet entitled *The Church, the Individual and the State*. The Church is the Body of Christ, the perfection of the world saved by the Son of God (3). The world freely transfigures itself, becoming the Church. The catholicity of the Church is not universality but *sobornost*—togetherness (5), "One in all and according to all"—i.e., the lovingly harmonized unity of many expressions of the Truth (6). The Church is an all-inclusive personality containing the symphonic personalities of local and national churches (7 f.).

The state is the necessary self-organization of the sinful world. If a state strives to follow the truths and ideals of the Church, it is Christian (12). In so far as man and the state are sinful, acts of violence, punishments, wars are inevitable, but they still remain a sin; they can only be overcome through union with Christ (13). But to renounce war, reckoning on a *miracle,* means to tempt God and is a serious crime, endangering the good of the citizens and of posterity (14). Tolstoy's absolute "nonresistance to evil by violence" shows lack of understanding the world's imperfection. To avoid using violence in struggling against evil is in truth an indirect and hypocritical resistance by violence, since other people wage wars and persecute criminals, and I leave it to them to do, while I stand aside. Only the person who is suffering from evil has a right not to resist it by violence; this is not nonresistance, but self-sacrifice, the best means of victory (28). A world striving for perfection contains inner contradictions that lead to tragic conflicts (30).

The state must strive to become a personality within the Church, but empirically it is only to a small degree Christian (67). The Church blesses not the activities of the state as such, in their partly evil nature, but only the *good* in them, thus, e.g., it prays for the *Christ-loving* army. In war time the Church prays for the Divine justice to prevail, and not for the empirical victory over the enemy. Thus, for instance, the feasts of the Intercession of Our Lady, so much loved in Russia, is connected with a miracle which led to the defeat of the Russians by the Greeks (19).

The modern idea of the separation of the Church from the state is absurd, says Karsavin: (1) a state separated from the Church would arrive at a religion of humanity, or at self-deification, or at relativism. (2) Such a separation is impossible in so far as a state has true ideals which are potentially Christian. But it is essential to delimit the activities of the Church and the state. The task of the Church is to urge the state freely to perfect itself for the Kingdom of Heaven, to denounce evil, to bless the good, but not to undertake political guidance.

The state must secure for the Church independence in its own sphere of activity—theological, educational, moral, missionary, liturgical; the Church must have the right to denounce wrong, to have rights of property, but it must not have the economic support of the state, or use the power of the state for persecuting heretics; the state must defend the Church against aggressive propaganda (23). A *symphony* between the Church and the state is the ideal relation between them.

Karsavin discusses the problem of the peculiarity of the Russian spirit in his pamphlet *The East, the West and the Russian Idea*. The Russian people, he says, is a unimultiplicity of peoples subordinated to the Great-Russian nation (7). The Russian people are great in the future which they must build and in what they have done already—in their state organization, spiritual culture, church, science, art (23).

The essential aspect of the Russian people according to Karsavin is their religiousness, including militant atheism (15). To find the central idea of Russian religiousness he compares East, West and Russia, and also draws a distinction between three ways of understanding the Absolute or God in relation to the world—theistic, pantheistic, and Christian (18). By "East" he means the non-Christian civilizations of Islam, Buddhism, Hinduism, Taoism, of the Greek and Roman naturalism and also barbarian nations (17); the West and Russia are the civilized Christian world. Theism means for Karsavin the doctrine that God transcends the world and stands in an external relation to it (18). He gives the name of pantheism to the view that the Deity is immanent in the world; it is not, however, the world as such that is divine, but only "the true essence of everything" (26 ff.), in the indeterminate potentiality without individual differentiation (the doctrine of Taoism, Buddhism, Brahmanism). Christianity is the doctrine about the Absolute triunity as the principle of pan-unity, irreducible to the undifferentiated potentiality of all things, as in pantheism (31). According to the Christian teaching, the relative is both distinct from the Absolute and one with it; everything actual is divine, it is a theophany; the creature receives God into itself (32). Such interpretations of Christianity, Karsavin says, are sometimes regarded as pantheistic, but that is not correct, especially on Karsavin's own definition of pantheism. Christianity affirms the absolute value of personality in its concrete realization; it furthers the development of culture and takes the purpose of life to be universal transfiguration and resurrection (35 f.).

The religion of the West, which has included in its creed the *filioque* clause—i.e., the doctrine of the procession of the Holy Spirit both from the Father and the Son—contains a perversion of the main basis of Christianity. Indeed, such a doctrine presupposes that the Holy

Spirit proceeds "from that in which the Father and the Son are one;" in that case, there is a special unity of the Father and the Son, not in substance or personality, but superpersonal. It follows then that the Holy Spirit is below the Father and the Son, which is "blasphemy against the Holy Ghost." But apart from the Holy Spirit the creature could not be deified; hence, belittling the Holy Spirit leads to belittling Christ in His humanity and to the idea that empirical existence *cannot be wholly deified* or become absolute; an impassable barrier is fixed between the absolute and the relative; knowledge is recognized to be limited (41). If man admits the weakness of his reason and will, he needs unquestionable truth on earth and an invincible earthly church; hence there arises an earthly organization of the church in the form of a hierarchical monarchy with the Pope at its head, having secular power (46). Further, this leads to renouncing the heavenly life, concentrating upon earthly welfare, to the flourishing of technics, capitalism, imperialism, and finally to relativism and self-disintegration (47 f.).

In Eastern Christianity—i.e., in Orthodoxy, which has not adopted any new dogmas after the seventh Ecumenical Council—there is no severance between the absolute and the relative (54). The relative is to be deified wholly and be made absolute; there are no limits to knowledge; knowledge is not only thought, but "living faith," unity of thought and activity; hence the problem which split the West into Catholicism and Protestantism does not arise (55). Redemption is not a juridical restitution achieved by Christ's sacrifice. Repentance in the Orthodox view is a transfiguration of the whole person and not an exact compensation for sin by a corresponding quantity of good works. Hence indulgences and the doctrine of purgatory are impossible in Orthodoxy (56). Orthodoxy is cosmic; in Orthodox ikons this is expressed by the symbolism of colors, the symbolism of cosmic life.

A characteristic feature of Russian thought is the struggle against empiricism and rationalism, and interest in metaphysical problems (57). Russian artistic literature is "heroic in character." In Russian foreign policy from the time of the Holy Alliance to the present day the ideological element is put in the forefront (58). The Russian ideal is mutual interpenetration between the Church and the state (70). But the Church represents the pan-unity of humanity as a whole. Since the Church has been divided into the Western and the Eastern, we must *wait* for the reunion of the churches before beginning our common task (70 f.). Meanwhile the task of Russian culture is to "actualize the potencies preserved since the eighth century," to accept the potencies actualized by the West ("europeanization") and complete them with its own principles. Reunion of the churches is not merely a formal act, but a union of cultures which is unnoticeably taking place already (73).

The defect of Russian Orthodoxy is its passivity and inaction; much that is valuable in it is merely "a tendency towards development" (58). Russians "contemplate the Absolute through a haze of dreams" (59). "Confidence in the deification to come renders the present sterile." The ideal is not attainable through "partial reforms and isolated efforts (62), and a Russian always wants to act in the name of something absolute or raised to the level of absolute." If a Russian doubts the absolute ideal, he can sink to complete indifference to everything or even to brutishness; he is capable of passing "from incredible law-abidingness to most unbridled total rebellion." In his striving for the infinite a Russian is afraid of definitions as limitations; hence the Russian genius for transmutation (79).

Karsavin's system is a form of pantheism. He regards the Absolute as the all-embracing unity. In criticizing the conception of pan-unity in the philosophy of Vladimir Soloviev and Father S. Bulgakov, I have been pointing out that God is a supersystematic principle creating the world system as something ontologically external to Him. He does not in consequence become a limited being, because the relation of limiting is only possible between homogenous objects. Karsavin says that if God is not a pan-unity, there may be another, a third . . . a tenth God beside Him. That objection is not convincing. We arrive of necessity at the conception of God as a supersystematic principle conditioning the existence of the world system with its actual and possible content. The world system together with the supersystematic principle, God, contains all that Karsavin includes in his conception of pan-unity. Just as his pan-unity is unique, so is the supersystematic principle, God, together with the universe whose ground He is. When Karsavin says that alongside such a God there might exist a second, a third . . . a tenth God, I ask him where does he find a second, a third . . . a tenth universe which compel us to admit the existence of a second, third or tenth God. No one can point out such universes; hence, the admission of many Gods is an arbitrary flight of fancy.

Karsavin distinguishes his system from pantheism by pointing to his theory of created being; but he himself explains that God does not create any positive "something" with a nature of its own. A created entity is in his view "nothing" to which the Absolute gives Itself, and in so far as that "nothing" receives the Divine content it becomes a "created something," "a second subject." This attempt to escape from pantheism is utterly unsatisfactory: "nothing" is not an empty vessel that can receive anything or still less to manifest pride which prevents it from accepting the *fullness* of the Divine life. That explains why in his system the creature, as Karsavin says himself, is not strictly speaking a personality: it receives all its content from the Divine pan-unity, it does not create anything itself, so that the whole of the created world is according to Karsavin a theophany (85, 175). The conception of theophany may be found in a theistic system as well, but there it means the manifestation of God in His works, namely in His creating entities ontologically distinct from Him, whose being nevertheless testifies that He exists as their creator. For Karsavin the word "theophany" means something different, namely, the manifestation of God in the creature in the sense that all the positive content of the creature is the content of the Divine being; the creature in so far as it is *something* is ontologically identical with God, as at any rate a part of the Divine being.

In criticizing Father S. Bulgakov's doctrine I have pointed out that pantheism is logically untenable. In Karsavin's system its logical impossibility is particularly clear since he refers absolutely everything real to God, leaving merely "nothing" to the creature. Like all forms of pantheism his system fails to explain the created entities' freedom in the sense of their independence of God and even of proud opposition to Him. He means by freedom simply being "self-grounded" or "self-conditioned." Nor can his system give a satisfactory answer as to the origin and nature of evil. To be consistent, Karsavin is bound to understand evil and the imperfection of the creature as merely incompleteness of the good. Such an interpretation is in sharp opposition to the real nature of evil which often has an evil content such as personal hatred, by no means reducible to insufficient love. It is not surprising therefore that Karsavin denies the existence of the devil: if he did not, he would have to admit that God realizes a theophany which consists in His hatred for Himself.

Karsavin is a personalist. He regards every entity as either potentially personal, or embryonically personal (animals), or actually personal. He thinks that nations, cultural units and mankind are symphonic personalities. Each of these personalities, however, is one and the same pan-unity, though "contracted" in every one of them in a different way. Accordingly, he has no conception of true and eternal individual uniqueness as an absolute value: all development consists in the fact that a created entity which existed alongside of God, becomes God, and in the end of development there exists "once more only God alone." Karsavin rejects the conception of the subject as an individual substance; i.e., as a superspatial and supertemporal and therefore eternal agent. This is not surprising, for such a conception would be in contradiction to his pantheistic monism. He wants to replace the superspatial and the supertemporal by the all-spatial and all-temporal; that means that for him the world entirely consists of events; i.e., of temporal and spatially temporal processes, though an entity that has attained to the highest stage of being realizes those processes in all time and in all space. It is not hard to show that the conception of being in all space and in all time cannot explain certain aspects of the world, which become intelligible on the view that the self, i.e., the substantival agent, is superspatial and supertemporal. Every event lasting in time, if it be only one second and occupying space even if it be only one millimeter, consists of an infinite number of segments that are external to one another. It can only be one whole on condition that it is created by a supertemporal and superspatial agent who unifies it. Even the perception of a temporal process such as a melody as something that happens in time requires that it should be apprehended at once, as a single whole—and this is only possible because the perceiving subject is supertemporal.

These objections against some of the fundamental positions of Karsavin's philosophy should not prevent one from attaching considerable value to several of his doctrines such for instance as his conception of history, of symphonic personality, of the Divinely human process, of the independent development of every entity, of the external and the individual body and so on.

Chapter 19

STUDIES IN LOGIC

Considering what a comparatively short time ago Russian philosophy began to develop, it must be admitted that a great deal has been done in the field of logic. Karinsky's *Classification of Conclusions* is an approach to the logic of relations and a theory of nonsyllogistic inferences. Vvedensky's *Logic As a Part of Epistemology* may be said to be a classical instance of a system of logic in the spirit of Kant's critical philosophy. Lossky's *Logic* is a theory of inference in the spirit of comprehensivism, contrasted with existential theories. All this has been mentioned already; now something must be said about the works of Povarnin and N. A. Vassilyev.

S. I. Povarnin, a lecturer at the Petrograd[1] University, expounded his system of logic in two books *The Logic of Relations* and *Logic* (printed in the Annals of the Petrograd University Faculty of Arts, 1915). In these books Povarnin pays even more attention than does Karinsky to the nonsyllogistic inferences. His theory is based on the idea that judgments are expressions of many and various relations between objects, e.g., relation of causality, equality, inequality, succession, coexistence, etc. A judgment, he says, is an idea "about two objects joined by a relation." On this interpretation the conception of affirmation or negation becomes of secondary importance, and primary significance is attached to the relation between two objects. Starting with this theory Povarnin formulates his doctrine of the classification of inferences.

Professor Lapshin discusses Povarnin's works in a long monograph *Epistemological Studies* (in the Annals of the Petrograd University Faculty of Arts, 1917). It contains interesting information about the history of logic, especially the logic of relations. Lapshin notes the connection between Povarnin's theory and symbolic logic.

Nicolay Alexandrovich Vassilyev, the son of Professor Vassilyev who held the chair of mathematics at the University of Kazan, was a

---

1. During the First World War St. Petersburg was renamed Petrograd.

lecturer at that University. In his article "Imaginary (non-Aristotelian) Logic"[2] he lays down the foundations of a new system of logic.

"Our Aristotelian logic," says Vassilyev, "is only one of many possible systems of logic." Just as Lobachevsky created a non-Euclidean system of geometry without the axiom about parallel lines, so we may think out a non-Aristotelian logic without the law of contradiction. Such a logic might serve the purposes of knowledge in a world different from ours. "The law of contradiction expresses the incompatibility of affirmation and denial. A red object is not blue, because red in incompatible with blue" (212). "Incompatibility is the only logical basis of negation" (214). This implies that the possibility of a non-Aristotelian logic may be proved on epistemological grounds as follows. We learn about incompatibility from experience. Hence, the law of contradiction in Aristotelian logic is "an empirical and real law." It is real because it refers "not to ideas, but to reality, not to judgments, but to objects." Consequently, Aristotelian logic is not purely formal. "Formal laws of thought are concerned with thought only and not with reality—with judgments and not with objects" (221). "But if the law of contradiction is a real and empirical law, we can dispense with it in thinking, and then we shall arrive at an imaginary logic." That logic denies the ontological law according to which "there is no contradiction in objects," but retains the formal law "judgments must not be mutually contradictory."

"To construct a logic without the ontological law of contradiction means to construct a logic in which there would be no negation in our sense of incompatibility. It is possible that in some object the grounds both for an affirmative and for a negative judgment may coincide" (216). In that case it would be necessary to recognize the possibility of judgments expressive of the contradiction present in the object, namely, of saying that "S both is and at the same time, is not, A." Vassilyev calls such judgments "neutral." Thus in his imaginary logic judgments would be divided in quality into three kinds; positive, negative, and neutral.

Vassilyev goes on to show that in his logic which denies the ontological law of contradiction it is possible to develop a theory of the syllogism. He shows in the case of the first figure of the syllogism, how his theory would differ from the traditional logic.

Vassilyev compares the peculiarities of non-Aristotelian logic with those of non-Euclidean geometry. Mathematicians have given a real interpretation of that geometry, and in a similar way he tries to show that "given a certain arrangement of the world or of our faculty of

---

2. *The Journal of the Ministry of Education*, August 1912.

perception, logic is bound to be non-Aristotelian." In our world, he says, all sensations are positive. "Sensations due to negative causes are positive too: stillness, darkness, rest are no less positive than sound, light, movement. Darkness becomes a negation of light only secondarily, through being incompatible with it. Hence, negativeness is something external to sensations, something that is added to them if they are considered in relation to other sensations. But we could conceive of a world with negative sensations, pure *non-A*. Such negation would be absolute" in contradistinction to our relative negation. It is conceivable that in such a world "some object S would at one and the same time give us both positive sensations A and negative non-A" and then we should have to form a neutral judgment "S is and is not A at one and the same time" (238 f.).

N. A. Vassilyev develops his theory of the possibility of a non-Aristotelian logic cleverly and consistently, but it is founded upon an error. Lossky explains in his *Logic* that the law of contradiction is certainly not the expression of the incompatibility of any two qualities, such as red and blue. It expresses something far more fundamental, namely, that "red is not not-red," or that "redness in so far as it is redness is not the absence of redness." Thus understood, the law of contradiction is an ontological law discovered through intellectual intuition and absolutely inviolable. Accepting this interpretation, Lossky shows that all attempts to prove the possibility of violating the law of contradiction, made, e.g., by Hegel, S. L. Frank, Vvedensky, Lapshin, dialectical materialists, are invalid.

Chapter 20

TRANSCENDENTAL-LOGICAL IDEALISM IN RUSSIA AND ITS CRITIC, V. ERN

1. REPRESENTATIVES OF TRANSCENDENTAL-LOGICAL IDEALISM

Throughout the nineteenth century most Russian philosophers, however original their line of thought might be, kept in touch with the German post-Kantian philosophy. In the twentieth century this intellectual intercourse was particularly close, for a number of young Russians worked in Germany in the seminars of Professors Windelband, Rickert, Hermann Cohen, Natorp, Husserl—prominent representatives of that form of neo-Kantianism which may be called transcendental-logical idealism. The chief Russian champions of this theory were S. Hessen, G. D. Gurvich, F. Stepun, V. Sezeman, B. Yakovenko, G. Lanz, V. Savalsky, N. V. Boldyrev, G. Shpet. On returning to Russia these young men founded in 1910 the Russian section of the international journal *Logos* under the editorship of Hessen, Stepun and Yakovenko.

Transcendental-logical idealism arose in Germany on a neo-Kantian basis and is a very radical modification of Kant's theory of knowledge. It resembles Kant's theory in so far as it too asserts that all objects of knowledge are objects of consciousness built up by the very process of cognition. Like Kant's theory it is a form of epistemological idealism. But in contradistinction to Kant the philosophers in question maintain that the knowing subject is not the individual human self, but a super-individual subject; at the same time they interpret the logical conditions of knowledge as neither mental nor physical but as belonging to the realm of ideal being, first discovered by Plato. They differ from Plato, however, in regarding ideal being not as a metaphysical reality, but as merely a logical condition of knowledge. This is why they can be best described as transcendental-logical idealists. The difference between their theory and Kant's is fully discussed in Lossky's *Introduc-

tion to Philosophy, Part I: "Introduction to the Theory of Knowledge." Lossky gives in this book two versions of Kant's critical theory, having in view the interpretations of *The Critique of Pure Reason* in the spirit of psychologism and phenomenalism, on the one hand, and of transcendental logic on the other hand. Lossky's purpose is to show that only the first interpretation gives a correct idea of Kant's theory of knowledge, while the transcendental-logical interpretation, which frees the *Critique* from all psychologism and phenomenalism—as e.g., Cohen does in his *Kant's Theorie der Erfahrung*—is a profound modification of Kantianism.

Transcendental-logical idealism was a development of neo-Kantianism tending to bring epistemology closer to ontology and thus to lead in the end to a revival of metaphysics. Valuable reflections upon this transition stage of transcendental-logical idealism are to be found in S. A. Alexeyev (Askoldov)'s article "The Inner Crisis of Transcendental Idealism," in *Voprosi filosofii*, 125, 1915, and S. L. Frank's article "The Crisis of Modern Philosophy," in *Russkaya Mysl*, September 1916.

The same evolution was taking place in the Russian transcendental-logical idealism, as one of its representatives S. Hessen pointed out in his article "Nejnovejsi ruská filosofie" in a Czech journal *Ruch filosofický*, I, 1923.

Russian young men studying philosophy in Germany were in lively contact both with their teachers and with the German students, and imparted to them information about Russian philosophy. It may therefore be said that at that time not only the German philosophy affected the Russian, but also Russian ontologism and intuitivism began to influence the German. This probably is the source of the "emotional intuitivism" in M. Scheler's theory of values. It is difficult to estimate this kind of influence with any certainty, but there can be no doubt that the Russian representatives of transcendental-logical idealism were affected by Russian intuitivism and ideal realism; this can be seen from the comparison between their earlier and their later writings. As they passed from the problems of epistemology to those of axiology, ethics and social philosophy, they came up more and more against the question of the knowledge of living reality, discussed in the metaphysics of concrete ideal realism. Since the time of Kant, philosophy has been faced with the following alternative: either there is intuition as the immediate contemplation of the object in itself, and then metaphysics is possible, or, as Kant thinks, there is no intuition and then, as he says, metaphysics as a science is impossible. As soon as the Russian transcendental-logical idealists felt the need of metaphysics they developed a tendency toward intuitivism. Some of them worked out the theory that there are many varieties of knowledge and experience, others admitted the existence of a practical as well as of a theoretical intuition. This change in point of view is particularly pronounced in the works of S. Hessen, G. D. Gurvich, V. Sezeman, F. Stepun, B. Yakovenko.

Sergey Iosifovich Hessen (1887–1950) received his philosophical education in Germany and at first was an adherent of Rickert's normative criticism. The thesis he submitted for his doctorate was called *Ueber individuelle Kausalität;* he dealt in it with the problem of individual causality on the basis of the distinction between "ideographic" and "nomothetic" sciences. After returning to Russia he was professor of philosophy at Tomsk and after the revolution at Warsaw and at Lodz.

S. Hessen's chief works are: "The Philosophy of Punishment," *Logos,* 1912–1913; *The Foundations of Pedagogics,* 1924; "The Problem of Constitutional Socialism," *Sovremenniya Zapiski,* 1924–1928; "The Tragedy of the Good in the Brothers Karamazov," *Sovremenniya Zapiski,* 1928.

In his inquiry into the problem of punishment Hessen says: "On its formal side a crime is the violation of the law by a responsible subject." A crime is a symptom of disharmony between legality and life. When a law is just and therefore ought to stand, justice which has suffered from the violation of it, is re-established when the legal norm is confirmed by the condemnation of the crime. This is the pure *form* of punishment. "Like every activity intended to establish justice in society, punishment serves the law and, consequently, the criminal himself, who is being punished as a subject possessed of legal rights. Punishment is inflicted upon him in his own interests, for, possessing rights, he is as much interested in the re-establishment of justice as are his judges." As a rule the *matter* of punishment is added to its *form;* i.e., the criminal is deprived of some concrete rights such as the right of property, freedom of movement, etc.

The question "what precise rights must be taken away in each particular case is decided entirely on the strength of material considerations. The decision is determined by reference to extraneous purposes such as the defense of the state and society from dangerous individuals, intimidation, correction, etc.;" the means which the state has at its disposal have also to be taken into consideration, as well as the individuality of the concrete psychophysical persons committing the crime.

On the strength of defining punishment as an act of legal justice Hessen determines its lower and upper limit; transgression of the upper limit means forsaking the domain of law and making punishment an act of vengeance, a measure of public safety, and not an act of justice. The lower limit of punishment is a public declaration of the sentence. The upper limit is "the deprivation of the criminal of all rights except one, which still allows him to be regarded as a subject of rights." Hence, complete deprivation of rights, "outlawry" or "surrendering the criminal to be despoiled" is not an act of legal justice. Similarly, "however wise it might sometimes seem from the point of view of the state to execute a man, it must be definitely recognized that capital punishment is opposed to the conception of legal justice." Death penalty destroys the subject of rights, and punishment ceases to be an expression of justice. "Or rather, it is not the subject of rights who is destroyed (like all that has significance, he is indestructible), but the possibility of his realization" (228).

In his book *The Foundations of Pedagogics* Hessen expounds the philosophical basis of the problem of education and upbringing, making a clever use of the dialectical method. The purpose of education is, in his view, to put a person in touch with the cultural values of science, art, morality, law, economics, and to make the natural man into a cultured man. He ends his book by the words "to overcome the past through connecting it with the eternal which constitutes its real meaning is the true aim of education" (368).

In working out the problems of ethics and social philosophy Hessen, like G. D. Gurvich comes close to intuitivism and seeks to enlarge it by the conception of practical conative intuition which he calls "volitional vision" (*Willensschau*). In his writings on the subject he approximates more and more to the general spirit of Russian concrete ideal realism. This can be seen, for instance, in his essay "The Tragedy of the Good in Dostoevsky's *Brothers Karamazov*." According to Hessen's interpretation the three brothers, Dmitri, Ivan and Alyosha, are the embodiments of the three stages of the good and of the corresponding three temptations of evil; evil itself, as represented by Smerdyakov, acts the part of servant to the three perverted images of the good. Dmitri Karamazov stands for "the natural basis of morality" expressed by the semi-instinctive feelings of shame, pity, and reverence (Soloviev's theory). Ivan represents the good which has become an object of reflection, and seeks for the rational meaning of life. It is the Kantian autonomous good, consisting in the free fulfillment of duty without love. The highest degree of goodness—the good as love—is embodied in Alyosha who loves every living being in its individual wholeness, "for nothing," and is at each given moment creatively participating in other people's life. Hessen regards Father Zossima as representative of the superethical holy life. He interprets Father Zossima's idea that "everyone is responsible for everyone else" as an indication that the Kingdom of God and the Principle in which it is rooted transcend the opposition between good and evil. Father Zossima, in his view, stands above the moral sphere, and Fyodor Pavlovich Karamazov—below it.

Hessen's extensive work *The Problem of Constitutional Socialism* deserves consideration as an attempt to give a synthesis of the valuable aspects of the individualistic structure of society with the valuable aspects of the socialist ideal. Hessen strives to show that such a line of development will lead not merely to preserving, but actually to giving a more perfect expression to the values of religion, nationality, the state, legal justice, freedom and even of private property.

George Davidovich Gurvich (born in 1894) was in his youth an adherent of transcendental-logical idealism. He left Russia after the Bolshevik revolution and was professor of philosophy at Strasbourg; at present he is living in Paris and working at sociology. Gurvich's chief works are: *Fichtes System der konkreten Ethik*, 1924; *Socialism and Property* (Sovremenniya Zapiski, 1928); *L'idée du droit social*, 1931; *Le temps présent et l'idée du droit social*, 1931; *Morale théorique et science des moeurs*, 1937.

G. D. Gurvich, like S. Hessen, came under the influence of intuitivism and concrete ideal realism. He maintains the existence of practical intuition which he calls "volitional vision" or *"l'intuition volitive."* He has made an original attempt to work out the conception of a special kind of property which he describes as *"soborny* property." He designates by that term property which belongs to a group of members, so that both the group as a whole and each co-member is the subject of property; each co-member (or several of them together) "has secured to him as his inalienable property a certain ideal part of the object, and he has a right to demand compensation for it if he leaves the group, which he is free to do. Since the whole group is as much the subject of property as each co-member, the property always remains in the hands of the group, and an individual member, on leaving it, receives only a money equivalent of his part."

Vassili Emilievich Sezeman (born 1884) was professor of philosophy at the University of Kovno in Lithuania and is now at Vilno.

His chief works are: "Platonism, Plotinus, and Modernity," *Logos* 1925; "Zum Problem des reinen Wissens," *Philosophischer Anzeiger* 1927; *Uebergegenständliches und ungegenständliches Wissen*, commentationes ordinis philologorum (Lib. II) of the Kovno University, 1927; *Beiträge Zum Erkenntnisproblem, Das Logisch-Rationale*, Eranus, commentationes societatis Philos. Lituanae, v. I, 1930; *Die logischen Gezetze und das Sein*, 1932.

In working out a doctrine of the different species of experience

V. Sezeman distinguishes objective knowledge, *Erkenntnis* and nonobjective cognition, *Wissen*. In objective knowledge there is opposition between subject and object, a distance between the knower and the known; that knowledge is reached by removing all subjective elements from the reality that is being cognized; the logical formulation which leads to objectification (*Vergegenständlichung*) expresses the content of knowledge by a concept and tends, so to speak, to stiffen in its verbal form, i.e., tends to assume the character of thinghood: objectification degenerates into "hypostacising abstractions." A typical form of objective knowledge is to be found in natural science. The nonobjective cognition of spiritual realities—e.g., the moral, religious, and aesthetic experience—is of a different nature. In it there is no separation between the subject and the object: the subject participates in the reality he apprehends; the given contents of experience are inevitably connected with self-consciousness and self-knowledge. Such a cognition of experiences "in its primary form can never become knowledge formulated by means of concepts."

According to Sezeman, nonobjective cognition covers the whole domain of the subjective—the subject himself and all his mental and spiritual living activities; it also includes all activity on the part of others, all living, creative manifestations of reality. Objective knowledge through concepts has a universal character, but is divorced from reality; it makes reality undergo a perspectival distortion. Nonobjective cognition, on the contrary, is plunged in reality, but is not universal. The absolute ideal of knowledge could only be attained in an absolute self-consciousness in which the object would not be transcendent to the subject, and reality would be directly revealed in all its wholeness. This ideal is unattainable for us, finite beings; our limited self-consciousness can only serve as the basis and the starting point of the knowledge of the world's existence (*Dasein*); but in order to know its manner of being (*Sosein*) we are compelled to objectify the data of experience. A philosophy which by means of self-consciousness discovers the defects of this objective knowledge incites us again and again to go beyond it and to establish new, nonobjective points of view. This is how we advance toward the ideal of absolute knowledge.

A criticism of "volitional vision" and Sezeman's theories is to be found in Lossky's articles "Fichte's konkrete Ethik im Lichte des modernen Transcendentalismus," *Logos* 1926 and "Die intellectuelle Anschauung als Methode der Philosophie," *Der Russische Gedanke*, I, 1929.

Fyodor Avgustovich Stepun was born in 1884. He left Russia after the Bolshevik revolution and was professor at the Dresden Polytechnicum. Stepun's chief works are: "The Tragedy of Creativeness," *Logos* 1910; "The Tragedy of Mystical Consciousness," *ibid.* 1911; *Life and Creativeness,* 1923; *The Basic Problems of the Theater,* Berlin, Slovo, 1923.

Stepun, like Sezeman, works out a theory of his own concerning the advance toward the ideal of absolute knowledge by distinguishing between two types of experience: the experiences of creativeness and the experiences of life. The former are subject to the dualism of the subject-object relation, while life is expressed by the idea of positive all-unity. The process of civilization is characterized by the struggle between the creative efforts of the spirit, marked by dualism, and the striving to rediscover the primary unity of life.

Boris Valentinovich Yakovenko (1884–1949) lived during the First War and the revolution in Italy and afterwards settled in Prague. In 1929–38 he edited the magazine *Der Russische Gedanke,* and later occasional volumes of the *Bibliothèque Internationale de Philosophie.*

Yakovenko's chief works are: "What Is Philosophy? An Introduction to Transcendentalism," *Logos* 1911; "Immanent Transcendentism, Transcendent Immanentism and Dualism in General," *ibid.* 1912; *Vom Wesen des Pluralismus,* 1928; "Die Grundvorurteile des menschlichen Denkens," *Der Russische Gedanke,* 1929; *Zur Kritik des Psychologismus; The Critique of the Russian Intuitivistic Ideal Realism,* the Works of the Russian Popular University in Prague, vol. II, 1929; *Dejiny Ruske filosofie,* Praha 1939.

Yakovenko's approach to ontologism is different from that of Sezeman and Stepun. His aim is to get rid, through critical analysis, of the network of dogmatic schemata and preconceptions which envelop reality in practical life, in sense apprehension, scientific hypothetical thinking, "religious" faith, etc., and ascend to an intuition in which "the absolute multifarious all is present as it actually is in itself." Yakovenko calls his philosophy critical or transcendental intuitivism and also philosophic absolutism in contradistinction to all relativism and agnosticism. Yakovenko's comprehensive work *The History of Russian Philosophy* has been published in Czech in Prague.

Gustav Gustavovich Shpet (born 1879) was professor of philosophy at the University of Moscow. His chief works are: *Appearance and Meaning,* 1914; *History As a Problem of Logic,* 1916; *Aesthetic Fragments,* 1922; *An Essay on the Development of the Russian Philosophy,* I, 1922; *Introduction to Ethnical Psychology,* 1927.

In his book *Appearance and Meaning* Shpet upholds Husserl's theories. Shpet was the first to write a valuable and detailed work on the history of Russian philosophy, but his contemptuous attitude to the beginnings of it produces an unpleasant impression. Only the first volume was published, the second was forbidden by the Soviet Government.

Henrich Ernestovich Lanz (died 1946) left Russia after the Bolshevik revolution and was professor at the Stanford University in U.S.A. He wrote a book *Das Problem der Gegenständlichkeit in der modernen Logik* in 1912 and an article "Speculative Transcendentalism in Plotinus," in *The Journal of the Ministry of Public Education*, I, 1914.

Leonid Yevgenyevich Gabrilovich (born 1878) left Russia after the Bolshevik revolution and at present is living in New York. In addition to many articles concerned with various cultural problems, literary criticism, politics, etc., Gabrilovich published two purely philosophical essays: "The Conceptions of Truth and Certainty in the Theory of Knowledge" in *Voprosi filosofii i psychologii*, IV, 1908; "Ueber Bedeutung und Wesen der Elementarbegriffe," *Archiv für system. Philos.*, XV, 4, 1910.

The cognitive act which is the starting point of knowledge and which excludes all doubt is, according to Gabrilovich, a statement of "actual experiences." Their verbal expression such as "I am warm" or "this circle is yellow" has the form of judgment although in truth it is not even a judgment but a statement of "actual givenness" (466, 468). Investigating the conditions of certainty with regard to judgments about not-present experiences Gabrilovich distinguishes "conditions of concreteness" and "conditions of reality." The condition of concreteness is that the opposite cannot be represented even in imagination, thus, e.g., a square with uneven diagonals is not representable. Those conditions are expressed in judgments of pure mathematics and geometry. The certainty of judgments the opposites of which are representable depends upon the conditions of "thinghood, objectivity or reality;" those judgments must not contradict the principle of causality.

Gabrilovich's article is an introduction to a book which was to have been an inquiry into truth, concreteness, and reality, but has never been published.

2. SHESTOV'S IRRATIONALISM

Lev Shestov (1866–1938) whose real name was Schwarzman emigrated from Kiev after the Bolshevik revolution and settled in Paris.

Shestov's chief works are: *Dostoevsky and Nietzsche*, 1903; *Apotheosis of Groundlessness*, 1905; *The Idea of the Good in Tolstoy and in Nietzsche*, 1907; *Potestas clavium*, 1923; *La nuit de Gethsemanie*, 1925; *On Job's Balances*, 1929; *Athènes et Jerusalem*, 1938. See N. Lossky, "Shestov's Philosophy" in *Russkiya Zapiski*, 1939.

Extreme skepticism manifested by Shestov in his work from the first has its source in the ideal of unrealizable superlogical absolute knowledge. In the book *Apotheosis of Groundlessness* Shestov disproves mutually contradictory scientific and philosophical theories, leaving the reader suspended in the void. In the book *Athens and Jerusalem* he contrasts rational thought dating back to the Greek philosophy with the superrational biblical apprehension of the world which denies the law of contradiction. The idea of God's omnipotence leads Shestov to affirm, like the medieval philosopher, Peter Damiani, that God can make the past to have never been; e.g., it is in His power to ordain that Socrates did not drink the cup of poison in the year 399 B.C.

3. V. ERN

Vladimir Franzevich Ern (1882–1917) worked in close contact with the Moscow philosophers S. Trubetskoy, Lopatin, and P. Florensky. His chief works are: *The Struggle for the Logos*, 1911; *G. S. Skovoroda*, Moscow 1912; *Rosmini and His Theory of Knowledge*, 1914; *The Philosophy of Gioberti*, 1916.

See also S. Askoldov (Alexeyev)'s article on Ern in *Russkaya Mysl*, May 1917.

Ern was mainly concerned with combatting West-European rationalism and the tendency to mechanize the whole structure of life and to subordinate it to technics. He opposes to these factors of civilization the Logos of the ancient and the Christian philosophy. This Logos is a concrete living Being, the Second Person of the Trinity, incarnate and present in the historical process. Ern calls his philosophy "Logism." His book *The Struggle for the Logos* is a collection of essays in which he contrasts two philosophical tendencies—rationalism and his "logism." Rationalism is concerned with the subjective data of experience and their elaboration in accordance with the formal rules of logic, i.e., of understanding. It is a dead philosophy for it severs the knowing subject from the living reality. Logism, on the contrary, is the doctrine of the unity of the knower and the known, the vision of living reality. In the rationalism and empiricism of modern philosophy there is no conception of nature. In ancient philosophy, in the Middle Ages and during the Renaissance nature was taken to be an integral being, creative and having an inner life of its own: such is Aristotle's *physis* as the principle of change having a creative entelechy; the spermatic *logos* of the Stoics; the *natura creata creans* of Eriugena; the *archeus* of Paracelsus and Jean Baptiste van Helmont. In Descartes, on the contrary, material nature is devastated: it has no inner life; matter has only external properties, extension and movement as change of position in space. This is but one step to Berkeley's theory that matter does not exist and is merely a subjective idea. After him, Hume interpreted the soul, too, as merely a bundle of perceptions and not as a living principle. All this is a meonic myth. Kant developed meonism to its final limit: his immanent philosophy transforms the whole of the knowable world into a system of lifeless presentations. During the First World War Ern published a pamphlet *From Kant to Krupp*. He explains in it the destructive technique which menaces the whole of our civilization by the influence of Kant's meonic philosophy.

When in 1910 young Russian converts to transcendental-logical idealism came home from Germany and founded the Russian section of the international periodical *Logos,* Ern wrote a propos of this an article called "Something About Logos, Russian Philosophy and the Scientific Mind." He drew attention to the fact that the cover of the magazine had on it an image of Heraclitus and a design from the frieze of Parthenon, under which was written in Greek *logos*. The appearance of such a magazine in Russia which lived by the religion of Logos, the Word, might be welcomed had it meant the Logos corresponding to the true Russian culture based upon the tradition of the Eastern Fathers of the Church. But in analyzing the tendency of the new magazine Ern found that its Logos was profoundly different from the ancient Greek and the Christian Logos. Under the Greek mask we can see the familiar phrase *"made in Germany."* The magazine stands for rationalism, meonism, schematism. The Greek speculation led to the personal, living and Divine Logos in whom thought and existence form an indivisible unity. Therefore original Russian philosophy connected with Orthodoxy has the character of ontologism and not of epistemological idealism. In the West, too, the philosophy of the Catholic church is ontologic. A culture based upon the Divine Logos does not reject logical discursive thought. The Logos has three aspects expressed in the three domains of culture: (1) the Divine, expressed in religion which trains the will to realize moral good; (2) the cosmic, expressed in art the aim of which is to reveal the world as one in beauty; (3) the discursively logical, expressed in philosophy, the purpose of which is to comprehend the world-whole in the unity of theoretical thought. But in contradistinction to rationalism, in logism thought is not severed from integral reason: it contains within itself Existence, Goodness and Beauty.

According to Ern, only a philosophy based on the Divine Logos can guide life and establish its final end; it works out for the first time the true conception of progress. The positivist idea of progress as a quantitative increase of material goods is "a bad infinity." The true idea of progress indicates movement toward an absolute completion, the Absolute Good, i.e., to the Kingdom of God. Entrance into that Kingdom is the end of history which takes place through a catastrophic cataclysm and a transition into a qualitatively different realm of being.

Ern formulates the main points of his philosophy in the following statements: logism is (1) not re-ism (not a system of things), but personalism; (2) not mechanism or determinism, but an organic structure of the world, freedom; (3) not illusionism or meonism, but ontologism; (4) not schematism, but a realistic symbolism; (5) not a negative, but an actual infinity; (6) it is discrete, catastrophic; (7) not static, but dynamic.

Ern was interested in the philosophy of Rosmini and Gioberti because it was a form of ontologism that grew out of the Catholic culture. Early death from tuberculosis prevented Ern from working out his theories in detail; but his book *The Struggle For the Logos* is highly valuable for it is an attempt to define the peculiar characteristics of the Russian philosophy.

Chapter 21

SCIENTIST-PHILOSOPHERS

Prince Peter Alexeyevich Kropotkin (1842–1921) was educated at the Corps des Pages and afterwards graduated at the Petersburg University. He did scientific research in geography and geology. When in 1872 he went abroad he was converted to socialism and anarchism. After returning to Russia he took part in the revolutionary movement, was arrested in 1874, spent two years in prison, in 1876 made his escape and left Russia. Kropotkin's chief works are *Anarchy, Its Philosophy and Its Ideal*, 1902; *Mutual Aid, a Factor of Evolution*, 1912 (published in English in 1902); *Ethics*, I, 1922.

In the book *Mutual Aid* Kropotkin gives a number of instances of mutual aid between animals, both of the same and of different species. He argues that struggle for existence leads not to greater perfection, but to the survival of more primitive organisms. Creatures that largely practice mutual aid greatly multiply, and thus mutual aid proves to be the most important factor in evolution.

Struggle for existence does not explain the origination of new characteristics of an organism: it only explains their prevalence or their gradual disappearance. Nor is mutual aid, which Kropotkin values so highly, a factor capable of creating new characteristics. But owing to mutual aid creatures that have developed new qualities, e.g., capacity for aesthetic creativeness, for intense intellectual activity, etc. —qualities that are often accompanied by a decrease in biological strength—find it possible to live and multiply. Thus mutual aid furthers the richness and fullness of life and the development of superbiological activities.

Kropotkin sought to found ethics upon the data of natural history and not upon religious metaphysics. Mentioning that Darwin pointed out the existence of mutual sympathy between animals, Kropotkin says that social life engenders social instincts both in human beings and animals. This instinct contains "the beginnings of the feeling of good will and of partial identification of the individual with his group, which is the starting point of all lofty moral sentiments. On this basis there develops a higher feeling of justice or equal rights, equality; and then that which is usually called self-sacrifice" (14).

Kropotkin devoted a number of pamphlets, speeches, and articles to preaching anarchism.

The conception of the world as an integral whole containing higher organizing principles is developed in the Russian literature not only by religious philosophers, but also by some naturalists who apply it to the solution of the main problems of the philosophy of nature. Special mention should be made of V. Karpov, professor of histology at the Moscow University. In his book *The Fundamental Features of an Organic Interpretation of Nature* (1910) he applies the conception of organic wholeness to all kingdoms of nature and all individual formations in it. K. Starynkevich, a botanist, wrote a book *The Structure of Life* which was published after his death by G. V. Vernadsky with an introduction by Lossky in 1931. To explain organic wholes Starynkevich establishes the conception of a "primary intuition" which connects every organism with the rest of the world and provides a basis for the development of physiological self-regulation, instinct and reason. He also works out a doctrine about living units which are higher than the individual body of a plant or an animal, e.g., such units as a bee-hive, a forest, a marsh, and particularly about the organic unity of life upon earth and even in the cosmos as a whole.

Schultz, professor of zoology at the Harkov University, wrote a very informative book *Organism As Creativeness,* in the series called "The Theory and the Psychology of Creativeness," VII, 1916. He argues that the development of forms in an organism come under the definition of instinctive acts.

Sergey Ivanovich Metalnikov (1870–1945), a specialist on immunity, who after the Bolshevik revolution worked in Paris as a member of the Pasteur Institute, maintained on the strength of his observations of unicellular organisms that even a reflex act is a creative way out of a situation in which an organism finds itself in its particular environment. His study of immunity reactions enabled him to prove that they may be developed into conditional reflexes. He introduced cholera microbes into the abdomen of a rabbit, while striking a tuning fork; after a series of such experiments he sounded the tuning fork without introducing cholera microbes, but on cutting open the rabbit he found that the anticholera blood corpuscles had appeared all the same. He thus proved that immunity reaction is a centrally conditioned process; he actually found in insects the nerve ganglion which must be intact for preserving the different kinds of immunity essential to insects. In his article "Science and Ethics" Metalnikov speaks of love as an evolutionary factor. Toward the end of his life he proposed to work out a theory of evolution proving that evolution is conditioned by a reason which lies at the root of nature. Illness and death prevented him from doing this.

Alexandr Gavrilovich Gurvich (born 1874), a professor in the University of Moscow, who discovered the mitogenetic radiations of organisms, built up an organic theory of the factors involved in life processes; he did so very cautiously, avoiding conceptions that could not be clearly defined; thus, he used statistical methods in studying the development of the embryo.

L. S. Berg, a professor in the Petersburg University, in his pamphlet *Theories of Evolution* and a detailed monograph *Nomogenesis,* published in 1922, proves that the evolution of organisms is not due to the accumulation of accidental changes, but is a nomogenesis, i.e., a process of regular change in a definite direction.

The psychiatrist Nicolay Yevgrafovich Osipov (died 1934) left Russia after the Bolshevik revolution and while living in Prague aimed at recasting the psychological theories of Freud in the spirit of Lossky's personalistic metaphysics. He thought that love was a basic factor in cosmic life, far earlier than sexual passion and not reducible to mere physiological attraction. "The empirical value of Freud's research will not be affected," Osipov writes "if the central place is ascribed not to physiological attraction, but to Love in the eidetic sense as an absolute value. In our spatiotemporal world Love is embodied in varying degrees, beginning with the very lowest, that of identification (I love this apple and, in virtue of that love, eat it, i.e., destroy it). Then love expresses itself in sensuality—genital and extragenital—and tenderness. Finally it finds expression in special experiences of intimacy between people—the highest form of Love's manifestation in the human world." Unfortunately, illness and death prevented Osipov from developing in detail his theory of love which was to explain the connections between persons in a way different from that of the Freudians with their tendency to pansexualism.

Osipov's works that have a bearing on philosophy are the following: *Tolstoy's Kindheitserinnerungen,* Imago Verlag; *Revolution and Dream* (Works of the Russian Popular University, Prague, 1931); "The Sick and the Healthy in Dostoevsky," in the *Revue v nevrologii a psychiatrii,* 1931; see also Lossky's "N. E. Osipov As a Philosopher," in the symposium *Life and Death* in memory of Osipov, V. I, Prague 1935.

Mihail Mihailovich Novikov was professor of zoology at the Moscow University and then at Bratislava and is now living in München. In his treatises *The Limits of Scientific Knowledge of Living Nature,*

1922, and *Problems of Life,* Berlin 1922, he tries to arrive at a compromise solution of the dispute between vitalists and mechanists. He accepts Bergson's view about the difference between rational and intuitive knowledge and believes that biology as an exact science must continue rationalistic physicochemical study of organisms in order to establish mechanistic uniformities, remembering, however, that on this path the mystery of life must remain insoluble; attempts to solve it require intuition and therefore, since they lie beyond the confines of exact knowledge, must be left to philosophers.

The academician Vladimir Ivanovich Vernadsky (died in 1945), a geologist and mineralogist, devoted many years to the study of the laws of the biosphere. At the end of his life he began, like the French mathematician Le Roy, to talk of man as a great geological power, namely as of the creator of the "noösphere." He means by that term the reconstruction of the biosphere in the interests of thinking humanity.[1]

1. "The Biosphere and the Noösphere," *American Scientist,* XXXIII, 1945, "Scientific World Conception," *Voprosi filosofii i psychologii,* No. 65, 1902.

Chapter 22

JURIST-PHILOSOPHERS

Pavel Ivanovich Novgorodtsev (died 1924), professor at the University of Moscow, left Russia after the Bolshevik revolution and was dean of the Russian faculty of Low in Prague. His chief works that have a philosophic significance are: *Kant's and Hegel's Theories of Law and the State,* 1901; *The Crisis of Modern Juridical Consciousness,* 1909; *The Social Ideal,* 1917; "*Ueber die eigentümlichen Elemente der russischen Rechtsphilosophie,*" in *Philosophie und Recht,* II, 1922–23.

The impossibility of realizing a perfect social order in the conditions of earthly existence, insisted upon by Russian religious philosophers, was explained long ago in the works of Novgorodtsev. He bases it upon the analysis of relations between the individual and society. Novgorodtsev is concerned not with the generic notion of man but with concrete individual persons, and he brings incontrovertible scientific evidence to prove that "the antinomy between the personal and the social principles" cannot be solved within the limits of earthly existence: "The harmony between the individual and society is possible only in the intelligible realm of freedom where absolute and all-pervading solidarity is combined with infinite individual differences. In the conditions of historical life there is no such harmony and there cannot be." This explains the fact, pointed out by Novgorodtsev, of "the collapse of faith in the perfect constitutional state" and also of faith in socialism and anarchism, in short, "the collapse of the idea of earthly paradise." Novgorodtsev does not deny that the attainments of the modern constitutional state, as well as the strivings of socialism and anarchism are relatively good, but he shows that they are incommensurable with the ideal of the absolute good. Therefore, if we are to avoid a hopeless impasse, we must build our ideal of the earthly society with a view to "the freedom of the infinite development of personality, and not the harmony of completed perfection" (*Social Ideal,* 3rd ed., 25).

Yevgeny Vassilyevich Spektorsky (1873–1951), the last elected Rector of the Kiev University, left Russia after the Bolshevik revolution He was professor at Ljublyana in Yugoslavia, and since 1947 is a professor at the Russian Orthodox Academy in New York.

Spektorsky's main works are: *Essays on the Philosophy of Social Sciences,* 1907; *The Problem of Social Physics in the Seventeenth Century,* 1910; *Christianity and Culture,* Prague 1925; *Christian Ethics.*

In his book *Christianity and Culture* Spektorsky makes abundantly clear the high positive significance of Christianity for all the spheres of spiritual, social, and even material culture—for philosophy, science and art, for the development of the idea of personality, of legal justice, the state, etc.

In Russian jurisprudence there was a strong movement against naturalism; after the Bolshevik revolution it has been carried on by the emigrés. As in Germany, the opposition to naturalism was first based upon post-Kantian metaphysical idealism or upon modern transcendental idealism. In the Russian philosophy naturalism is opposed on even deeper grounds in connection with a religious interpretation of the world. An excellent analytic survey of the literature on the subject is made in the magazine *Philosophie und Recht* in a special supplement *Russische Rechtsphilosophie,* 1922–23 (Heft 2). The tendency to base jurisprudence on religious principles is described in Novgorodtsev's article "Ueber die eigentümlichen Elemente der russischen Rechtsphilosophie." G. Gurvich in his article "Die zwei grössten russischen Rechtsphilosophen Boris Tschitscherin und Wladimir Ssolowijew" compares the views of Chicherin based upon Kant's and Hegel's idealism with the views of Soloviev that have their source in religious metaphysics; he also explains the significance of the works of Novgorodtsev who tries to synthesize these two tendencies. Petrazhitsky's psychologism is expounded in an article by G. Landau. Finally, the article "Uebersicht der neueren rechtsphilosophischen Literatur in Russland" gives an idea of the Russian philosophy of law as a whole. It speaks of B. Kistyakovsky's works based upon the transcendental idealism of the Freiburg school, of Iosif Pokrovsky's ethical personalism, of the quest for the ideal bases of jurisprudence in the works of Spektorsky, N. N. Alexeyev and others.

Chapter 23

PHILOSOPHICAL IDEAS OF POET-SYMBOLISTS

1. ANDREI BELYI

The following four of the symbolist poets have written most on philosophical subjects: Andrei Belyi, Vyacheslav Ivanov, N. M. Minsky, and D. S. Merezhkovsky.

Andrei Belyi (1880–1934) is known under this penname. His real name was Boris Nikolaevich Bugaev. He was the son of professor Bugaev who held the chair of mathematics at the Moscow University. He studied natural sciences as well as the humanities. His chief philosophical work is *Symbolism,* published by Musaget, 1910.

According to Andrei Belyi symbolism is the world conception which provides a basis for symbolic art and embodies "certain features of Taoism in a realistic philosophy" (49, 106). Symbolism is a synthesis of India, Persia, Egypt, Greece, and the Middle Ages (50). Being under the strong influence of Rickert, Andrei Belyi maintained that exact science gives no interpretation of the world as a whole: it works by *limiting* the object of knowledge and therefore "systematizes the absence of knowledge." Life reveals itself not through scientific knowledge, but through creative activity which is "unanalyzable, integral and omnipotent;" it is only expressible in symbolic images which clothe the idea (72). The unity of life is expressed by such symbols as Adam Kadmon of the Kabbalah, the Atman of the Hindu philosophy, the Logos—Christ. On the whole Andrei Belyi's philosophy is a variety of pantheism.

In the process of cognitive or creative symbolization the symbol becomes reality. The living word is intimately connected with reality and therefore has magic power (see chapter "The Magic of Words"). Poetry, says Andrei Belyi, is connected with the creation of words—a gift which he himself possessed to a remarkable degree. Some of the words he invented ought to be introduced into general usage, but others express such subtle and fleeting shades of the subject he is describing that they could only be used once in a life time. A considerable part of his book is devoted to the analysis of the style of various poetical works, to the discussion of the significance of metrical forms, rhymes, alliteration, assonance, etc.

2. V. IVANOV—N. MINSKY

Vyacheslav Ivanovich Ivanov (born 1866) left Russia after the Bolshevik revolution, became a Catholic and is living in Rome. His chief works that have a bearing on philosophy are the following: *By the Stars*, 1909; *The Hellenic Religion of the Suffering God*, 1910; *Boundaries and Furrows*, 1916; *A Correspondence Between Two Corners*, Ogonki, Moscow-Berlin 1922; *Dostojewskij*, J. C. B. Mohr, 1932.

According to V. Ivanov symbols are suggestions of a reality inexpressible in words; they give rise to myths which express the truth in the form of images. This truth must lead to a theurgic synthesis of the personal and the communal principles. V. Ivanov's social ideal is communal (*soborny*) anarchy.

A Correspondence Between Two Corners consists of twelve letters exchanged between V. Ivanov and Gershenson in the summer of 1920 when they shared a room in a Moscow sanatorium. Mihail Osipovich Gershenson (1869–1925) was a gifted historian of Russian literature and culture. In their correspondence those two remarkable representatives of Russian and universal culture discussed their relation to history and civilization. V. Ivanov says that "the universal and the ecumenical in me" is a "bright guest who made his abode with me," and that "if I do not forsake God, He will raise me and give me immortality" (Letter I). Gershenson answers that he too does not doubt personal immortality, but that he would like "to plunge into Lethe" and wash off his soul all the past, all religions, all knowledge, all arts" (II). Ivanov remarks that this is a wrong path based on the feeling "that culture is not a living treasure house of gifts but a system of subtle compulsions; for me," he adds, culture is "a hierarchy of reverences, and my reverences are free" (III). He describes Gershenson's negative attitude to history as utopian anarchism and cultural nihilism; it was Tolstoy's path of "simplification" which was inferior to Dostoevsky's path of rising above one's environment, rather than of forsaking it, and of "fiery death in the spirit" (XI). Gershenson, however, expresses a hope that his path too will lead to the same goal as V. Ivanov's: "In the Father's house the same mansion is prepared for you and me" (XII).

In his book on Dostoevsky V. Ivanov speaks of two phases in the development of Satan's activity. Lucifer is the devil at the height of his energies, engrossed in a lively struggle against God. Ariman is the devil in a state of hopeless dejection and longing for non-being, after the experience of a long series of failures and disappointments. With regard to great saints Ivanov thinks that they not merely enter into individual communion with particular people, but also affect entire historical epochs. He sees a connection between St. Francis of Assisi and the work of Dante, and detects the influence of St. Seraphim of Sarov's spirit in Russian art and thought of the nineteenth century.

N. M. Minsky (born 1855) whose real name was Vilenkin, was a poet. Like many other Russian writers of his time he was carried away by Nietzsche's doctrine of the superman and in 1905 wrote a book *The Religion of the Future*. Minsky called his theory a "meonic philosophy" because he designated the absolute by the word "non-being" contrasting it with our being. This led him to conceive of the whole of our life and civilization as permeated by contradictions.

3. D. MEREZHKOVSKY

Dmitri Sergeyevich Merezhkovsky (1865–1941) was a very prolific and many-sided writer. He left Russia after the Bolshevik revolution and settled in Paris. In all his writings—artistic, critical, political— Merezhkovsky invariably touched upon religious problems and expressed his religious and philosophical views. He always wanted not merely theoretically to work out definite religious doctrines, but also to bring practical influence to bear on the life of the Church, the clergy and the general public. Together with Filosofov, Rozanov, Mirolyubov and Ternavtsev, Merezhkovsky organized in 1901 "Religious and Philosophical Meetings" with the object of bringing together "the intellectuals and the Church." At those meetings the attitude of the Church to the state and to autocracy was so sharply criticized that they were closed by the Government in April 1903; but after the revolution of 1905 the meetings were renewed.

Merezhkovsky's chief works that have a bearing on religion and philosophy are: *Tolstoy and Dostoevsky,* 1905; *The Birth of the Gods,* Prague 1925; *The Mystery of Three,* 1925; *The Mystery of the West: Atlantis—Europe,* 1931; *Jesus the Unknown,* 1932 (translated into English by Helen Matheson, Cape, and Scribners & Sons, 1934). The three novels that form the trilogy "Christ and Antichrist" are: *The Death of the Gods: Julian the Apostate; The Risen Gods: Leonardo da Vinci; Antichrist: Peter and Alexis.* Merezhkovsky's collected works comprised fifteen volumes in 1914.

Three problems came from the first into the foreground in Merezhkovsky's thought: the problem of sex; in connection with it, the problem of holy flesh; the problem of social justice and its solution through the christianization of the life of society. Merezhkovsky introduces these problems even into the doctrine of the Holy Trinity. In his book *The Mystery of Three* he says that the mystery of One, of God the Father, is the mystery of the Divine Self, of personality; the mystery of Two is the relation between the Self and the not-Self; the not-self excludes me, kills me or is killed by me, except in one point—sex: in sex there is the entrance of one being into another, "of another body into mine and of mine into another." Hence the birth of a new being; in the Trinity it is the birth of the Son. Thus, the mystery of the Second Person is Sex (50). The mystery of Three is the mystery of the Holy Spirit, the unity of the Three Persons in the Spirit; thus, it is the mystery of Society, the image of the Kingdom of God.

Merezhkovsky dwells on the idea of sex because through sex the highest unity is attainable: "I am conscious of myself in my own body—this is the root of personality; I am conscious of myself in another's body—this is the root of sex; I am conscious of myself in all other bodies—this is the root of society" (58). "The twain shall be one flesh" is said not only of marriage, but of the Divine society: "That they all may be one." The highest unity, the Divine society is connected with the Third Person of the Trinity, the Holy Spirit. In Aramaic the word "spirit," *Rucha,* is of feminine gender. One of the *agrapha*—i.e., of the sayings of Our Lord preserved in oral tradition only—runs thus "My mother is the Holy Spirit." This is how Merezhkovsky interprets the nature of the Holy Trinity: Father, Son, Mother-Spirit. The Third covenant will be the Kingdom of the Spirit-Mother. We should pray to the "warm Protectress of the cold world" (*Jesus the Unknown,* 112 f.).

The division into two sexes is according to Merezhkovsky the decay of personality, its halving. A complete division is so impossible that "in every man there is a secret woman, and in every woman—a secret man" (Weininger's idea). The ideal of personality is for Merezhkovsky, as for Soloviev and Berdyaev, an androgyn, a man-woman (*The Mystery of Three,* 187). The idea is repulsive if an androgyn is taken to mean a hermaphrodite, i.e., a being combining the physical characteristics of both sexes. Merezhkovsky says it should not be understood so crudely; earthly sexual love is a unity, and yet "it is, and it is not" (189). "Divine androgynism is neither masculine nor feminine." Merezhkovsky puts the question whether sinful sex is annulled or transfigured by holy sex (196). That question is of essential importance: on the first alternative, the ideal is supersexuality, i.e., the abolition of sex; on the second, the ideal is the transfiguration and therefore, in a sense, the preservation of sex. Merezhkovsky gives no final answer to this question.

He closely connects with sex the problem of the flesh. Much is said about it in his remarkable book *Tolstoy and Dostoevsky*. He discovers in Tolstoy a religious contemplation of the flesh, and in Dostoevsky a religious contemplation of the spirit; Tolstoy is a seer of the flesh, Dostoevsky of the spirit. Merezhkovsky highly values paganism for understanding the dignity of the body and religiously hallowing it. The ideal for him is not incorporeal holiness but holy flesh, the Kingdom of God in which the mystical unity of the Flesh and the Spirit is realized. In Christianity and more particularly in the Gospel Merezhkovsky discovers three mysteries relating to the problem of the holy flesh: the Incarnation of the Son of God, the partaking of His Body and Blood in communion, and Resurrection in the flesh. He accuses the Christian church of overestimating asceticism and bodiless spirituality, of not attaching sufficient value to the marriage union, and on the other hand of submitting to "unholy flesh"—the pagan state.

Merezhkovsky finds two infinities in the world, the upper and the lower, the spirit and the flesh, which are mystically identical; accordingly he is fond of repeating in his trilogy *Christ and Antichrist* the lines:

> Heaven above, heaven below,
> Stars above, stars below.
> All that's above is also below.

This idea, interpreted in the spirit of certain representatives of gnosticism, leads to a diabolical temptation of believing that there are two ways to perfection and holiness—that of bridling one's passions and, on the contrary, of giving them full rein. Merezhkovsky understood that he was on the brink of an abyss. "I know," he said, "that my question contains the danger of a heresy which might be called, in contradistinction to asceticism, the heresy of astartism; i.e., not of the holy union, but of blasphemous confusion and the pollution of the spirit by the flesh. If this is so, let those who stand on guard warn me." This probably is the reason why in his later works Merezhkovsky ceased to make use of the idea of "heaven above and heaven below."

The final union of the two infinites, the Flesh and the Spirit, will lead, in Merezhkovsky's idea, to the true realization of Christian freedom which is "beyond good and evil." The danger hidden in this thought is explained away by Merezhkovsky's definition of Christian freedom: "One day people will give up eating meat, not because they ought, but solely because they want to do so, because their hearts are drawn to this freely and irresistibly; not because such is the law, but because such is freedom." In other words, Christian freedom is present wherever there is love of the good, of absolute values. This is why the unknown name of Christ is the Liberator (*Jesus the Unknown*, 53). Christianity is salvation through freedom, anti-Christianity is salvation through slavery. "To fear freedom, to disbelieve in it means to disbelieve in the Holy Spirit," says Merezhkovsky.

He thinks that a new revelation and new dogmas are needed if the mystery of holy flesh is to be revealed and the Divine society realized. That will be the era of the Holy Spirit, the Third Covenant, "the eternal Gospel," of which Joachim of Flore spoke. "The Father has not saved the world, the Son has not saved it, the Mother shall save it; the Mother is the Holy Spirit" (*The Mystery of Three*, 364). The purpose of the historical process is to make mankind and the whole world realize the Kingdom of God, not in the world beyond, but here on earth as well. At one of the Religious Philosophical Meetings Merezhkovsky said that the earth is a place of preparation not only for heaven, but for the new, righteous earth. At the present time the problem that has come forward in this process of perfecting the earth is the social problem, the quest for social justice. This is the creative task of Christianity.[1]

The Church is to blame for not having worked in this direction. Seeing that "in Christianity there is no water to quench the social thirst" a number of people have turned away from the Church, and atheism is widely prevalent. There have appeared "learned troglodytes" with diabolical miracles, the most savage of savages, for they "do away with personality" and absolute ideals (*The Mystery of Three*, 10–16). They act upon nature from without "by mechanics;" in the Atlantis, Merezhkovsky thinks, man acted upon nature magically, from within, through organic power over it (*Jesus the Unknown*, 259).

In our era, Merezhkovsky says, the struggle of the man-god against the God-man has grown more fierce than ever. This is the secret of the whole Russian culture of the future—the struggle between the Eastern and the Western spirit, "the spirit of war and the spirit of grace" (*Tolstoy and Dostoevsky*, I, 10). In that struggle the love of the God-man Christ leads to the miracle of multiplying the loaves, or more exactly, to the brotherly satisfaction of the common need; in the kingdom of the man-god there takes place the diabolical miracle of the diminution of loaves (*Jesus the Unknown*, II, 185). In the kingdom of

---

[1]. See Z. Hippius, "The First Meeting," in the newspaper *Latest News*, February 13, 1931.

atheistic socialism love for the individual is replaced by "the will for the impersonal" and an ant heap is being built (*The Mystery of Three*, 55); instead of the sacrament of communion there is cannibalism. If the man-god wins the victory on the earth, that will mean that humanity has been a failure. Then the button maker will be needed,[2] the button maker who came to Peer Gynt in order to recast him because he was not himself (*ibid.*, 59). Merezhkovsky pictured this recasting as the conflagration in which Earth will perish. In his later years he had more and more often a presentiment of such an end of the Earth and of human history: "The world has never yet been conscious of such a yawning abyss in itself, ready to engulf everything at any moment; the axe is laid unto the root of the trees" (*Jesus the Unknown*, I, 116). This does not mean, however, that humanity will disappear: the fiery end of the second, after-the-deluge, humanity may not be the end of the world: there shall be a third humanity, a hiliastic one foretold in the Apocalypse (*ibid.*, II, 94). It will be the kingdom of the saints, the kingdom of love and freedom.

The whole of Merezhkovsky's religious philosophy is based upon the idea of Christianity as the religion of love and therefore of freedom. This combination of love and freedom brings him close to the religious and philosophical movement which was begun by Vladimir Soloviev.

The ideal of personality, according to Merezhkovsky, and also according to Soloviev and Berdyaev, is an androgyn, i.e., one integral personality which combines both man and woman. Such a theory can only be adopted by philosophers who deny the substantiality of the self, that is, who fail to recognize that the individual self is a supertemporal and superspatial entity. By virtue of its substantiality the self is an *individual* in the exact sense of that term; i.e., a being which is absolutely *indivisible* and not made up of two halves. Both man and woman are persons, imperfect only in the sense that a man has spiritual qualities which as a rule are lacking in a woman, and a woman has spiritual qualities which as a rule are absent in a man. The ideal of personality consists in combining in oneself the masculine and the feminine virtues; it is realized through the development of one's own self and not through an impossible mergence of two selves into one. That ideal is wholly realizable in the Kingdom of God, in which the transfigured bodies have no sex organs or sex functions. Consequently, in that Kingdom persons are supersexual and not bisexual. Similarly, the Persons of the Holy Trinity are neither men nor women.

2. See Ibsen's *Peer Gynt*.

4. V. ROZANOV

Vassili Vassilyevich Rozanov (1856–1919) after having graduated in the Faculty of Arts at the Moscow University taught history and geography in provincial Russian towns; he found his work very irksome. For many years, as he puts it, "he was bored with high-school atheism," but when he was thirty-five there was a sudden change in him which brought him to religion and to a decision to live in accordance with God's will. Thanks to N. N. Strahov he managed to move to Petersburg in 1893 and get a post in the Excise Department. In 1899 he retired, became a regular contributor of the conservative newspaper *Novoe Vremya* and wholly devoted himself to literary work. Rozanov was not a poet, but like the poet-symbolists he was "a seeker after God."

Rozanov's chief works are the following: *About Understanding*, Moscow 1886; *The Legend of the Great Inquisitor*, 1893; *Essays on Marriage*, 1898; *The Twilight of Enlightenment*, 1899; *Literary Essays*, 1899; *Religion and Culture*, 1901; *In the Realm of the Vague and the Uncertain*, 1904; *Near the Church Walls*, 1906; *The Dark Image: Metaphysics of Christianity*, 1911; *Fallen Leaves* (English translation by Koteliansky, London 1929); *Solitaria*, 1916; *The Apocalypse of Our Time*, 1918.

In 1922 Erich Hollerbach wrote a book *V. V. Rozanov* which is translated into English.

Rozanov had a great literary gift and was a highly original thinker and observer of life. His writings are not systematic or even coherent, but often show flashes of genius. Unfortunately his personality was in many ways pathological; the most striking instance of this was his abnormal preoccupation with sex. He might have been a character in one of Dostoevsky's novels. Erich Hollerbach in his book gives a magnificent characteristic of Rozanov. He says that in his striving to penetrate into the depths of the human soul Rozanov was interested in other writers' "domestic affairs," in their "underclothes." I know something about this from personal experience. Rozanov's three daughters attended a High School for girls the headmistress of which was my mother-in-law, Madame Stoyunin. Our flat adjoined the school. When Rozanov came to the school on business, he always called on me. As soon as I said "come in" in answer to his knock, he would quickly open the study door, rush to my desk on which a book lay open and peep to see what I was reading. He may have tried to catch everyone unawares in the same way so as to learn their real interests.

Rozanov's book *About Understanding* is the only one of his works

concerned with purely philosophical questions. He tries to work out a
conception of "understanding" which would overcome the antagonism
between science and philosophy. Reason, he says, contains speculative
schemata which are seven: the ideas of existence, of essence, of property,
of cause (or origin), of consequence (or purpose), of similarity and difference, and of number. By combining speculation and experience we
arrive at "understanding" as "integral knowledge." The human spirit
is an independent, immaterial entity, capable of creating various forms,
i.e., ideas, and imposing them upon material substance; such forms are,
e.g., sculpture, music, the state, and so on. The spirit is "the form of
forms." After the destruction of the body, the spirit survives as "the
form of pure existence, not confined to any limit." The book is written
in a dull, colorless style, very different from Rozanov's other writings
which clearly show his literary gift and originality.

Rozanov's books and articles are largely taken up with criticism of
Christianity. He regards the bright Christianity of Father Zossima and
Alyosha Karamazov an invention of Dostoevsky's. The true, historical
Christianity is in his view, a gloomy religion of death, preaching
celibacy, fasting and asceticism. Instead of love for man it devoted
itself to theology: the final result of such a religion is the Old Believers'
self-immolation by burning themselves or being buried alive as in 1896
near Tiraspol (it happened among the Old Believers who feared the
national census, regarding it as the work of antichrist). Rozanov wants
a bright religion, but he does not know spiritual joy because he does
not know Christianity as a religion of light; he wants the pagan carnal
joy. The Old Testament attracts him more than the New. In the Old
Testament, he says, "punishment is short and physical," and at bottom
Israel is never afraid. There is a wonderful spirit of freedom and even
of unruliness in it, and it is as though Jehovah and the prophets liked
that unruliness. They struggle with it as a groom struggles with a vicious
horse, or a mother with a child of genius; but they would be horrified
at the idea of making something timid and obedient out of the ardent
and lively "that we may lead a quiet and peaceable life" (*Dark Image*,
235). The Old Testament religion attracts Rozanov by its care for man
and its love for family life. But the pagan cult of the flesh, especially
the phallic cult attracts him even more. The phallus is in his opinion
"the source of all inspiration." Hollerbach says that by deifying sex,
Rozanov "transforms religion into sexual pantheism" (46).

In spite of his praises of the Old Testament Rozanov at one time
wrote as an anti-Semite. Such duality on his part was ascribed to a lack
of principle, and in 1913 he was expelled from the Petersburg Re-

ligious and Philosophical Meetings. As Hollerbach puts it, Rozanov was psychologically a Judophil and politically an anti-Semite, so that he was not "double-dealing" but rather "double-faced" (98).

After the Bolshevik revolution Rozanov lived at Father Pavel Florensky's in the Sergiev Posad by the Monastery of St. Sergius. He was writing there his *Apocalypse of Our Time* in which he went on denouncing Christianity. Indignant at this, Father Pavel, a lecturer of the Moscow Theological Academy Andreyev, and another person whose name I have forgotten, came to see Rozanov. Andreyev told me, they said to Rozanov that if he went on attacking Christianity they would not be his friends any more. Rozanov answered to this, evidently conscious of some demoniacal power in himself or near him: "Don't interfere with Rozanov; it will go badly with you." And indeed in the course of the following year all these three persons had serious misfortunes happen to them. Rozanov died, however, as a good Christian. Before death his heart was full of joy at Christ's Resurrection. Several times he received holy communion and extreme unction. He died while the last rites were being performed.

Chapter 24

DIALECTICAL MATERIALISM IN THE U.S.S.R.

1. HEGEL'S DIALECTICAL METHOD

Marxists say that their philosophy, dialectical materialism, is historically connected with the philosophy of Hegel, namely with his conception of the dialectical method. They point out, of course, that their philosophy profoundly differs from Hegel's: Hegel defends idealism and maintains that the ground of the world is the Absolute Spirit, while Marxists are materialists and believe that the only reality is matter. In spite of this difference, however, an exposition of dialectical materialism should be preceded by a discussion of Hegel's dialectical method and a critical examination of the Hegelian and the Marxist doctrine of the identity of opposites.

On Hegel's view the cosmic process is the development of the Absolute idea or the Absolute Spirit. Thought and existence are identical in this process. Since the cosmic process develops dialectically, philosophical interpretation of it develops by means of the dialectical method which is nothing other than objective dialectic itself, attaining self-consciousness in the philosopher's mind.

The starting point of dialectic is a one-sided and limited conception of the understanding, determined in accordance with the laws of identity and contradiction. It cannot remain in its one-sidedness: its own content compels it to transcend its limits and to become its opposite which is also rationalistic, limited and one-sided; thus the conception passes from the *thesis* to the *antithesis*. But it cannot rest there: the content of the antithesis also demands self-transcendence and transition into its opposite. This transcendence—i.e., the *negation of the negation*—takes the form not of a return to the thesis, but of a further development of the idea and of ascent toward *synthesis*—i.e., to a conception in which the identity of the opposites is realized. This identity is not the abstract identity of the understanding, but a concrete identity of reason: it consists in the fact that living reality is not afraid of contradiction, but on the contrary gives embodiment to it.

The third level of development, the synthesis, proves on closer inspection to contain in addition to the living identity of opposites some further elements of rationalistic one-sidedness which requires a new negation, and so on; thus the self-development of the idea takes place every time in the form of a triad—i.e., along the three stages of thesis, antithesis, synthesis.

An example of it is to be found at the beginning of Hegel's *Logic*. Starting with pure *being* and finding no content in it, Hegel identifies it with *nothing*. "Thus," he says, "the beginning contains being and nothing, it is the unity of being and nothing, for it is non-being which is at the same time being, and being which at the same time is non-being." Hegel discovers the true expression of this identity between being and non-being in becoming (*Werden*).[1]

According to traditional formal logic everything is subject to the laws of identity, contradiction and excluded middle, so that "every *A* is *A*" and "no *A* can be non-*A*." Hegel regards such logic as an expression of rationalistic abstractions inapplicable to the concrete living reality in which, on the contrary, everything is contradictory and "every *A* is *B*," since the presence of contradictions, conflicts and struggle between opposed principles compels being to progress and develop. Dialectical logic thus sharply differs from the logic of the understanding.

For purposes of criticism, let us take a more concrete instance, namely, the relation between the outer and the inner. Hegel discusses it in his *Logic* with reference to force as the inner form of reality, and to its external manifestation as the form of being; he tries to show that in this case the inner and the outer is "only an identity" (*nur eine Identität ausmachen*).[2] He expresses the same idea, though less emphatically, in other sections of his *Logic*, e.g., when he speaks of inner sensations (feelings) and their bodily expressions in weeping, laughter, etc.[3]

Let us take some particular instance of mental states and their bodily expression. Suppose two rival and mutually hostile thinkers engaged upon some philosophical problem are having a lively discussion. One of them succeeds in proving that his opponent's theory obviously contains an absurdity. He demolishes his rival's arguments, conscious of his own superiority, his head held high, and a jerky sarcastic laugh escaping him from time to time. It is certainly impossible in this case to speak of the identity between the inner and the outer, between the mental experience and its bodily expression. The bodily

---

1. Hegel, *Wissenschaft der Logik*, I, 68, 77–80. (Vol. III, 1833 ed.)
2. II, sec. 2, chap. 3, 178. (Vol. IV, 1834 ed.)
3. *The Encyclopaedia of Philosophical Sciences*, §§ 393–400.

expression consists of spatial processes: changes in the position of the head, periodical contractions and expansions of the chest, movement of the particles of air, sound waves, and so on. The inner mental experience of the disputant—the expression of his own self—is proud delight in his own superiority and ironically contemptuous triumph over his rival. All his intimate, inner, i.e., mental processes have only a temporal form, and the outer, i.e., bodily expression are spatiotemporal. Separating one side from the other by intellectual analysis, one can easily see that the qualitative difference between the psychical and the physical is enormous. An inability to concentrate attention now chiefly on the one and now on the other, in order to detect the difference between them, leads to their confusion, which is as absurd an error as it would be to assert the identity of color and extension when looking at a red disk, and not being able mentally to distinguish its redness from its spatial form (the circle).

The profound difference between the psychical and its physical manifestation does not prevent them forming the closest possible unity, closer even than the unity of the red color and its extendedness. In the instance we have been considering there is *interpenetration* between different and even opposite processes (inner and outer), though it is not an identity of opposites but only their *unity*. Identity of opposites, violating the law of contradiction, is absolutely unrealizable because it is absolutely meaningless. The violation of the law of contradiction would mean, for instance, that "redness in its very redness is not red." An absurdity of this kind can be merely verbally expressed as a puzzle, but it is absolutely impossible to realize it even in thought.

Hegel considers every change to be an embodied contradiction. In truth, however, every change is a unity of opposites, but not their identity violating the law of contradiction.

2. DIALECTICAL MATERIALISM

In U.S.S.R. the state compulsorily upholds a certain philosophical system, namely, the materialism of Marx and Engels called dialectical (abridged form *diamat*). Up to 1925 many Soviet philosophers, especially the naturalists, while emphasizing their loyalty to Marxism were not sufficiently clear in their minds about the distinction between dialectical and mechanistic materialism. In 1925 there was published for the first time Engel's manuscript *The Dialectics of Nature* (written in 1873, 1878–1882), which caused a sharp division of Soviet Marxists into "dialecticians" and "mechanists." A fierce struggle "on two fronts" broke out against "menshevik-minded idealism and mechanistic materialism." The outlines of dialectical materialism were clearly defined.[1]

Let us see first of all what its adherents mean by the term "materialism." Engels, and Lenin following him, say that philosophers are divided into materialists, idealists and agnostics. For the materialists, says Lenin, matter, nature (physical being) is primary, and spirit, consciousness, sensation, the psychical, is secondary. For the idealists, on the contrary, spirit is primary. Agnostics deny that the world and its basic principles are knowable.[2]

"There is nothing in the world but matter in motion, and matter cannot move save in space and time" (Lenin). The fundamental forms of all being are space and time; being outside of time is just as much of an absurdity as being outside of space" (Engels, *Anti-Dühring*, 4th Russian ed., 39).

On the strength of this it may appear that dialectical materialism is based upon as clear and definite a conception of matter as the mechanistic materialism: matter is extended, impenetrable being, moving, i.e., changing position in space. We shall see, however, that this is not the case.

"The conception of matter," says Byhovsky, "is used in two senses. We distinguish between the philosophical and the physical conception of matter. They are not mutually contradictory, but they define matter from two different points of view" (78). Following Holbach and Plehanov and quoting Lenin he defines matter from the philosophical, epistemological point of view as that "which acting upon our sense organs produces sensation; matter is the objective reality, given to us in sensation" (Lenin, 116). This definition contains merely the recognition of the objective reality of matter, i.e., of its existing independently of our consciousness, and asserts that "our knowledge of it originates through the senses" (Byhovsky, 78) but does not indicate its nature. One would expect that this would be done by the definition of matter from the point of view of physics. Vain hope! "What is meant by giving a 'definition'?" ask Lenin, Byhovsky and others. It means first of all to subsume a given concept under another, a more inclusive generic one, as

---

1. In my exposition of dialectical materialism I shall be referring chiefly to the following books and articles: Engels, *The Dialectics of Nature*, with an introduction by D. Ryazanov, 4th ed., 1930; Lenin, *Materialism and Empirio-Criticism*, 1908, Collected Works, X; Deborin, *Hegel and Dialectical Materialism*, introductory article in the translation of Hegel's *Collected Works*, I, 2nd ed., 1929; B. Byhovsky, *An Outline of the Philosophy of Dialectical Materialism*; I. Luppol, *On Two Fronts*, 1930; V. Pozner, *Dialectical Materialism—the Philosophy of the Proletariat*, 1933; M. A. Leonov, *An Outline of Dialectical Materialism*, 1948. In referring to these books I will not give their full titles.

2. Lenin, *Materialism and Empirio-Criticism;* the references are to the English translation by I. Kvitko, Marks & Lawrence, 1927; Engels, *Ludwig Feuerbach*.

one of its species and indicate its specific difference (e.g., in the definition "a square is an equilateral rectangle," "rectangle" is a generic notion and "equilateral" the specific distinguishing characteristic). But "matter cannot be defined *per genus et differentiam* since matter is *all* that exists, the most general conception, the genus of all genera. All that exists is some aspect of matter, but matter itself cannot be defined as a particular instance of some genus. For the same reason it is impossible to indicate the specific difference of matter. If matter is *all* that exists, it is unthinkable to seek for the characteristics that distinguish it from something else, since that something else could only be nonexistence, i.e., it could not exist."[3]

Dialectical materialists have thus greatly simplified their task of providing the grounds for a materialistic world conception. Without any proof they affirm that "matter is *all* that exists, being from its very nature is a *material* category" (Deborin, XLI). This makes it possible, in accordance with the requirements of modern science and philosophy, to ascribe to "being" all kinds of manifestations, properties and faculties which are very far from being material, and yet to call one's theory materialism on the ground that "matter is *all that exists*." Engels in his *Dialectics of Nature* indicates the way which may lead us to the knowledge of what matter is: "Once we have come to know the forms of the motion of matter (though our knowledge of this is still very deficient, since natural science is of recent origin) we have come to know matter itself, and this exhausts the knowledge of it" (17). This statement sounds very materialistic if the word motion is taken in the sense, generally accepted in science, of transposition in space. On the very next page, however, Engels explains that in dialectical materialism motion means "change in general" (18, 163). All dialectical materialists accept this use: by the word "motion" they designate not merely transposition in space, but also every qualitative change. Thus so far all we have been told about matter is that matter is everything that exists and changes. But we need not despair: the consideration of the "dialecticians" struggle against mechanistic materialism and of their other theories will give us a more definite idea of the nature of their philosophy.

A metaphysical philosophy, says Engels—including under this term mechanistic materialism—is concerned with "unchangeable categories," and dialectical materialism with "fluid" ones (1 f.). Thus, e.g., according to mechanistic materialism the smallest particles are unchangeable and uniform. But, says Engels, "natural science that strives to discover matter as such and to reduce qualitative distinctions to purely quantitative differences in the composition of identical tiniest particles is doing

3. Byhovsky, 78; Lenin, 118.

the same thing as it would be doing if it sought for fruit as such, instead of cherries, pears, apples, etc., if it sought for a mammal as such, instead of cats, dogs, sheep, etc., or if it sought for gas as such, for metal as such, for stone as such, for chemical fusion, or for movement as such. This one-sided mathematical point of view according to which matter is only quantitatively determined is the point of view of French eighteenth century materialism" (Engels, 103; Luppol, 146 f.). Dialectical materialism is free from the one-sidedness of the mechanistic view, since it is guided by the following three laws of dialectics derived "from the history of nature and of human society: the law of the transition of quantity into quality, and vice versa; the law of the mutual interpenetration of opposites; the law of the negation of negation" (157).

The second and the third law have been mentioned in connection with Hegel's dialectical method; the first law is that at a certain stage quantitative changes result in sudden changes in quality. Besides, speaking generally "there is no quality apart from quantity, and no quantity without quality" (Deborin, XX).

Motion—i.e., every kind of change—is dialectical through and through. "The chief basic feature of every change consists, as we know, in the fact that a certain thing is negated in its movement, that it ceases to be what it was and acquires new forms of existence. In its transition into a new quality, in the process of the appearance of the new, the former quality is not destroyed without a trace, but enters into the new quality as a subordinate element. Negation is "lifting," to use a customary dialectical term. "Lifting" is a form of negation in which a thing comes to an end and at the same time is preserved at a new level. "This is how food or oxygen is assimilated by the organism and transmuted in it, this is how a plant preserves the nutritive elements of the soil, this is how history of science and art absorbs the legacy of the past. That which remains of the past is subordinated to new laws of development, comes into the orbit of new movements, is harnessed to the chariot of the new quality. The transformation of energy is at the same time the preservation of energy. The destruction of capitalism is at the same time the absorption of technical and cultural results of capitalist development. The appearance of higher forms of motion is not the destruction of the lower, but their sublimation. Mechanical laws exist within the limits of the higher forms of motion as subsidiary, subordinate, sublimated."

"How does the further development take place? When a particular thing has been changed into its opposite and its preceding state been sublimated, development continues on the new basis, and at a certain stage of it the thing again for a second time changes into its opposite.

Does this mean that, with the second negation, the thing returns to its original state? No, it does not. The second negation or, in dialectical terminology, the negation of negation is not a return to the original state. Negation of the negation means 'lifting' both of the first and the second stage of development or rising above both" (Byhovsky, 208 f.). "It is not a circular but a spiral movement."[4]

The opposite into which a thing is transformed in its development is "something more than mere difference," Byhovsky explains. Opposition "is qualified difference, an inner, essential, necessary and irreconcilable difference in a certain definite respect. The world as a whole is nothing other than the unity of such opposites, a divided unity, containing polarities. Electrical and magnetic processes are an instance of the unity of opposites. Matter is the unity of protons and electrons, the unity of a continuous wave and discrete particles. There is no action without counteraction. Every origination is at the same time necessarily a destruction of something. The survival of the fittest is the dying out of the unfit. A class society is a unity of opposites. The proletariat and the bourgeoisie are social categories, the distinction between which amounts to opposition" (Byhovsky, 211). Thus "the moving world is a unity containing contradictions" (Byhovsky, 213). The basic principle of the dialectical interpretation of the world is that "the world is a unity divided in itself, a unity of opposites, the bearer of inner contradictions" (Byhovsky, 213; Pozner, 59). "Objective dialectics," i.e., movement by means of contradictions, "reigns throughout nature" (Engels, 42; Deborin, LXXXI). "Detection of the unity of opposites in nature," says Lenin, "conditions the possibility of knowing all the processes of the world in their *self-movement,* in their spontaneous development, in their actual life."[5]

At this point the profound difference between the dialectical and the mechanistic materialism becomes apparent. "For a mechanist," Byhovsky points out, "contradiction is mechanical, it is the contradiction of conflicting things, or of mutually opposed forces. On a mechanistic interpretation of motion, contradiction can only be external and not inward, it is not contained and does not take place in a unity, there is no inner necessary connection between its elements. The theory of equilibrium (A. Bogdanov, N. Buharin) is a clear instance of a methodology based upon the substitution of the mechanical principle of conflict between forces moving in opposite direction for the dialectical principle of the unity of opposites." According to that theory "equilib-

---

4. Lenin, "Karl Marx," *Collected Works,* 2nd ed., XVIII, 11.
5. Lenin, "The Question of Dialectics," *Under the Banner of Marxism,* V–VI, 14, 1925.

rium is the state of a thing in which it cannot change its condition of itself, without the help of an outside force. Disturbance of the balance is the result of conflict between mutually opposed forces;" i.e., of the forces in some system and its environment. The fundamental differences between this mechanistic view of balance and the dialectical theory are as follows: in the first place, "according to the theory of equilibrium there is no immanent origination of differences, no immanent splitting up of the unity, no mutual interpenetration between the opposites. Opposition is severed from the unity, the antagonistic elements are mutually independent, alien and external, their contradiction appears accidental. Secondly, inner contradictions as the moving power of development are replaced by external contradictions, by the conflict between a system and its environment. Self-movement is replaced by movement caused by an impetus from without. Internal relations in a system are reduced to the level of derivative and made dependent upon external relations. The inner uniformities of qualitatively determined things are regarded as a function of external relations between objects and not as the moving force of development. Thirdly, the theory of equilibrium reduces all the multiplicity of the forms of movement to mechanical impact between bodies. The conception of equilibrium borrowed from mechanics does away with the wealth of the higher, supermechanical (biological and social) forms of development. Fourthly, in the theory of balance the relation between movement and rest is reversed. Equilibrium is said to be mobile and relative; thus motion in this view is a form of rest, and not vice versa. It is not motion that bears within it rest and balance, but on the contrary, balance proves to be the bearer of movement. Fifthly, the theory of equilibrium is the theory of abstract quantitative change. The greater force determines the direction of the lesser. Transmutation into a new quality, the appearance of new forms of development, of new uniformities—all this cannot be fitted into the flat crude scheme of equilibrium. Finally in the sixth place, the negation of negation, the "lifting" of the positive and the negative movements of development, the appearance of the new, is replaced, on the mechanistic theory, by the reinstatement of equilibrium between the system and the environment" (Byhovsky, 237 f.).

In so far as change is dialectical self-movement, based upon inner contradictions, it deserves the name of *"development"* and, as Lenin says and Deborin repeats after him, has an *immanent* character. "The object *necessarily* develops in a *definite* direction, but may develop in another direction owing to its essence or immanent nature" (Deborin, XCVI).

Accordingly, it is not surprising to find Lenin pointing out that development has a *creative* character. He distinguishes "two conceptions of development (or evolution): development as increase and decrease, as repetition, and development as the unity of opposites (the division of a unit into mutually exclusive opposites and the interrelation between them). The first conception is dead, poor, arid. The second is vital; it alone explains the self-movement of all that is, the sudden changes, the breaks in continuity, the transformation into the opposite, the destruction of the old and the birth of the new."[6]

In his article on "Karl Marx" Lenin points out the following features of the dialectical theory of development: "Development repeats, as it were, the past stages, but in a different way, on a higher level (negation of the negation), proceeding so to speak along a spiral and not in a straight line; development is catastrophic and revolutionary, by sudden jumps; there are breaks in continuity, quantity is transformed into quality; there are inner impulses to development, given by contradiction, by the conflict between different forces and tendencies affecting the given body, or acting within the limits of a given fact, or of a particular society; there is interdependence and the closest possible, indissoluble bond between *all* the aspects of every event (and history keeps discovering new aspects)—a bond which results in a single, uniform cosmic process of movement. These are some of the characteristics of dialectics as a theory of development, more significant than the usual theory."[7]

If, according to Lenin, evolution is *creative,* and is immanent and *spontaneous* self-movement containing "inner impulses," it is clearly possible to speak of the transition from some stages of being to others as having value and not merely being a fact. "Every process of development," says Deborin, "is an ascent from the lower forms or stages to the higher, from abstract determinations comparatively poor in content to the more concrete, with a richer and fuller content. The highest stage contains the lower as "sublimated," i.e., as no longer independent. The lower form has developed into the higher; in doing so it has not disappeared without a trace, but has itself become a different and higher form" (Deborin, XCV). Further, it is clear from this that dialectical development may be called a *historical* process. "The higher form is connected with the lower," Deborin goes on, "and therefore a result does not exist apart from the *path of development* that has led to it. Every given event or every given form must be regarded as *having developed,* as *having become;* i.e., we must regard it as a historical forma-

---

6. Lenin, "The Question of Dialectics," 15.
7. Lenin, "Karl Marx," 11.

tion." As Ryazanov puts it, "Marx and Engels establish the *historical* character of events in nature and society."[8]

Even inorganic nature is in a state of development and transformation. Ryazanov quotes the following words of Marx: "Even elements do not remain in a state of rest. They continually change into one another, and this change forms the first level of the earth's life—the metereological process. In the life of the organism all trace of the different elements as such disappears."[9] These words clearly express Marx's conviction that the higher stages of cosmic being profoundly differ from the lower in quality and therefore cannot be interpreted as merely more and more complex aggregates of the lower, simple elements. This idea is strongly emphasized in the Soviet dialectical materialism. It sharply distinguishes it from mechanistic materialism. "To reduce the complex to the simple means refusing to understand the complex," says Byhovsky. "To reduce the whole multiplicity of cosmic laws to mechanical ones means refusing to understand any laws except the simplest mechanical ones; it means limiting one's knowledge to the elementary forms of motion. An atom consists of electrons, but the laws of an atom's existence are not limited to the laws of motion of the separate electrons. A molecule consists of atoms, but it transcends the laws of an atom's life. A cell consists of molecules, an organism consists of cells, a biological species consists of organisms, but their life is not confined to the laws that determine the life of their components. Society consists of organisms, but its development cannot be deduced from the laws that govern the life of organisms. There exist three chief, fundamental realms of being: the inorganic world, the organic world (in which the appearance of consciousness marks a break of the utmost significance) and the social world. The forms of movement in each of these realms are qualitatively unique and irreducible to other forms, though derived from them." A mechanistic materialist reduces organic laws to the mechanical "and at the same time, social laws, reduced to the biological, are also absorbed in the laws of mechanics." Sociology becomes for him a collective reflexology (Behterev). In reality, however, each higher stage is subject to special laws of its own, and these "specific uniformities, these supermechanical kinds of development do not contradict mechani-

---

8. Deborin, XCV f.; Ryazanov, XVIII. The conception of historical development as a system in which the present arises under the influence of the *past itself* and not only of its consequences immediately adjoining the present is discussed in N. Lossky's essay "Bergson's Intuitive Philosophy."

9. The quotation is taken by Ryazanov from Marx's article "On Class Commissions in Prussia."

cal laws and do not exclude them, but transcend them as secondary and subordinate.[10]

Engels says: "Each of the higher forms of motion is always necessarily connected with real mechanical motion (external or molecular), and at the same time produces other kinds of motion; chemical activity is impossible without electrical changes and changes in temperature, organic life is impossible without mechanical, molecular, chemical, thermic, electrical and other changes. But the presence of these secondary forms does not exhaust the nature of the main form in each case. We shall no doubt one day 'reduce' thought to molecular and chemical changes in the brain; but will that exhaust the nature of thought?" (Engels, 18). Thus everything is subject to the laws of mechanics, but not to them alone.

The view that the laws of the higher forms of being cannot be completely reduced to those of the lower is widely prevalent in philosophy. Thus, it is to be found in Comte's positivism; in German philosophy it is connected with the theories that the higher stages of being are based upon the lower but are qualitatively distinct; in English philosophy it takes the form of the theory of "emergent evolution;" i.e., of a creative evolution that builds up new stages of being, the qualities of which are not merely due to the qualities of their components.[11]

Those who maintain that "matter is all that exists" and at the same time recognize creative evolution must endow matter with the capacity for creative activity. "Matter," says Yegorshin, "is extremely rich and has a variety of forms. It does not receive its qualities from the spirit, but has itself the power to create them, including spirit as well" (168).

What, then, is this mysterious matter, so rich in potencies and faculties and yet left without any ontological definition in dialectical materialism? Let us ask the question essential for ontology (the science about the elements and aspects of being) whether matter is a *substance* or merely a complex of events, i.e., of temporal and spatiotemporal processes. If it is a substance, it is the bearer and the creative source of events—a principle which is as such more than an event.

Revolutionary materialists who study philosophy not out of love for truth but for the strictly practical purpose of acquiring a weapon to break up the old social life avoid questions that require subtle

---

10. Byhovsky, 202–204; Yegorshin, *Natural Science, Philosophy and Marxism*, 138, 1930; Pozner, 62, 64.

11. Cf., e.g., Lloyd Morgan, *Emergent Evolution;* S. Alexander, *Space, Time and Deity;* and others.

analysis. Nevertheless Lenin in his attacks on Mach and Avenarius, who deny the substantival bases of reality, provides some data for answering the question we are concerned with.

In criticizing Mach and Avenarius, Lenin says that their rejection of the idea of substance lands them with "sensation without matter, and thought without brain" (138). He regards as absurd a theory in which "instead of the thought, idea and sensation of a living man, a dead abstraction is posited, that is, nobody's thought, nobody's idea, nobody's sensation" (225). But perhaps Lenin thinks that sensitive matter (brain) is itself merely a complex of motions? No, in the paragraph entitled "Is Motion Without Matter Conceivable?" he sharply criticizes all attempts to conceive of movement apart from matter and quotes Engels and Dietzgen in support of his view (223). "The dialectical materialist not only regards motion as the inseparable property of matter but rejects even the simplified interpretation of motion" (226); i.e., the view according to which motion is "nobody's" motion: "It moves—and that is all" (224). Deborin therefore is right in introducing the term substance ("in a materialistic system of logic the central idea must be that of *matter* as substance") and in supporting Spinoza's conception of substance interpreted as a "creative force" (XC, XCI). Lenin himself does not use the term substance; he says it is "a word which the professors like to employ for the sake of 'importance' instead of the clearer and more exact word 'matter'" (138); but the passages that have been quoted show that he had sufficient insight to distinguish two important aspects in the structure of reality—events on the one hand, and the creative source of events on the other. He ought therefore to have understood that the term "substance" is needed for clearness and definiteness, and not for "importance" sake.

Let us now pass to the question which is of decisive importance both for the defense of and for the disproof of materialism, as to the place of consciousness and psychical processes in nature. Unfortunately, in speaking about this dialectical materialists do not distinguish between such different subjects of inquiry as consciousness, psychical process and thought. They also include in this series sensation as the lowest form of consciousness. A few words should be said about the difference between these facts so that we may form a better idea of the theories of the dialectical materialists. Let us begin with the analysis of human consciousness.

Consciousness always has two aspects: there is someone who is conscious and something of which he is conscious; let us call these two aspects, respectively, the subject and the object of consciousness. In the case of human consciousness, the conscious subject is the human self.

The nature of consciousness consists in the fact that the object of it (the joy that is felt, the sound that is heard, the color that is seen, etc.) exists not only for itself but in some intimate way *for the subject* as well. Most modern philosophers and psychologists maintain that for cognition to take place there must be, in addition to the subject and the object, a special mental *act of awareness* directed by the subject upon the object (upon the joy, the sound, the color). Such mental acts are called *intentional:* they are directed upon the object and have no meaning apart from it; they do not change the object, but bring it into the field of the subject's consciousness and knowledge. To be conscious of an object does not as yet mean to know it; a member of a victorious football team may be wildly excited with joy without in the least *observing* that feeling in himself while engaged in giving a lively account of the game. If he happens to be a psychologist he can concentrate attention on his feeling of joy and *cognize* it as, e.g., elation with a tinge of triumph over the vanquished opponent; he will then have not only the experience of the feeling, but an idea of it and even a judgment about it. In order to gain this knowledge about the feeling, it is necessary to perform, in addition to the act of awareness, a number of other supplementary intentional acts such as an act of comparing the given feeling with other mental states, an act of distinguishing, etc.

According to the theory of knowledge which I call intuitivism my cognition of my feeling in the form of a presentation or even of judgment does not mean that the feeling is replaced by an image, a copy, or a symbol of it: my knowledge about my feeling of joy is a direct contemplation of that feeling as it is in itself, or an *intuition* directed upon that feeling in such a way that through comparing it with other states and tracing its relations to them, I can give to myself and to others an account of it, discriminate various aspects of it (mentally analyze it) and point out its connection with the world.

One may be conscious of a mental state without directing upon it intentional acts of discriminating, comparing, etc.; in that case there is awareness of it, but not knowledge. The psychic life may, indeed, take an even simpler form: a mental state may exist without an act of awareness being directed upon it; then it remains a subconscious or an unconscious mental experience. Thus, a singer may make critical remarks about her rival's performance under the influence of an unconscious feeling of envy, which another person may detect in her expression and the tone of her voice. It would be quite erroneous to say that an unconscious mental state is not mental at all, but is a purely physical process in the central nervous system. Even so simple an act as an unconscious desire during a lively conversation at table to take and eat a piece of bread lying before me cannot be regarded as a purely physical process unaccompanied by inner psychical states and consisting merely of centrifugal currents in the nervous system. It has already been pointed out that even in inorganic nature an act of attraction or repulsion can only take place on the strength of a preceding inner psychoid striving to attraction or repulsion in a given direction. If we are conscious of such an *inner* state as *striving*, and of such an external process as *transposition* of material particles *in space*, we see with absolute certainty that they are two profoundly different events, though closely welded together.

Thus, consciousness and mental life are not identical: there may be an unconscious or subconscious mental life. Indeed, the difference between "the conscious" and "the psychical" goes even further. According to the theory of intuitivism, the knowing subject is able to direct his acts of awareness and of knowing not only upon his mental states, but also upon his bodily processes and upon the external world as it is in itself: I can be directly aware and have a direct knowledge of the fall of a stone and of a weeping child who has trapped his finger in the door, as they actually are apart from my acts of attention, etc., directed upon them. The human self is so closely bound up with the world that it can look right into other entities' being.

According to this theory, when I watch a stone falling, this material process becomes *immanent* in my *consciousness* while remaining *transcendent* to me as a knowing *subject;* i.e., it does not become one of my mental processes. If I am conscious of this object and know it, my acts of attending, distinguishing, etc., belong to the mental sphere, but that which I distinguish—the color and form of the stone, its movement, etc.—is a physical process. In consciousness and in knowledge distinction must be drawn between the subjective and the objective side: only the subjective side, i.e., my intentional acts, are bound to be mental; the objective side may be anything in the world—material processes, other mental lives, my own mental states, social phenomena, ideal being (nonspatial and nontemporal), and so on.

It is clear from this that "the mental" and "consciousness" are not identical: the mental may be unconscious, and consciousness may contain nonmental elements.

Thinking is the most important side of the cognitive process: it is an intentional mental act directed upon the intelligible (nonsensory) or the ideal (i.e., nonspatial and nontemporal) aspect of things, e.g., upon *relations*. The object of thought such as relations is present in the knowing consciousness as it is in itself and, as already said, it is neither a mental nor a material process: it is ideal.

What is the sensation, say, of red color, of the note la_3, of warmth, etc.? Obviously colors, sounds, etc., are something radically different from the subject's *mental* states, from his feelings, desires and strivings. They are physical qualities connected with mechanical material processes; e.g., sound is connected with air waves or in general, with vibrations of material particles. Only the acts of *awareness*, the acts of *sensing* directed upon them are mental processes.

After this long digression we may try to sort out the confused theories of dialectical materialism with regard to mental life.

"Sensation, thought, consciousness are the highest products of matter organized in a certain way. This is the doctrine of materialism in general and of Marx and Engels in particular," says Lenin (34). Lenin seems to identify sensation with thought, consciousness, and mental states (see e.g., page 34 where he speaks of sensation as thought). He maintains that "sensations are images of the external world" (83); namely its copies, *Abbild or Spiegelbild*, according to Engels. "Save through sensations, we cannot know of the existence of forms of substance, or of forms of motion; sensations are produced by the effect of matter in motion upon our sense organs" (258). "The sensation of red reflects ether vibrations whose frequency approximately amounts to 450 trillions per second. The sensation of blue reflects ether vibrations whose frequency is approximately 620 trillions per second. The vibrations of the ether exist independently of our visual sensations. Our visual sensations depend upon the effects of the vibrations of ether upon our organs of vision. Our sensations reflect objective reality, something which exists independently of humanity and human sensations" (259).

This would seem to imply that Lenin holds the "mechanist" view, according to which sensations and mental states in general are caused by mechanical processes of motion taking place in the sense organs and the cortex (e.g., 36). That doctrine has always been regarded as the weak point of materialism. Dialectical materialists understand this, and reject it, but there is nothing clear and definite that they put in its place. Lenin says that the real materialistic doctrine "consists not in the derivation of sensation from the movement of matter or in the identification of sensation with the movement of matter, but in the recognition that sensation is one of the properties of matter in motion. On this particular question Engels held Diderot's views. Engels opposed the vulgar materialists, Vogt, Büchner and Moleschott because they assumed that thought is secreted by the brain as bile is secreted by the liver" (28).

Logical consistency requires us to admit further, that in addition to movement, sensation (or some other, simpler, but analogous inner state or psychical process) is also a primary characteristic of matter.

This is precisely the idea we find in Lenin: "Materialism in full agreement with natural science takes matter as the *prius;* regarding consciousness, reason and sensation as derivative, because in a well-expressed form it is connected only with the higher forms of matter (organic matter). It becomes possible, therefore, to assume the existence of a property similar to sensation 'in the foundation stones of the structure of matter itself.' Such for example is the supposition of the well-known German naturalist Ernst Haeckel, the English biologist Lloyd Morgan and others, not to speak of Diderot's conjecture, mentioned above" (26). Obviously Lenin is here referring to what I have called psychoid processes. V. Pozner, quoting Lenin, also says that "the sensing faculty" is the property of highly organized matter but that nonorganized matter too has *inner* states (46). The adherents of metaphysical and mechanistic materialism fail to see, he says, that consciousness, i.e., "the faculty of reflecting, cannot be simply reduced to an external transposition of material particles; it is connected with the inner state of matter in motion" (64). At the same time he attacks Plehanov for holding a hylozoistic theory about matter being animate (64), and does not even attempt to show in what way Plehanov's view differs from Lenin's contention that even nonorganized matter has inner states analogous to sensation.

Byhovsky is equally vague. He says that "consciousness is the property of a definite kind of matter, of definitely organized matter, extremely complex in structure, that comes into being at a very high stage of evolution. Consciousness inherent in matter makes it as it were two-sided: physiological objective processes are accompanied by their inner subjective reflection. Consciousness is an inner state of matter, an introspective expression of certain physiological processes. What kind of connection is there between consciousness and matter? Can it be said that consciousness is causally determined by material processes, that matter affects consciousness and produces changes in it? A material change can only result in another material change." Admitting that mechanical processes are not the cause of consciousness and of mental states, Byhovsky comes to the conclusion that "consciousness and matter are not two heterogenous realities. The physical and the psychical are one and the same process considered from two sides. That which on the face of it, from the objective side, appears as a physical process is apprehended from within by the material entity itself as a fact of will, or as a fact of sensation, as something spiritual" (Byhovsky, 83–84). He goes on to say that "this faculty of being conscious is a property conditioned by the physical organization similarly to its other properties" (84). This statement contradicts his assertion that "a material change can only result in another material change." The only way to avoid inconsistency is to interpret his words as follows: The material ground of the world (not defined in dialectical materialism) creates, first, its mechanical manifestations and then at a certain stage of evolution—namely, in animal organisms—creates, in addition to the external material processes, also inner psychical processes. With regard to this interpretation the difference between Lenin's and Pozner's theories on the one hand and Byhovsky's on the other, is this: according to Lenin and Pozner the material ground of the world creates from the very beginning, at all stages of evolution, not only external material processes but also inner processes or sensations, or at any rate something very similar to sensations; according to Byhovsky the material ground of the world superadds inner processes to the outer only at a comparatively high level of evolution. But whichever of these alternatives be adopted, the question to be answered is this: if the principle at the basis of cosmic processes creates two series of events which form a single whole but cannot be reduced one to the other—namely, external material and inner psychic (or psychoid) events—what right have we to call this creative source and bearer of events "matter"? That principle obviously transcends both series and is a *metapsychophysical* principle. The true conception of the world is to be found not in one-sided materialism or one-sided idealism, but in ideal-realism, which is indeed a unity of opposites. It is significant that Engels and Lenin when speaking of the ultimate reality often call it _nature_ which implies something more complex than matter.

The use of the term "matter" with reference to the primary reality might be defended on the strength of the doctrine that the psychical is always secondary in the sense of always being a copy or "reflection" of the material process; i.e., of always serving the purposes of *knowledge about material* changes. Such an intellectualistic theory of psychical life is, however, obviously untenable: the foremost place in psychical life belongs to feelings and conative processes which, clearly, are not copies or "reflections" of material changes with which they are connected. As we have seen, striving is the starting point of all interaction, even of so simple a form of it as impact.

Dialectical materialists understand that psychical processes are something *sui generis,* different from material processes. It must now be asked whether in their opinion psychical processes have any *influence* upon the further course of cosmic changes, or are purely *passive* so that there is no need to refer to them in explaining the world's development. According to Lenin, materialism does not by any means assert "the lesser reality of consciousness" (238); consequently, consciousness is as real as material processes. One would have thought this implies that psychical processes may have a bearing upon the course of material processes, just as the latter have a bearing upon the origination of mental events. Marx maintains, however, that consciousness does not determine existence, but existence determines consciousness. And so all dialectical materialists invariably repeat this dictum, understanding by the word "consciousness" all mental processes. If Marx's dictum is taken to be a law of nature it would compel us to admit that all the higher expressions of mental and spiritual life, religion, art, philosophy and so on, are a *passive* superstructure over social material processes. The essence of historical and economic materialism preached by Marxists consists precisely in the doctrine that the history of social life is conditioned by the development of productive forces and relations. Economic relations, Marxists say, are the *real basis* of social life, while political forms, law, religion, art, philosophy, etc., are only a *superstructure* over this basis, and dependent upon it.

Marx, Engels, and true social democrats held this doctrine, believing that social revolution will take place in highly industrialized countries where the dictatorship of the proletariat will arise spontaneously, owing to the enormous numerical preponderance of workers and employees over the small group of property owners. But Russia was industrially a backward country, and the communistic revolution in it was made by a comparatively small Bolshevik party. The revolution has resulted in the development in U.S.S.R. of a terrible form of tyrannical state capitalism; the state is the property owner and, concentrating in its hands the military and police force as well as the power of wealth, it exploits the workers to an extent undreamed of by bourgeois capitalists. Now that the state has shown itself in its true colors and the peasants have been transformed from small landowners into Collective Farm laborers, there can be no doubt that the Soviet regime is supported by a small group of communists against the will of the enormous majority of the population; to preserve it, those in authority must exert their will to the utmost and use skillful propaganda, advertisement, care in bringing up the young and other methods which clearly prove the importance of ideology and of deliberate voluntary activity for the maintenance and development of social life. Accordingly, Bolsheviks have now definitely begun to talk of the influence of ideology upon the economic basis of life. Political and legal relations, philosophy, art and other ideological developments, says Pozner, "are based upon economics, but they all influence one another and their economic basis." Curiously enough he says on the same page that "it is not people's consciousness that determines their existence but, on the contrary, their social existence determines their consciousness" (68). And then he goes on to say "when the enormous productive forces will create a classless society, there shall be planned, conscious guidance of the process of social production and of social life as a whole; there will take place then, according to Engels, a leap from the realm of necessity into the realm of freedom" (68). Luppol says that Lenin admitted "final causes" to be real and knowable; i.e., he maintained that certain processes were purposive or teleological (186).

Byhovsky, who is on the whole more systematic than Pozner, proves to be just as vague with reference to this question. "According to the materialistic interpretation of society," he writes, "it is not the social consciousness in all its forms and aspects that determines social existence, but material conditions of human existence determine social consciousness. The reason or the will of individuals or peoples, or races, or nations do not determine the course, the direction and the character of the historical process, but on the contrary they are merely the product, the expression and the reflection of the conditions of life. They are merely a link in the objective course of historical events; i.e., a result of the way in which the relations between nature and society, and inter-social relations are formed independently of human will" (Byhovsky, 93). Further on, however, he declares that "it is a malicious and false caricature of the Marxist interpretation of society to affirm that it *reduces* all social life to economics and denies all historical significance to the state, science and religion, transforming them into shadows that accompany economic changes. Materialism does not deny the reciprocal influence of the superstructure on its basis, but explains the direction of that influence and its possible limits. Thus, religion is not merely the outcome of certain definite social relations, but affects them in its turn, influencing, for instance, the institution of marriage. Manifestations of social life that are more remote from the economic basis than other manifestations of it depend upon the latter, but affect them in their turn. On the basis of a given method of production and of economic relations corresponding with them there grows up a powerful system of interacting and interconnected relations and ideas. A materialist interpretation of history is by no means favorable to arid schematism" (106).

Finding that other sociologists (Jaurès, Kareyev) "maintain that existence affects consciousness, but consciousness also affects existence," he declares that their view is "eclectic;" but he feels justified in saying the same thing himself because his materialism "explains the direction" of the influence of consciousness and "its possible limits." As though his opponents overlooked the direction of the influence of consciousness or imagined that this influence was unlimited!

The vagueness of the dialectical materialists' conception of consciousness is due both to their determination at all costs to subordinate nonmaterial processes to the material and to the fact that they do not discriminate between "consciousness" and "mental process." Consciousness means the existence of some reality *for* the subject; it is consciousness of reality. In this sense all consciousness is always determined by reality. In the same way, all knowledge and thought has reality for its object and, according to the intuitive theory, actually includes it in itself as directly contemplated; hence, all knowledge and thought is always determined by reality. The psychical side of consciousness, knowledge and thought consists solely of *intentional psychical acts* directed upon reality but not affecting it; therefore consciousness, knowledge and thought are, *as such,* determined by reality and do not determine it. But other psychical processes—namely, conative processes always connected with emotions, strivings, attractions, desires—powerfully affect reality and determine it. Moreover, in so far as acts of will are based upon knowledge and thought, through them knowledge also vitally affects reality.

The fact that modern Marxists admit the influence of mental life upon material processes clearly shows that dialectical materialism is in reality not materialism at all. We know from the history of philosophy that one of the most difficult problems for human thought is to account for the possibility of influence of mind upon matter and *vice versa*. Monistic and dualistic systems of philosophy cannot solve this problem because of the profound difference in kind between physical and mental processes.

The only way to account for their interconnection and for the possibility of their influencing each other without being causally interrelated is through discovering a third principle which creates and unites them and is neither mental nor material. According to the theory of ideal realism, delineated above, this third principle is concretely ideal being—superspatial and supertemporal substantival agents.[12]

Being opposed to mechanistic materialism, dialectical materialists are not prepared to replace philosophy by natural science. Engels says that naturalists who revile philosophy and reject it are, unconsciously to themselves, enslaved by poor, homemade philosophy (25). He thinks that for developing the faculty of theoretical thinking it is necessary to study the history of philosophy. Such study is needed both for improving our powers of theoretical thought, and for working out the science of epistemology. Byhovsky says that "philosophy is the theory

---

12. See N. Lossky's books, *Types of World Conception* (in Russian); *The World As an Organic Whole* and *Freedom of Will*.

of science" (9). According to Lenin "dialectics is the theory of knowledge."[13]

The dialectical materialists' interest in the theory of knowledge is understandable. They struggle against skepticism, relativism and agnosticism, and insist that reality is knowable. If they are to vindicate their contention, they must work out a theory of knowledge.

Referring to Engels, Lenin says: "Human reason in its nature is capable of yielding and does yield the absolute truth which is composed of the sum total of relative truths. Each step in the development of science adds new fragments of truth, and from this the absolute truth is constituted, but the limits of the truth of each scientific statement are relative, now expanding, now shrinking with the growth of science."[14]

Lenin thinks that the source of true knowledge is *sensations;* i.e., data of experience interpreted as "the action of matter in motion upon our sense organs." Luppol rightly describes such a theory of knowledge as materialistic *sensualism* (182) (sensus-sensation). One would have thought this necessarily leads to solipsism; i.e., to the doctrine that we know only our own subjective states produced by an unknown cause, and perhaps not in the least like it. Lenin, however, does not make this deduction. He confidently asserts that "our sensations are copies of the external world" (79). Like Engels, he is convinced that they *agree* with or *correspond* to the reality outside us (88). He contemptuously rejects Plehanov's contention that human sensations and ideas are "hieroglyphics," i.e., are "not the copy of real things and nature's processes, not their images, but only arbitrary signs and symbols of them" (195). He understands that "the theory of symbols" logically leads to agnosticism and insists that Engels is right when he speaks "neither of symbols or hieroglyphics but of copies, photographs, images, mirror reflections of things" (195). Engels "constantly and exclusively speaks in his works of things and their mental images or reflections (*Gedankenabbilder*). It is obvious that these mental images arise only from sensations" (22).

Thus, Engel's and Lenin's theory of knowledge is a sensualistic theory of copying or reflection. It is obvious, however, that if truth were a subjective copy of transsubjective things, it would be impossible in any given case to prove that we possess an exact copy of a thing, i.e., the truth about it, and the very theory of copying could never be really proved.

Indeed, according to that theory all we have in consciousness are copies only and it is utterly impossible to observe the copy together with

---

13. "The Question of Dialectics," 16.
14. Lenin, *Materialism and Empirio-Criticism,* 106; similar arguments are advanced by Engels in *Anti-Dühring.*

the original so as to establish by direct comparison the degree of likeness between them—as one can do, for instance, in comparing a marble bust with the person whom it represents. Besides, for materialism the case is further complicated, for how can a *mental* image be an exact copy of a *material* thing? To avoid the absurdity of such an assertion one would have to adopt the theory of *panpsychism;* i.e., to admit that the external world entirely consists of psychical processes and that my ideas, say, of another person's anger or striving are exact copies of that anger or striving.

The example given by Lenin of sensation as a "reflection" of reality gives him away completely. "The sensation of red," he says, "reflects ether vibrations whose frequency approximately amounts to 450 trillions per second. The sensation of blue reflects ether vibrations whose frequency is approximately 620 trillions per second. The vibrations of the ether exist independently of our visual sensations. Our visual sensations depend upon the effect of the vibrations of ether upon our organs of vision. Our sensations reflect objective reality, something which exists independently of humanity and human sensations" (259). The red and the blue color cannot in any sense of the term be said "to resemble" ether vibrations; and considering that, according to Lenin, those vibrations themselves are only known to us as "images" in our mind composed of our sensations, what possible grounds can there be for asserting that those images correspond to an external reality? Plehanov understood that theories of reflection, symbolism and so on cannot account for our knowledge of the properties of the external world or indeed prove the existence of that world. He was therefore driven to the admission that our belief in the existence of the external world is an act of faith and argued that "such faith is a necessary precondition of *critical* thought in the best sense of the term."[15]

Lenin is aware, of course, of the comic nature of Plehanov's contention that critical thought is based upon faith, and he does not agree with it. We shall see in a moment what his own solution of the difficulty is, but let us first conclude our examination of his sensualistic theory. Does human knowledge really consist of sensations alone? Relations such as the *unity* of the properties of an object, causal connection and so on, cannot possibly be sensations; it is absurd to say that the yellowness, hardness and coldness of an apple are given us in three sensations (visual, tactile and thermic) and the unity of those qualities is a fourth sensation. People who have a better knowledge of philosophy than Lenin, even if they be dialectical materialists, understand that knowl-

---

15. Plehanov, Commentary on the Russian translation of Engels' book on Feuerbach, 86, 1918 (Geneva Edition, 111, 1905).

edge includes nonsensory as well as sensory elements. Thus Byhovsky says, "Man has at his disposal two main instruments by means of which knowledge is attained—his experience, i.e., the totality of data acquired through his sense organs, and reason which systematizes and works out those data" (13). "The data of observation and experiment must be understood, thought out, put together. The connections and interrelations between facts must be established by means of thought; they must be systematized and estimated, their laws and principles must be discovered. In such thinking many general notions are used by means of which connections between things are expressed, defined and scientifically evaluated. Those notions and logical categories are an absolutely essential element in every cognitive process in all branches of knowledge. Their significance for science cannot be overestimated and their part in forming knowledge is enormous" (18–19).

Knowledge of these aspects of the world is obtained of course by abstraction from experience; "the forms of being cannot be drawn or deduced by thought from itself, but only from the external world," says Lenin quoting Engels.[16] This is true, but it means that experience certainly does not consist of sensations alone and that nature from which ideal principles are abstracted contains those principles in its very structure. Deborin rightly says that categories "are simply reflections, results and generalizations of *experience*. But observation and experience can by no means be reduced to immediate sensation and perception. Without thought there can be no scientific experience" (XXIV).

These quotations from Byhovsky and Deborin show that having a certain knowledge of Kant, Hegel and modern epistemology they cannot defend pure sensualism or deny the presence of nonsensuous elements in knowledge; but they are unable to account for those elements. The habits of mechanistic materialism have too great a hold upon them. For mechanistic materialists the world consists of impenetrable moving particles, the only interaction between which is impact; our sense organs react to those impacts by *sensations;* the whole of knowledge, on such a theory, is obtained from experience produced by impacts and consists of sensations only (Lenin develops exactly the same theory as the mechanistic materialists; e.g., 80).

For dialectical materialists true knowledge consists of subjective mental states which must copy external reality. But why do they suppose that this miracle of material things being copied by mental processes really takes place? Engel's answer to the question is as follows: "Our subjective thought and the objective world are subject to the same laws and therefore in their final results they cannot contradict each other but

16. Engels, *Anti-Dühring*.

must be in agreement" (94). This assertion, he says, is the "preconception" of our theoretical thought (94). Pozner, quoting Lenin, says that dialectic is the law of objective reality and at the same time the law of knowledge (34).

The doctrine that the subjective dialectic corresponds to the objective cannot be proved if we adopt the dialectical materialists' theory of knowledge. According to that theory we always have in consciousness the subjective dialectic only, and its correspondence to the objective dialectic must forever remain a hypothesis incapable of proof. Moreover, this hypothesis does not explain how truth about the external world is possible. The law of dialectical development is held by the dialectical materialists to have a universal application. Hence, not only thought but all other subjective processes, such as for instance imagination are subject to it. But if the subjective process of imagination does not copy external reality, although it is subject to the same law, the subjective process of thought may not copy it either.

In trying to establish the criterion of *agreement* between the subjective knowledge of the external world with the actual structure of that world Engels, following Marx, finds it in practice, namely, in experiment and industry. "If we can prove the correctness of our idea of an actual occurrence by experiencing it ourselves and producing it from its constituent elements, and using it for our own purposes into the bargain, the Kantian phrase *Ding an Sich* (thing in itself) ceases to have any meaning. The chemical substances which go to form the bodies of plants and animals remained just such a thing-in-itself until organic chemistry undertook to show them one after the other, whereupon the thing in itself became a thing for us as the coloring matter in the roots of the madder, alizarine, which we no longer allow to grow in the roots of the madder in the field, but make much more cheaply and simply from coal tar."[17]

Dialectical materialists were greatly pleased with this argument of Engels; they repeat it with delight and develop it further (Lenin, 77, 109–114; Byhovsky, 69 f.). And indeed, successful practical activity and its progressive development gives us a right to affirm that we *can* have a true knowledge about the world. This, however, leads to a conclusion unfavorable to a sensualistic theory of "copying" reality. It is essential to work out a theory of knowledge and of the world which would reasonably explain how a subject can have true knowledge not only about his experiences but about the external world in its real nature independent of our subjective acts of cognition. The dialectical materialist

---

16.
17. Quoted by Lenin on page 75, from Engel's *L. Feuerbach*, 4th German edition,

theory of knowledge, according to which only our subjective *psychical* processes (images, reflections, etc.) are immediately given in consciousness, cannot explain how true knowledge about the external, especially the material, world is possible. It cannot even explain how, starting with its subjective psychical processes, the human self could ever have arrived at the idea that matter exists at all.

Modern epistemology can help the materialists with regard to this point, but only on condition that they renounce their one-sided theory and admit that cosmic being is complex and that, although matter does form part of it, it is not a basic principle. Such a view of the world is to be found for instance in the intuitive theory of knowledge combined with ideal realism in metaphysics. The doctrine of ideal realism implies among other things "pansomatism;" i.e., the conception that every concrete event has a bodily aspect.

Lenin who admitted "at the basis of the very structure of matter" the existence of "a faculty similar to sensation" apparently approached the ideal-realist position. He says, "From the point of view of the crude, simple, metaphysical materialism philosophical idealism is sheer nonsense. But from the point of view of dialectical materialism philosophical idealism is a one-sided, exaggerated, *überschwängliches*[18] (Dietzgen) development of one of the features, aspects or facets of knowledge, making it into an absolute, *severed* from matter and deified."[19]

It should be added, however, that an adequate expression of truth free from a one-sided exaggeration of any one particular element of the world is to be found neither in idealism nor in any form of materialism (including dialectical materialism) but only in ideal realism.

Dialectical materialists reject traditional logic with its laws of identity, contradiction and excluded middle and want to replace it by a dialectical logic, which Byhovsky calls "a logic of contradictions" because "contradiction is its distinguishing principle" (32). It has already been shown above that attacks upon the traditional logic are due to a wrong interpretation of the laws of identity and contradiction.[20]

Materialists who seek to base their whole world conception upon experience and at the same time are compelled by their theory of knowledge to assert that matter is not given in experience, but only mental images of it are given, find themselves in a desperate predicament. It is therefore to be expected that an attempt should be made to put an intuitivistic interpretation upon Lenin's words that "all matter has a property essentially akin to sensation, namely, the property of 'mirroring' or reflection." Such an attempt has actually been made by a Bul-

18. Expansive, swelling out.
20. E.g. Byhovsky, 218–242.

19. "The Question of Dialectics," 17.

garian, T. Pavlov (P. Dosev) in his book *The Theory of Reflection*, published in Russian in Moscow.[21]

In this book Pavlov attacks the intuitivism of Bergson and especially of Lossky. Bergson's name occurs in his book fifteen times, and Lossky's more than forty times. And yet in discussing the relation between "a thing and the idea of a thing" Pavlov says "dialectical materialism does not create an impassable gulf between the ideas of things and the things themselves. Its solution of the problem is that in form (that is, in being present in consciousness) ideas differ from things, but in *content* they coincide with things, though not completely or absolutely and not at once" (187); but this view is precisely Lossky's intuitivism.

Party fanaticism like every strong passion, is accompanied by a lowering of intellectual power, especially of the capacity to understand and criticize other people's ideas. Pavlov's book is a striking instance of this. He continually draws absurd and utterly unwarranted deductions from Lossky's theories. For instance he says that Bergson and Lossky have discredited the word "intuition" and that for intuitivists discursive thinking "has no really scientific value." Pavlov fails to notice the fundamental difference between the intuitivism of Bergson and that of Lossky. Bergson's theory of knowledge is dualistic: he thinks that there are two essentially different kinds of knowledge—the intuitive and the rational. Intuitive knowledge is the contemplation of a thing in its true living essence, it is absolute knowledge; rationalistic knowledge—i.e., discursive conceptual thought, consists, according to Bergson, of symbols only and therefore has but a relative significance. Lossky's theory of knowledge is *monistic* in the sense that he regards all species of knowledge as intuitive. He sets a special value upon discursive thinking, interpreting it as a highly important species of intuition, namely, as intellectual intuition, or contemplation of the ideal bases of the world which impart a systematic character to it (e.g., the contemplation of the mathematical forms of the world).

The following circumstance shows how superficial is Pavlov's knowledge of the theories he criticizes. Professor Mihalchev, a Bulgarian admirer of Rehmke's philosophy, says in his book *Forms and Relations* that Lossky has borrowed his theory from Rehmke while pretending to have discovered it himself. Pavlov quotes these words, adding that Mihalchev "has uttered a holy truth" (98). As a matter of fact, however, Lossky devotes a whole chapter in his *Intuitive Bases of Knowledge* to the consideration of his predecessors' views: "The Doctrine of the Immediate Apprehension of the Transsubjective World in the Philosophy of the Nineteenth Century." He finds the doctrine of the immediate

21. *Teoria otrazheniya*, Socekgiz, 1936.

perception of the external world in Fichte, Schelling, Hegel, Schopenhauer, in positivistic empiricism (e.g., in R. Avenarius), in Schuppe's "immanent philosophy," in Rickert's "normative criticism" and, of course, in Russian philosophy, in Vladimir Soloviev and Prince S. N. Trubetskoy. Lossky mentions Rehmke alongside of Schuppe, regarding him as an adherent of "immanent philosophy" on the strength of his book *Die Welt als Wahrnehmung und Begriff;* German historians of philosophy regard him in the same way. How Mihalchev and Pavlov (Dosev) could have missed such an important chapter in the *Intuitive Basis of Knowledge* is a riddle that might be an interesting subject of inquiry for psychologists investigating the workings of the human mind.

In spite of being philosophically untenable, materialism attracts a great number of people. It must therefore be supposed that it contains a grain of truth which is hard to express in a clear form and, if insufficiently analyzed, is easily misinterpreted in a materialistic sense. This truth is as follows. All agents forming part of the world perform not only *inner* spiritual and mental actions but also *external* actions that have a spatial form; i.e., have the character of corporeality. Thus, *everything spiritual and mental is incarnate.* This doctrine may be described as *pansomatism (soma* = body). Of course the truth of pansomatism is profoundly different from materialism. Alll that exists has a bodily aspect but is not exhausted by it; moreover, this bodily aspect is not a basic manifestation of being but a derivative one, realized under the guidance of inner, spiritual and mental processes. At the lower stages of evolution in inorganic nature the inner processes are so simplified that it is very difficult to establish their presence. Through misunderstanding, the truth of pansomatism may be expressed in a form that suggests materialism; for instance, the metaphysics of the Stoics is apparently materialistic, but in reality it is a variety of ideal realism.[22] The type of ideal realism worked out in N. Lossky's books and briefly indicated above includes pansomatism in the sense just defined.

Many people get accustomed, especially under the influence of their occupation, to concentrate attention solely on the corporeal aspect of reality and thus develop a tendency to a materialistic interpretation of the world; this is the case, e.g., with factory workers, engineers, doctors, etc.

One may thus discover *psychological* motives inclining certain persons toward materialism, but it is impossible to find *logical* reasons showing it to be true. We have seen that dialectical materialism is based upon the arbitrary assumption that "matter is all that exists." But in

22. N. Lossky, "The Metaphysics of the Stoics," *Journal of Philos. Studies,* 1929.

working out this theory dialectical materialists endow this basic reality with such properties as "the faculty akin to sensation," creative activity, the power of *immanent spontaneous* development which proceeds in *a definite* direction and creates more and more *valuable* grades of being subject to laws irreducible to the laws of the preceding lower stages of evolution. Berdyaev rightly says that "the dialectical materialism of Leninist Marxists' endows matter with divine attributes."[23] It is incomprehensible on what grounds they call such a basic reality "matter."

Not being materialists in the true sense of the word, Marxists make their world conception appear materialistic because they leave things unsaid or make vague and inaccurate statements. They derive much help in this respect from the word "motion" which they apply both to transposition in space and to creative acts producing new qualities. The word "nature" often used by them instead of "matter" also proves very useful. Their specific doctrine borrowed from Hegel's dialectic, about the identity of opposites and therefore of the realization of contradictions is in truth simply an inaccurate expression of the idea of the unity of opposites which does not in the least cancel the law of contradiction. Dialectical materialists themselves almost understand this. Lenin speaks of "the identity of opposites (or perhaps it would be more true to say 'their unity')."[24] It is not surprising therefore that very often dialectical materialists put those terms side by side and speak of "identity or inseparability" (e.g., Engels, 24) "identity or unity." M. Leonov who published his *Study of Dialectical Materialism* in 1948 no longer speaks of the identity of opposites but only of their unity (285, 287).

It is much to the credit of dialectical materialists that they strive to get rid of the poverty-stricken mechanistic theory and to do justice to the wealth of the individual content of events, as for instance Lenin does in the quotation cited above from his article on "Karl Marx." But dialecticity which necessarily implies complexity, and materialism which leads to narrow one-sidedness are as impossible to mix as oil and water. The fear to lose their hold on materialism compels Marxists to cling to materialistic theories which inevitably impoverish the world. I will point out the following of them: the world must be interpreted as a *monistic* system (Byhovsky, 32 f.); all reality must be conceived as spatial and temporal; the contents of consciousness are to be interpreted in the spirit of *sensualism*, i.e., reduced to sensations; consciousness must be regarded as passive (consciousness is determined by existence, and not

---

23. Berdyaev, *The General Line of Soviet Philosophy and Militant Atheism*, 16, Paris Y.M.C.A. 1932.
24. "The Question of Dialectics," 22.

vice versa); *determinism* is compulsory, the doctrine of free will must be rejected.

These materialistic preconceptions lead either to one-sided theories or to inconsistencies:

(1) Dialectical materialists preach monism, while truth is to be found in the synthesis of monism and pluralism: the fundamental principles and the meaning of existence are a unity, and its qualitative contents a plurality. Their attempts to admit a creative evolution producing qualitatively different grades of being is incompatible with the theory that the ultimate reality is matter.

(2) The temporal process presupposes a combination of temporal and nontemporal elements; the spatial process presupposes a combination of spatial and nonspatial elements; in other words, one-sided realism which admits only spatial and temporal being is an error; the truth about the world is to be found in ideal realism.

(3) While virtually admitting the wealth and diversity of the world, dialectical Marxists want to reduce the whole content of experience to sense data (sensualism); in truth, however, experience combines sensuous and nonsensuous data. But dialectical materialists are afraid even to mention the non-sensuous aspect of the world: recognition of the non-sensuous is connected with the recognition of the spiritual, and they fear the spiritual as the devil fears holy water.

(4) Engels and the modern dialectical materialists say that Hegel's dialectic was *abstract* and idealistic, and that they replace it by a concrete one, since they have sensuous reality in view (see e.g., Deborin, XXVII f.). As a matter of fact, sense data such as colors, sounds, etc., taken as particular "here and now" realities, apart from their interconnection with all the other rich and complex content of the world, are as poor and abstract as the discursive notions, e.g., as mathematical ideas. Dialectical materialists are aware of two extremes only, which are both abstractions: discursive general notions on the one hand, and particular sense data on the other, they do not see the depths of mental and spiritual being, for in speaking of it they generally have in mind not the whole wealth of the mental and the spiritual life but only one comparatively unimportant function of it, namely, abstract thinking. They have not the remotest idea of true concreteness which is the fullness of spiritual and mental creativeness, of the emotional experience of personal and cosmic values, of voluntary purposive participation in the life of the world, and of embodying all these functions in physical life. Hegel who was in fact not an idealist but an ideal-realist, though he failed to give adequate expression to this aspect of his philosophy, was infinitely nearer the truth than dialectical materialists.

(5) The paucity and one-sidedness of dialectical materialism are particularly apparent in the treatment of the historical processes which are the most complex of all. As we have seen, its adherents verbally admit that "manifestations of social life that are more remote from the economic basis than other manifestations of it depend upon the latter, but affect them in their turn. On the basis of a given method of production and of economic relations corresponding to it there grows up a powerful system of interacting and interconnected relations and ideas. A materialistic interpretation of history is by no means favorable to arid schematism" (Byhovsky, 106). In fact, however, we find in all their writings a boring, arid, and at the same time superficial and futile schematism. The most various and profound spiritual tendencies that have an abiding significance are explained by the influence of "the feudal system," of "the bourgeois society," of "the landed gentry," of the "development of commercial capital," and so on.

A good instance of this way of thinking is the use Pozner makes of the theories of psychoanalysis: "The pettiness of the German bourgeoisie, its cowardice and incapacity for a decisive struggle with feudalism, have led to a fine flowering of literature and philosophy by which it seemed to compensate itself for what it had failed to attain in the political domain" (16). Apparently, it is sufficient to be cowardly in order to create a fine literature and philosophy—as though a negative condition could account for creative achievements requiring complex positive abilities.

Materialistic philosophy is so obviously invalid and superficial that the stubbornness and fantastical intolerance with which the representative Russian Bolsheviks uphold and defend it can only be explained by some deep psychological motives and enthralling passions. The chief of those motives is that materialism is more closely and directly connected with atheism than any other theory; it is most suitable for destroying all Christian religious feelings and ideas and is therefore particularly attractive to the Bolsheviks who furiously hate Christianity. Christianity preaches love and consideration for other people even when struggling with them; it fosters respect for tradition, for the older generation, for authority, and a healthy conservatism which is not opposed to progress but avoids violent destruction of the past. Bolshevism is characterized by qualities which are the direct opposite of the Christian culture. It preaches hatred for the past. This connection of the Bolshevist mentality with the past rather than with the future is made admirably clear by Berdyaev. The Bolsheviks live by hatred for the former society—not of its unsatisfactory *institutions*, but of its *actual* representatives—the bourgeois, the gentlemen, the priest, the idealist philosopher. Hatred of actual individual people is a satanic feeling; Scheler justly remarks that it is accompanied by sorrow at observing the other person's good qualities and malicious joy at his defects. Such a feeling is never inspired by noble motives. With the revolutionaries it is based upon personal injuries deeply buried in the subconscious: social and family wrongs, wounded self-love, pride, vanity, love of power. Those motives of conduct find clear expression in the Bolsheviks: they carry out the destruction of the old without any compunction by the most cruel means and with utter contempt for human personality; the new social order by which they intend to benefit humanity is introduced by them against the will of the "beneficiaries" in the proud conviction that they know best what is good for people. In their conduct they are guided by the conviction that "all things are permissible" for attaining their aim. Materialism and atheism is just the philosophy that gives them the sanction they want.

Dialectical materialism is more convenient for the Bolsheviks than the mechanistic. Being entirely centered upon social and economic problems they want to be independent of natural science in their domain (see e.g., Ryazanov, XI f.). The conviction based upon the principles of dialectics that all levels of being are changeable is a good weapon for the revolutionary destruction of the actual state of things (Pozner, 30). The freedom to violate the law of contradiction is particularly useful. However absurd the results of the Soviet mismanagement might be, however much their policy might be opposed to their own ideals, they only have to call the contradiction "vital," and their activities are justified. Thus, e.g., the Bolsheviks are breaking up Russia into a number of autonomous national republics, artificially cultivating the language and literature of tribes not in the least inclined to independent national development (apparently, this policy is based on the idea *divide et impera!*). Stalin said a propos of this in one of his speeches that it is necessary for national cultures to develop in order to be merged "into one common culture with one common language." According to Marxism the state is always a form of exploitation of society and should be totally abolished; Stalin says of it "the greatest development of the power of the state as a preparation of conditions for the disappearance of the power of the state—such is the Marxist formula ... this contradiction is vital and entirely reflects the Marxist dialectic" (see Pozner, 50).

It is not truth that Bolsheviks seek in philosophy, but only a convenient weapon for attaining their revolutionary aims. This is why, following Lenin, they sing praises of "party loyalties" in philosophy. "From the beginning to the end Marx and Engels were 'partial' in philosophy; in each and every 'new' tendency they were able to discover deviations from materialism and an unwarranted indulgence in idealism and fideism" (293). Under the influence of party loyalties independent observation and inquiry become atrophied and the only thing that develops is interest in defending petrified dogmas at all costs. The means of defense grow more and more naive: there is either appeal to authority, or abuse, denunciation, threats. Luppol in his book *On Two Fronts* directed against "menshevizing idealism" and "mechanistic materialism" calls these deviations from Marxism "sabotage" which ought to be liquidated and describes their supporters as "secret wreckers" (9). We know that Bolsheviks liquidate "wreckers" by shooting or concentration camps. Tornstein is even more bitter: she says in her book (4) that to ignore Leninism which is the highest stage of dialectical materialism is "planned sabotage."

The style of Bolshevik writings is strikingly offensive. It is not uncommon to find in them such revolting metaphors as that used by Lenin "a hundred thousand readers of Haeckel meant a hundred thousand expectorations into the face of Mach's and Avenarius's philosophy" (306).

But even more disgusting than malice is sneaking servility largely characteristic of Soviet writers, anxiety not to lag behind "the general line of the party" and to testify their orthodoxy by everything they say. Thus in the whole social structure of the U.S.S.R. and in all Soviet theories the foremost place is given to the communal as against the personal individual being. And so Pozner, repeating Lenin's words that sensation is the image of the corresponding external event, goes on to say "dialectical materialism goes further; it teaches that sensations arise not simply as a passive result of the action of external objects upon our sense organs, but as the result of the active influence of the social man upon nature and of his reaction to his environment" (47). One would have to suppose that the yellow color of the sand can be perceived not by an individual man, but only by a member of a gang of workmen digging a pond.

The above exposition and analysis of dialectical materialism gives us the right to draw the following conclusion. True materialism, i.e., the doctrine that the ultimate reality consists of impenetrable particles of matter moving through space, and that mental events are the passive product of matter in motion, is a poor theory incapable of further development. Dialectical materialism in speaking of matter or nature as the primary reality richly endows it with qualities and faculties, but has no right whatever to call it matter. It assumes the guise of materialism partly owing to its terminology, partly through inconsistently holding on to certain fragmentary dogmas of genuine materialism, and partly through vagueness and confusion of thought. In the U.S.S.R. dialectical materialism is a party philosophy concerned not with the quest for truth, but with the practical needs of the revolution. So long as the U.S.S.R. is ruled by a power that suppresses all free inquiry, dialectical materialism cannot develop as a philosophy. Unhampered thinking would soon transform dialectical materialism into some complex system of ideal realism.

Chapter 25

THE INFLUENCE OF E. MACH AND R. AVENARIUS ON MARXISTS

The French and English form of positivism—the theories of Auguste Comte, J. S. Mill and Spencer—were widely prevalent in Russia in the second half of the nineteenth century but toward the end of it and the beginning of the twentieth there developed a tendency to seek new and more subtle forms of it. This was the case, for instance, with V. V. Lesevitch.

Vladimir Victorovich Lesevitch (1837–1905) received his higher education at the Petersburg School of Engineering and the Academy of the General Staff. For his political activities he was exiled first to Siberia and then Kazan, Poltava and Tver (1879–1888). In his youth Lesevitch was a follower of Comte as interpreted by Littré and Vyrubov but later he adopted the theory of empirio-criticism. R. Avenarius's *Kritik der reinen Erfahrung* (Critique of pure experience) became for him the pattern of scientific philosophy.[1]

The influence of Mach and Avenarius was particularly prevalent at the beginning of the twentieth century among Russian Marxists. For the most part they adhered to dialectical materialism. But some of them had a gift for philosophy and a good training in the subject. They understood how untenable was the theory of knowledge expounded by Engels under the name of the theory of reflection. They gave up materialism and began to seek for Marxism an epistemological basis consistent with the recent developments in philosophy. Bogdanov in particular has given much attention to the subject.

Alexandr Alexandrovich Bogdanov (his real name was Malinovsky, 1873–1928) graduated in medicine. When he took up philosophy, he came under the influence of Mach and Avenarius and worked out a theory which he called empiriomonism. According to it, knowledge is a

---

1. Lesevitch's writings include *A Critical Inquiry Into the Fundamental Principles of Positivist Philosophy*, 1877; *Letters on Scientific Philosophy*, 1878; *What Is Scientific Philosophy?* 1891; *Collected Works*, 2 vols., Petrograd 1915.

social adaptation, aimed at giving as exact as possible a description of experience under the conditions of the greatest possible economy of thought. Bogdanov claims that his theory differs from empirio-criticism by its monistic character: the psychical is the individually organized experience, and the physical the socially organized experience. Thus the psychical and the physical are simply the differently organized elements of one experience. That which has social significance for a given epoch is regarded as true. Since 1913 Bogdanov took up the subject of "techtology": he gives that name to the general science of organization, and it is dealt with in his book *Universal Organizational Science*. All the problems which confront mankind are problems of organization. Man must transform the world into an organized whole. Philosophy must be discarded and replaced by techtology. The difference between "I" and "thou" exists only in so far as there exists a conflict of interests. When complete universal harmony is reached, the conception of the "I" will disappear.[2]

Other writers who came under the influence of Mach and Avenarius were A. Lunacharsky (1873–1933), Bazarov, P. Yushkevich, I. A. Berman (born 1868), S. A. Suvorov (1869–1918), N. Valentinov (born 1879).

Vladimir Alexandrovich Bazarov (his real name is Rudnev) was born in 1874; like Bogdanov he is a relativist in epistemology. In the book *Essays on the Philosophy of Marxism* he criticizes dialectical materialism; in *Sketches of a Realistic World Conception* (1904) he attacks idealism as it is presented in Almanach's *Problems of Idealism* (1902). In 1906 Bazarov, Lunacharsky and Yushkevich together with some adherents of dialectical materialism published a symposium *Literary Disintegration*, containing a critique of Russian and Western-European philosophical and literary works incompatible with Marxism.[3]

Pavel Solomonovitch Yushkevich (born 1873) calls his theory empirio-symbolism. He regards the data of sensuous experience and also conceptional theories as symbols. In addition to the human reason he admits the existence of a supreme reason, the Logos, the bearer of highest empirio-symbols or laws of nature.[4]

---

2. Besides techtology, Bogdanov's works include *The Basic Principles of the Historical View of Nature*, 1899; *Knowledge From the Historical Point of View*, 1901; *Empiriomonism*, 3 vols., 1905–6; *The Adventures of a School of Philosophy*, 1908; *The Philosophy of Living Experience*, 1922.

3. Bazarov, *Essays on the Philosophy of Collectivism*, 1909; *On Two Fronts*, 1910; *On the Way to Socialism* (a collection of articles), 1919. A. Lunacharsky, *Religion and Socialism*, 1903.

4. Yushkevich's works: *Materialism and Critical Realism*, 1908; *New Currents*, 1910; *The World Conception and World Conceptions*, 1912.

The Marxists who fell under the influence of Mach and Avenarius were sharply attacked by Lenin (under the assumed name V. Ilyin) in his book *Materialism and Empirio-Criticism* (Moscow 1909). All schools of thought that reject materialism are pronounced by him to be reactionary.

Chapter 26

RECENT DEVELOPMENTS IN RUSSIAN PHILOSOPHY

1. S. ALEXEYEV (ASKOLDOV)

Sergey Alexeyevich Alexeyev (penname, Askoldov, 1870–1945) was the son of the philosopher A. A. Kozlov. He could not inherit his father's name for the following reason. Kozlov as a young man was an ardent "Populist" and married a peasant. He soon parted from her, but his wife would not divorce him. When he fell in love with Marya Alexandrovna Chelishchev, a girl of noble birth and a cultured family, and formed a stable marriage alliance with her, his children could not legally bear his name, and his son's surname had to be Alexeyev, i.e., son of Alexis.

After graduating in the Faculty of Science at the Petersburg University, Alexeyev took a post in the Department of Customs and Excise as an expert in chemistry hoping that he could devote all his spare time to philosophy. It appeared, however, that conscientious work at his job left him little time and energy for philosophy. Accordingly, at the age of forty Alexeyev decided, like his father, to take up academic work. In 1914 he wrote a book *Thought and Reality* for which he obtained the degree of M.A. in philosophy at the Moscow University. After the Bolshevik revolution he had of course to abandon the hope of professorship. In 1921 Alexeyev founded a secret religious and philosophical society known as S. A. Askoldov's but in 1926 it was renamed "The Brotherhood of St. Seraphim of Sarov." In 1928 the Soviet Government arrested all the members of the Brotherhood and Alexeyev was exiled to the Zyrian Region (Kama Basin) where he lived in very trying conditions. In 1935 he was allowed to move to Novgorod. In 1941 when Novgorod was occupied by the Germans Alexeyev found himself on this side of the "iron curtain" and wrote a few articles against Marxism. In 1944 he received a premium for his book *The Critique of Dialectical Materialism*. During the last years of his life Alexeyev suffered from a severe form of angina, which he bore with great fortitude. He died at Potsdam.[1]

Alexeyev (Askoldov) was a highly gifted philosopher but circumstances did not give him a chance fully to express his ideas in print. His chief works are the following: *The Fundamental Problems of the Theory of Knowledge and Ontology,* 1900; "In Defense of the Miraculous," *Voprosy Filosofii i psikhologii,* V, 1903; "On Love For God and For One's Neighbor," *ibid.*, I, 1907; *A. A. Kozlov,* 1912; *Thought and Reality,* 1914; *Consciousness As a Whole,* 1918; "Time," *Mysl,* III, 1922; "Spirit and Matter," in the symposium *Noviye Vehi,* No. 2, Prague 1945.

S. A. Alexeyev, like his father A. A. Kozlov, is a representative of personalism, closely approaching Leibniz's monadology. In his book *Thought and Reality* he argues against Lossky's absolute intuitivism, but to a certain extent he himself is an intuitivist, for although he regards sense qualities as subjective, he admits the presence of a transsubjective element in perception. The intuitive part of perception, however, is according to him "too insignificant in relation to the whole content of perception" and is only "a kind of scanty framework clothed by the act of apperception with a variegated and multicolored garment, numerically different for every percipient" (chap. X).

In his article on "Time" Alexeyev distinguishes between ontological, psychological and physical time. He says that physical time, with which the modern theory of relativity is concerned, is obtained by measurement in connection with movement in space. It is a relative time, considered not *sub specie mundi,* but only *sub specie mensionis* (83). Ontological time is cognized by thought apart from connection with movement in space; in that time there exists a "now" univalent for all world systems (84).

Alexeyev's conception of overcoming time is as follows. In our time new contents of being crowd out the old ones, and they die. There may, however, be a higher temporal order in which the past does not fade away, but retains its vitality alongside of the ever-increasing new contents. In the realm of being where time is of such a type "the sting of death is taken out" (94).

Alexeyev's article "In Defense of the Miraculous" is particularly valuable in our day when among the Protestants there are persons even among the clergy who, under the influence of pseudoscientific ideas, deny the possibility of miracles. According to Alexeyev's definition "a miracle is an event happening within the domain of objective human experience, but conditioned by the powers of higher spiritual beings and

---

1. Information about Alexeyev's life and activity after 1922, when I was exiled from U.S.S.R., has been given me by Professor I. M. Andreyevsky.

not following from the laws of material nature" (440). He divides the objections against the miraculous into three categories—epistemological, metaphysical and ethical, and shows that they are invalid. Particular importance attaches to his argument that the individual self is one of the causes of events and that the activities of the self have the character of individual causality and not of a uniform law.

On the ground of his metaphysics, closely akin to Leibniz's theories, Alexeyev admitted reincarnation. At the end of his life he wrote a book *On Reincarnation*. Before his death he said in a letter to Professor Andreyevsky: "As I prayed to Father John of Kronstadt and to St. Seraphim, I felt that I must burn my book on reincarnation. I may be right in theory, but they would have rejected my work. And I cannot pray to them without first destroying that which they would have condemned in the sense of saying 'don't!' pronouncing it 'not wanted.' I've burnt it today!"

2. V. SZYLKARSKI

Vladimir Semyonovich Szylkarski (born 1882) was Professor at the Yuryev (Dorpat) University; after the Bolshevik revolution was professor at the Kovno University in Lithuania and at present at the University of Bonn.

Szylkarski's chief works are *The Typological Method in the History of Philosophy*, 1916; *The Problem of Being*, 1917; *Soloviev's Philosophie der All-Einheit*, 1932; *Teichmüllers philosophischer Entwicklungsgang*, 1939; *Adolf Dyroff*, 1947.

In his book *The Typological Method in the History of Philosophy* Szylkarski considers the typical philosophical conceptions as stages in the self-knowledge of our active "self." He recognizes four such stages: naive realism, concerned with material objects of the external world; sensualism, dealing with sensations; intellectualism, concerned with the activity of thought and leading to abstract idealism as, e.g., in the philosophy of Hegel; concrete idealism which is concrete spiritualism. Those stages express the movement of philosophic thought from the periphery to the center, from objects of the external world to the substantival human self. A philosophy that puts the substantival self at the basis of its interpretation of the world is personalism.

Dmitri Ivanovich Tschizewski (Chizhevski), born 1895, emigrated after the Bolshevik revolution, and for a number of years was professor at Halle. He has written many books and articles on the history of philosophy of the Slav peoples. His chief works are: *Philosophy in the Ukraine*, 1926; *Formalism in Ethics* (Works of the Russian Popular University in Prague, I, 1929); *The Problem of the Double* in the symposium on *Dostoevsky* edited by A. Behm, I, Prague 1929; *The Philosophy of Skovoroda*, 1934; *Hegel in Russia*, Paris 1939; also in German in the symposium *Hegel bei den Slaven*, edited by Chizhevski, Reichenberg, 1934.

In his article on *Formalism in Ethics* Chizhevski expounds an original plan of developing ethics in the spirit of concrete ideal realism. In his study of Dostoevsky's creative work Chizhevski has made valuable suggestions on the problem of "the double" explaining this strange phenomenon by the moral decay of personality.

3. L. KOBILINSKY

Lev Lvovitch Kobilinsky (1874–1947) who wrote under the name of Kobilinsky-Ellis, left Russia in 1911. The instructive story of his emigration is told in Andrey Bely's *Memoirs*. He became a disciple of Rudolf Steiner, the founder of anthroposophy. As he listened to his lectures, he began to wonder whether Steiner worshipped the powers of light or of darkness. One day, while waiting for the lecture to begin, Kobilinsky asked the German ladies, followers of Steiner, whether he served Christ or Beelzebub, and they answered *"Wir sind ein Luciferianisches Volk"* ("we are a Luciferian people"). Then Kobilinsky renounced anthroposophy, became a Catholic and settled in Switzerland at Locarno-Monti. I know about Kobilinsky's attitude to Steiner from his letters to me.

Kobilinsky-Ellis's chief works are: *Monarchia Sancti Petri, Christliche Weisheit*, 1929; *Jukowski*.

Kobilinsky's Christian world conception is not always in accord with traditional Christianity; thus, he maintains that the plurality of selves is a consequence of sin; a believer in reincarnation, he expressed his view one day to his father confessor, a Capuchin monk. The Capuchin replied: "Almighty God can send a man's soul to be born on earth three hundred times if it is necessary."

Kobilinsky wanted to acquaint Western Europe with the lofty spirit of Russian literature; he published in German a book on Zhukovsky and wrote a long monograph on Pushkin which he had not had time to publish. In this monograph Kobilinsky convincingly proves, by analyzing such poetical works as *Mozart and Salieri, Boris Godunov, The Avaricious Knight*, etc., that Pushkin was a realist, but he depicted reality in the light of the Divine truth.

4. B. VYSHESLAVTSEV

Boris Petrovich Vysheslavtsev was born in 1879. He was professor of philosophy of law at the University of Moscow. After leaving Russia he worked in the Russian section of the Y.M.C.A. Press in Paris. At present he is living in Switzerland.

Vysheslavtsev's chief works are *Fichte's Ethics*, 1914; *The Heart of Man in the Indian and Christian Mysticism*, Y.M.C.A. Press, Paris 1929; *The Ethics of Transfigured Eros*, Y.M.C.A. Press, Paris 1932.

The small but very valuable book *The Heart of Man* is concerned with a problem that occupies a prominent place in modern philosophy. The German philosopher Max Scheler in his book *Der Formalismus in der Ethik und die materielle Wertethik* worked out a theory of "emotional intuitivism" according to which feeling is an intentional mental act directed upon objective values and bringing them into the subject's consciousness. Scheler's theory drew many philosophers' attention to Pascal's conception of the "logic of the heart" different from the logic of the intellect. In the Russian philosophy that problem had been raised long before: recall, for instance, Yurkevich's philosophy and Soloviev's article about it. D. Chizhevsky in his *History of the Ukrainian Philosophy* points out that one of the characteristics of Ukrainian thought is its preoccupation with the philosophy of the heart, and devotes a whole chapter to the subject.

Vysheslavtsev states the problem in all its implications. In accordance with the teachings of Christian and Hindu mystics he means by the heart not merely the faculty of feeling, but something far more significant, namely the ontological, superrational principle which forms the personality's real selfhood. Indian mysticism interprets that principle as the identical basis of all living creatures, while Christianity insists that individual selves are a plurality from the first. This is the explanation, Vysheslavtsev thinks, of the difference between Christian love and Buddhist "compassion without love."

Transcending the division between soul and body the metaphysical principle finds realization in the heart which is both the source of love and of creative freedom and the most important bodily organ. This leads Vysheslavtsev to see the meaning of the Catholic cult of the Sacred Heart. He defends it from the charge of materialism made against it by "false spiritualism," though he points out that the particular setting of that cult makes it unacceptable to the Orthodox religious feeling.

In conclusion Vysheslavtsev examines the antinomy of the heart which is both an infallible judge and the source of evil as well as of good; he finds the solution of the antinomy in the concept of freedom as the essence of the self.

In his book *The Ethics of the Transfigured Eros* Vysheslavtsev shows, by quoting a number of passages from the Gospel and from St. Paul's Epistles that Christianity is meant to be a religion that replaces slavery to the law by the freedom of grace, and the ethics of law by the ethics of sublimation, of the transfigured Eros. Law cannot be the highest guide in life, for it is merely an abstract norm forbidding crimes, a negative norm devoid of creative power. The worst of it is that the imperative character of law and of the conscious effort of will is that it provokes the spirit of resistance which rises from the depths of subconscious instincts and strivings, in accordance with the *loi de l'effort converti* discovered by the Nancy school (Coué, Baudouin). Christianity points out another path: it directs man's spiritual powers toward the Absolute, toward God and the Kingdom of God as the fullness of being, as absolute beauty and perfection which calls forth our love and increases the power of free creativeness. That power finds a right solution in each concrete case of moral conflict. It is the path of the sublimation of the soul through Eros for the Logos (86). The highest and holiest values appear to the Christian mind not in the form of abstract law but as concrete living images of the actual Person of the God-man Jesus Christ and of His saints whom He loves and finds "loveable." Imagination transforms the instincts by introducing beautiful images into the dark realm of the subconscious and arousing love for them; it thus leads to their embodiment, to the magical creation of a new reality (75–82).

By the beauty of the Divine image, imagination sublimates Eros in which distinct stages may be distinguished: Eros may be physical, mental, spiritual, angelic and divine. The doctrine of Dionysius the Areopagite and St. Maxim the Confessor about Eros leading up to the Absolute and to deification by grace is, Vysheslavtsev thinks, the Christian theory of the sublimation of the soul.

In contradistinction to the Nancy school, Vysheslavtsev maintains that sublimation is reached not through the activity of imagination alone, but through the power of free will. It is not imagination but free will which decides whether man is to enter the path of the sublimation or the profanation of Eros (153). Having made the choice, the will calls in the help of imagination so as to overcome in an indirect way the resistance of the flesh and the still more dangerous satanic resistance of proud self-well (143). Here as elsewhere man rules over nature by obeying it (134). The freedom of the personality striving for perfection is preserved because God wants us to do His will not as slaves, but "as friends and sons" (180): grace cannot be simply given, it must also be freely taken by man (147).

Vysheslavtsev's doctrine of sublimation is of the utmost value. The terrible discoveries made by Freud and his school may prove fatal to man unless ways are pointed out for transfiguring the low instincts lurking in the realm of the subconscious. Particular importance attaches to his arguments that this purpose can only be attained through connecting our imagination and will with the concrete goodness of the Absolute, the living personality of the God-man and the saints. Vysheslavtsev shows that the training of imagination, feeling and will in the spirit of Christianity is the only way of attaining the fullness of perfect life. He succeeds in finding new arguments to prove that Christianity can only serve this purpose if it is interpreted as truly the religion of love and freedom, as the good news of the kingdom of grace, and not distorted by legalism or fanatical intolerance.

5. I. ILYIN

Ivan Alexandrovich Ilyin was born in 1882. He was professor of the philosophy of law in the Moscow University, was exiled from Russia by the Soviet Government in 1922 and is now living in Switzerland. His chief works are: *The Philosophy of Hegel as a Concrete Teaching About God and Man*, 2 vols., 1918; *Of Resistance to Evil by Force*, Berlin 1925; *The Religious Meaning of Philosophy*, Paris 1925; *Of Perfect Art*, Riga; *The Path of Spiritual Renewal*, Paris 1937.

Russian philosophers have a distinct tendency toward concrete ideal realism. It is therefore not accidental that they should have produced works about Fichte and Hegel pointing out the concrete character of those thinkers' teachings. Vysheslavtsev studied the concrete ethics of Fichte in the last period of his creative development, and Ilyin proved the falsity of the prevalent conception of Hegel's philosophy as a system of abstract panlogism. He has demonstrated that the idea is for Hegel a concrete principle, i.e., what Lossky calls a concretely ideal entity; further, he has shown that Hegel's concrete speculation is intuition directed upon concretely ideal being. The meaning of philosophy consists for Ilyin in the knowledge of God and the divine basis of the world, namely, in the study of truth, goodness and beauty as having their source in God. Ilyin explains the decadence of modern art by the lack of religion among the people of the present day, and hopes that there will again come a period of religious revival, when art will flourish anew.

Ilyin's inquiry into *Resisting Evil by Force* is a valuable piece of work. He sharply criticizes in it Tolstoy's doctrine of nonresistance. Ilyin says that Tolstoy calls all recourse to force in the struggle with evil "violence" and regards it as an attempt "sacrilegiously" to usurp God's will by invading another person's inner life which is in God's hands. Ilyin thinks that Tolstoy's doctrine contains the following absurdity: "When a villain injures an honest man or demoralizes a child, that, apparently, is God's will; but when an honest man tries to hinder the villain, that is not God's will."

Ilyin begins the constructive part of his book by pointing out that not every application of force should be described as "violence," for it is an opprobrious term and prejudges the issue. The name "violence" should only be given to arbitrary, unreasonable compulsion preceding from an evil mind or directed toward evil (29 f.). In order to prevent the irremediable consequences of a blunder or of an evil passion a man who strives after the good must in the first instance seek mental and spiritual means to overcome evil by good. But if he has no such means at his disposal, he is bound to use mental or physical compulsion and prevention. "It is right to push away from the brink of a precipice an absent-minded wayfarer; to snatch the bottle of poison from an embittered suicide; to strike at the right moment the hand of a political assassin aiming at his victim; to knock down an incendiary in the nick of time; to drive out of a church shameless desecrators; to make an armed attack against a crowd of soldiers raping a child" (54). "Resistance to evil by force and by the sword is permissible not when it is possible, but when it is necessary because there are no other means available;" in that case it is not only a man's right but his duty to enter that path (195 f.) even though it may lead to the malefactor's death.

Does this imply that the end justifies the means? No, certainly not. The evil of physical compulsion or prevention does not become good because it is used as the only means in our power for attaining a good end. In such cases, says Ilyin, the way of force and of the sword "is both obligatory and unrighteous" (197). "Only the best of men can carry out this unrighteousness without being infected by it, can find and observe the proper limits in it, can remember that it is wrong and spiritually dangerous, and discover personal and social antidotes for it. By comparison with the rulers of the state happy are the monks, the scholars, the artists and thinkers: it is given to them to do clean work with clean hands. They must not, however, judge or condemn the soldiers and politicians, but be grateful to them and pray that they may be cleansed from their sin and made wise: their own hands are clean for doing clean work only because other people had clean hands for doing dirty work" (209). "If the principle of state compulsion and prevention were expressed by the figure of a warrior, and the principle of religious purification, prayer and righteousness by the figure of a monk—the solution of the problem would consist in recognizing their necessity to each other" (219).

The possibility of situations that inevitably lead to the contradiction between a good purpose and imperfect means is man's *moral tragedy,* as Ilyin and other thinkers sharing his view express it.

6. FATHER VASSILI ZENKOVSKY

Vassili Vassilyevich Zenkovsky was born in 1881. He was lecturer at the Kiev University. Since 1925 he has been professor of philosophy and psychology at the Orthodox Theological Academy in Paris, and in 1942 was ordained priest.

Zenkovsky's chief works are: *The Problem of Psychical Causality,* 1914; *The Hierarchical Structure of the Soul,* in the Scientific works of the Russian Popular University in Prague, II, 1929; "Die religiöse Erfahrung," in *Der Russische Gedanke,* II, 1930; "The Overcoming of Platonism and the Problem of Sophia in the Created World," *Put,* XXIV, 1930; "Of the Image of God in Man," in the symposium *Orthodox Thought,* II, Paris 1930; *Questions of Education in the Light of Christian Anthropology,* Y.M.C.A. Press, Paris 1934; "The Problem of the Cosmos in Christianity," in the symposium *The Living Tradition, The Fundamental Principles of Christian Cosmology; The History of Russian Philosophy,* 2 vols.

After a thorough investigation of the problem of psychic causality Zenkovsky concludes that such causality is a fact, and turns it to good account in his further works. In his article on religious experience Zenkovsky means by experience contents of consciousness that can be described as "given," that are conditioned by the interaction between the subject and the object, and are related to an object. He argues against Dürkheim, Freud and others who attempt to explain religious experiences as derivative from other experiences. Thus, Dürkheim deduces them from the experiences of social ties, but those experiences already contain a religious element. It must be admitted that there are to be found in consciousness religious data which are not derivative and can only be explained by the interaction between the subject and a transsubjective principle. As to the nature of that principle, it is given in mystical experience as a conceptually inexpressible, all-embracing all, which leads many religious minds to interpret it in a pantheistic spirit. Humanity does not, however, stop at that form of religious experience; some people have also the experience of communion with a higher principle as a personal or superpersonal Being which makes itself known to us through the Word and the Revelation as a Supercosmic transcendental principle. True, there are many revelations and to some extent they contradict one another, but this does not prove that revelation is subjective—any more than the existence of hallucinations and illusions compels us to regard all sense perception as false. Zenkovsky gets over the contradiction between the pantheistic and the theistic religious experience by interpreting the pantheistic experience as the vision of the Sophian created aspect of the world, mistaken for the vision of God Himself. He does not wholly reject Troeltsch's conception of a special religious a priori, but points out that it cannot be developed within a system of immanent philosophy: transcendental functions do not generate the *contents* of experience and can only be realized in connection with data which point to a transsubjective source.

Zenkovsky maintains that the soul has a hierarchical structure and that the highest element in it is "the heart," understood in accordance with Christian anthropology as the life of feeling that establishes a spiritual bond with God and the divine foundations of the world.

In dealing with the problems of Christian cosmology Father Vassili argues against a-cosmism, pantheism and atheistic naturalism. Those mistaken theories can only be avoided, he says, if we have a correct conception of the creation of the world by God. Following Father Sergius Bulgakov, though considerably modifying his doctrine, Zenkovsky works out a theory of the Divine Sophia and the created Sophia. The Divine Sophia, the Wisdom of God, is the totality of ideas about the world, κοσμος νοητος as God's conception of the world; ideas that lie at the basis of cosmic processes are the created Sophia. The ideas in God are related to the ideas in the world as "primary images" to "images." To avoid confusion, Father Vassili gives the name of "ideas" to primary images only, and calls images "logoses;" he has in mind the Stoic and the Patristic doctrine of the spermatic logos. (*Fundamental Problems*, 65 f.) The World Soul contains the logoses in their unity. The conception of the World Soul has been discredited in the eyes of many of the Fathers of the Church by its connection with pantheism. In truth, however, it can be worked out apart from pantheism and be used for overcoming mechanistic naturalism (60 f.).

A-cosmism and occasionalism can only be disproved if we recognize the existence of active, though created substance in the world (73). Father Vassili distinguishes two kinds of activity: the empirical and the substantial causal correlations (*causae ad fieri* and *causae ad esse* of the scholastics). Empirical causality manifests itself in the transition from one event to another, and substantial causality embraces a particular entity's whole cycle of being (66).

The doctrine of the creation of the world by God compels us, in Father Vassili's opinion, to admit that time is in God, since the idea that time begins in the world "leads us to inquire about the time which was before the beginning of the present time" (69).

The tendency of certain theologians to interpret all activity as proceeding from God and to explain everything good in man solely by the action of God in him leads, Father Vassili says, to a-cosmism and occasionalism. Those fallacies can be avoided by recognizing the existence of active created substances and the active nature of the Divine image in man.

Zenkovsky's inquiry into the problems of Christian cosmology is of great value, but it is impossible to agree with him that the idea of the beginning of the world and of time in it compels us to recognize the existence of time in God before the creation of the world. The word "beginning" does not always mean the appearance of process A after the process B; it may also mean the first moments of the process A.

7. FATHER GEORGE FLOROVSKY

George Vassilievich Florovsky was born in 1893. He graduated in the Faculty of Arts at the University of Odessa and did post-graduate work in philosophy under Professor N. Lange with a view to becoming a university lecturer. He left Russia after the Bolshevik revolution and in 1925 was appointed professor of Patristics at the Orthodox Theological Academy in Paris; since 1947 he occupies the chair of dogmatic theology and patrology in the Orthodox Theological Academy in New York. He was ordained priest in 1932. Father Florovsky is active in the modern ecumenical movement.

Father George's chief works are as follows: *Human and Divine Wisdom*, 1922; "The Foundations of Logical Relativism," *Uchoniya Zapiski*, I, Prague; *The Death on the Cross*, Paris 1930; "Creature and Createdness," *Pravoslavnaya Mysl*, I, Paris 1930; "Evolution und Epigenesis," *Der Russische Gedanke*, 1930; *The Eastern Fathers of the Fourth to Eighth Centuries*, Paris; *The Ways of Russian Theology*, Y.M.C.A. Press, Paris 1937; "The Problems of Christian Reunion," *Put*, 1933; *The Eastern Tradition in Christianity*, Hewett Lectures, 1949.

Florovsky's relativism differs profoundly from that of Protagoras: he simply means by it that human knowledge is formal and unfinished and its progress is *in indefinitum*.

Father George is the most Orthodox of modern Russian theologians:

he is anxious strictly to adhere to the Holy Writ and patristic tradition. He rejects the doctrine of God as pan-unity: in creating the world, God creates a reality that is different from Him. He is definitely opposed to the Sophiology of Father Pavel Florensky and Father Sergius Bulgakov and thinks that liturgic texts and Orthodox iconography do not confirm their theories.

The creation of man as a free agent is a kenosis of the Divine will due to God's love for the creature. Man's soul and body are two aspects of one single living entity. In consequence of sin the connection between soul and body becomes unstable; man becomes mortal, and death is not simply the separation of the soul from the body, but the death of man himself, since "the soul without the body is a phantom. Man's death becomes a cosmic catastrophe, for in the dying man nature loses its immortal center and itself as it were dies in man" (*Death on the Cross*, 157). Victory over death is achieved by Christ. When in accordance with His human nature He died on the cross, His soul and body were parted, but His Divinity remained inseparable both from His soul and His body, says Father George on the authority of St. John Damascene. Consequently His body was not subject to corruption after death and was resuscitated by Him. His descent into hell means the descent not into the nethermost pit, but into Hades (*sheol*), the abode of the Old Testament saints; it signifies "breaking the fetters of death." Thanks to Christ who reestablishes the unity of the soul and body, our death too is no longer death, but "falling asleep" as St. John Chrysostom says.

Father George emphasizes the historical character of the Christian, as opposed to the Greek, conception of the world and ascribes great value to it. For the Greeks everything temporal belongs to the lower realm of being; there is no creativeness in time, but only cycles, periodical repetitions of all the past. On the Christian view time is not a circle, but a line that has a beginning, end, and aim. The historical process is unique in time and consists of creative acts that determine the fate of the human personality. Father George denies reincarnation and maintains that universal resurrection is not universal salvation; one life on earth is sufficient for man to make his choice and to manifest either a striving toward the good or a stubbornness of will that deserves condemnation and eternal torments.

Father George confirms all his important theological statements by references to the Eastern Fathers and says that his purpose is to make a "neopatristic synthesis." In his articles "The Problems of Christian Reunion" he argues against "the theory of church ramifications." He says that there are "no branches with equal rights" but admits that "the sick branches do not dry off at once" (13 f.). Speaking of the Roman Church he says that in it "there is no sufficiently firm and clear expression of the feeling that even after ascending into heaven Christ really and directly, though invisibly, abides in the earthly historical Church and governs it. Hence the need and the possibility of the idea of the Vicar of Christ who in a sense replaces Him in history" (11). For Christian reunion "actual work in common is more important than the direct approach to the question of reunion. In this respect collaboration in theological studies and exchange of knowledge is indubitably a real act of union in so far as it is an expression of solidarity in striving for Christian truth" (14).

Father George has done great service to the development of Russian theology by his remarkable work *The Ways of Russian Theology*. At the beginning of his book he asks the interesting and significant question as to the reason for "the late and belated awakening of the Russian thought?"—a surprising fact, for the Russians are a gifted people. The Russian ikons, for instance, "testify to the depth, complexity and subtlety of the ancient Russian spiritual experience and to the creative power of the Russian spirit." To answer that question Father George inquires into the religious life of the Russian people throughout their history as well as into their theology. He depicts that life as an arduous struggle, first, with external, and afterwards, in modern times, with internal obstacles. In the first chapter "The Crisis of Russian Byzantism" he gives a vivid account of the conflict "between the two truths," that of Iosif Volokolamsky and of Nil Sorsky. Equally stirring is his presentation of such moments in the spiritual life of the nation as "The Meeting with the West" in the sixteenth century, of "the contradictions of the seventeenth century," the two wrongs—the Old Believers, and the reforms of Nikon, the influence of Peter the Great's reforms upon the life of the church, and the significance of the masonic movement in the eighteenth century. His description of the events in the Russian religious life from the time of Alexander I onwards throws much light on the present position: he deals with the half-century long struggle for the translation of the Scriptures into Russian from the Slavonic, the activity of the Metropolitans Philaret of Moscow, Philaret of Kiev and Philaret of Chernigov, the Slavophils, nihilism, the works of the "historical school" in the second half of the nineteenth century, the activity of K. P. Pobedonostsev, the Procurator of the Holy Synod, the teachings of Vladimir Soloviev, the religious and philosophical works of his numerous successors, the argument about dogmatic development, and finally the treatment of religious subjects in the works of the "decadent" and "symbolist" poets at the beginning of the twentieth century.

Father George quotes some remarkable facts relating to the youth of Pisarev, Dobrolyubov and other outstanding persons, showing that the Russian intellectuals, even when they come to reject the Church and the historical religion are, for the most part, deeply religious by temperament. In their passionate search for new ways leading to the fullness of truth Russian people often find themselves at the edge of an abyss; thus, e.g., Merezhkovsky began to fear that he was falling into the "heresy of Astartism, which means not the holy union between the spirit and the flesh, but their sacrilegious confusion and pollution of the spirit by the flesh."

Father George gives much information about valuable works that were never published or long delayed owing to the immoderate vigilance of the State and the Synod. For instance, "a brilliant book by Professor M. D. Muretov against Renan was stopped by the censor, for the author began by giving an exposition of the false doctrine which he proceeded to criticize, and that was not considered a wise thing to do. The public went on reading Renan in secret, and Muretov's attack on him was delayed by some fifteen years. Thus the impression was produced that prohibitions were due to the inability for self-defense. Besides, only too often attempts were made to defend that which could not be defended, and this undermined confidence. People lost heart when the duties of an envigilator were substituted for the vocation of the teacher" (421).

Father George's book contains many pointed and clever remarks about prominent people, events and tendencies of the religious life. One cannot always agree with them; often they are too severe, for instance when the author accuses many of the persons whom he criticizes of having no sense of the meaning of history or of the reality of the Church. But his judgments are always interesting and attract the reader's attention. The book has an extensive bibliography occupying fifty-four pages.

At the end of his book Father George asks why the history of the Russian culture has so many breaks in it, so many instances of rejecting the old and passionately embracing the new, so many disappointments and lacerations. Among other things, he points to the Russian "universal responsiveness" as a "fatal and ambiguous gift." Too impressive a mind produces a "syncretion" instead of the longed for synthesis. He accuses the Russian national character of instability and inconstancy in love, of the tendency "to languish on fateful crossroads" without venturing to make a responsible choice. Divided love, he says, often brings the Russian soul to the tragedy of demoniac possession. The way out of these calamities is to be found in spiritual discipline, and, for the theological thought in particular, in the return to the style and the methods of the Fathers. He does not by any means suggest neglecting the Western thought. On the contrary, his advice is to utilize "the centuries old experience of the Catholic West," the great systems of "high scholastics," the experience of Catholic mystics and the theological experience of modern Catholicism because "theology is in its essence a Catholic task." A new era has recently begun in the history of the Christian world, says Father George; it is characterized by the enormous range of godless rebellion and struggle against God. One of the ways to combat it, to heal people's minds from possession by evil forces lies in the development of theology, the task of which is to work out an integral system of Christian thought.

Father George's book is a valuable contribution to the study of the history of Russian culture. The questions he asks in it concerning the peculiarities of the Russian religious life and its development, and his answers to them may also be helpful for the understanding of other domains of Russian culture.

8. V. LOSSKY

Vladimir Nicolaevich Lossky, the son of the philosopher N. O. Lossky, was born in 1903. He studied at the Faculty of Arts of the Petrograd University, continued his studies in Prague and finally graduated at the Sorbonne in Paris where he specialized in medieval philosophy.

His chief works are *Essai sur la theologie mystique de l'Eglise d'Orient*, Aubier, Paris 1944; *Meister Eckehardt* (in the press).

The work on the mystical theology of the Eastern Church is of the type of a "neopatristic synthesis," to use Father George Florovsky's term. Lossky confirms all the main contentions of his book by references to patristic writings. Theology and mysticism, he says, are closely interconnected in the tradition of the Eastern Church. The aim of that theology is not theoretical but practical: it leads to that which is above knowledge, "to the union with God, i.e., to deification, the δέωσις of the Greek Fathers" (7). The main portion of the book consists in showing that apophatic theology interpenetrates all the fundamental doctrines of the Eastern Fathers. He dwells at length upon the mysticism of pseudo-Dionysius the Areopagite and the doctrine of St. Gregory Palama about the Divine "energies." The apophatic theology of Dionysius the Areopagite differs profoundly from that of Plotinus. According to Plotinus, God is unknowable because He is simple; hence he regards ecstasy as ἅπλωσις (simplification, 29) in which the original ontological unity of the human soul and God is made manifest; according to

Dionysius, God is unknowable because He is ontologically superior to the world, and union with God is deification; i.e., a new state never before attained by the natural man (36).

Cataphatic theology does not essentially differ from the apophatic. "It may even be said that they are one and the same path trodden in two different directions: God comes down to us in His energies which manifest Him to us, and we ascend to Him through a series of unions, while He remains unknowable in His own nature. Even the highest theophany, the perfect manifestation of God in the world through the incarnation of the Word, retains for us its apophatic character" (37). God's unknowability does not lead to agnosticism; it demands "contemplative theology leading the spirit to realities which are above reason. That is why Church dogmas often appear to the human reason in the form of antinomies." This is particularly true of the Trinitarian dogma (40 f.). Plotinus has a doctrine of the Trinity (the One, the Spirit and the World Soul), and even uses the expression "to be consubstantial." But Plotinus's Trinity is a descending hierarchy of three principles, while the Christian doctrine of the Holy Trinity is the contemplation of the unity and the difference of the Three Persons that are co-equal.

The Western theologians in dealing with the Trinitarian dogma usually start with the conception of the Divine nature passing from it to the conception of the Three Persons, while the Greeks proceed in the reverse order, from the Three Persons to a single nature; but there is no question of the superiority or priority of nature over personality or *vice versa*. The case is different with the Western doctrine of the procession of the Holy Spirit from the Father and the Son (*Filioque*), which led to the schism between the Western and the Eastern churches. The Greeks detect in this formula a tendency to put in the foreground "the unity of nature at the expense of the real difference between the Persons: the relations of procession, not directly connecting both the Son and the Holy Spirit with one single source, the Father, become a system of relations in one nature and prove to be logically posterior to nature." The Holy Spirit is for the Western theologians "the bond between the Father and the Son." Nature "becomes in the Trinity a principle of unity differentiated by relations. Relations, instead of being the characteristics of the Persons, are identified with them." St. Thomas Aquinas says "a person's name signifies relation" (56 f.). Teachings which put the nature of God in the foreground "put the universal above the individual" (61); this leads to impersonal apophatic mysticism, e.g., Master Eckehart's doctrine of *Gottheit* (63). "In insisting upon the monarchy of the Father as the sole source and principle of the unity of the Three

Persons, the Eastern theologians were defending, as they thought, a more concrete and personal conception of the Trinity."

It may be asked whether according to such a triadology the conception of the Person is higher than that of the Divine Nature. V. Lossky thinks this is the fallacy of Father Sergius Bulgakov's sophiology, for according to him the Divine nature is the manifestation of all the Three Persons of the Holy Trinity. The Eastern Fathers do not fall into either extreme: they maintain that in the Holy Trinity nature and personality are apophatically equivalent. Their conception of the monarchy of the Father is not subordinationism. The difference is reflected even in the doctrine of beatitude: for the West, bliss is contemplation of the Divine Nature, and for the East it is participation in the Divine life of the Holy Trinity (61–64).

V. Lossky devotes special attention to the doctrine of the Divine "energies," which was worked out in detail by St. Gregory Palama, but was foreshadowed by Athenagoras, St. Basil, St. Gregory the Divine, Dionysius and St. John Damascene. God dwells "in the light which no man can approach unto," but in His "energies" He comes outwards, manifests and gives Himself. "The Divine grace that gives deification," says St. Gregory Palama, "is not God's nature, but His energy;" it is "the rays of Divinity" which penetrate the world, "the uncreated light" or "grace": God is not limited in His energies: He is wholly present in each ray of His Divinity; this manifestation of Him is "the glory of God" (72). "Union with God in His energies, i.e., by means of grace, allows us to participate in the nature of God, but our nature does not therefore become God's nature." In deification the creature "remains creature, while becoming God through grace" (84).

Western theologians deny the distinction between God's nature and energies, but admit other distinctions such as the created light of grace, the created supernatural gifts and so on. "The Eastern theology recognizes no supernatural order between God and the created world, added on to the creature as a new creation." The difference lies in the fact that the Western conception of grace contains the idea of causality —grace is understood as the effect of a Divine cause, but for Eastern theology grace is the radiation of the Divine nature, i.e., of "energies": it is "the presence of the eternal and uncreated light" in the created world, "the real omnipresence of God in all things, greater than His causal presence" (85 f.). In the world nature and grace "are mutually interpenetrated, one exists within the other" (121).

The "nothing" to which we must descend in thinking of the creation of the world by God is, according to V. Lossky, as much of a mystery as the Divine Nothing to which we must ascend in apophatic theology (88). The creation of the world by God is an act of creating absolutely new being, not contained in God's nature. "Creation is the work of God's will and not of His nature" (89). The ideas in accordance with which the world is created are not κόσμος νοητός within the nature of God: in the words of Dionysius they are not in the Divine Nature (as Father Sergius Bulgakov teaches) but "in that which comes after nature," in the Divine energies. Containing within them the will of God, ideas are dynamic: they are ideas-volitions external to the creature and predetermining the different stages of the creature's participation in the Divine energies. The world is "a hierarchy of real analogies" called to deification through "synergy;" i.e., through free co-operation of the created will with the Divine ideas-volitions (92 f.).

Eastern theology is always soteriological. Bent on the problem of union with God, it does not enter into alliance with philosophy as does scholasticism (99). Man is by nature connected with the whole world. If Adam had been guided by the love of God and had wholly given himself to God, he would have united the whole world and led it up to God, while God in His turn would have given Himself to man, who would then have received through grace all that God has by nature (St. Maxim). But Adam failed in his cosmic task and it was taken over by the Son of God, the God-man, the Second Adam. Eastern thought is always concerned with the world as a whole. "This finds expression in theology, in liturgic poetry, in iconography, and perhaps most of all in the works of the Eastern Church ascetic teachers of the spiritual life" (105). The whole of the world's history is regarded as "the history of the Church which is the mystical basis of the world" (106 f.).

The words of Genesis that in creating man God "breathed" into him the breath of life should not be taken to mean that the spirit of man is a particle of the Deity. That would imply that man is "God burdened by a body" or "a combination of God and animal;" then the origin of evil would be incomprehensible and "God Himself would have sinned in Adam." The words of the Bible should be interpreted as meaning that "the spirit of man is intimately connected with the grace of God" (112 f.).

In man as in God distinction must be drawn between nature and personality. Nature is the same in all men. Adam before the Fall was a universal man, but owing to the Fall human nature was broken up and divided between many individuals (115 f.). Each personality is unique, and is undefinable and unknowable in its perfection as the image of God, according to St. Gregory of Nissa. "Personality is not a part of the whole, it contains the whole" (102); it is capable of being free from its own nature and of subordinating it to itself. Because of the

Fall man loses his true freedom and acts in accordance with his natural qualities or his "character;" he becomes less personal, a "mixture of personality and nature." This mixture is called in the ascetic literature of the East "selfhood." The reinstatement of personality is achieved through the renunciation of selfhood, through a free sacrifice of one's individual will. In ceasing to exist for itself, the personality "expands infinitely and is enriched by all that belongs to all." It becomes the perfect image of God and acquires Divine likeness; i.e., becomes "a created god" or "god by grace." This deification is attained through the co-operation of two wills—the will of the Holy Spirit bestowing grace, and the will of man receiving the grace (122).

Sin, nature and death must be conquered if deification is to be attained. Those three obstacles have been overcome by the God-man Jesus Christ, the New Adam who united together the created and the uncreated being. His body is the Church in which two aspects must be distinguished—the christological and the pneumatological, the organic and the personal (181). In its christological aspect the Church is a theo-andric organism "with two natures, two wills, two activities, inseparable and yet distinct from each other." Therefore in the history of dogma all christological heresies are repeated in ecclesiology (183). The work of Christ is directed upon human nature the whole of which is unified in His Person. The pneumatological aspect of the Church consists in the fact that the Holy Spirit endows every personality with the fullness of divinity in accordance with its unique individual character (162 f.). The oneness of human nature is connected with the Person of Christ, the multiplicity of human persons—with the grace of the Holy Spirit (180). The work of Christ and the work of the Holy Spirit are inseparable from each other. The "catholicity" of the Church consists in the harmony or, to a certain extent, in the identity, of unity and multiplicity: the fullness of the whole is not the sum of the parts, since each part possesses the same fullness as the whole. The Holy Trinity is the ideal of this catholicity, "the canon of all canons of the Church" (173 f.). The Church with its sacraments is the objective condition of our union with God, and the subjective conditions depend upon ourselves.

Christ is the head of the Church in the same sense in which the husband is the head of the single body of the two partners in marriage: the Church is His Wife, and the heart of the Church is the Mother of God. St. Gregory Palama says that in the Virgin Mary "God united all the partial aspects of beauty distributed among other creatures and made her the common adornment of the kingdom of all beings, visible and invisible. Through her men and angels obtain grace" (189 ff.).

Deification must begin on earth by our fitting ourselves for the eternal life, and however much we may succeed in this, we cannot make a merit of it. "The conception of merit is foreign to the Eastern Church tradition" (194). In order to begin the spiritual life we must direct our will toward God, renounce the world, and attain a harmony between reason and heart. "Without reason the heart is blind, without the heart which is the center of all activity reason is impotent." Reasonable consciousness, "vocation," is the necessary condition of ascetic life (198 f.).

The soul cannot be healed unless man turns his will to God with perfect faith in prayer, which is "a personal meeting with God" and trains us in the love of God (204). At first prayer finds expression in words but at the higher stages, when the will is fully given to God, spiritual prayer takes place without words: it is contemplation, "absolute rest and peace, participation in the energies of the Holy Spirit," says St. Isaac the Syrian. Prayer must become continuous. The ascetics of the Eastern Church have worked out the practice of inner or spiritual prayer known as ἡσυχάσμα (206). The short prayer to Jesus "Lord Jesus Christ, Son of God, have mercy upon me, a sinner" is repeated all the time and becomes the monk's second nature. The purpose of that prayer is to attain continual "standing before God" (207 f.). Prayer must not be accompanied by the desire to experience ecstasy or to have sensuous images of the angels, Christ or Our Lady. Nilus the Sinaite gave warning against this mistake as early as the fourth century (208 f.).

Free renunciation of one's own nature and union with God leads to a perfect realization of the human personality with the help of grace, to full consciousness or "gnosis," and makes man into a "son of light" (Ephes. V, 9–14). Holy Writ is full of expressions relating to light, and God Himself is called Light. St. Simeon the New Theologian says that "the light of the glory of God precedes His face." In the fourteenth century there were arguments about that light between the Eastern Tomists and the adherents of the Eastern Church tradition. They were discussing "the reality of the mystical experience, the possibility of consciously contemplating God, the created or uncreated nature of grace." St. Gregory Palama says that "God is called Light not in His nature but in His energies" (218). That light is "the visible character of the Deity, of the energies or grace by which God makes Himself known. That light fills simultaneously the senses and the intellect, revealing itself to the whole man and not only to some one of his faculties." Therefore St. Simeon the New Theologian calls that light invisible and at the same time affirms that it can be seen (219). It is the uncreated immaterial light of the glory of God. That light was always inherent in Christ's body invisibly to men, but on Mount Thabor the Apostles' nature underwent a gracious change necessary for mystical experience and for the vision of that light" (221 f.). At the eschatological end of history this transfiguration of personality and its union with God "will be manifested differently in each human being that has acquired the grace of the Holy Spirit in the Church. But the limits of the Church on the other side of death and the possibility of salvation for those who have not seen the light in this life remain for us a mystery of God's mercy, upon which we dare not reckon, but which we may not limit in accordance with human standards" (234).

At the conclusion of his book V. Lossky says that the apophatic theology of the Eastern Church striving for the perfect fullness of being rises from concepts to contemplation and transforms dogmas into the experience of the unutterable Divine mysteries. Christ always appears in the Church "in the fullness of His divinity, triumphant and glorified even in His passion, even in the sepulchre." The worship of Christ's humanity is foreign to the Eastern tradition or, rather, His deified humanity appears in it in the same glorified form in which the Apostles saw it on Mount Thabor. The saints of the Eastern Church never had stigmata" but they "were often transfigured by the inward light of uncreated grace and appeared radiant as Christ at the Transfiguring" (241 f.). "Awareness of the fullness of the Holy Spirit, given to each member of the Church in proportion to his spiritual growth, banishes the darkness of death, the fear of Judgment, the abyss of hell, and directs our gaze solely upon the Lord approaching in His glory. This joy of resurrection and the eternal life makes the Easter night the feast of faith when everyone shares in however small a measure if only for a few moments in the fullness of the eighth day to which there shall be no end." Therefore every year at Easter Matins there is read aloud the sermon of St. John Chrysostom in which he says that the Lord God receives with equal love those who come at the eleventh hour as those who come at the beginning (246).

Chapter 27

CHARACTERISTIC FEATURES OF RUSSIAN PHILOSOPHY

Philosophy is a science and therefore, like every other science, it seeks to establish truths that have been strictly proved and are therefore binding for every thinking being and not only for a particular people or nation. It must be borne in mind, however, that philosophy is a unique kind of science differing from other sciences in two following ways. In analyzing the nature of cosmic being, philosophy aims at carrying this analysis to its furthest limits, i.e., it is concerned not only with sections of the world but also with such aspects of it as are not further analyzable and form the content of ideas and judgments of the highest degree of generality. To carry out this task successfully a philosopher must have the faculty of speculation, i.e., of intellectual intuition, developed even more fully than, e.g., a mathematician's. On the other hand, having studied the basic elements and aspects of the world, philosophy must detect the interconnection between them which forms the world-whole. Moreover, the world-whole, studied by the branch of metaphysics called cosmology, contains concrete individual elements of such significance as for instance, the biological evolution, the history of humanity—and philosophy must answer the question as to their meaning and their place in the world-whole. In dealing with such problems a philosopher finds it helpful to use the faculty of aesthetic contemplation of concrete unities. Thus, the highest achievements of philosophy require the union of two opposed and not easily combinable faculties: the highest degree of abstract thinking and a high degree of concrete contemplation of reality.

The tasks of philosophy are so stupendous and the faculties necessary for carrying them out are so little developed in man that philosophy up to the present stands at a much lower level of development than, e.g., mathematics or physics. This can be seen from the fact that there exist many schools of philosophy, sometimes sharply opposed and bitterly hostile to one another and at times indeed scarcely capable of mutual understanding. The worst thing is that even the most important philosophical systems contain, together with great achievements, unquestionable errors. Not infrequently there appear schools of thought that are strikingly one-sided. It is not surprising that in contradistinction to special sciences—i.e., sciences about particular sections and aspects of the world—philosophy bears the stamp of the character and interests of the different nations concerned with it. One may speak, accordingly, of the national peculiarities of German, French, English, American, Russian philosophy. The differences between the philosophy of different nations depend upon the particular choice of subjects for study, the greater or lesser capacity for philosophic speculation, the greater or lesser degree of confidence in the different kinds of experience such as the sensuous or the religious experience, and so on.

It is generally said that the Russian philosophy is chiefly concerned with ethical problems, but this is not the case. All departments of philosophy—epistemology, logic, ethics, aesthetics, the history of philosophy—were investigated in Russia before the Bolshevik revolution. A certain amount of truth contained in the idea that Russian philosophers are particularly interested in problems of ethics will be dealt with later. Let us begin with the question of epistemology, a science that is of vital importance for all other philosophical problems, both as regards their nature and their solution.

The view that the external world is knowable is widely prevalent in Russian philosophy, and indeed is often stated in its extreme form, namely, as the doctrine of intuition or immediate contemplation of objects as they are in themselves. A keen sense of reality, opposed to regarding the contents of external perception as mental or subjective, seems to be a characteristic feature of Russian philosophy. The Slavophils already urged that our knowledge of reality was immediate;[1] unfortunately they described such knowledge by the misleading term "faith." Different forms of intuitivism in epistemology, varying in degree of completeness, have been worked out by V. Soloviev, Prince S. Trubetskoy, Prince Eugene Trubetskoy, N. Lossky, Florensky, S. Frank, Babynin, Berezhkov, Ogniev, Kozlov (in his teaching about the apprehension of God), Ern, Losev, D. Boldyrev, S. Levitsky, I. A. Ilyin and, partly, Karsavin. Even the representatives of transcendental logical idealism, S. Hessen and G. D. Gurvich may be included in the list, in so far as they admit the existence of "will-intuition." Thinkers like Kudriavtsev, Nesmelov, who maintain that religious faith is the highest form of knowledge also belong to the same group.

1. As pointed out by E. Radlov in his article "The Slavophils' Theory of Knowledge," *The Journal of the Ministry of Public Education*, February 1916.

In contradistinction to Kantian epistemological idealism Russian intuitivism is a form of epistemological realism. It found expression, among other things, in the fact that Russian philosophy as represented by the brothers Trubetskoy forestalled the Western in discarding the doctrine that sense data are subjective mental states of the observer, and admitted their transsubjective character. Another expression of this realism is the Russian philosophers' confidence in the mystical intuition which gives knowledge about metalogical principles.

The ideal of *integral* knowledge—i.e., of knowledge as an organic all-embracing unity, proclaimed by Kireyevsky and Khomiakov—appealed to many other Russian thinkers; but it can only be attained if the subrational aspect of the world (sense qualities), its rational (or ideal) aspect, and the superrational principles are all given together in experience which combines sensuous, intellectual and mystical intuition. The whole truth is only revealed to the whole man, said Kireyevsky and Khomiakov. It is only through combining all his spiritual powers —sense experience, rational thought, aesthetic perception, moral experience and religious contemplation—that man begins to apprehend the world's true being and grasp the superrational truths about God. It is precisely such integral experience that underlies the creative work of many Russian thinkers—V. Soloviev, Prince S. Trubetskoy, Prince E. Trubetskoy, Florensky, Bulgakov, Berdyaev, N. Lossky, S. Frank, Karsavin, Losev, I. A. Ilyin, and others; in connection with it they attempt to work out a philosophy which would be an all-embracing synthesis. A striking instance of the spiritual path that leads to integral experience is provided by the biography of the brothers Trubetskoy; they both suffered from the spiritual devastation which results from living solely by theoretical thought based upon sensuous experience, and both found the fullness of life and a wealth of thought when in working out their world conception they made use of all the varieties of experience, including such subtle forms of it as aesthetic apprehension, moral consciousness and religious contemplation.

It is remarkable that even the most important of Russian positivists, Lavrov and Mihailovsky, developed their philosophy with the object (insisted upon by Mihailovsky) of combining theoretical truth with truth as righteousness, thus showing their absolute confidence in the testimony of moral experience. This explains why Russian thinkers are opposed to the doctrine of the struggle for existence as an evolutionary factor. Not only Mihailovsky, Kropotkin, Danilevsky, Chicherin, but even the materialist Chernyshevsky, definitely reject such a conception of evolution. The assertion that Russian thinkers are pre-eminently concerned with ethics contains a certain amount of truth, for even when they are dealing with departments of philosophy remote from ethics they do not, as a rule, lose sight of their subject's connection with ethical problems. Father Vassili Zenkovsky, the author of *History of Russian Philosophy*, the first volume of which he submitted as his M.A. thesis at the Paris Theological Academy, says that "Ethics has a special importance for the development of Russian philosophical thought. Even the champions of extreme naturalism and positivism assign to ethics an independent and indeed a dominating position: the primacy of ethics is fully clear in Hertsen, and still more so in Lavrov, Mihailovsky, Tolstoy and others. Down to our own day ethical personalism is perhaps the most characteristic standpoint of Russian thought."

The connecting link between the subrational sense data and superrational principles is abstractly ideal being; it is cognized by means of speculation, i.e., of intellectual intuition. The speculative faculty is as highly developed in the Russian philosophers as in the German. True, positivism and mechanistic materialism were widely prevalent in Russia, but a tendency to such views existed, and no doubt still exists, as in all other countries, among scientists, engineers, doctors, lawyers and other educated people who are not philosophically minded, and they are always in the majority. As to professional Russian philosophers, not many of them were positivists or materialists.

The striving for integral knowledge and a keen sense of reality are bound up in Russian philosophy with confidence in all the varieties of experience, both sensuous and more subtle, which go deeper into the structure of being. Russian thinkers trust intellectual intuition, moral and aesthetic experiences which reveal the highest values, and above all they trust mystical religious experience that establishes man's connection with God and His kingdom.

The main task of philosophy is to work out a theory about the world as a whole, based upon all the varieties of experience. Religious experience provides data that are most important for this purpose, giving final completeness to our world conception and revealing the supreme meaning of cosmic existence. A philosophy that takes this experience into consideration inevitably proves to be *religious*. Since the highest and most complete stage of religious experience is that attained by Christianity, it is natural that a philosophy that probes into the inmost depths of being should have a Christian character. The most characteristic feature of the Russian philosophy is that in it a number of thinkers devote their energies to working out a comprehensive Christian world conception. Some of them, e.g., Soloviev, Florensky, Bulgakov, are remarkable for their wide erudition; many have a distinct literary gift; many have written a number of various works that are translated into English, French and German. If all this is taken into consideration, it will be seen that the development of Russian philosophy aiming at a Christian interpretation of the world is a fact of considerable importance, capable of noticeably affecting human culture.

I have only expounded the religious teachings of philosophers who, like Soloviev, started with the general traditions of European philosophy and worked out a Christian world conception in a style different from that which is usually adopted in theological Academies and among the clergy. Alongside of them one might mention valuable works approaching the traditional style of the Russian Orthodox Church—for instance those of Bishop Feofan Vyshinsky, Metropolitan Antony Hrapovitsky and others. Most of those works are discussed in Father George Florovsky's extremely informative book *The Ways of Russian Theology* which I commend to my readers.

These general remarks on the peculiar nature of Russian christian philosophy may be supplemented by pointing out the following specific features of it. The Christian systems of the thinkers referred to are decidedly *realistic*. In their teaching about sacraments, redemption, grace, deification, the Church, Russian Orthodox philosophers are opposed to one-sided moralism and subjectivism: they put into the foreground *ontological* combinations and changes in the personal and cosmic life, leading to changes in the moral and mental conditions. They maintain that concrete entities form the basis of reality and that the world is an organic whole.

In their teaching about God and His connection with the world Russian philosophers rely not so much upon inferences as upon the living experience of "personal encounter with God." Striking descriptions of mystical experience are to be found in Soloviev, Prince Eugene Trubetskoy, Father P. Florensky and Father S. Bulgakov.

Many religious philosophers are chiefly concerned with cosmological problems, and their Christianity as a whole acquires a *cosmological* character. A particularly clear instance of this is afforded by Sophiology —a doctrine highly characteristic of Russian religious philosophy. It is combined with interest in superhuman spiritual beings. Vladimir Soloviev was the first exponent of Sophiology; it was further developed by Father P. Florensky, Father S. Bulgakov, Father V. Zenkovsky, but met with decisive opposition on the part of the Moscow Synod and also of Father G. Florovsky, Vladimir Lossky and others. Nevertheless in a modified form, consistent with the dogmas of the Orthodox Church, it is sure to play a significant part in the future development of religious philosophy.

The conception of *consubstantiality* introduced into metaphysics from Trinitarian theology by Father Pavel Florensky is of vital importance for theories about the structure of the world. This conception existed before Christianity and outside it. Thus Plato, Aristotle and Plotinus recognized the presence of intimate ontological connections between all the entities in the world—connections that overcome the divisions in time and space. The same idea is found in all Christian thinkers—the Fathers of the Church and the great scholastics and also in the philosophy of Fichte, Schelling, Hegel and all Russian religious thinkers. But Florensky's merit is to have deliberately introduced the principle of consubstantiality into metaphysics on the analogy of its theological meaning and thus given an impetus to a systematic application of it in every possible way. Florensky himself made it the basis of his doctrine of Christian love as the bond between personal beings that brings about their real transfiguration. Other Russian philosophers have made use of it in working out a theory of intuition, a theory of values and many other problems.

The idea of *sobornost* developed by Khomiakov is also of great importance. *Sobornost* means a combination of unity and freedom of many persons on the basis of common love for God and for all absolute values. It will be easily seen that the principle of *sobornost* is of value not only for the life of the church but also for solving many problems in the spirit of synthesis between individualism and universalism. Many Russian philosophers have begun to make use of it in discussing various questions of spiritual and social life. This principle is so valuable that it ought to be designated by a special term. It is best to introduce for the purpose the Russian word *sobornost* which already is used sometimes in English, French and German literature. The Anglican-Orthodox Fellowship of St. Alban and St. Sergius publishes a magazine called *Sobornost*.

Many Russian religious philosophers are concerned with the meaning of the historical process. They criticize positivist theories of progress and point out that within earthly conditions it is impossible to realize a perfect social order. Every new social order brings about only partial improvements and at the same time contains new defects and possibilities of abuse. The failures of history show that the purpose of historical process is to prepare humanity for passing from history to *meta-history* —to the "life of the world to come" in the Kingdom of God. The essential condition of perfection in that Kingdom is the transfiguration of the soul and body or deification by grace.

People who are out of sympathy with metaphysics and especially with religion say that in the Russian history there was no period similar to that of medieval scholasticism when people's intellectual energies were entirely devoted to working out systems of Christian philosophy. They think that Russian society at the end of the nineteenth and the beginning of the twentieth century entered for the first time into the phase of thought corresponding to the Middle Ages, and regard it therefore as backward. Such a view leaves out of account the fact that culture develops not along a straight upward line, but along a spiral; the upper curves of the spiral contain processes parallel to the lower and similar to them but more subtle, perfected by the preceding process of development. Russian religious philosophy is not a repetition of scholasticism; it makes use of all the achievements of science and modern philosophy, especially of the highly developed epistemology of our day. It may therefore be said to be a progressive achievement capable of giving a new impetus to Western thought.

Russian Orthodox people accustomed in dealing with religious problems to the traditional style prevalent in the old Theological Academies will regard with distrust philosophical works which introduce into religious thought many features of secular literature. They should be reminded, however, that in our time a number of people in all nations and at all levels of society have fallen away from the Church and believe that a Christian world conception is incompatible with science and philosophy. In order to combat this error it is essential that religious and philosophic literature should include works of different types to suit the requirements of different social circles. The literature we have been considering is useful for arousing a sympathetic interest in Christianity in the minds of highly cultured people who have grown indifferent to religion under the influence of the general character of modern civilization.

In the life of society every ideological tendency develops against the background of another, opposite tendency with which it has to struggle. At the present time in the U.S.S.R. all religious philosophy is furiously attacked by the adherents of dialectical materialism. All Soviet philosophers whose works appear in print belong to that school. The significance of this fact for the history of Russian culture should not, however, be exaggerated. Dialectical materialism is the only philosophy allowed by the Soviet Government. A philosopher who attempted to write a book or an article in a different line of thought could not have his work published and moreover would be in danger of being sent to a concentration camp. As soon as Russia becomes free of the communist dictatorship and has freedom of thought, there will at once appear many different schools of philosophy just as in any other free and civilized country.

Russian philosophy contains many valuable ideas not only with regard to religious problems, but also in the realm of epistemology, metaphysics and ethics. Acquaintance with them will be useful for the development of universal human culture. But the history of the philosophy of a whole nation is so complex a subject that justice cannot be done to it in one single work. It is to be hoped therefore that there will soon appear surveys of Russian philosophy by writers who hold other views than the author of the present book. Such works will supplement and correct one another.

INDEX OF NAMES

Hyphenated page numbers refer to the places where the doctrines of the philosophers listed are discussed.

Aksakov, C. S., 26, 38, 40, 41-45, 51, 118, 173
Aksakov, S. T., 41, 42
Alexander I, 48, 51, 393
Alexander II, 17, 29, 40, 44, 83, 171, 201
Alexander III, 84, 135
Alexander, Samuel, 296, 355
Alexeyev, N. N., 334
Alexeyev (Askoldov), S. A., 29, 158, 160, 162, 172, 247, 319, 326, 381-383
Almazov, B. N., 173
Ambodic, 179
Andreyevsky, I. M., 382, 383
Angelus Silesius, 282
Annenkov, P. V., 52, 197
Anselm of Canterbury, 274
Antony (Hrapovicky), 218, 406
Antony, 85, 89
Arbeneva, N. P., 16, 18
Aristotle, 189, 293, 294, 326, 407
Arndt, Johann, 11
Arseniev, N. S., 14, 247, 298
Askoldov, *see* Alexeyev, S. A.
Astafiev, P., 158, 162
Athenagoras, 397
Avenarius, R., 175, 356, 371, 376, 378, 379, 380

Baader, F., 131
Babynin, B., 296, 403
Bach, Johann Sebastian, 177
Baer, Karl von, 67, 72
Bakunin, L. A., 52
Bakunin, Michael A., 51, 52, 53, 54, 55, 58, 59-60, 63, 144
Bakunin, P. A., 144-145
Barghoorn, F., 63
Baron, P., 41
Barsukov, N. P., 18
Baudouin, Charles, 386
Bazarov, V. A., 379

Beethoven, Ludwig van, 51, 150, 151, 152, 177
Behterev, V. M., 64, 354
Beliayev, 86
Belinsky, V. G., 41, 42, 51, 53-56, 141
Belyi (Bugaev), Andrey, 132, 172, 335-336, 384
Berdyaev, N. A., 14, 29, 41, 72, 172, 173, 187, 192, 193, 233-250, 277, 338, 341, 372, 374, 404
Berezhkov, F., 296, 403
Berg, L. S., 143, 331
Bergson, Henri, 161, 252, 253, 281, 370
Berkeley, George, Bishop, 327
Berman, I. A., 379
Bestujev-Riumin, C. N., 83
Block, A., 132, 172
Bludov, D. N., 45
Bobrov, E. A., 158, 162
Boehme, Jacob, 10, 11, 13, 131, 204, 205, 235, 277
Boethius, 249
Bogdanov (Malinovsky), A. A., 351, 378-379
Bogolubov, V., 11
Boivin, 30
Boldyrev, D. V., 296, 403
Boldyrev, N. V., 318
Bolshakoff, S., 41
Borodin, A. P., 150
Bossuet, J. B., 22
Botkin, V., 51, 53, 54
Bruno, Giordano, 149, 204, 299
Bryusov, V., 172
Büchner, L., 63, 82, 359
Bugaev, N. V., 158, 161-162
Buharin, N., 351
Bulgakov, Sergius, 14, 26, 29, 172, 173, 174, 192-232, 233, 245, 247, 294, 295, 302, 312, 313, 390, 392, 404, 405, 406
Byhovsky, B., 348, 349, 351, 352, 354,

411

355, 360, 361, 363, 364, 365, 366, 367, 368, 369, 374
Byron, George, 214

Caats, A., 29
Carr, E. H., 60
Cassirer, E., 280
Catherine the Great, 11
Chaadaev, P. Y., 47–51
Chelishchev, M. A., 381
Chernyshevsky, N. G., 59, 60–62, 73, 170, 200
Chicherin, B. N., 134–143, 171, 334, 404
Chizhevsky (Tschizevski), D. I., 10, 72, 73, 134, 383–384, 385
Christiansen, Broder, 184
Cohen, H., 280, 318
Comte, Auguste, 65, 104, 142, 355, 378
Coué, Emile, 386
Cousin, Victor, 23

Damascius, 292
Damiani, Peter, 326
Danilevsky, N. Y., 70–72, 117, 404
Dante, 337
Darwin, Charles, 61, 64, 66, 72, 329
Debolsky, N. G., 143–144, 171
Deborin, 348, 349, 350, 351, 352, 353, 354, 356, 366, 367, 373
De Roberty, E. V., 66
Descartes, 22, 57, 139, 140, 254, 326
D'Herbigny, M., 93
Diderot, 359, 360
Dietzgen, Josef, 356, 369
Diminsky, 123
Dionysius the Areopagite, 10, 138, 235, 248, 386, 395, 396, 397, 398
Dobrolubov, N. A., 59, 62, 170, 200, 394
Dorn, N., 29
Dostoevsky, F. M., 17, 71, 75, 79, 93, 119, 151, 169, 187, 200, 214, 233, 234, 243, 247, 252, 321, 325, 331, 336, 337, 339, 340, 342, 343, 384
Drews, Arthur, 205
Duddington, N. A., 93, 251
Duff, James, 41
Dunphy, William H., 93
Du-Prel, K., 191
Durkheim, Emile, 389
Dyroff, A., 383

Eckehart, Johann, 204, 205, 235, 270, 395, 396
Ehrenfels, Christian von, 168
Elagin, A. A., 15
Engels, Friedrich, 59, 347, 348, 349, 350,

351, 354, 355, 356, 359, 361, 362, 365, 367, 368, 372, 373, 375, 378
Eriugena, John Scotus, 204, 205, 326
Ern, F., 10, 14, 29, 247, 318, 326–328, 403
Eulogius, Metropolitan, 231, 232
Evers, 42
Ezekiel, 185

Fedorov, N. F., 14, 75–80, 142, 247
Fénélon, François, 13, 22
Feofan (Prokopovich), 10, 46
Feofan (Vyshinsky), 406
Feuerbach, Ludwig, 55, 56, 57, 60, 65, 82, 197, 348, 366, 368
Fichte, J. G., 13, 22, 53, 59, 127, 159, 163, 189, 203, 322, 323, 371, 385, 407
Filipov, T., 118
Filistinsky, V., 176, 177
Filosofov, D., 337
Florensky, Pavel, 14, 26, 29, 176–191, 204, 208, 210, 247, 259, 326, 344, 392, 403, 404, 405, 406, 407
Florovsky, George, 14, 29, 190, 191, 247, 391–395, 406
Fourier, Charles, 60, 70, 158
Francis of Assisi, 337
Frank, S. L., 14, 29, 128, 172, 173, 174, 192, 193, 227, 230, 233, 247, 266–292, 296, 299, 302, 317, 319, 403, 404
Freud, Sigmund, 331, 387, 389

Gabrilovich, L. E., 325
Gabry, R., 58
Gagarin, P. I., 75
Gagarin, Prince, 50
Galich, A. I., 13
Gershenson, M. O., 45, 49, 173, 336
Gioberti, 326, 328
Gippius, Zinaida, 172, 340
Goethe, J. W., 42, 51, 56, 57
Gogol, N. V., 31, 55, 169, 240
Gogotsky, S. S., 134
Golubinsky, N., 10
Granovsky, T., 24, 51, 52, 134
Gratiaux, A., 41
Gredeskul, N. A., 174
Gregory VII, 154
Gregory the Divine, 397
Gregory of Nyssa, 398
Gregory Palamas, 395, 397, 399, 400
Griboyedov, A. S., 53
Grot, N. Y., 149, 160
Gurvich, A. G., 331
Gurvich, G. D., 141, 318, 320, 321, 322, 334, 403
Guyon, 13, 22

INDEX

Haag, Luise, 56
Haeckel, Ernest, 360, 376
Hanka, 31
Hartmann, Eduard, 82, 158, 205
Haydn, F. J., 150
Hegel, Georg W. F., 13, 16, 22, 23, 32, 42, 46, 51, 52, 53, 54, 56, 57, 59, 60, 61, 68, 72, 73, 82, 96, 134, 135, 136, 137, 138, 139, 140, 141, 144, 154, 159, 163, 189, 198, 205, 288, 289, 292, 317, 333, 334, 345, 346, 348, 350, 367, 371, 372, 373, 383, 384, 387, 407
Helmont, Jean Baptista van, 326
Helvetius, 11, 12
Heracleitus, 129, 327
Herder, I. G., 11
Hertsen, A. I., 17, 51, 53, 56–58, 405
Hessen, S. I., 318, 319, 320–322, 403
Hoffmann, E. T., 51
Hollerbach, E., 342, 343, 344
Hume, David, 146, 148, 327
Husserl, E., 253, 292, 318, 324

Iamblichus, 191
Ibsen, Henrik, 341
Ilyin, I. A., 14, 29, 32, 52, 140, 193, 233, 247, 387–389, 403, 404
Iosif Volokolamsky, 393
Isaac the Syrian, 182, 400
Ivanov, Viacheslav, 29, 172, 335, 336–337
Izgoev, A. S., 173

Jacobi, F. H., 33, 97, 298
Jaurès, Jean, 363
Joachim of Flore, 340
John Chrysostom, 392, 401
John Damascene, 10, 392, 397
John of Kronstadt, 383
John of Leyden, 200
John of the Cross, 13
Julian the Apostate, 337

Kant, I., 13, 49, 59, 69, 74, 96, 135, 139, 140, 146, 151, 154, 163, 164, 165, 166, 167, 170, 180, 190, 192, 203, 238, 240, 292, 298, 315, 318, 319, 327, 333, 334, 367
Kareyev, N. I., 69, 363
Karinsky, M. I., 145–149, 171, 315
Karpov, V., 330
Karsavin, L. P., 14, 29, 230, 233, 247, 299–314, 403, 404
Karsavina, T., 299
Kartashev, A. V., 92
Katkov, M., 51, 118
Kavelin, K. D., 51, 68–69

Khitroveo, S. P., 89
Khomyakov, A. S., 13, 14, 21, 25, 26, 29–40, 42, 43, 45, 46, 117, 118, 127, 135, 151, 179, 187, 190, 234, 239, 247, 404, 407
Kireyevsky, I. V., 13, 14, 15–29, 31, 32, 40, 41, 42, 43, 45, 68, 117, 127, 135, 247, 404
Kireyevsky, Marie A., 29
Kistiakovsky, B. A., 173, 334
Kobilinsky-Ellis, L. L., 384
Kokovtsev, V. N., 174
Koltsov, A., 51
Komensky, Amos, 170
Kondakov, N. P., 157
Korkunov, N. M., 69
Kornilov, A. A., 60, 145
Koshelev, A. I., 18, 23, 26
Kovalevsky, M. M., 174
Koyré, A., 29
Kozhevnikov, V. A., 76, 297–298
Kozlov, A. A., 158–160, 381, 382, 403
Kraevich, 53
Kropotkin, P. A., 329–330, 404
Kudriavtsev-Platonov, V. D., 73, 74, 403

Lagrange, Joseph Louis, 169
Laird, John, 296
Lamansky, 118
Lamennais, H. de, 48
Landau, G., 334
Lang, Andrew, 46
Lange, N., 391
Lanz, G. E., 318, 325
Lapshin, I. I., 12, 63, 166–170, 193, 233, 315, 317
Lavrov, P. L., 65, 66, 404, 405
Leibniz, Gottfried, W., 11, 12, 22, 74, 130, 139, 140, 151, 158, 161, 185, 246, 254, 255, 256, 264, 280, 382, 383
Lenin, Vladimir, 57, 348, 349, 351, 352, 353, 356, 359, 360, 361, 363, 365, 366, 367, 368, 369, 372, 375, 376, 380
Leonardo da Vinci, 176, 177, 337
Leonov, M. A., 348, 372
Leontiev, K. N., 16, 72, 118, 234, 247
Lermontov, M., 51, 119, 214
Leroux, P., 54, 60, 158
Lesgaft, P. F., 64
Lesevitch, V. V., 378
Levitsky, S. A., 296, 297, 403
Liaskovsky, V., 29
Littré, Emile, 66, 378
Lobachevsky, N. I., 316
Locke, John, 11, 151
Lomonosov, M. O., 42

INDEX

Lopatin, L. M., 129, 130, 158, 160–161, 171, 326
Lorancey, 31
Losev, A. F., 292–295, 403, 404
Lossky, N. O., 12, 14, 26, 29, 32, 52, 107, 140, 158, 162, 163, 166, 180, 193, 251–266, 267, 295, 296, 297, 315, 317, 318, 319, 323, 325, 330, 331, 354, 364, 370, 371, 382, 387, 395, 403, 404
Lossky, V. N., 227, 231, 395–401, 406
Lukyanov, S., 81, 109, 178
Lunacharsky, A., 379
Luppol, I., 348, 350, 365, 376

Macarius the Great, 182
Mach, Ernst, 175, 356, 376, 378, 379, 380
Makarius, Bishop, 26
Makary, Rev., 17
Maklakov, V. A., 172, 173
Malebranche, Nicolas, 274
Marat, Jean P., 55
Marshall, John S., 251
Martynov, 85
Marx, Karl, 59, 197, 198, 244, 245, 347, 351, 353, 354, 359, 362, 368, 375
Masaryk, T. G., 225
Maximus the Confessor, 10, 15, 386, 398
Mendeleyev, D., 142
Menzel, Wolfgang, 53
Merezhkovsky, D. S., 29, 172, 335, 337–341, 394
Metalnikov, S. I., 330–331
Michelet, K. L., 16
Mihailovsky, N. K., 66–68, 233, 404, 405
Mihalchev, 370, 371
Miliukov, P. N., 45, 174
Mill, John Stuart, 65, 82, 146, 147, 148, 149, 150, 151, 378
Miller, Orest, 118
Minsky, N. M., 172, 335, 337
Mirolyubov, 337
Mitzkevitch (Mickiewicz), 119
Mochulsky, G., 93
Mogila, Pyotr, 10
Moleschott, Jakob, 63, 359
Molinos, Miguel de, 13
Montague, William P., 296
Montesquieu, 11
Morgan, Lloyd, 355, 360
Mozart, W. A., 150
Muckermann, F., 94
Müller, Max, 46
Muretov, M. D., 394
Mussorgsky, M. P., 150, 169

Nadezhdin, N. I., 13, 48, 51

Natorp, Paul, 318
Neander, 31
Nekrassov, 84
Nesmelov, 403
Nettlau, 60
Newman, Cardinal, 93
Newton, Isaac, 57
Nicholas I, 16, 17, 45, 48, 53, 54, 56
Nicholas II, 153
Nicholas of Cusa, 204, 268, 270, 274, 299
Nietzsche, Friedrich, 325, 337
Nikiforov, L. P., 87
Nikon, 393
Nil Sorsky, 393
Nilus the Sinaite, 400
Novalis, F., 127
Novgorodtsev, P. I., 14, 29, 132, 172, 247, 333, 334
Novikov, M. M., 331–332
Novikov, N. I., 11

Odoevsky, V., Prince, 16, 50
Ogaryov, N. P., 51
Ognyov, A., 296, 403
Oken, L., 16
Origen, 13, 129
Osipov, N. E., 186, 331
Ossipovsky, 163
Osten-Saken, 30
Ostromirov, 75
Ostwald, W., 149
Otto, Rudolf, 248

Palmer, William, 35
Pamphilius, 13
Paracelsus, 326
Parmenides, 159
Pascal, Blaise, 22, 27, 49
Pasternak, 76
Paul I, 11
Pavlov (Dosev), T., 370–371
Pavlov, I. P., 64
Pavlov, M. G., 13, 15, 51
Pavlov-Silvansky, 59
Peter the Great, 10, 40, 43, 115, 337, 393
Peterson, N., 76
Petrashevsky, M. B., 70
Petrazhitsky, L., 334
Petrunkevitch, I. I., 174
Philaret (Metropolitan of Chernigov), 393
Philaret (Metropolitan of Kiev), 393
Philaret (Metropolitan of Moscow), 393
Philaret (hermit), 24
Philip II, 54
Philo Judaeus, 10
Philopon, 292

INDEX

Picasso, Pablo, 184
Pico de Mirandola, 31
Pierling, Paul, 88, 132
Pisarev, D. I., 59, 62–63, 82, 170, 394
Pius IX, 35, 116
Plato, 20, 74, 87, 112, 119, 183, 185, 188, 189, 204, 211, 273, 292, 293, 294, 318, 407
Platon, Metropolitan, 74
Plehanov, G. V., 348, 360, 365, 366
Plotinus, 163, 189, 204, 205, 273, 294, 322, 325, 395, 396, 407
Plotkin, L. A., 63
Plutarch, 185
Pobedonostsev, K. P., 393
Pogodin, M. P., 16, 31, 42, 45
Pokrovsky, I., 334
Popov, P., 296
Pordage, 13
Povarnin, S. I., 315
Pozner, 351, 360, 361, 362, 363, 368, 374, 375
Proclus, 292, 293
Protagoras, 391
Proudhon, P. J., 56, 60
Pushkin, A. S., 50, 119, 169, 384

Quénet, 48

Rachky. M., Canon, 89
Radishchev, A. N., 11–12
Radlov, E. L., 87, 90, 145, 163, 403
Redkin, P. T., 134
Rehmke, J., 370, 371
Renan, Ernest, 394
Rickert, H., 253, 318, 320, 335, 371
Rimsky-Korsakov, N., 150, 169, 170
Rodin, Auguste, 184
Romanov, E. K., 82, 89, 94
Rosenberg, O. O., 284
Rosmini, 326, 328
Rousseau, J. J., 11
Rozanov, V. V., 122, 124, 125, 172, 337, 342–344
Rubinstein, Anton, 151
Rückert, Friedrich, 70
Ruge, A., 59
Russell, Bertrand, 63
Ruysbruck, 13
Ryazanov, D., 348, 354, 375

Safarik, 31
Saint-Martin, 10, 11
Saint-Simon, Claude Henri, 50, 54, 56, 60
Samarin, D. Y., 46
Samarin, Y. F., 39, 42, 45, 46, 69, 85

Savalsky, V., 318
Savich, 64
Scheler, M., 28, 319, 385
Schelling, Friedrich W., 13, 15, 16, 23, 31, 48, 51, 82, 127, 155, 161, 163, 189, 277, 371, 407
Schleiermacher, Friedrich Daniel, 19, 20
Schiller, Friedrich, 42, 51, 56
Schmidt, Wilhelm, 46
Schopenhauer, Arthur, 82, 128, 151, 158, 205, 371
Schubert, Franz, 51
Schuppe, 371
Schwarz, I. G., 11
Scriabin, N., 169
Sechenov, I., 59, 63, 68
Seraphim, Archbishop, 227
Seraphim of Sarov, 337, 381, 383
Sergius of Radonezh, 101, 407
Sergius, Metropolitan, 172, 231, 232
Setnitsky, N. A., 78
Setschkareff, V., 13
Sezeman, V., 318, 322–323, 324
Shahovskoy, D., 49
Shakespeare, W., 51, 63
Shestov, L., 238, 325–326
Shevyrev, N., 16, 45
Shirinsky-Shihmatov, Platon A., 171
Shpet (Spet), G. G., 58, 318, 324
Simeon the New Theologian, 400
Simplicius, 292
Skobtsova, E., 41
Skovoroda, Gregory, 10, 326, 384
Smetana, B., 170
Smolitsch, I., 29
Soloviev, S. M. (historian), 42, 81
Soloviev, S. M. (nephew of Vladimir S. Soloviev), 91
Soloviev, Vladimir S., 14, 26, 29, 33, 41, 71, 72, 73, 74, 75, 76, 80–133, 138, 140, 141, 143, 149, 151, 153, 154, 155, 157, 161, 164, 171, 175, 176, 178, 183, 187, 189, 192, 206, 213, 230, 233, 244, 247, 277, 298, 302, 313, 321, 334, 338, 341, 371, 383, 385, 393, 403, 404, 405, 406
Spektorsky, E. V., 14, 29, 247, 333–334
Spencer, Herbert, 46, 65, 67, 146, 147, 148, 149, 150, 151, 378
Spengler, Oswald, 70, 117
Speransky, M. M., 12–13
Spinoza, 22, 74, 82, 176, 230, 356
St. Alban, 407
St. Augustine, 154, 274
St. Basil, 397
St. Bonaventura, 274

INDEX

St. Cyril, "Apostle of the Slavs," 189, 190
St. Cyril of Jerusalem, 31
St. Methodius, 13
St. Paul, 38, 157, 272, 386
Stalin, J., 375
Stankevich, N. V., 24, 41, 42, 51–53, 54, 59
Starynkevich, K., 330
Stassiulevich, M. M., 87, 91, 118
Stchedrin, E., 124
Steiner, Rudolf, 384
Steklov, Y. M., 60, 62
Stepun, F. A., 318, 323–324
Stern, William, 254
Stoyunin, Marie, 342
Strakhov, N. N., 70, 72, 121, 342
Stremooukhov, D., 86, 89, 93, 95, 131
Strossmayer, Bishop of Zagreb, 84, 88
Struve, P. B., 172, 173, 192, 278
Suk, J., 170
Suvorov, S. A., 379
Swedenborg, Emanuel, 184
Synesius, 13
Szylkarski, V. S., 93, 383

Tauler, J., 13
Tavernier, 87, 94
Teichmüller, G., 158, 159, 383
Ternavtsev, 337
Thomas Aquinas, 204, 396
Thomas à Kempis, 10, 13
Tikhomirov, L., 124
Tiutchev, F. J., 116, 117, 272
Tolstoy, Leo N., 75, 76, 169, 203, 249, 325, 331, 336, 337, 339, 340, 388, 405
Tolstoy, Nicholas, Rev., 85, 87
Tornstein, 376
Torquemada, 141
Towianski, 116
Troeltsch, Ernst, 390
Troitsky, M. M., 69
Trubetskoy, E. N., 14, 29, 84, 85, 88, 90, 91, 93, 94, 95, 129, 130, 131, 150–157, 172, 247, 403, 404, 406
Trubetskoy, Peter, 86
Trubetskoy, S. N., 14, 29, 86, 150–154, 155, 169, 172, 247, 326, 371, 403, 404
Tschizevski, D. I., see Chizhevsky
Tsertelev, D., 92

Tugan-Baranovsky, M. I., 174, 192
Tukalevsky, V., 11
Turgenev, A. I., 50
Turgenev, I. S., 62, 169

Uexküll, V. I., 92
Uvarov, S. S., 45

Valentinov, N., 379
Varnava, 85
Vassilyev, A., 315
Vassilyev, N. A., 315–317
Veliaminov, 92
Vellansky, D. M., 13
Venevitinov, D., 16
Vengerov, S. A., 44
Vernadsky, G. V., 11, 173, 330
Vernadsky, V. I., 332
Virubov, G. N., 66, 378
Vladislavlev, M. I., 163
Vogt, K., 63, 359
Voltaire, 10, 22
Vvedensky, A. I., 143, 146, 149, 163–166, 168, 171, 315, 317
Vyelgorsky, M., 18
Vysheslavtsev, B. P., 14, 29, 247, 385–387

Weininger, Otto, 338
Werder, K., 52
Windelband, W., 318

Yakovenko, B. V., 318, 324
Yakovlev, A., 56
Yarosh, 118
Yavorsky, Stefan, 46
Yegorshin, 355
Yelchaninov, A., 13
Yurkevich, P. D., 73–74, 127, 385
Yushkevich, P., 379

Zander, L. A., 193, 232
Zavitnevich, V., 30, 32, 41, 187
Zenkovsky, Vassili, 14, 29, 247, 389–391, 405, 406
Zeno of Elea, 159
Zernov, N., 41
Zhukovsky, V. A., 15, 17, 19, 384
Zouboff, P. P., 82, 93

Integral knowledge —
    LS — TL ay
+ art, phil., religion